Informal Assessment in Education

GILBERT R. GUERIN
San Jose State University

ARLEE S. MAIER
San Francisco State University

Informal Assessment in Education

MAYFIELD PUBLISHING COMPANY

First edition 1983

Library of Congress Catalog Card Number: 81-84695
International Standard Book Number: 0-87484-533-5

Manufactured in the United States of America
Mayfield Publishing Company
1240 Villa Street, Mountain View, CA 94041

Special projects editor: Liz J. Currie
Manuscript editor: Carol Dondrea
Designer: Nancy Sears
Cover photographer: Elizabeth Crews
Production manager: Cathy Willkie
Compositor: Graphic Typesetting Service
Printer and binder: George Banta Company

Contents

Preface

The idea for this book grew out of the expressed needs of teachers and psychologists for practical methods for evaluating the behavior and skills of children and youth. Our focus is on assessment strategies that can be used to organize and interpret information gathered through daily observation and interactions with students. We feel that this type of information plays the pivotal role in the instructional decisions made by classroom teachers.

Testing is one part of assessment, and in recent years there has been an explosion in the use of tests. More students now receive more testing and at an earlier age than ever before. Battery testing, which starts as early as kindergarten, continues through the grades, occurring with regularity once or twice a year. At the same time, textbook and materials manufacturers provide tests with their products; special education teachers do extensive diagnostic testing; health and speech services use screening and diagnostic tests; guidance and psychological services are involved in group or individual testing; and classroom teachers test students as part of their ongoing programs.

At least equally important, however, are the many other assessment strategies that are crucial for understanding students' behavior and growth. Observations, surveys, measures, records, and interviews occur regularly. Information from these procedures, when combined with that obtained from formal and informal testing, provides the professional with the background for informed decisions.

This book is an introduction to informal assessment, assessment that does not involve sophisticated statistical descriptions or comparative data. We describe procedures that can increase the effectiveness of teachers, counselors, speech therapists, psychologists, and other personnel who help young people. The text is, in part, a collection of procedures and strategies that we have developed over the years, and that have evolved to meet contemporary needs. We also offer new strategies and methods that place greater emphasis on student participation, teacher-student interaction, and analysis of the instructional setting.

We have made every attempt to select strategies that have proven both useful and manageable. One of the strengths of informal assessment is that the procedures can be modified to take advantage of natural conditions and events. Unworkable procedures can be discarded and replaced by more appropriate methods. We encourage the reader to make the modifications and adaptations that are needed to fit an approach to his or her classroom.

Prior knowledge of either testing or assessment is not required to understand or apply these methods. We have provided the basic information the user needs. Reading lists are included, and we encourage the reader to use those sources for relevant information. Most texts on testing explain the underlying concepts, and we recommend these sources if further elaboration is needed. Such reference information is useful to those seeking a more comprehensive understanding of specific aspects of assessment. A broad knowledge of complementary and divergent points of view can help broaden assessment skills and can provide a basis for examining one's personal beliefs and attitudes toward assessment.

The book is divided into four parts. In each of the first three parts, we examine an important aspect of assessment: the process, the techniques, and the application. Part Four presents some special concerns. The three process chapters in Part One deal with the purpose, the accuracy, and special conditions of assessment. Chapter 1 contrasts formal with informal assessment, describes the various purposes for which assessment can be used, identifies the focus of assessment, and reviews basic statistical concerns. Chapter 2 describes in detail several approaches to assessment and discusses test construction and strategies. Chapter 3 is concerned with identifying a problem and collecting relevant data. Several recording and reporting formats are also discussed.

The second part of the book deals with the basic techniques of informal assessment. Chapter 4 is devoted to methods of observation—direct views of behavior that provide the teacher with most of the information on which classroom decisions are based. Chapter 5 deals with methods of obtaining information by inquiry, including the interview-conference and the questionnaire. Chapter 6 focuses on methods for reporting assessment information; it also details common errors that occur during the assessment process.

In Part Three, we discuss methods for assessing the skill areas commonly taught in school, as well as for assessing behavior. Skill chapters cover sensorimotor development, thinking and language, spelling and handwriting, and reading and arithmetic.

Part Four covers special topics, including careers, classroom management, and assessment of minority students. Chapter 13, on classroom management, gives a comprehensive view of student and classroom analysis. The chapter is based on the assumption that simple and ordinary procedures have been used and a broader analysis is required.

The forms and formats we have provided as demonstrations, illustrations, or applications were selected from a wide range of useful procedures. They represent generic examples and are not the only instruments available. The reader is encouraged to select those that best fit the purpose of assessment and the student under consideration.

We would like to thank the following reviewers for their comments on the manuscript: Robert F. Busch, University of Missouri; Bill Curtis, Middle Tennessee State University; LeJeune H. Ellison, University of Arkansas; Jeannette E. Fleischner, Teachers College, Columbia University; Richard M. New, Northwest Missouri State University; Dennis M. Nulman, California Polytechnic State University; Nancy Riley, Northwest Missouri State University; Susan Vogel, Barat College; and Ruth Waugh, University of Oregon.

G. R. G.
A. S. M.

Informal Assessment in Education

Part One
The Process of Informal Assessment

The assessment process involves collecting data that can be used for planning educational programs, identifying educational goals, selecting instructional strategies and materials, implementing educational plans, and monitoring students' progress toward goal attainment. Continuous data gathering is required not only for measuring student progress but for determining what modifications of planned interventions are necessary. This section provides a theory and rationale for informal assessment, including discussion of the process of gathering, interpreting, and applying data to educational planning.

Chapter 1
What Is Informal Assessment?

Formal vs. Informal Assessment
Purposes of Assessment
  Placement
  Instruction
  Reporting and Counseling
Pupil Involvement
The Focus of Assessment
  Students
  The Instructional Setting
  Instruction
  Out-of-School Factors
Guides to Informal Assessment

Strategies of informal assessment are a critically important part of a teacher's repertoire of skills. Information gathered through observations of everyday student behavior, through the examination of student products such as papers, tests, and presentations, and through discussion with students provides the basis for many teacher decisions. What children and adolescents are observed to say and do within the context of the school forms the data base on which teacher opinions, judgments, and actions are made. The process of informal assessment is a means by which teachers, either through ability or training, are able to collect, evaluate, and use information about the students they instruct. Evaluation information is used to establish goals, select strategies, and measure outcomes.

Ordinary methods of gathering information about the average student, such as cursory reviews of the cumulative record or previous test scores, are usually insufficient to help the teacher cope with the needs of exceptional students, especially those with learning disabilities. In spite of good intentions and conscientious effort, teachers often find that exceptional children and adolescents fail to achieve the expected learning growth or that they behave in ways that interfere with effective learning. Observations, tests, queries, or discussions that work well with the average student may produce little in the way of useful information about atypical students because the data may be incomplete, lack focus, or be inappropriate for the task at hand. Although information on exceptional students is as available as information on average students, such information is often difficult either to interpret or to translate into positive action. An organized and systematic use of informal assessment can significantly improve the teacher's ability to understand students and to make appropriate decisions.

The daily products, behavior, and comments of a student are an immediately available source of information upon which to make classroom decisions. Such information is easily gathered, occurs in the natural setting, and allows for immediate and continual verification. Such information is "there to see, all the time."

Typically, informal assessment is subjective and private; it is neither shared nor verified with students, colleagues, or parents. By casual and ordinary methods of observation teachers notice those dominant details of a student's behavior that are readily observable and can be easily recalled to memory. Such observations tend to focus on the extraordinary features of a student's behavior and are, in part, limited by the perceptual skill of the teacher. For the exceptional pupil the information gathered by the teacher often results in an incomplete patchwork of knowledge, and new data, casually gathered, tend to reinforce previously developed opinions. At its usual level of sophistication, informal assessment is only marginally valuable, and may keep a teacher "stuck" in a particular point of view. Group data are also of little help when trying to design an individual educational plan for an exceptional pupil. Test scores that define general levels of achievement give few clues as to the specific action needed to help the student who does not respond to ordinary teacher interventions.

A student who has spent many hours in classroom activities has produced a myriad of clues as to his or her motivation, ability, and needs. Teachers skilled in selecting, collecting, and analyzing daily information can capitalize on available information and use it to understand the unique nature of the student. Such information can lead to more appropriate goals and teaching strategies, to improved management of student behavior, and to effective systems for monitoring student growth.

FORMAL VS. INFORMAL ASSESSMENT

Differences between formal and informal assessment center on six basic testing dimensions: setting, activities, dialogue, statistics, data, and format. Formal assessment procedures employ tightly organized test materials, structured test situations, and group-based comparisons. These tests often have a highly prescribed test format and are designed to reveal data that can be compared to that obtained on children who were tested during the instrument's construction. Formal tests tend to be specific in nature and most frequently address the issues of intelligence, achievement, ability, or personality. Many formal tests require administration under ideal conditions. The test situation is to be relatively free from distractions; the interaction is adult-dominated; and the student's performance is taken in isolation, separate from group process or group productions. Table 1-1 lists the six most common dimensions and indicates the polar differences between formal and informal assessment.

Table 1-1.
Dimensions and Polar Differences Between Formal and Informal Assessment

DIMENSIONS	FORMAL	←——→	INFORMAL
Setting	Structured	←——→	Naturalistic
Activities	Ordered	←——→	Flexible
Dialogue	Prescribed	←——→	Open
Statistics	Standardized	←——→	Idiosyncratic
Data	Codified	←——→	Enumerated
Format	Numerical	←——→	Descriptive

Informal assessment, which does not require a formal or defined reference group, often includes information that is idiosyncratic. Such information is obtained in a setting that is natural to the student's daily experience and that involves ordinary classroom interactions. Data may also include subjective opinions that, in part, reflect either the teacher's teaching style and needs, or the student's learning style and needs. Informal assessment is often directed at answering specific, practical, and immediate questions. Tests are designed to answer specific questions about individual performance, and case histories are developed to identify the individual's unique experiences. Informal assessment encompasses information that is ongoing and cumulative rather than information that is drawn from a fixed point in time and is static.

Both informal and formal assessment procedures are used in most evaluation situations. The teacher, specialist, or psychologist who must evaluate a student in order to make a placement decision will attend to the reactions, comments, and general behavior of the child, as well as to the performance on specific test items. A complete report by the assessor will include both informal observations and formal test data. In a well-written report all relevant data will be integrated into a comprehensive description of the student. The evaluation decisions will be based on both comparative and idiosyncratic data. Formal information may provide the basis for the eligibility decisions, whereas less formal data may provide the information necessary to implement an instructional or behavioral program.

Thus, both formal and informal data are necessary for a comprehensive assessment of a student since each provides information on different aspects of student performance. Group or individual standardized tests tend to provide entry or diagnostic data, and daily informal assessment provides information on such areas as behavioral or academic progress, nature and degree of student involvement, relationship between the student, his or her peers, and the teacher.

PURPOSES OF ASSESSMENT

Educational assessment is a process by which characteristics of the individual, the group of individuals, the setting, goals and objectives, and materials or teaching strategies are identified and understood for the purpose of making judgments and decisions relevant to educational activities. Assessment is most often used to develop information relating to identification and placement, to programming and instruction, or to reporting and counseling. Although the same information can be used to accomplish several purposes, prior knowledge about the purpose or use of assessment information can lead to the selection of more appropriate strategies and data.

Traditionally, formal assessment has been used to make decisions on student placement or grouping and to diagnose group instruction problems. Informal assessment, on the other hand, has been used to analyze ongoing skills, interests, and behavior. This distinction is workable only where identification and placement are separated from instructional planning. For instance, data used to determine eligibility of children for a traditional special education class did not need to provide information that was useful to the teacher. When, however, the activities of diagnosis, placement, and instruction became closely interrelated, the purpose of assessment expanded, and both informal and formal information became necessary in order to make informed decisions.

Legal commitments to children influence the purpose of pupil assessment. Public Law 94-142 expressly guarantees a free public education to all handicapped children. It requires that instruction be given in the least restrictive environment, a concept commonly held to mean in a setting and manner as nearly like that of regular pupils as possible. Also required are an individualized educational program and the use of nondiscriminatory tests. Each of these mandates influences the purpose of pupil assessment; and in the case of individualized program and nondiscriminatory testing, they parallel what has been commonly held to be good practice in regular education programs.

In addition to the general purposes and those that have been identified by law, a number of activities involved in instruction require assessment data. These have been identified in Table 1-2; they are classified according to whether they help prepare for instruction, relate directly to instruction, or are auxiliary to instruction. In each case the teacher needs an information base upon which to take some action. Assessment data are also used to monitor teaching styles, check classroom management, and select instructional materials.

Table 1-2.
Instructional Activities and Related Assessment Needs

PREPARATION	INSTRUCTION	AUXILIARY
Identifying	Placing	Reporting
Diagnosis	Monitoring	Counseling
Planning	Evaluating	Recognizing

Placement

When the term *placement* is used in the regular education program, it usually refers to the act of selecting a child for a particular class or instructional group. Group placement is often made on the basis of skill level, interest, or behavioral compatibility. In special education, *placement* takes on a more critical meaning in that it can result in the interruption of a student's existing program and possible separation from his or her peers. It is obvious that the more drastic and irrevocable the placement decision, the greater the need for clear, accurate, and comprehensive assessment information. In a decision to place a child in a school outside his neighborhood and away from his or her friends, the social ramifications, as well as the educational implications of that decision, need to be considered.

In placement decisions two considerations are foremost: (1) What are the needs of the student? (2) What educational provisions can best meet those needs? These concerns may appear obvious; however, in the past many placement decisions were based on a narrow view of the student's needs and on a fixed set of solutions.

The old adage, "If the only tool you have is a hammer, everything you see will look like a nail," describes assessment data based on a narrow range of assessment strategies. For instance, the use of ability (intelligence) testing as the primary tool of assessment may lead to errors by oversimplifying pupil problems. Low intelligence was often given as the reason for low skill development. To get around the "hammer-nail" problem, a full range of functions—intellectual abilities, physical and perceptual skills, academic skills, motivation and interests, and social skills—needs to be considered. The areas of assessment need to be broad enough to identify a range of possible "causes."

Another area of consideration relates to the instructional options available to the teacher. The selection of assessment strategies is, in part, determined by the types of assistance that are available. Yet, although it is foolish to assess a child for a nonexistent program, it is only when assessment is allowed to suggest unique solutions that a truly individualized program can be realized. The teacher must often choose between gathering data that are immediately useful or gathering data that can have long-term or broad implications. Some combination is usually preferred.

An example will illustrate how assessment with limited purpose both satisfies and perpetuates a narrow view of the kinds of instructional programs children need. The focus of traditional special education assessment was on the placement or admission of a student to predetermined special education classes. The purpose was to determine the eligibility and appropriateness of the child for an existing program. The emphasis was on whether a child would fit, not on what program modifications would best suit a given child. The child was evaluated and delivered to programs on the basis of this limited purpose and procedure. Seldom did the procedure help the child within his or her regular class setting.

Assessment strategies that provide comprehensive data can identify a series of options rather than fixed, predetermined solutions. For instance, the data might suggest that, before a decision is made to remove the student for remedial instruction, an aide using appropriate material work with the child within a regular classroom. Radical solutions such as total removal should be taken only after reasonable alternatives are fairly tried and all the ramifications of the placement have been examined. Options that don't work within a reasonable amount of time should be abandoned and others tried. Assessment provides the data that lead to such a series of possible teaching interventions.

Instruction

Informal assessment is as much a part of the everyday process of instruction as the materials used in the classroom. Assessments are made at each step in the process and are a constant feature in instruction. Most classroom decisions are made without conscious effort but are nonetheless the result of informally gathered information. It is only when the resulting teaching strategies do not produce results that the teacher should question the original judgment and the basis on which that judgment was made.

A simple example will illustrate the number of times assessment can be used in a simple instructional problem. In this example the teacher's action will be successful. The class has been given a workbook assignment involving column addition and carrying. One student, Mike, makes frequent errors. The following steps occur.

1. The teacher reviews a work sample, which shows that some column additions are in error and there are frequent carrying errors.
2. The teacher assigns simple problems on preceding pages; these reveal consistent addition errors in some number combinations, as well as repeated errors in carrying from one column to another.
3. The teacher gives instruction through verbal explanation, demonstration, trial, and practice.
4. The student is successful in calculations made in each preparation step after direct teacher instruction.
5. The student returns to the original page, completes it correctly, and is monitored closely when new processes are introduced.

This brief and simplified description illustrates that there are a variety of points at which the teacher makes evaluations and chooses the next step in instruction. Recognition of the problem led to a review of the student's work product and was followed by a simple test of the child's ability to perform component parts of the task. Standard instruction was employed and the student successfully learned each task required to master the skill successfully. The student's subsequent performance was monitored and success was verified.

Instructional questions can be relatively simple and straightforward, for example, "What is Mike's computational skill level?" Or they can be more detailed, as in "What are Mike's specific strengths and weaknesses in computation?" A still more complex question is, "What attitudes and skills influence Mike's computational achievement?" Each can be answered by informal methods of assessment. Each set of answers will define Mike's behavior in a somewhat different manner, and each will provide data that lead to different instructional interventions.

Assessment occurs at each step in the process of instruction (Figure 1-1). Student data are used to establish goals and objectives and to select appropriate instructional methods. The monitoring of instruction is an assessment activity that parallels teaching. The evaluation of instruction involves the use of assessment information to judge the effectiveness of the teaching process.

Figure 1-1.
Steps in the Process of Instruction

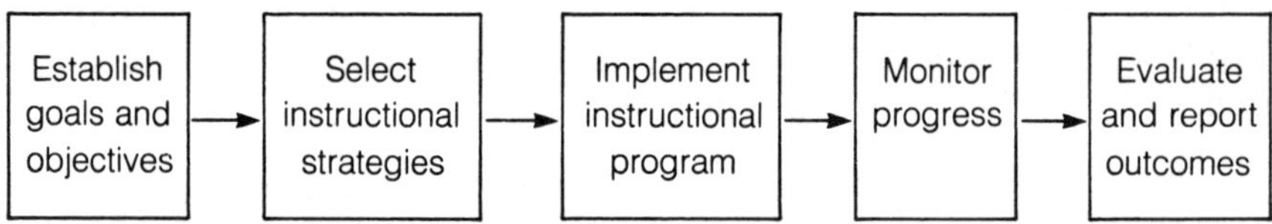

Typically, assessment provides information that is used to explain why rather than how a child performs poorly. The data "explain" the performance. Once this reason is determined, the teacher's effort to improve the child's performance diminishes. When informal assessment data have been used to give a simplistic reason for a student's failure to learn, they tend to limit rather than enhance the student's chance to improve. Information on intelligence, for instance, has often been used to explain poor performance. In other situations, a student's bilingualism is sometimes accepted as a natural explanation for low achievement; or poor reading skill is used to explain poor performance in social studies. In each of these examples, assessment data are used to explain *why* a pupil performed poorly. Such answers or reasons tend to justify poor performance and stifle the search for solutions. "Reasons" that are not easily corrected become the rationalizations for subsequent failure and thwart the search for improved instruction. However, data about the "why" of performance are relevant only to the extent that they lead to an improved instructional setting, content, or procedure. Answers to questions of "how" are usually more helpful to the teacher and the student.

An example will illustrate how the "why" answer can restrict thinking. Lisa is having serious problems in social studies. An assessment of Lisa's performance reveals that she is unable to complete the assignments or participate in class because her low reading ability does not allow her access to the data she needs. It is rightfully assumed that improved reading skill will probably improve her performance in social studies, and she is enrolled in remedial reading instruction. If assessment stops at this point, it will fail to identify Lisa's immediate needs. Remedial instruction in reading, at best a slow process, will not solve Lisa's immediate problem. In fact, it may be months, possibly years, before remedial reading instruction will significantly improve Lisa's classroom performance.

Lisa's social studies problem can be better understood by a more thorough examination of her situation. Informal assessment would determine that Lisa has many of the skills required in social studies. She remembers relevant facts, can analyze and synthesize data, can express her ideas verbally, and has a low but functional ability to make written reports. When data are given to Lisa by tape, through oral reading, through demonstrations or selected television and radio news programs, she is able to understand and remember them. When provided with appropriate data and with writing assistance, Lisa can successfully complete her assignments and become a participating member of the class. Launched on such a program Lisa can succeed in social studies and eventually will have the reading skill to learn through ordinary instruction.

The purpose of assessment in Lisa's case is to determine what is needed to assist her in day-to-day classroom activities (social studies), as well as to identify long-range goals (remedial reading). The knowledge that reading problems rendered Lisa unable to complete her social studies assignment is not sufficient to help in the design of a corrective or adaptive program. A more complete assessment of the tasks she is to perform and the skills she has at her disposal will provide the basis for an individualized program.

Reporting and Counseling

Informal assessment data can be shared with others, and therefore are useful in the teacher's communications with parents, students, and fellow professionals. They can also help a pupil in self-understanding and self-monitoring.

Assessment data give parents an opportunity to better understand their children's performance. Formal assessment data, such as standardized tests, provide parents with information that compares their children with other children on a given dimension. They also give parents a rough estimate of their child's academic strengths and weaknesses. Informal assessment information, such as observations, work samples, and class tests, can expand and personalize that understanding. It can provide parents with practical examples and data that clarify performance, skills, and limitations. It can provide the basis for a cooperative exchange and planning.

Written reports to parents usually focus on a child's skills or behavior. Grades or other marking systems are the common shorthand of the teacher-to-parent communication and serve several purposes. They require the teacher to make periodic assessments and to keep the parent informed on student progress. In a way, they are a form of accountability for both teacher and child. They reflect successes and failures in both teaching and learning.

Conferences and interviews can serve a purpose similar to that of the written report, and at the same time provide an opportunity for a broad exchange of information. Both reporting strategies require the use of information gained through informal assessment. The interview approach, however, gives the teacher access to an important source of data, the parent. Data gathered through careful interviewing methods can yield information that is helpful to teaching decisions. For example, if it is determined that the parent is an unwilling or ineffective "home teacher," the teacher may choose to provide all instruction within the school. On the other hand, if parents are comfortable with a subject area, are interested in helping their children, and are capable of actively supporting instruction, they can be enlisted to take an active part in teaching their children.

Teacher decisions based on the interview data gained in parent conferences are often critical to the child's performance. It is therefore important that accurate data and conclusions be drawn from parent–teacher exchanges. Skillful interviewing is an important and often neglected part of teacher training; it is an invaluable assessment strategy.

On the parents' side, they must obtain information from the teacher that is clear, accurate, and practical. Written reports must represent the best assessment of the child that the teacher can provide, and face-to-face meetings should include relevant information on such areas as social skills, creative abilities, interest areas, skill development, and learning styles. Informal assessment is invaluable in developing this data.

Students rely on both formal and informal assessment data to determine how they are doing in class and in a subject area. Feedback on student performance is the most common classroom assessment process. The form varies but the result is the same: The student receives a judgment from his or her teacher. On a daily basis and in simple form, such judgment can be a check, a score, a grade, a smile, or a word. It is part of the natural flow that occurs in every classroom. It is the bedrock of shared, informal assessment. It is, for the most part, focused on skill development and is the product of the teacher's informed judgment.

A less common, but no less important, assessment strategy is one that allows students to explore, discover, and understand their own skills, values, expectations, aspirations, and interests. The purpose of this form of assessment is to allow student self-examination. This form of evaluation is one step in helping students take responsibility for their own educational plans, decisions, and actions.

The fourth class of participants in informal assessment are fellow teachers and other professionals. Information that is vigorously gathered and recorded in understandable form is useful to peers and support personnel. These data can be the basis upon which educational plans are formed and administrative decisions made. A clearly recorded observation can be shared with a fellow teacher or psychologist to help generate ideas for new teaching approaches. Student interview data, conscientiously gathered and recorded, can provide the initial information needed in a placement decision. The amount of respect given to informal data is related to their preciseness, their clarity, and their objectivity. The clear, accurate description of a student's performance in a classroom is one of the most appropriate sources of data for educational decisions.

PUPIL INVOLVEMENT

When assessment includes active student participation, it provides the teacher with data upon which to make judgments and the student with the opportunity to help shape the instructional program. Active student involvement in assessment can result in personally relevant data, greater student responsibility for instruction, and improved student motivation. Drawbacks center around the time required to achieve student involvement and the possible conflicts between teacher and student goals. However, teachers who seek a cooperative and participatory atmosphere and who value high student motivation should encourage pupil involvement in assessment.

Assessment information that is gathered cooperatively allows the student full participation in the process of instruction. The amount of information a student has about himself can result in an increase in the student's role in instruction. When assessment data are limited to those held by the teacher, they tend to result in a teacher-dominated instructional plan and program. The teacher's data become the basis of action. The teacher selects goals and instructional strategies and is charged with motivating the student. In this procedure the student has a passive role.

A student who participates in assessment can share in planning and can make commitments based on his or her knowledge of the process and expected outcomes. A crossover occurs as the information held by the student is used to help the teacher carry out instructional objectives. The student is often able to provide information about his own learning that is relatively unavailable through less direct means of inquiry. For instance, many students are both knowledgeable and candid about their strengths and weaknesses. Many students, once they realize that the teacher respects their judgments and is sensitive to their needs, will provide clear insights into the barriers they experience in learning, their willingness to cooperate, the strengths and weaknesses of a particular instructional approach, and the likelihood of the success of alternate strategies.

A cooperative plan may develop as follows. A student is doing poorly in most subjects; the student's skills are low and the effort she makes is negligible. The teacher discusses the situation with the student, sharing his concern for her. He asks the student to suggest what help would be useful in each subject and to rank the subjects in order of importance. The teacher describes how he thinks he might best assist, and he and the student reach an agreement on the responsibilities of each. A reasonable time line is developed, and follow-up points are identified.

Participation in an assessment plan carries with it an implied commitment to involvement. Assessment planning allows the student to consider the expected learning outcomes and to establish how they should be reported and evaluated. Such planning acts as rehearsal for the instruction that is to follow and allows both the teacher and the student to "think through" the educational plan. Possible obstacles can be anticipated and plans developed to make the learning as efficient and effective as possible. Student suggestions can be incorporated whenever they appear feasible and are compatible with the instructional objectives.

Knowledge about his or her progress is a critical element in a student's learning. This is especially true for the exceptional student, where growth is small and the opportunity to praise, meager. Such students often expect failure, and this expectation overshadows or conceals legitimate improvement. Periodic and consistent information on progress is often necessary to maintain motivation. Assessment strategies used when working with slow learning students can emphasize growth and minimize learning problems. Assessment data in all student participation programs are designed to be easily understood and simple to collect.

The case of Lisa illustrates how a student's participation can influence planning, goal setting, and instruction. It was determined that Lisa's reading skills were deficient but that most of her social studies skills were quite adequate. This observation was shared with Lisa and verified by her. Lisa agreed that she would like to do better in social studies and accepted remedial assistance in reading as one step to improving her performance. She then participated in planning an adapted program in social studies. A variety of data collection options—such as having parents, aides, or classmates read to her; listening to radio news broadcasts; watching television news programs; or listening to tapes of textbook material—were explained to her. She was encouraged to identify other ways by which she could gather relevant social studies information. She eventually chose to use tapes and television news broadcasts as her prime data sources. She was asked to help the teacher evaluate how well the adapted program worked. Lisa chose to participate in class discussion three times a week. On other days, she made either brief notes on what she had learned or a brief oral report to the teacher or adult helper. Lisa agreed to follow a daily study program and to monitor her own progress. She kept daily records and evaluated her own progress in brief discussions with the teacher. The teacher kept a daily record on Lisa's performance, and, with the child's help, determined the degree to which Lisa kept her agreements for that day.

The daily monitor of Lisa's performance was an important feature in the early stages of Lisa's social studies plan. It not only actively involved Lisa in her own instruction, but it provided the teacher with a simple method of tracking Lisa's progress. Informal assessment provided the teacher with a continual flow of information that was current, accurate, and task-related. Assessment information in this case was both objective, such as an analysis of Lisa's written products, and subjective, such as the report of Lisa's feelings about her accomplishments.

THE FOCUS OF ASSESSMENT

Assessment has traditionally centered on the student. If there was a problem in learning, the student was considered the obvious source. It was the student who was expected to change; it was the student who was easiest to measure. Unfortunately, such a narrow focus masks problems that have as their source other aspects of education. For example, inappropriate materials, poor adult models, low expectations, problems in communication, ineffective teaching, or lack of parental support are easily overlooked when attention is focused on the student. It is easier to find the student at fault than to consider other serious problems.

Informal assessment can be focused either narrowly or broadly; in a brief time, the inquiring professional can examine a specific area or a wide variety of causes or related conditions. A narrow focus is most appropriately concerned with specific skills or behavior. A more comprehensive student assessment touches on relevant data drawn from several areas. The usual areas of consideration are the student, the setting, the instruction, and the out-of-school conditions. Table 1-3 cites these areas and lists some of the elements in each.

Table 1-3.
The Focus and Content of Assessment

STUDENT	INSTRUCTION
Skills	Goals and objectives
Behavior	Materials
Personality	Methods
Interests	Style
Ability	Reporting
Style	Teachers
History	
SETTING	**OUT-OF-SCHOOL**
Grouping	Adaptability
Peers	Parents
Friendship	Community
Aides	Religion
Facilities	Culture
System	Peers
	Nutrition
	Economics
	Work
	Recreation

Students

Many student characteristics become evident upon close informal examination. Skills or deficiencies in academic, artistic, or physical competency are often fairly evident. Behavior is also apparent and relatively easy to observe and describe. The overall personality evident in such behavior as showing humor, persistence, and friendliness, is more elusive and may reflect the student's response within the setting rather than a consistent personality pattern. Student interests are often not apparent to the teacher but become evident upon close examination. Ability is the power or capacity to perform, and in school ability is often seen as an anticipated rate of growth based on other observations of performance. Learning style is often apparent only upon careful examination. The student's history can provide clues to some of these characteristics, but, unfortunately, can also bias a teacher and create unrealistic expectations. Each element in a student's personality is worth understanding; each can provide data that can help improve instruction and each is available to some degree through informal assessment.

The Instructional Setting

The setting in which a student is instructed subtly influences performance and can also be the subject of assessment. The pattern of relationships in the class and the school can have an impact on performance. The groupings used in public schools, for instance, are unique to the field of education. In few other places does a person work together in a group of, say, thirty, all intent on a single task and all dependent on a single leader. The student in school is required to perform in a variety of ways not duplicated in the world of work. Students must function well individually, in pairs, in small groups, and in large groups. Since groupings are seldom based on student choice, peer support fluctuates significantly depending on how the class is arranged. Friends and enemies are mixed in a mandatory and closed environment. In addition, the teacher is preselected and aides are assigned. Each condition can improve or inhibit performance.

School is a system, and as such it structures the experiences of the student. Goals and objectives are based on tradition or adult expectations. The goals may or may not be appropriate or relevant to the student, his or her family, or the family culture. Grade level groupings, reporting styles, support systems, length of year, hours of class, seating arrangements, and out-of-class activities are all preset and may impede as well as facilitate learning. As in other social systems, success may be based as much on the degree of fit as on the degree of growth. System failure can go undetected when assessment is narrow and student-focused. The school plant itself, for instance, can be so constructed that it limits flexible student grouping. Solutions will be critically limited if the system itself is not open to examination and change. Some informal assessment strategies allow for examining the system, its facilities, and procedures.

Instruction

The student is an obvious focus for assessment, but the instructional program deserves equal attention. When learning does not occur, it is just as appropriate to question instructional procedures as it is to examine student performance. The teacher faces the problem of gaining a perspective on his or her own methods in order to get a perspective on the student's problem. Since the teacher is a part of the process and is intimately related to each step in instruction, it can be difficult for him or her to make an objective, detached assessment. For instance, in the midst of many competing demands, such as providing behavior management and learning at several different levels, it is difficult for a teacher to notice that a style of teaching is not compatible with a given student's style of learning. Weaknesses in teaching methods or classroom management procedures are equally difficult to detect. Yet, weaknesses in some classrooms are clearly those of the teacher and not the student. Informal assessment can, and must, be used to pinpoint these problems.

Instructional objectives, methods, and materials all affect student performance. Students who must wait after each assignment for special assistance from the teacher will demonstrate little initiative or self-reliance. Students who continually fail to reach unrealistic expectations will usually lose self-confidence and exhibit low motivation. A systematic check of objectives, methods, and materials can reveal the source of some student problems and lead to improved instruction. Monitoring and reporting strategies can be designed to improve student performance, and to suggest what support services could be employed to enhance instruction. Clearly, defined needs can be addressed by specific changes in instructional procedures.

Out-of-School Factors

The out-of-school influence on a student has long been recognized in education. Parents and community, culture and religion, peers and peer groups all have an effect on a student's performance. They provide roles, goals, and expectations, and can support or undermine the efforts of the teacher. The nutritional and economic level of the family also influence student behavior, as do the student's work and recreational experiences. Some understanding of the role these elements play can help the teacher in planning and providing instruction. Cooperation between school and home and between school and the community can lead to improved programs.

Informal assessment is the indispensable tool of the teacher. It can focus on teaching, on learning, or on the relationships between people. It can examine the supervision; the community and family; the student and his or her peers; and the teacher, teaching methods, or teaching materials. Selecting the focus is essential to the assessment process.

GUIDES TO INFORMAL ASSESSMENT

Basic tenets in informal assessment are that it is a *skill that all possess* and that it is used daily. It does not involve a mysterious set of strategies, and it is not reserved for an elite group. Informal assessment strategies allow the teacher or other professional to expand and perfect existing skills. Observation provides most classroom information. Other methods of assessment can be used when data are not readily observable. Often, improved assessment results when structure and detail are added to otherwise ordinary methods of data collection. For instance, a fully described event, including the antecedent behavior and subsequent activities, provides significantly more useful information than the ordinary observation that John hit Peter while on the play yard. Quantifying adds another important dimension to informal assessment. In other situations, task analysis helps determine appropriate instructional steps.

Informal assessment is used when a teacher must make a judgment about instruction or behavior. Informal assessment helps to answer questions such as "What do I do now?" and "Is what I'm doing working?" The *need* for assessment *springs from a concern* or question about performance. Appropriate action is based on the teacher's ability to gather relevant information and to translate that information into instructional procedures. It is an ongoing process in any instructional situation.

As a general guiding principle, the teacher selects the easiest and most convenient assessment strategy that will produce the necessary information. It is *selection based on economy.* The teacher starts with the obvious, and only if that is not sufficient for effective decisions does the teacher turn to more sophisticated methods of inquiry and observation. This general guide is also appropriate in selecting instructional strategies. A simple, direct procedure that works is usually preferable to an equally effective but more elaborate and time-consuming method. Assessment strategies can be modified, adapted, and simplified to fill the need or the situation. Just as learning can take place under the most primitive of conditions, so useful assessment data can also arise from the simplest and most accidental circumstances. The teacher needs to be alert to relevant examples of behavior and sensitive to the demonstrated needs and characteristics of the student.

It is easy to let personal bias enter into judgments about pupils. It is also difficult at times to detect bias in ourselves. Subtle expectations about student behavior can influence judgments and lead to inappropriate teacher attitudes and behavior. Expectations, such as those based on sexual, racial, and ethnic group stereotypes, can seriously predetermine a teacher's actions and negatively affect the course of student learning. Legal action against bias has tended to elevate awareness of this problem, but many subtle forms remain even in well-intentioned teachers. It is useful to know and recognize the feelings and attitudes that have come to shape and color perceptions. Recognition and acceptance of these feelings as real and influential can help reveal the influence such attitudes have on assessment and instructional activities. This recognition can further help clarify observations and allow a more accurate perception of conditions as they exist for the student. Teacher decisions can then be reasonably free of prejudgments and biased expectations.

It has been said that psychology is the study of human behavior within a particular culture. A similar statement can be made about educational assessment: It is the appraisal of educationally related behavior within a given setting that is often unlike the world outside. Data drawn from the school situation are most appropriately interpreted in that setting—*generalization* outside the classroom *is risky.* This is obviously true for the student who is quiet within the class but outgoing and vocal on the playground. Not so obvious is the student who is inconspicuous in the classroom but a leader in the street, or one who uses classroom-appropriate language in the class and dialect language in the schoolyard or in private. Observations made in the classroom may not reflect the "soul" of the student; they may describe the student only within specific settings and under certain conditions. Generalizing to behavior outside the classroom is safest when there is verifiable or collaborative information from other settings.

In addition to these general guides, two considerations need to be addressed any time information is gathered from a sample of a student's behavior or performance. The first is the problem of *reliability.* Reliability refers to the consistency and repeatability of data. Reliability asks these questions: Do the data give consistent results? Would the results be similar if gathered in a slightly different manner or if gathered at some other hour, day, and so on? If the answer to either question is no, the data are unreliable and should not be used in decision making. Increasing the amount of data or the length of a sample tends to improve reliability.

The second consideration rests in whether information is *valid* or representative. This consideration asks of the data, Does this really measure or represent what I claim it measures? For instance, is an oral spelling test a valid measure of spelling as found in written compositions? For some children it will be valid; for others it will not accurately represent their daily spelling proficiency. Validity tends to improve when evaluation data closely represent the task that is to be judged.

Assessment guides can improve the accuracy and usefulness of data gathered informally. Unbiased data collection and reporting can result in a more accurate representation of the facts. When instructional strategies are open to examination, and when the setting can be evaluated, the possibility of blaming the child is reduced. Examples of behavior that continue long enough and appear frequently enough to be representative will ensure both data consistency and information that accurately represents the problem under consideration. Such behavior examples will be the most relevant for decision making.

Summary

Informal assessment plays a critical role in the decisions that are made daily in schools. This assessment is based on data generated from observations, interviews, case histories, and tests. It is the result of careful attention to behavior and performance, and to appropriate recording and reporting. When informal data are combined with information from standardized tests they result in a comprehensive understanding of student performance and provide the basis for carefully considered judgments.

The assessment process is an ongoing activity within the schools. It provides information used to identify pupil needs; to plan and deliver instruction; to monitor, evaluate, and report progress; and to counsel and otherwise assist students and their parents. Informal data are readily available and immediately applicable in the classroom setting. Greater sophistication in selecting, gathering, and recording informal data is needed, however, in order to meet the challenges of the atypical student.

There are several options when selecting the focus of informal assessment. Data can be gathered about the skills, behavior, and attitudes of a particular student or group of students; about the setting or ecology in which a student functions; about the methods and strategies of instruction; and about behavior and experiences outside of school. Each will provide information that may be useful in decision making, but the area that is given the greatest emphasis will set the parameters for subsequent decisions. Data generated from a particular area of information will result in action that affects that area of experience. The knowledgeable assessor takes care in selecting the area of focus and recognizes the inherent influence and limitation created by that choice.

Bibliography

Broadfoot, Patricia. *Assessment in Schools and Society.* London: Methuen, 1979.

Eaves, Ronald C., and McLaughlin, Phillip. "A Systems Approach for the Assessment of the Child and His Environment: Getting Back to Basics." *The Journal of Special Education* 11, no. 1 (1977): 99–111.

Freijo, Tom D., and Jaeger, Richard M. "Social Class and Race as Concomitants of Composite Halo in Teachers' Evaluative Rating of Pupils." *American Education Research Journal* 13, no. 1 (1976): 1–14.

Gray-Little, Bernadette, and Applebaum, Mark I. "Instrumentality Effect in the Assessment of Racial Differences in Self-Esteem." *Journal of Personality and Social Psychology* 37, no. 7 (1979): 1221–1229.

Haney, Walt. "Trouble over Testing." *Educational Leadership* 37, no. 8 (1980): 640–650.

Lahey, Benjamine B.; Vosk, Barbara N.; and Habif, Valerie L. "Behavioral Assessment of Learning Disabled Children: A Rationale and Strategy." *Behavioral Assessment* 3, no. 1 (1981): 3–14.

Levin, Murray. "The Academic Achievement Test: Its Historical Context and Social Functions." *American Psychologist* 31, no. 3 (1976): 228–238.

Poole, Richard L. "Evaluating and Victimizing Elementary School Children." *Education* 97, no. 1 (1976): 115–120.

Salili, Farideh; Maehr, Martin L.; Sorensen, Richard L.; and Fyans, Leslie J., Jr. "A Further Consideration of the Effects of Evaluation on Motivation." *American Educational Research Journal* 13, no. 2 (1976): 85–102.

Scherr, Judith E. "Danger: Testing in Progress." *AMICUS* 4, no. 2 (March/April 1979): 74–81.

Shager, Rodney W. *The Great Criterion-referenced Test Myth.* CSE Report No. 95. Los Angeles: Center for the Study of Evaluation, School of Education, University of California, 1978.

Shavelson, Richard J.; Cadwell, Joel; and Izu, Tonia. "Teachers' Sensitivity to the Reliability of Information in Making Pedagogical Decisions." *American Educational Research Journal* 14, no. 2 (1977): 83–97.

Ysseldyke, James E., and Algozzine, Bob. "Perspectives on Assessment of Learning Disabled Students." *Learning Disability Quarterly* 2, no. 4 (1979): 3–13.

Chapter 2
Assessment Approaches

There are several ways to approach the analysis of students' performance. Assessment can compare one student's performance to that of other students; it can determine a student's level of achievement in relation to a specific goal; it can identify a student's ability to complete successfully a group of activities critical to the completion of a task; it can view performance within the context of developmental and deviation expectancies; and it can provide a comprehensive understanding of a student's behavior. Comparison is most frequently found in formal tests. All the other approaches involve informal assessment and are augmented by formal testing. Each type of assessment provides the teacher with different information and each satisfies different assessment needs. All have a legitimate and important place in student assessment.

STUDENT COMPARISON

Assessment that compares a student to other students is called *norm-referenced* and is the most common kind of measurement found in the schools. Such assessment involves testing, and is useful when comparisons are important. Competitive grading, for instance, requires accurate assessment of student differences and rankings. Norm-referenced information answers such questions as these: How is my son doing in comparison to other children his age? Who are the best and the poorest spellers in the class? Information on the relative standing of a student can also be used, together with data obtained in earlier grades, to determine growth rates and identify patterns of strengths and weaknesses. Significant fluctuations can reflect changes in learning styles, and downturns can signal emerging problems. Norm-referenced tests are discussed in more detail later in the chapter.

SKILL ASSESSMENT

Assessment that measures a learner's skill in accomplishing a given task uses *criterion* tests. The term, suggested by Glaser (1963), refers to the measurement of an individual's performance relative to a specific behavioral objective. The focus is on the student's level of performance, what the student can do, and what is needed to reach a success level. The performance of other students has little relevance. Criterion-referenced information answers such questions as these: What specific functions in math can John perform? How much improvement does Mary need in order to type 50 words per minute?

The strengths of criterion-referenced assessment lie in its flexibility and adaptability to different curriculums, its inclusion of specific performance skills and levels, and its identification of acceptability levels for success or mastery. Items are drawn directly from instruction and results are easily translated into instructional plans. The teacher and the student usually agree about the appropriateness of the measurement, and subsequent goals are often self-evident. Since the sequence of questions is generally linear, students can easily see the growth they have made and the direction in which they are headed. Assessment can be continuous, and disagreements about results are easily resolved by demonstrating the skill in question.

The limitations of this approach rest in the time and detail that is required to construct criterion tests, in the narrowness of the focus, and in the appropriateness of the criterion. Individual records are needed to track each student's development and, at times, individualized instruction is needed. Criterion items tend to focus on the obvious and avoid the subtle and elaborate detail of a subject that is necessary to the instruction of bright students. Instruction limited to criterion-referenced assessment and material can be bland and stiff.

The criterion-referenced approach may also overlook general causes of poor performance that run through several areas of instruction. An analysis of math performance, for instance, might not reveal a student's general aversion and poor performance in all paper-and-pencil tasks. The focus on the specific can obscure subtle and pervasive conditions. Criterion tests are discussed in more detail later in the chapter.

TASK ANALYSIS

The *task analysis* approach is a more detailed form of student assessment. In this procedure a skill is reduced to units and sequenced in teachable subskills, each with a hierarchy of tasks and subtasks. The use of this process in academic areas is foreign to many teachers because text publishers and other curriculum developers have typically provided a ready-made plan of sequenced steps and knowledges within a subject area. Even assessment instruments are often constructed around a predetermined sequence of elements within a subject area, and questions are arranged in ascending order of difficulty. When, however, the usual order and steps in teaching a skill do not lead to learning, the teacher who wishes to determine where the breakdown has occurred can turn to task analysis.

Most teachers actually have an unrecognized understanding of the essential steps in task analysis because they have used the process when instructing in nonacademic subjects such as sports, art, dancing, construction, and so on. When preparing a student to master a dance step, to use a baseball bat, to prepare a planting area, or to make a paper head, the teacher first identifies each small step needed to carry out the task. These steps are then taught in a sequenced and orderly fashion. The teacher can apply these same strategies to academic and behavioral tasks and help guide a failing student to success.

The strengths of this assessment procedure lie in its selection of a target objective, identification of the steps needed to reach an acceptable level of success, and breakdown of the tasks into learning units that the student can manage. The procedure provides the answers to a number of questions including these: Where should I begin teaching? What is the precise level of this student's skills? What progress is being made? Is the student ready for the next step?

The drawbacks to task analysis center around the time needed to conduct the analysis and to design and implement an instructional sequence.

Task analysis also has the tendency to restrict the teacher's focus. The procedure is helpful in pinpointing student strengths and weaknesses, but it can result in the neglect of more general needs and disorders.

Task analysis is examined in greater detail later in the chapter.

SURVEY ANALYSIS

A *survey analysis* extends student assessment beyond the task or the skill. A survey is undertaken to confirm the suspicion that a student is falling behind his or her peers and that the lag in learning extends over a range of subject areas. The survey includes those areas where the student is experiencing difficulty and a determination of the achievement that is expected.

The survey assessment is curriculum-oriented; that is, it lists the skills required to accomplish reading, spelling, writing, arithmetic, and other classroom tasks. If the survey reveals a modest discrepancy between what the child is doing and what is expected of him or her, then a remedial plan is developed. Thus, it may be determined that a student will receive added practice or instruction during recess or after school for a few days, may be given a peer tutor, or may receive teacher-directed tutoring over an extended period of time. If the discrepancy is great, the diagnostic analysis, described later, should be used.

The strength of the survey analysis rests on its extension of the assessment procedure into a variety of curriculum-related areas. The identification of a problem triggers a wider examination of student progress. Common problems that may affect more than one learning area are identified, and both the depth and the range of the problem are determined.

One limitation of the approach is the time it takes to complete a thorough survey of all subject areas. This approach can also lead to superficial attention to a problem that requires precise task or criterion analysis. It is also possible to become overwhelmed by the pervasiveness of a problem and to neglect the fact that a direct and successful remedial intervention in a single area may in turn reduce problems in other subject areas.

Survey analysis is discussed in greater detail later in the chapter.

DIAGNOSTIC ANALYSIS

A fifth approach to assessment is the comprehensive *diagnostic analysis*. This assessment is undertaken only after it has been established that (1) the student's skill or behavior is significantly different from what can be expected in normal development, (2) the discrepancy is persistent, or escalating, (3) the discrepancy falls significantly outside the range of normal variation, and (4) a variety of interventions have failed to bring about a change. Often one or more of the previously described assessment approaches have been tried, teaching strategies have been instituted, and either there has not been a noticeable change in the student's performance or the problem has shifted from one area to another. Diagnostic assessment can be performed by the classroom teacher, but often, because of the time required, it is performed by a learning specialist.

Diagnostic analysis is child-oriented; the assessor observes the student under a variety of conditions and along several dimensions. Data in different skill areas and from different indices of behavior are compared and combined to provide a comprehensive picture of the student. Judgments based on a composite understanding of the student lead to instructional priorities. The intent of the assessment is to achieve maximum understanding of the student's problem and to select areas for assistance that are most likely to affect total performance.

The strength of this procedure lies in the comprehensive nature of the assessment. While previously mentioned assessment procedures generally focus on the behavior of the student or the task to be accomplished, the diagnostic process develops a broad spectrum of assessment information including history, skill, ability, and attitude evaluation. The data may lead to teaching interventions that deal with an underlying problem rather than with an observable skill deficiency.

There are several difficulties with this approach. First, it is more time-consuming than the other methods. Also, it is possible to reduce an underlying problem and still not improve the student's academic skill. This approach, therefore, should be used only after more direct methods have been tried or seriously considered and have been abandoned as inadequate.

Diagnostic analysis is discussed in greater detail later in the chapter.

Table 2-1 briefly summarizes the characteristics of all the assessment procedures.

TEST CONSTRUCTION AND STRATEGIES

Tests are an important part of assessment; consequently, their construction is also important. Tests must be reliable and valid, and test items must be constructed according to certain guidelines. Five test strategies are considered here: norm-referenced tests, criterion tests, task analysis, survey analysis, and diagnostic analysis.

Table 2-1.
Basic Characteristics of Five Assessment Approaches

	BRIEF DESCRIPTION	STRENGTHS	LIMITATIONS	USES
Norm-referenced test	Makes comparisons among students	Describes the student's level compared to other students	General data; inappropriate norms	Giving grades; communicating with parents; measuring growth
Criterion test	Focuses on skill level in a subject area	Identifies the exact level of skill mastery	Lacks data on relative standing; narrow focus	Skill analysis; small-step instruction; skill level measure
Task analysis	Examines all the activities required in a task	Provides details on all steps needed to achieve mastery	Time demands; limited focus	Analysis of overall tasks; identification of related areas of needs; sequenced training
Survey analysis	Measures all curricular areas where difficulties are experienced	Determines skill needs for a variety of learning areas	Useful only for mild, nonescalating problems	Classroom examination of student deficiencies for remediation by standard methods
Diagnostic analysis	Leads to a comprehensive understanding of a condition	Gives overall understanding of strengths and weaknesses	Time demands; no assurance that improvement will generalize	Comprehensive assessment; identifying underlying problems; integrated instruction

Reliability and Validity

A basic concern in all assessment is test reliability and validity. In commercially produced, formal tests, data on these two test characteristics are included in the manual and should be reviewed by the teacher. In teacher-made tests, the responsibility for reliability and validity rests with the teacher.

Reliability Good reliability requires that the teacher provide enough test items so that students' chance errors, their misunderstandings and small voids in knowledge and understanding, do not result in an inaccurate report of their actual achievement, belief, opinion, or attitude. Experience, however, provides the following counsel against overlong testing: Keep it short enough so that fatigue and inattention do not occur. Two or more sessions may be needed when intensive testing is done.

As a general rule, the more items there are in a test, the more reliable the results. The response on a single item is very unreliable. The minimum number of items required to ensure reliability depends on the type of item used. Multiple-choice tests of fifteen or more items are generally desirable. A short answer essay test of three items is considerably less reliable and trustworthy than a test of six or more items. A long answer essay test of one item is not recommended for assessment and should be reserved for learning exercises. Twenty or more true-false items are required to partly offset the fact that 50 percent of the responses could be correct just on the basis of chance. And it would take sixty true-false items to get as reliable a measure as 15 multiple-choice items. Matching items poses unusual problems and requires careful construction. Since confusion and error occur in long matching exercises, no more than six items should be included in a single question.

Validity Validity addresses the issue of whether a test actually measures what it claims to measure. Test items in teacher-made tests are often selected from the exact subject area and written in the same format in which they were taught. As a result, assuming the student is in good health and is motivated, the score is likely to be a valid measure of the student's specific skill. As items become less representative of a subject area or as test form differs from actual application, validity diminishes. For instance, a spelling test that requires a student to identify a correctly spelled word from among a number of incorrect spellings may not accurately measure a particular student's ability to spell correctly when writing a composition.

The more directly a subject can be measured, the more likely it is that the results will be valid. Math tests, for instance, tend to take examples directly from skill or application areas. As such, they tend to be valid measures. It is less likely that attitudes, beliefs, or interests can be as accurately measured. Information drawn indirectly or tangently from a content area tends to have low validity.

Good validity is most likely to occur when

1. Test-taking conditions are ideal and motivation is high
2. Test items are clearly written and the question structure and format are easily understood and consistent
3. Test items are representative of the actual skill, achievement, ability, or behavior that is being measured

Test Items

Five types of test items have been briefly mentioned: multiple-choice, short answer essay, long essay, true-false, and matching. Other useful forms are completion items, ratings, and checklists. Each can provide useful information and has a place in the repertoire of assessment instruments. Samples of item form and general construction guidelines follow.

Multiple-choice questions The multiple-choice form includes a statement item and usually four answer choices. Here is an example:

What form of test item allows 50 percent of the responses to be correct on the basis of chance?
- a. Multiple-choice
- b. True-false
- c. Short essay
- d. Sentence completion

Items should be prepared following these general guidelines:

1. The stem of the question should be able to stand as a complete statement or question.
2. Answers should be nearly equal in length.
3. Grammar should be consistent throughout the stem and answers.
4. The position of the correct answer should be varied.
5. Determiners such as *all, none, some, often,* and *usually* sound be avoided.
6. Negative statements in the stem or answers should be avoided.

Short-answer essay The length of the response to an essay question is determined by the knowledge of the respondent, the space provided, the limitations set in the question, and the time allocated for the response. Statements that limit the length of the response include "In the space provided . . . ," "Limit your answer to three paragraphs," "Spend approximately 15 minutes on each question," and "Consider only those items that are mentioned in the text." In both short-answer and long-answer essay questions, the format includes the question and a clear statement of the expected parameters of the response. Here is an example of a short-answer essay question:

> What is the difference between multiple-choice and sentence completion questions? Briefly describe each, tell how they differ, and give an example of each.

Long-answer essay This type of question is used when a comprehensive and lengthy response is required. The format gives the respondent a large amount of response freedom and allows him or her to demonstrate organizational ability, creativity, and breadth of understanding. Such latitude, however, makes this form of response difficult to score or grade. Here is an example of a long-answer essay question:

> Describe the purposes of test questions in school. Include in your response the various ways in which questions are used, the type of question formats available, and the strengths and weaknesses of each type.

True-false questions In the true-false format, a single statement is presented and the respondent is to determine whether the item is true or false. The difficulty in constructing test items like these lies in the fact that important concepts almost always have exceptions, and thus this test format is often inappropriate. At the same time, trivial information is hardly worth examining.

The true-false format is usually presented as follows:

T F 1. Multiple-choice items tend to be more trivial than true-false items.

General guidelines for preparing true-false items are as follows:

1. Items should in general be easy.
2. Items should be brief and clear.

3. Items should be balanced as to the number that are true and false, with any advantage given to the number of false items.
4. Items must be unequivocally true or false.

Matching questions In the matching format, two columns of information are given. One column provides the statement or premise and the other the list of terms or phrases that correspond to it. The following is an illustration:

Match the test type with the correct description and place the letter of the description in the space before the test type.

_____ Multiple choice	a. Stem is required
_____ True-false	b. Validity is low
_____ Matching	c. Chance factor is high
_____ Short essay	d. Correcting is laborious
	e. Premise is used

The guidelines for constructing matching questions are as follows:

1. Responses should exceed the number of premises.
2. A response can be used for one or more premises or not used at all.
3. Premise and response content should be homogeneous.
4. A premise should not have more than one response.
5. Items should be short and clear.

Completion items With completion items, a statement is constructed so that the respondent must complete the item. For example:

_______________ test items are likely to be trivial.

The guidelines for constructing good completion items are:

1. The given portions of the statement must be clear and suggest a single correct answer.
2. Items should be easily completed by those familiar with the content area.
3. The response should be limited to a single missing item for each statement.
4. The length of the blank space and the articles *a* and *an* should not provide clues to the correct answer.

Ratings With ratings, a variety of formats are available. Statements can be used that rank, describe, or identify. Here are examples of several rating forms.

1. Compare Susan Smith to other students in the classroom:

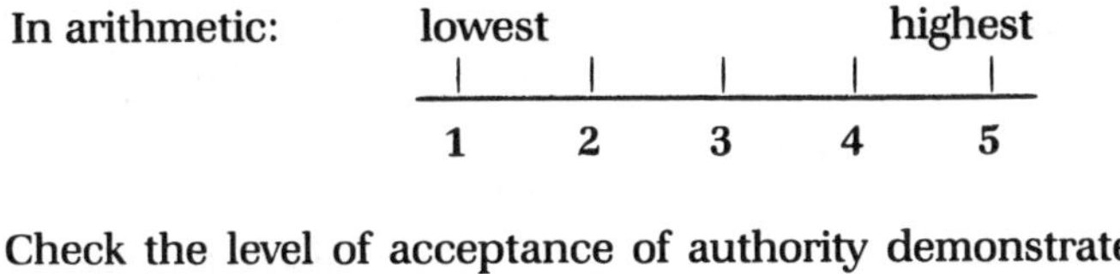

2. Check the level of acceptance of authority demonstrated by this student.

Defiant	Critical or resistant	Usually obedient	Compliant and respectful	Submissive

3. The part of this class that I enjoyed the most was:

____

The part I enjoyed the least was:

____

Ratings should be constructed according to the following guidelines:

1. The rating task must be clear enough that the respondent understands what he or she is to do.
2. The response format should be concise and easy to complete.
3. Several variations on the same question should be given in order to increase reliability.
4. Interpretation should be made cautiously for tests that measure areas other than verifiable skills.
5. Item descriptors at different points of the scale should be equally distant in meaning.
6. Stability of the response over time should be questioned in areas other than verifiable skills.

Checklists A checklist provides a series of items that allow the respondent to complete a rapid survey of critical identifiers in the area under investigation. A variety of formats are available. For example:

1. When I have free time in class, I like to: (Check two)

Watch others ____	Talk to friends ____
Read ____	Play games ____
Think about things ____	Draw ____
Work on projects ____	Other ____

2. Check those items that describe the student's regular behavior.

Dislikes school ____	Has problems following directions ____
Is uncooperative with teacher ____	Has short attention span ____
Is not liked by peers ____	Is unorganized in class work ____
Has fights or arguments ____	Gives up easily ____
Does not contribute to class discussion ____	Does not take responsibility ____
Does not work independently ____	Is late in turning in work ____
Demonstrates low skills in two or more areas ____	Is late or frequently absent ____
Does not complete assignments ____	Has problems on the yard ____
Other ____	Speaks out inappropriately ____

3. The teacher in the classroom:

	Yes	No
Prepares daily plans	____	____
Provides some individualized material	____	____
Can see the entire class during activities	____	____
Verbally attends to correct behaviors	____	____
Recognizes students seeking attention	____	____
Is polite to students	____	____
Moves about the room to facilitate order	____	____
Can make limit-setting statements	____	____
Makes verbal statements clear, concise, and audible	____	____

Guidelines for the construction of checklists are as follows:

1. The list of identifiers should be comprehensive enough to cover the critical elements in the subject area.
2. Identifiers should be concise and clearly descriptive of the element to be examined.
3. Identifiers should be grouped so that all those related to a particular area fall in consecutive order.

4. Whenever possible, identifiers should be behavioral descriptions that are subject to verification.

Norm-Referenced Tests

Most commercially produced tests are norm-referenced. That is, they have carefully selected items that have been administered to a large sample of students. The publisher provides a manual that includes the directions for administration and scoring, as well as the statistics developed from the original test trials. The statistics generally include a description of the sample population, the average results of the sample, and the variations and deviations that occurred. Grade-level scores or other forms of standard measures are often provided. These are formal tests and have the advantages of professionally constructed questions and comparative data. They are easily explained to other professionals and their results are commonly accepted as creditable.

The limitations of commercially produced norm-referenced tests lie in the limited application of the resulting information and the inappropriateness of some comparison groups. In an attempt to cover the wide variation in skill levels that exists among students, the norm-referenced test often lacks the refinements needed to actually assess the strengths and weakness of a given student at a given level of performance. It thus provides little information upon which a teacher can plan an instructional program for a particular student. The second limitation occurs when there is a significant difference between an individual student and the larger norm group with whom he is compared. Assessment questions reflect both the content of a subject area and a context within which that subject occurs. The context includes such areas as culture, economics, behavior, and language. Students who lack experience in the context from which questions are drawn and in which tests are given perform poorly, and their strengths and potential go unnoticed.

The traditional teacher-made test can also be normed, but it will be far less sophisticated than the commercial tests. Score averages, score ranking, and score variations are relatively easy to compute. Tests that are reused can provide accumulated data and, therefore, can reflect an individual's standing within a larger multiyear group of students.

The advantage of teacher-made tests is that they can be tied directly to classroom instruction. Such tests allow the teacher to measure knowledge and skill before and after instruction, and the test results can provide students with information directly related to their classroom experience.

The weakness in such tests is most frequently found in poor item construction. Concerns about test reliability and validity are especially critical in teacher-made tests, especially when results are used to make serious decisions about student grades, progress, and placement. These tests are often created to meet an immediate and unique need and are administered and scored in haste. However, together with criterion-referenced tests, they are at the heart of instruction and deserve serious consideration.

The following are general guides for norm-referenced tests.

1. Select tests that reflect the goals and objectives of your instructional program.
2. Use tests with items that will measure the range of skill levels present in your class.
3. Review the publisher's information on reliability, validity, and normative data.
4. Use tests that have a norm group similar to your class or represent an intentional comparison group.
5. Determine if the resulting test data can be clearly and accurately interpreted.
6. Follow the publisher's recommended testing procedures.

Criterion Tests

Criterion tests measure the student's performance in relation to specific instructional objectives. These tests can be teacher-made or commercially prepared. The items on the tests are directly related to the subjects of instruction and they focus on skill levels.

Criterion tests measure the skill level a student has achieved on the road to mastery. The acceptable level of mastery is set, and it becomes the criterion for successful completion of the learning sequence. In this way criterion tests specifically focus on the content of instruction and provide direct evidence about the level of a student's achievement. Criterion tests continuously measure, in an organized way, an individual's performance. By using criterion tests, the teacher can pinpoint student skill levels, as well as strengths and weaknesses. Such tests can be used to determine how far a student must progress to reach a given standard and the degree of accuracy required at that level. Criterion tests help to identify the skill level at which a student enters the hierarchy of steps in instruction; such tests can also be used to measure the effectiveness of instructional procedures. In these ways the criterion tests tend to outperform norm-referenced tests.

The criterion test has several drawbacks. It implies a commitment to individualized instruction, to frequent measurement, and to adherence to skill mastery. Individualized instruction in some form is, of course, the natural outcome of an assessment technique that identifies the specific functioning level of each student. The data can be used to group students for instruction, but individual variations are magnified and demand some individual attention. This can pose a serious problem to a teacher who is unable to individualize because of large class size and insufficient assistance.

A closely related problem is the amount of time required in criterion testing. At a minimum, the testing occurs before and after (pre-post) a given teaching sequence. Testing can also occur weekly or in short daily probes. Thus, a large pool of test items must be available; time must be set aside to test; and test reviews and instructional modifications must be conducted. All this can lead to appropriate and responsive instruction; at the same time, it can place a significant burden on the classroom teacher. Several strategies can improve the manageability of criterion instruction. One strategy is to limit the procedure to one or two subject areas; another is to restrict the number of students with whom it is used. The teacher can also use commercially produced systems and obtain help from trained aides or peers.

Criterion measurement requires that test items measure performance, that they be sequenced to follow the steps in learning, and that an appropriate level of mastery be identified. The use of skill mastery has a number of implications in instruction. There is the danger that test items will become the goal rather than examples of instruction and that instruction will become chained to the test. If this occurs, instruction narrows to meet the specific criteria of the test and loses those elements that allow the student to generalize the information. A slavish adherence to criterion and mastery instruction tends to overlook the elaborate breadth and quality of knowledge and avoids those areas that are not easily subjected to criterion measures, such as attitudes, appreciation, and creativity.

Limitations, however, are a reality with any single form of measurement and should not detract from the essential value and use of criterion measures. Nor should criterion testing be taken as a new form of measurement. It is, in a systematic way, what effective teachers have always done. When confronted by a student who had difficulty learning, the teacher broke the subject into small steps, determined where the student was failing, and began instruction at that point.

The following is a brief example of two formats of criterion testing in basic two-digit addition:

$$\begin{array}{r}2\\+3\\\hline\end{array}\quad\begin{array}{r}1\\+8\\\hline\end{array}\quad\begin{array}{r}0\\+9\\\hline\end{array}\quad\begin{array}{r}5\\+8\\\hline\end{array}\qquad\begin{array}{l}2+4=\\0+8=\end{array}\qquad\begin{array}{l}1+7=\\6+5=\end{array}$$

The following are general guidelines for constructing criterion-referenced tests.

1. Reduce instructional goals to a sequence of objectives that lead to each goal.
2. Construct items that measure performance that is directly related to the skill steps leading to an objective.
3. Establish criterion levels to reflect the degree of performance that ensures consistent success and provides the basic entry skill needed for subsequent objectives.
4. Include enough items (four to ten) to establish clearly that the results accurately represent the student's level of performance.
5. Create a pool of pretested items so that the same item does not need to be used in repeated testing.
6. Evaluate and redesign items so that they are clear and accurate measurements of a learning step.

Task Analysis

Some student problems involve more than a specific skill deficiency. Even when a simple task is to be completed, it requires the integration of a complex array of activities. Task analysis examines all the activities required to complete a task. It can be used to identify the skills required to enter the task, the types of related abilities that are needed, the steps required to reach the goal, the possible alternative procedures, and the expected outcomes.

In both criterion-referenced testing and task analysis, it is important to specify the objective of the instruction, the learning outcome that is to be achieved. In criterion testing a clear statement of the objective is essential because it becomes the standard toward which learning is geared. In task analysis the objective is important because it sets the parameters of the needs of the task. Task analysis is a method well suited to examining the complex array of skills required to carry out a class assignment. It can provide a comprehensive understanding of the component steps, options, and accommodations that are appropriate for the completion of a task. Approaches to task analysis vary, depending partly on assessor preference. Five approaches are described.

1. *Watch and question.* The teacher can carefully watch a student perform an activity and notice at what point the student begins to fail. In a social studies assignment, for instance, a student may attend to the directions, select the appropriate text, read the book, and then falter in the

preparation of a written report. The steps are apparent. Further examination may reveal that the student did not understand the assignment but did grasp the appropriate content of the text. The breakdown occurred when the student attempted to organize the material, develop an appropriate sentence and paragraph content, and write the report.

2. *Watch an expert.* It is often helpful, especially in the analysis of a physical task, to watch someone who is proficient in the task. Such watching allows the observer to chronicle each step in the process and to notice the details required in a successful performance. It also allows the observer to match proper and improper performance in analyzing discrepancies.

3. *Do-it-yourself.* One of the most frequent approaches to task analysis is for the teacher to perform the task, and note the required actions. This procedure puts a strain on objectivity, but it allows the teacher to experience the complexity of the task personally. It also gives the teacher the skill necessary to model or demonstrate the task.

4. *Backward stepping.* Many tasks lend themselves to a deductive form of backward analysis. Starting with the successfully performed task, the teacher asks what is immediately required to perform the task. The answer is the first step backward from the point of completion. Continuing backward, preceding steps are identified until the skill level of the student is reached. This procedure allows the teacher to stop the analysis at the point where the student is proficient.

5. *Goal examination.* Goals in the affective (feeling) and behavioral (action) areas are often best understood in terms of an analysis of the expected behavior. If, for instance, peer cooperation is a student goal, it is necessary to break the goal into specific observable behaviors, such as shares books and materials with peers, accepts papers from peers, and so on. In this form of analysis it is important to identify concrete examples of successful behavior and also the level and frequency required to achieve an acceptable performance.

The following are guidelines for constructing task analysis items.

1. Identify a specific task and determine the level of acceptable performance.
2. Identify and record the skills and behaviors necessary to complete the task.
3. Determine the student's skill level required for each step.
4. Determine appropriate alternative, compensatory, or adapted methods of completing the task.
5. Begin instruction or adaptation for those steps where the student needs assistance.

6. Keep the focus on the task and describe necessary skills in observable, behavioral terms.

Survey Analysis

Survey analysis systematically examines a student's skills in one or more curriculum areas. In this procedure the required skills in each area in which the student is experiencing difficulty are outlined. The outline(s) can be constructed by the teacher or other assessor and can be tailored to the particular subject and level under consideration. The inventories that are provided in each of the skill-related chapters (Chapters 7–10) are examples of survey analysis instruments.

The purpose of the survey analysis is to systematically address student performance so as to identify the exact nature of the difficulty. Attention is focused on clearly identifying features within a subject area and establishing the degree of the discrepancy between a student's actual and expected performance.

The starting point of the analysis is the subject area the assessor believes to be either the most troublesome or central to other problems. In the primary grades this tends to be one of the basic skill areas—reading, writing, or arithmetic. In the upper elementary grades the problem is often located in a subject area that requires a cluster of basic skills, such as social studies. Problems in higher grade levels also tend to involve clusters of basic skills, as well as related learning skills such as motivation, analysis, organization, and planning.

The survey analysis outline is developed in a manner similar to that used in task analysis, but it does not pay the same precise and narrow attention to step and sequence. The process of outline construction allows the assessor to determine skill needs that are common across different subject areas, such as the impact of illegible handwriting on all written assignments. The items in the survey outline can be determined using the same steps that are described for task analysis, or they can be drawn from text or workbook skill breakdowns, from those in standardized tests, or those generated in student reports about themselves.

The following are guidelines for constructing survey analysis items.

1. Write outline items in a form that allows them to be checked as to the degree of presence or absence.
2. Devise item statements that are short, describe clearly defined skills, and are measurable.
3. Create items that can be verified by observation in several settings.
4. It is desirable to develop a sequence of subskills.

5. Determine ways to estimate levels of performance.
6. Create items that suggest instructional categories.

The student learning profile presented in Figure 2-1 is an example of a survey analysis outline. This profile is also appropriate for use in summarizing data from the diagnostic analysis, a procedure that is described generally in the next section and in greater detail in those chapters that deal with the assessment of academic subjects. The profile can be filled in by using information gained through observation or testing. A checkmark should be placed at the appropriate location on the rating scale. For example, in the area of language skills, the profile provides for assessing three areas, one of which has as many as three subareas. After observing and recording the child's performance in each area and subarea two or three times, the teacher will be able to determine if the child's general ability to process information is poor, below average, average, above average, or good, and mark the profile accordingly. Making the two or three observations in each area to obtain this general impression may be time-consuming, but it is essential in order to come up with an opinion that is less subject to error.

Figure 2-1.
Student Learning Profile

	POOR	BELOW AVERAGE	AVERAGE	ABOVE AVERAGE	GOOD
I. General intelligence (if known)					
Verbal	______	______	______	______	______
Performance	______	______	______	______	______
II. Language					
Concepts (inner)	______	______	______	______	______
Comprehension	______	______	______	______	______
Problem solving	______	______	______	______	______
Receptive	______	______	______	______	______
Vocabulary	______	______	______	______	______
Comprehension	______	______	______	______	______
Expressive	______	______	______	______	______
Vocabulary	______	______	______	______	______
Sentence formation	______	______	______	______	______
Fluency	______	______	______	______	______

(continued)

Figure 2-1 continued

	POOR	BELOW AVERAGE	AVERAGE	ABOVE AVERAGE	GOOD
III. Sensorimotor					
Gross motor	____	____	____	____	____
Coordination	____	____	____	____	____
Sports participation	____	____	____	____	____
Fine motor	____	____	____	____	____
Dexterity	____	____	____	____	____
Motor-planning	____	____	____	____	____
Coordination	____	____	____	____	____
Organization	____	____	____	____	____
Auditory development	____	____	____	____	____
Nonverbal	____	____	____	____	____
Verbal	____	____	____	____	____
Visual development	____	____	____	____	____
Perception	____	____	____	____	____
Spatial relationships	____	____	____	____	____
IV. Academic					
Reading	____	____	____	____	____
Oral	____	____	____	____	____
Silent	____	____	____	____	____
Word recognition	____	____	____	____	____
Comprehension	____	____	____	____	____
Functional use	____	____	____	____	____
Recreational use	____	____	____	____	____
Arithmetic	____	____	____	____	____
Concepts	____	____	____	____	____
Mental arithmetic	____	____	____	____	____
Computation	____	____	____	____	____
Spelling	____	____	____	____	____
Spelling lists	____	____	____	____	____
Written work	____	____	____	____	____
Handwriting	____	____	____	____	____
Quality	____	____	____	____	____
Speed	____	____	____	____	____
Written language	____	____	____	____	____
Productivity	____	____	____	____	____
Syntax	____	____	____	____	____
Form	____	____	____	____	____
Ideation	____	____	____	____	____

	POOR	BELOW AVERAGE	AVERAGE	ABOVE AVERAGE	GOOD
V. Social Skills					
Adults	____	____	____	____	____
Peers	____	____	____	____	____
Classroom	____	____	____	____	____
Playground	____	____	____	____	____
Outside community	____	____	____	____	____

SOURCE: Developed by Arlee S. Maier. Copyright © 1980 by Arlee S. Maier.

Diagnostic Analysis

Diagnostic analysis is a process for determining the cause and nature of a disorder or a learning problem. It is a comprehensive examination of a student's characteristics, and it assumes an interrelatedness of underlying functional processes. It often includes some attention to the cognitive, behavioral, and affective development of the student. Each of these generic areas separates into a large number of subareas such as thinking, memory, attention, social relationships, attitudes, motivation, and interests.

The diagnostic analysis uses a variety of assessment methods. A broad spectrum approach to assessment is used and is appropriate for those problems that have resisted simpler correction procedures such as direct remedial instruction or standard behavior management strategies.

In diagnostic analysis the problem is stated in enough detail to provide a comprehensive understanding of the scope and persistence of the behavior. A review is then made to determine what information is available and to identify those areas that require further investigation. Assessment strategies are then selected and data are developed. The information is analyzed, and interventions are designed to modify the student's performance.

The profile presented in Figure 2-1, when used as a part of the diagnostic assessment, will help the teacher organize and interpret the information obtained, as well as understand what problem areas have contributed to the child's lack of success in the classroom. The profile will also help the teacher determine what kind of remedial program should be used and what kind of accommodation should be made in assignments or teaching methods in order for the child to succeed.

When the profile has been completed, the teacher will have a graphic outline of the assessment findings. Now, if both reading comprehension and inner language functioning are low, the teacher understands that oral language activities, based on listening and understanding, will need to be strengthened before he or she can expect reading comprehension to improve. Or, the profile may reveal weakness in spatial relations, motor-planning, and arithmetic computation, while arithmetic concepts appear to be satisfactory. The teacher will then be able to identify that understanding arithmetic is not really the child's problem, but that writing the computations down on the paper is the problem. In this case the remediation will consist of helping the child set the computations on paper in an organized fashion so that the columns and rows line up properly and the problems do not run off the page.

The diagnostic analysis consists of four parts: obtaining the background information, making and recording the observations of performance, developing the learning profile, and providing a report when necessary. The first three are necessary to make a careful and complete informal assessment. The report is required when other persons are to judge or to carry out part of an intervention.

In the review and development of information a number of questions are to be answered about the seriousness and cause(s) of the problem, the appropriateness of interventions, and the priorities for the actions to be taken. The questions develop along the following lines. A yes response indicates the need for diagnostic rather than survey assessment.

1. Is the performance at a developmental level significantly (one or two years) different from that of other students his or her age?
2. Are there significant lags in development in several skill areas?
3. Is the lag in development or the nature of the dysfunction in an area likely to affect or be affected by learning and behavior in other areas?
4. Is the lag in development or the dysfunction something that can be expected to require some extraordinary effort?
5. Is the problem area pivotal to a large student problem?

The diagnostic analysis includes data from a number of areas. A listing of the usual areas considered, along with examples of the content of those areas, follows:

AREAS	CONTENT EXAMPLES
Academic achievement	Skill areas in reading, mathematics, and language (written)
Cognitive functioning	General ability, learning styles, thinking skills, problem-solving ability

AREAS	CONTENT EXAMPLES
Perceptional-motor development	Visual-motor coordination; motor skills; auditory, tactile, and visual discrimination and memory
Language development	Receptive understanding, vocabulary, syntax, expressive skill
Social skill and behavior	Interpersonal relations, role taking, group functioning, impulse control, leadership
Affective functioning	Emotional control and expression, self-concept, feelings, beliefs and values
Adaptive development	Independence, responsibility, self-sufficiency, attention, out-of-school behavior, self-direction
Interests and aptitudes	Special skills, personal interests, and goals

Once data have been developed in each of the areas thought to be most relevant to the problems, the data are organized into a comprehensive statement about the condition of the student and the problem. This synthesis is extremely important in that it brings together isolated pieces of information and provides a comprehensive view of the problem. The interrelationships between different student functions then often become clear, and appropriate corrective action can be planned.

A basic format for a diagnostic assessment synthesis section (report summary) includes the following:

1. A clear restatement of the problem
2. A description of the pupil's function in the classroom and other related activities
3. A review of relevant history
4. Observations made during any testing
5. A summary of the data from each test, organized by domain areas such as (a) academic, (b) social, (c) ability
6. An overall summary of the major findings

A recommendation section, which is a logical outcome from the synthesis of the data, follows. Substantive findings are translated directly into application. Tentative findings based on data interpretation provide the basis for suggestions for possible action.

Summary

The five procedures—student comparison, skill assessment, task analysis, survey analysis, and diagnostic analysis—are the basic strategies used in student assessment. They allow an assessor to make comparisons among students, check student growth, analyze learning steps, and understand learning problems. Formal group testing is frequently used to produce comparison data. Subject-oriented tests, designed to measure growth on a continuum toward a goal, represent a form of criterion tests and are often based on informal procedures. The analysis of entry skills and the steps needed to complete a learning activity constitute the process of task analysis. The multitest, comprehensive assessment of a student constitutes diagnostic analysis, while a checklist of subskills in one or more curricular areas allows for a survey analysis of student performance.

Testing is a continuous classroom activity. Different procedures generate different data and lead to unique views of the student. Results from an appropriate test strategy can lead to significant instructional improvements.

Bibliography

Carr, Rey A. "Goal Attainment Scaling As a Useful Tool for Evaluating Progress in Special Education." *Exceptional Children* 46, no. 2 (1978): 88–95.

Crocker, Linda, and Benson, Jeri. "Achievement, Guessing and Risk Taking Behavior under Norm Referenced and Criterion Referenced Testing Conditions," *American Educational Research Journal* 13, no. 3 (1976): 207–215.

Dunlap, William P., and Brennan, Alison H. "Diagnosing Learning Difficulties via the IAI (Informal Arithmetic Inventory)." *Academic Therapy* 12, no. 4 (1978): 389–397.

Ewing, Norma, and Brecht, Richard. "Diagnostic Prescriptive Instruction: A Reconsideration of Some Issues." *The Journal of Special Education* 11, no. 3 (1977): 323–327.

Glaser, Robert. "Instructional Technology and the Measurement of Learning Outcomes: Some Questions." *American Psychologist* 18, no. 8 (1963): 510–522.

Hambleton, Ronald K.; Swaminathan, Hariharan; Algina, James; and Coulson, Douglas B. "Criterion-referenced Testing and Measurement: A Review of Technical Issues and Developments." *Review of Educational Research* 48, no. 1 (1978): 1–47.

Harris, Larry P., and Wolf, Steven R. "Validity and Reliability of Criterion-referenced Measures: Issues and Procedures for Special Educators." *Learning Disability Quarterly* 3 (1979): 84–88.

Ironson, Gail H., and Suboviak, Michael. "A Comparison of Several Methods of Assessing Item Bias." *Journal of Educational Measurement* 16, no. 4 (1979): 209–225.

Kratochwill, Thomas R. "The Movement of Psychological Extras into Ability Assessment." *The Journal of Special Education* 11, no. 3 (1977): 298–311.

Loe, David C. "Informal Assessment during Clinical Teaching." *Academic Therapy* 10, no. 4 (1975): 467–472.

Mercer, L. R., and Ysseldyke, J. E. "Designing Diagnostic-Prescriptive Programs." In *With Bias toward None.* Lexington: University of Kentucky, Coordinating Office for Regional Resources Center, 1976. Pp. 40–41.

Moyer, J. R., and Dardig, J. C. "Practical Task Analysis for Special Educators." *Teaching Exceptional Children* 11, no. 1 (1978): 16–18.

Popham, W. James. *Criterion-Referenced Measurement.* Englewood Cliffs, N.J.: Prentice-Hall, 1978.

Popham, W. James "Education Measurement for Improvement of Instruction." *Phi Delta Kappan* 61, no. 8 (1980): 531–534.

Smead, Valerie S. "Ability Training and Task Analysis in Diagnostic/Prescriptive Teaching." *The Journal of Special Education* 11, no. 1 (1977): 113–125.

Sugarman, Alan. "Is Psychodiagnostic Assessment Humanistic?" *Journal of Personality Assessment* 42, no. 1 (1978): 11–21.

Vance, Hubert B. "Informal Assessment Techniques with LD Children." *Academic Therapy* 12, no. 3 (1977): 291–303.

Chapter 3
Problem Identification, Data Collection, and Interaction Recording

Assessment of skill growth and student behavior is an essential and unavoidable part of instruction; it is a key element in the movement toward individualizing instruction. It is through assessment that both individual and group strengths, weaknesses, interests, and needs become known, and as a result of this information appropriate planning can take place. Assessment is the constant companion of both ordinary and special instruction.

In the ordinary process of instruction data are casually gathered in order to follow student progress. When expected learning or behavior does not occur, more exacting measures are required. The teacher or other professional must examine the nature of the problem, gather specific data documenting the situation, and record the information so that it can be used to select and implement some form of action.

IDENTIFYING THE PROBLEM

The suspicion of a problem occurs when the learning and behavior of a student varies significantly from those of other students in the same setting or when there is a marked change in the student's general pattern of growth or behavior. Such a discrepancy becomes significant to the degree that it exceeds the range of variation expected as a result of differences in age and general ability or from temporary plateaus in learning. A discrepancy is cause for concern if it is persistent, chronic, or has long-term implications. Occasional learning lags or misbehaviors occur within the normal variations expected in children and youth.

Five guides can help in determining the seriousness of a problem. These guides separate cultural, transient, and developmental differences from those that reflect more basic and persistent disorders in learning and behavior.

1. *The significance of a problem is related to the degree to which the problem permeates the skill or behavior area.* The larger the affected skill or behavioral area, the more likely that special assessment and instruction will be necessary. For instance, it is generally easier to understand and assist a student who is awkward when meeting new adults than it is to evaluate and assist a student who is shy and withdrawn in the presence of all adults. It is also less serious for a sixth grade student to have problems with fractions than to have problems with basic addition, subtraction, multiplication, and division. In each case the student with good basic skills is more likely to respond to ordinary assistance. The student with the more pervasive problem will require a more comprehensive evaluation and help.

It is the task of the assessor to sort out those problems that are relatively simple from those that are complex. This determination has implications for the type of assessment and instruction that will be used.

2. *The significance of a problem is related to the number of performance areas involved.* Problems have a tendency to affect related areas. Poor academic performance, for instance, can result in generally poor behavior. The assessor is faced with identifying the underlying problem. This is a more difficult and complex task than dealing with a problem where there is a direct correspondence between symptom and cause. Tracing a symptom to its root can take time. For example, a student's poor self-concept is found to be the result of poor performance in sports. The physical performance might be the result of poor visual-motor perception and coordination. The same basic root may have affected reading and resulted in failures in academic areas that depend on reading. The seriousness arises from the number of areas that have been affected by the basic problem and by its underlying cause.

At times the cause of the original problem has been outgrown and yet the original attitudes and behavioral patterns persist. For this student the present lies in the shadow of the past, and the assessor is in search of a "phantom cause" that may have created problems in many areas and then disappeared. The seriousness results from the spread of the problem and its persistence in spite of the absence of the initial cause.

The assessor's task is to understand the symptom, identify the possible underlying problem, determine the essential needs of the task, and then plan a program of assistance. The focus is twofold: (1) to determine the behavior or the skill that is desired and (2) to determine the root of the problem and the areas affected. An analysis of the size of the problem, of the number of areas of performance affected, will suggest how serious the problem is and what assessment steps might be taken.

3. *The significance of a problem decreases to the extent that the performance can be explained by a cultural difference, second language, consistent development, unusual current circumstances, or differences in group values.* A number of factors that affect learning and performance are partly outside the immediate domain of the school. An understanding of these influences can help the teacher in planning a program of assessment. The impact of language and culture is profound and is considered in a separate chapter (Chapter 14). Developmental and current circumstances are a continuum of experiences that affect performance. Individual characteristics and group values are the personal and social factors that help determine the individual's selection and interpretation of learning experiences.

Developmental history and current circumstances include the maturational and environmental conditions that influence a child's performance. A historical review of the student's development includes attention to physical growth and health conditions and their probable impact on learning and behavior. Social, psychological, and school histories provide information on the formation of the attitudinal, learning, and behavioral patterns that influence current performance.

An inventory of current circumstances answers questions related to the environmental and social conditions that influence behavior and learning. This evaluation includes attention to current health, nutritional, and drug conditions. Home conditions including love and security also play an important role in student performance. Student participation in activities such as out-of-school sports, recreation, or work can both reinforce and hinder school performance. Knowledge about the nature of the outside influence, the permanence of that influence, and the history of the behavior is useful information in estimating the persistence of the current problem and possible immediate and long-run solutions.

There is a temptation to accept developmental and current circumstances as the reasons and justifications for performance problems, thereby relieving the professional of further responsibility. Effective assessment, however, avoids this trap and generates historical and situational data to assist in planning and implementing instruction. The basic responsibility for the instruction of the student in the skills and knowledge required in the culture remains with the schools.

4. *The significance of a problem is influenced by the length of time it has gone uncorrected.* There are at least three important reasons for determining the history of a problem. First, the longer a problem has existed, the more likely it is that previous assessments have been made and have not corrected the problem. The current assessor must review what has been done and decide whether to select a new method of assessment, reinterpret the original material, or repeat the earlier assessment. The recommended assessment procedure for a long-term problem is to identify the type of information needed, decide what assessment data would be useful, review the results of previous assessment, and determine what remains to be done.

The second reason for using historic information is to determine the types of intervention strategies that have already been used and the effectiveness of each procedure. It is safe to assume that previous teachers have attempted to cope with the problem and that they met with varying degrees of success. Although changes due to maturation and a new teacher may turn previously unsuccessful strategies into effective ones, it is discouraging for a student to be confronted with the same procedures and material associated with earlier failure. Repeated use of similar materials should be avoided.

The last consideration for determining the history of a problem is that an old problem is less likely to be easily corrected than an emerging problem. An emerging problem may, by its nature, be temporary, the result of immediate or fleeting problems. A long-term problem, however, has a history of resistance to accurate assessment or successful instruction. The problem has also encased itself in layers of attitudes, beliefs, and related behaviors. A student who reads poorly in the sixth grade views herself as a poor reader and has many beliefs and attitudes about what that means. Years of failure can result in an evolutionary change from the belief that "I read poorly" to the acceptance that "I am a poor reader." Instead of acknowledging the skill deficiency, the student comes to accept a negative attribute so strongly that it becomes a barrier to improvement. A comprehensive assessment is the recommended procedure for such a long-term, persistent problem.

5. *Significance is indicated by persistent resistance to ordinary remedial and corrective methods.* A diagnostic assessment presupposes that the teacher has used those corrective methods available in the classroom. Individual attention and standard remedial approaches should be attempted before an extensive assessment is undertaken. It is important not to prejudge a student's skill or performance level from previous records or notations. A student who is a problem in one classroom may fit easily into the groupings of another class. The teaching style in a new class may naturally fit the learning style of the student. A student's performance may also improve as the result of maturation or situational circumstances.

At the same time, it is possible to pass a problem up from one grade to the next without giving it the attention it deserves. A student who consistently and persistently fails to achieve, a student who has an area of difficulty that is incompatible with other higher areas of performance, a student whose achievement or behavior puzzles a teacher—each of these warrants further assessment.

SELECTING ASSESSMENT PROCEDURES

There are several approaches to collecting assessment data. To determine which approach to follow, check the seriousness of the problem and its resistance to change. The basic choices, in order of time invested, are: ordinary classroom assessment, direct assessment, and comprehensive assessment. The teacher with good assessment skills is able to generate "ordinary" assessment data that are accurate, appropriate, and sophisticated. When these data fail to provide the necessary information, the teacher or professional can move to a second level of assessment. At this level more detailed information is gathered on the specific problem under consideration. When this information is still inadequate, a third level is available. This is the level of the comprehensive assessment, and in addition to a thorough examination of the specific problem, it may include attention to intelligence, related skills and abilities, personality, and developmental history.

Information upon which decisions and judgments are based is conceptually clustered under major domain areas. It is helpful, when deciding what information is needed, to check each domain area to determine whether that type of information will be useful in answering the questions generated by student problems. The major domains are:

Achievement areas: Basic skill and subject areas such as reading, math, language, history, physical education, music, and science

Behavior areas: Those areas of personal behavior that include emotions, self-control, responsibility, motivation, humor, attitudes, values, empathy, and interests

Perceptual-motor development: A group of sensory-related skills including auditory-visual-tactile-haptic perception, sensory integration, and perceptual-motor integration

Social interaction: The student's ability to relate effectively with others in one-to-one and group experiences and including skills such as cooperation, leadership, and support

Language development: The comprehensive ability to receive, understand, and express language in an oral or manual communication mode

Adaptive behavior: The student's ability and skill to manage needs, interactions, responsibility, and self-care in a variety of settings outside the school

Vocational/careers: Those interests, aptitudes, and skills that make success and satisfaction likely in current and future work and recreation

Ability measure: A varied group of indices that suggest the general growth rate in cognitive and behavioral areas and speculate as to potential for growth in specific areas

Learning style: The student's preferred sensory mode, interest areas, priorities, choice of teaching methods, and organizing processes

The domains provide an informational framework in which a problem can be viewed. In a skill problem such as may occur in reading, the need for specific diagnostic skill information is apparent. If the problem resists all standard remedial techniques, information from related domains needs to be examined. The following questions reflect the range of related information that might be useful in planning a corrective program for a student:

What are the specific strengths and weaknesses in the skill area?

Are the perceptual-motor skills sufficiently developed for the reading task?

Are the behavioral indices of motivation, attention, and persistence appropriate for the task?

Is language development sufficient to carry out the task?

Is the growth rate in reading significantly different from other cognitive and behavioral growth?

What is the learning style of the student?

In a diagnostic assessment both developmental and current performance information is gathered in those domain areas that are most closely related to the problem. In the series of questions just posed the information starts with diagnostic testing of the skill and then, if necessary, questions the areas of perceptual-motor development; attitudes, values, and motivation toward the skill; related language development; general ability; and learning style. Interview data can provide information on the interest, willingness, and ability of the parent(s) to help improve their child's performance.

The choice of method or procedure for examining the domain area depends in part on appropriateness, availability, and economy of the measures. The steps in selection, along with examples of the questions the assessor asks of himself or herself, follow.

QUESTIONS	STEPS
What problem am I trying to solve and what questions do I have?	Define problem
What decisions and judgments do I need to make and what information will be useful?	Identify purpose
What available procedures will provide the information I seek?	Identify appropriate procedure
Are other procedures available that will provide similar information in an easier manner?	Identify assessment options
Is there enough time to use the procedure and to record and interpret the information?	Determine practicality
Is it likely that the student, the parents, and so on, will respond to the procedure in a helpful way?	Determine feasibility

RECORDING INFORMATION

It is a sad commentary on student assessment that the great wealth of student information held by the classroom teacher typically plays a small role in major program and placement decisions. In some states the classroom teacher or the special education teacher is not an official member of the committee that places students in special education. One reason for the omission of these teachers has been that the information they hold is often not in a form that can be easily shared, quickly communicated, or acceptably verified. The teacher's primary role has been to initiate the action and provide a statement of the problem. Even the problem statement is often radically changed by other professionals in the course of committee decisions. The teacher is seen as an initiator, not a diagnostician. The teacher with good assessment and reporting skills, however, can reverse this trend and become a major contributor to important program and placement decisions. Recording and reporting information are critical ingredients in this change.

The sheer volume of information that is available to a teacher can make recording time-consuming; and the various forms in which information exists can make recording cumbersome. To ease the congestion of information, organizing schemes must be used. Grouping information by domains is a practical and logical organizing schema. In this way data on academic skills can be organized into one cluster of information, behavioral data into another, language data into another, and so on. Data from separate domains can then be drawn together for analysis.

The method of recording can reduce the volume of data so that it is easier to locate information when it is needed. The use of standard formats and simple procedures for quantifying information speeds both recording and reporting. The method of recording and the resultant ease with which information can be recovered affects the likelihood that data will be used. Recording is the first and critical step in processing assessment data. The following guides address important considerations in the selection of a recording procedure.

1. *Use recording procedures that are as simple and as efficient as possible.* Awkward and time-consuming procedures discourage recording and lead to incomplete records. Every recording procedure should be occasionally reexamined to determine if there is an easier method. Time is an important factor in assessment, and every effort should be made to simplify the recording process.

2. *Have students or aides, when appropriate, participate in the recording process.* Many informal assessment procedures make it possible for students to correct, check, enter, or otherwise record their own behavior. Student recordings are most often used in self-monitoring activities. Other informal assessment procedures can be carried out by a trained aide. Aide training involves explanation, demonstration, practice, and trials. The reliability of aide records can be improved by having the aide and the assessor conduct simultaneous assessments until observations are essentially similar.

3. *Record information so that it accurately represents the critical elements of the history or event.* The format used in recording data tends to influence what is perceived. What is requested is recorded, and other behavior tends to be ignored or omitted. The recording format is therefore

very important. The elements need to be clearly and precisely identified, labeled, stated, or described. Categories, whenever possible, should be stated in behavioral terms so events can be easily recognized and confirmed.

4. *Use a recording format that does not require the transfer of the raw data to another form.* The transfer of data is both time-wasting and error prone; it should be avoided if possible. Carefully planned recording sheets can act as the permanent record of the activity even when completed by students. When transfer must be made, the accuracy of the new data needs to be thoroughly checked.

Assessment data must often be converted from a raw form to a descriptive or summarized form. This conversion is the basic step in data analysis. Quantitative material such as frequency counts and error counts is easily displayed in graphs on which raw data are recorded directly. For example, in Figure 3-1, the student records from 0 to 15 correctly spelled

Figure 3-1.
Record Chart for the Number of Words Spelled Correctly on Each of Sixteen Days

Each day, mark the number of words spelled correctly.

Number of Words

15	15	15	15	15	15	15	15	15	15	15	15	15	15	15	15
14	14	14	14	14	14	14	14	14	14	14	14	14	14	14	14
13	13	13	13	13	13	13	13	13	13	13	13	13	13	13	13
12	12	12	12	12	12	12	12	12	12	12	12	12	12	12	12
11	11	11	11	11	11	11	11	11	11	11	11	11	11	11	11
10	10	10	10	10	10	10	10	10	10	10	10	10	10	10	10
9	9	9	9	9	9	9	9	9	9	9	9	9	9	9	9
8	8	8	8	8	8	8	8	8	8	8	8	8	8	8	8
7	7	7	7	7	7	7	7	7	7	7	7	7	7	7	7
6	6	6	6	6	6	6	6	6	6	6	6	6	6	6	6
5	5	5	5	5	5	5	5	5	5	5	5	5	5	5	5
4	4	4	4	4	4	4	4	4	4	4	4	4	4	4	4
3	3	3	3	3	3	3	3	3	3	3	3	3	3	3	3
2	2	2	2	2	2	2	2	2	2	2	2	2	2	2	2
1	1	1	1	1	1	1	1	1	1	1	1	1	1	1	1
0	0	0	0	0	0	0	0	0	0	0	0	0	0	0	0
1	2	3	4	5	6	7	8	9	10	11	12	13	14	15	16

Days

words for each of sixteen days. The data recorded and display occur on the same page. This procedure allows the student to enter daily scores on a chart that the teacher can read easily.

Tabulation is another way to record a score and transform it directly to a descriptive computation. Sociometric choices provide an example. Students in a class are asked the question, "If you have a social studies project to do and you can choose another person in this group to work with you, who would it be?" After the first choice is written, a new question is introduced: "If the person you chose could not join you, who would you now pick to work with you?" The matrix of choices is expressed in Figure 3-2.

Figure 3-2.
Sociometric Matrix of Social Studies Choices

	Chosen									
	Ann	Bill	Cheryl	Frank	Gary	Jim	Joy	Lisa	Peter	Susan
Ann			1			2				
Bill					2			1		
Cheryl		1			2					
Frank		1							2	
Gary			1						2	
Jim			2					1		
Joy								2		1
Lisa	2								1	
Peter							2	1		
Susan			1				2			

1st Choice	0	2	3	0	0	0	0	3	1	1
2nd Choice	1	0	1	0	2	1	2	1	2	0
Frequency chosen	1	2	4	0	2	1	2	4	3	1
Rating	1	4	7	0	2	1	2	7	4	2

The rating is calculated by adding the "frequency chosen" to the number of "first choices" (thus giving double weighting to first choices). In this tabular presentation high ratings indicate a high degree of fellow student acceptance, low scores indicate social isolation.

Descriptive statistics such as percentages or averages provide another type of data conversion. Although the entries can be made on the record sheet, as in Figure 3-3 and 3-4, a third step is required to post the scores in a display format. In Figure 3-3 the "correct" count is converted to a percentile and plotted on the graph. In Figure 3-4 weekly averages are calculated and the resulting data are plotted each week.

In Figure 3-3 the students' scores are entered in the "number correct" row. The "percentage correct" figures are calculated by dividing the num-

Figure 3-3.
Chart of Percentage of Words Spelled Correctly over Sixteen Days

Maximum words each day = 15

Day:	1	2	3	4	5	6	7	8	9	10	11	12	13	14	15	16
Number correct:	3	4	3	6	7	10	9	11	12	11	12	10	13	13	12	13
Percentage correct (number ÷ 15):	20	26	20	40	46	66	60	73	80	73	80	66	86	86	80	86

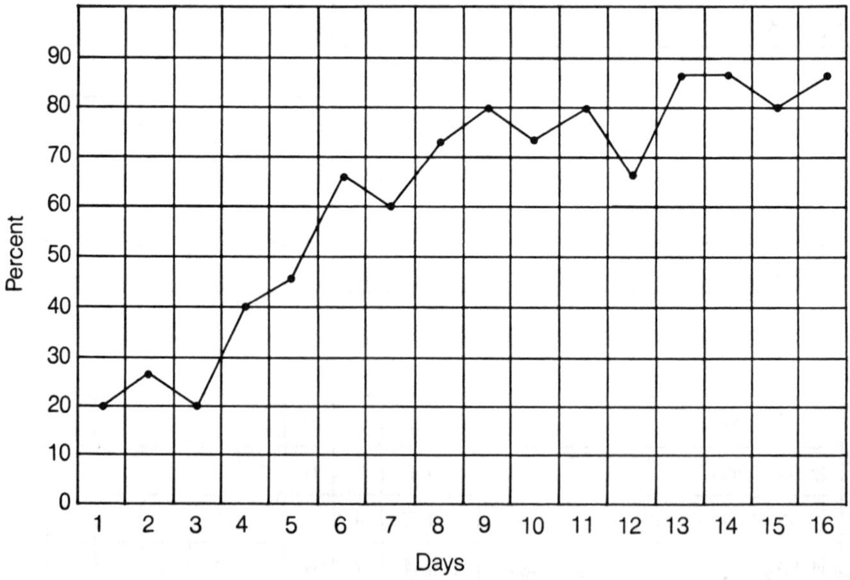

ber correct by the number of correct possible (15). The percentage for each day is entered into the graph as a point and connecting lines are drawn to complete the display.

Figure 3-4.
Average Number of Words Spelled Correctly Each Week

Maximum words each day = 15

Day:	1	2	3	4	5	6	7	8	9	10	11	12	13	14	15
Number correct:	3	4	3	6	7	10	9	11	12	11	12	10	13	13	12

Weekly average:	1st week	2nd week	3rd week
$\frac{\text{Total weekly score}}{\text{Number of days}}$:	$\frac{23}{5} = 4.6$	$\frac{53}{5} = 10.6$	$\frac{60}{5} = 12$

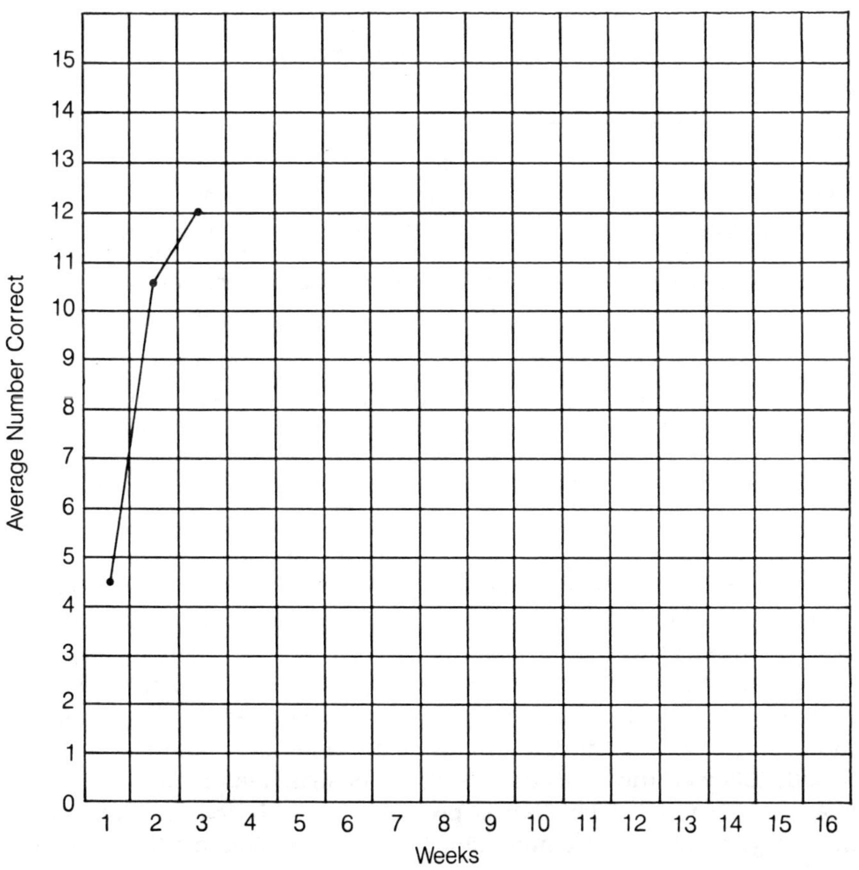

In Figure 3-4 the same data are averaged for each five-day period and provide a stable measure of spelling performance over an extended period. The figure covers weekly averages for sixteen weeks.

Informal assessment that results in verbal data can also be recorded in such a way that the transfer from raw data to descriptive data occurs within the recording format. Interviewing formats can be designed, for example, so the teacher's data are presented, parent information is solicited, and a plan is proposed, discussed, and evaluated. This procedure not only preorganizes the session but also facilitates the recording of the proceedings during or immediately after the conference. Figure 3-5 describes such a recording format.

Figure 3-5.
Problem-Focused Parent Conference Format

Student ____________________ Subject Behavior ____________________

Date	*Data*	*Parent Contributions*	*Plan*
	Interviewer lists data before conference and shares with parents	Parent information, attitudes, reactions, suggestions recorded after conference	Plan outlined before conference, shared and modified as a result of the conference, and recorded
Date	Process is repeated for subsequent conference, and conference data are held in the student's file until the goal is reached or the semester or year is completed.		

Academic performance can also be examined and recorded in functional terms that act both as raw data and descriptors. This is especially appropriate when assessing a range of behaviors such as thinking skills, class attitudes, general interests, language proficiency, listening skills, and social interaction. The easiest method to ensure a comprehensive evaluation is to follow a schema that outlines or specifies the range of performance possible within the skill under consideration. Formal tests have usually followed this procedure in their construction but lack the practical and personal detail that is possible in an observation, interview, inventory, or tailored examination. In Table 3-1, Bloom's taxonomy of cognitive objectives has been modified to provide a schema from which questions can be generated and used to examine informally a student's level of thinking. The results provide concrete illustrations of a student's functional response, and provide the basis for an estimate of developmental level.

Table 3-1.
Informal Evaluation Based on Bloom's Cognitive Objectives

TOPIC AREA: INDIAN TRIBES NATIVE TO THIS AREA

LEVELS OF OBJECTIVES (DEFINITION)	TEACHER QUESTIONS (EXAMPLES OF VERBS)	STUDENT RESPONSES	RESPONSE LEVEL
1. Knowledge: Recalls, identifies, or otherwise recognizes facts	"Name the tribes" (Define, draw, repeat, record, recall, recite, recognize, identify, write)	"The Apaches and Sioux"	Knowledge
2. Comprehension: Understands the meaning of information and ideas	"Describe how they lived" (Classify, compare, contrast, describe, discuss, interpret, translate)	"Both tribes lived on the plains and moved to find food"	Comprehension
3. Application: Uses information methods, theories, and principles in new or appropriate situations	"How is that similar to people today?" (Apply, calculate, complete, demonstrate, illustrate, practice, solve, use)	"We moved here when my father got a job here."	Application
4. Analysis: Breaks information into component elements or parts	"How did families divide the work?" (Analyze, classify, discuss, divide, explain, infer, inspect, separate, sort)	"The men were hunters and gatherers and guarded the family, and the women cooked, made clothes, and took care of the children."	Analysis

(continued)

Table 3-1. *continued*

LEVELS OF OBJECTIVES (DEFINITION)	TEACHER QUESTIONS (EXAMPLES OF VERBS)	STUDENT RESPONSES	RESPONSE LEVEL
5. Synthesis: Combines elements or parts into a whole unit	"What would a family need to do to prepare to move?" (Arrange, combine, construct, create, design, develop, generalize, organize, plan, predict, prepare)	"Take their tent down." "Have food ready, get packed, herd horses, get the tribe together, decide where to go, and move out."	Comprehension Synthesis
6. Evaluation: Makes judgments about value usefulness	"What are the good and bad parts of being a nomadic people?" (Appraise, assess, critique, estimate, evaluate, grade, judge, rank, rate, recommend, test, value)	"It's good to see new places and feel free, and it was hard when food was low and other people made you move."	Evaluation

There is no more exasperating experience than finding that an important piece of descriptive information is missing from an informal record. As a general rule, it is better to overrecord than underrecord. Observations that are vivid at the time of an evaluation soon fade from memory, and only written documentation can ensure their immortality. The following list includes items of information that should be noted for each activity in informal assessment.

1. Date, time, and assessor
2. Purpose of the assessment
3. Instructional goal or objective
4. Subject, activity, and students involved
5. Type of assessment procedure
6. Method for scoring and/or summarizing

7. Results on others who had similar assessment
8. Estimate of degree behavior is typical, estimate of accuracy, estimate of reliability of the measure
9. Notation of any unusual conditions

COMPREHENSIVE RECORD

A recording format can act as an outline and guide in an assessment. A comprehensive format ensures the assessor that important areas have been covered in as much detail as the problem warrants. A checklist of individual history and abilities provides such a format and is relatively easy to use. The checklist can be kept in an accessible place and used during observations. Careful documentation is important and several observations should be made in order to arrive at a reliable statement about behavior. Observations can be made of spontaneous performance in the classroom or on the playground, or the situation can be highly structured and created to provide an opportunity for a behavior to occur.

A model of a checklist is shown in Figure 3-6. When the checklist is adapted for classroom use, space should be left between each item so recordings can be made. The use of multiple observations cannot be overemphasized. Further, a consensus of observations is important and the unusual occurrence is generally discounted. For instance, behaviors that occur after an unusual fight on the playground or on the day before the student develops chickenpox can give false impressions. In the end it is the student who suffers from a misdiagnosis—only care in observing and recording can help ensure an accurate understanding of a student's progress and problems. When a comprehensive record has been completed, the characteristics of the student form a total picture of strengths and weaknesses, which allows a more adequate understanding of the student's learning style.

A more complete explanation of each item in the background section of Figure 3-6 follows. Other sections are described in detail in Part Three. The descriptions can be used to improve the record that is obtained.

BACKGROUND INFORMATION

The background information section of this checklist should be documented and filled out briefly. Only the history that appears to contribute to the child's school problems need be included. Teachers sometimes have a tendency to overemphasize family problems, and while such things as a parent's divorce and/or being raised by a single parent do

Figure 3-6.
Comprehensive Development and Ability Record Checklist

I. Background
  A. Developmental
    1. Birth
    2. Developmental signs
      a. Sitting
      b. Standing
      c. Walking
    3. Problem first observed
  B. Health
    1. Infancy
    2. Early childhood
    3. Chronic conditions
    4. Medications
  C. Language
    1. First words
    2. Complete sentences
    3. Vocabulary
    4. Communication
    5. Articulation
  D. School
    1. Present school
    2. Type of class
    3. School history
      a. Preschool
      b. Kindergarten
      c. Grades 1–3
      d. Grades 4–6
      e. Junior High
      f. High school
    4. Type of assistance
  E. Social/emotional
    1. Traumatic experiences
    2. Family relationships
      a. Parents
      b. Siblings
    3. Neighbors
    4. Peers
      a. Age preference
      b. Friendships
  F. Previous studies
    1. Group tests
    2. Individual tests
      a. Academic
      b. Psychological
      c. Speech

II. Sensorimotor
  A. Gross-motor development
    1. Basic
      a. Rolling
      b. Sitting
      c. Crawling
      d. Walking
      e. Running
    2. Advanced
      a. Throwing
        (1) Two hands
        (2) One hand
      b. Jumping
        (1) Two feet
        (2) One foot
      c. Skipping
      d. Dancing
    3. Coordination
  B. Fine-motor development
    1. Finger movement
    2. Handling objects
    3. Tracing
    4. Coloring
    5. Cutting
    6. Geometric forms
    7. Pictures
    8. Handwriting
    9. Motor-planning
    10. Laterality
      a. Hand
      b. Foot
      c. Eye
      d. Right/left orientation
        (1) Self
        (2) Other
        (3) Position-in-space
      e. Left-to-right progression (directionality)
        (1) Reading
        (2) Writing
    11. Organization
  C. Auditory development
    1. Nonverbal
      a. Hearing
      b. Localization

- c. Perception
- d. Figure-ground identification
- 2. Verbal
  - a. Auditory discrimination
  - b. Auditory closure
  - c. Auditory memory
    - (1) Numbers
    - (2) Words
    - (3) Sentences
    - (4) Directions
  - d. Auditory sequencing
    - (1) Sounds
    - (2) Sound blending
- D. Visual development
  - 1. Perception
    - a. Multiple-choice
    - b. Copying
  - 2. Speed of perception
  - 3. Figure-ground discrimination
  - 4. Visual discrimination
    - a. Nonverbal
    - b. Verbal
  - 5. Visual memory
    - a. Color
    - b. Designs
    - c. Letters
    - d. Words
  - 6. Form constancy
  - 7. Spatial relations
    - a. Position-in-space
    - b. Size
    - c. Relationship
- III. Language/cognition
  - A. Inner language
    - 1. Categorization
      - a. Pictures
      - b. Words
      - c. Similarities and differences
      - d. Common characteristics
    - 2. Play behavior
    - 3. Associations
      - a. Nonverbal
        - (1) Picture opposites
        - (2) Picture associations
        - (3) Picture interpretation
        - (4) Picture absurdities
      - b. Verbal
        - (1) Opposites
        - (2) Reasoning (syllogisms)
        - (3) Associations
        - (4) Inferences
        - (5) Outcomes
    - 4. Size
    - 5. Body parts identification
      - a. Point
      - b. Name
    - 6. Sequence
      - a. Pictures
      - b. Verbal
      - c. Abstract
        - (1) Visual
        - (2) Verbal
      - d. Predicting outcomes
    - 7. Time concepts
      - a. Social
      - b. Automatic
        - (1) Days
        - (2) Months
        - (3) Seasons
      - c. Clock
        - (1) Set
        - (2) Read
    - 8. Problem solving
      - a. Visual
        - (1) Searching for details
        - (2) Finding hidden objects
        - (3) Answering questions
      - b. Verbal
        - (1) Recalling details
        - (2) Resolving situations
      - c. Abstraction
        - (1) Determining design sequence
        - (2) Determining number sequence
  - B. Receptive language
    - 1. Nonverbal
      - a. Response to gestures
      - b. Identification of pictures
      - c. Identification of function of objects
      - d. Identification of actions in pictures
      - e. Identification of noises by persons
      - f. Identification of environment noises
      - g. "Reads" picture story
      - h. "Reads" maps

(continued)

Figure 3-6 continued

i. "Reads" graphs
j. "Reads" diagrams
2. Verbal
 a. Listening
  (1) Auditory closure
  (2) Vocabulary
  (3) Prepositions (location)
  (4) Adverbs (sequence)
  (5) Conversation
  (6) Speed of listening
 b. Comprehension
  (1) Words
  (2) Sentences
  (3) Paragraphs
  (4) Understanding sequence
  (5) Recalling details
  (6) Getting the main idea
  (7) Drawing conclusions
  (8) Making inferences
  (9) Critical listening

C. Expressive language
 1. Nonverbal: gestures
 2. Verbal
  a. Articulation
  b. Voice
  c. Intonation
  d. Fluency
 3. Word finding
  a. Conversation
  b. Description
   (1) Objects
   (2) Pictures
   (3) Stories
   (4) Directions
 4. Sentence formation
  a. Conversation
   (1) Participates with group
   (2) Adjusts language to social situations
  b. Description
   (1) Communication
   (2) Oral reports
  c. Creative expression
 5. Written language
  a. Productivity
  b. Sentence structure
  c. Punctuation
  d. Form
   (1) Creative writing
   (2) Paragraphs
   (3) Written reports
   (4) Correspondence
  e. Ability to abstract
   (1) Use of vocabulary
   (2) Development
   (3) Elaborations
   (4) Developing major theme
   (5) Developing minor points
   (6) Use of summation, conclusion, prediction
   (7) Constructing plot
   (8) Figurative language
  f. Spelling
  g. Handwriting
  h. Self-correction

IV. Academic
 A. Spelling
  1. Achievement scores
  2. Word attack skills
 B. Handwriting
 C. Reading
  1. Grade levels
   a. Listening comprehension
   b. Silent reading
   c. Oral reading
  2. Reading rate
   a. Oral
   b. Silent
  3. Word attack skills
   a. Phonetic patterns
   b. Structural patterns
   c. Syllabication patterns
   d. Motor patterns
  4. Comprehension
   a. Literal
   b. Interpretive
   c. Critical
  5. Functional reading
   a. Study skills
   b. Library skills
   c. Life skills
 D. Arithmetic
  1. Achievement scores
  2. Concepts
  3. Computation

V. Student behavior
 A. Observed action
  1. Chronology

2. Frequency	B. Self-reporting
3. Sequence	1. Attitudes
4. Traits	2. Sociograms
5. Options	3. Projections
6. Environment	4. Personal inventories

SOURCE: Developed by Arlee S. Maier. Copyright © 1980 by Arlee S. Maier.

contribute to the quality of a child's home life, they are common enough today that they frequently cannot be considered the reason for the child's problems.

It is important, however, to document school history in detail, because it may lead to a significant insight into why the child is not doing well. In the following sections each background area of the checklist is examined, and factors to which the teacher should particularly attend are described.

Developmental

It is important for the teacher to document when problems were first observed, in order to see if the difficulties the child is currently experiencing are of recent origin or are part of a long-term pattern. Specific dates and documentation are not important, but a parent's impression of whether the child seemed to be early, average, or late in such things as sitting, walking, standing, and so on can be helpful.

1. Was there anything developmentally unusual about this child before, during or after birth? Was weight and health normal at birth?
2. Did the child sit, stand, and walk at a normal age?
3. When did the child's problem first come to your attention?

Health

Medical reports are not necessary, but information that may have contributed to learning problems should be noted. Parents can be asked:

1. Was the child generally healthy during infancy and early childhood?
2. Did the child have any serious illnesses or injuries that resulted in prolonged hospitalization or absence from school?
3. Does the child suffer from any chronic problems that may have caused frequent absences or affected learning? Such things as epilepsy, asthma or other allergies, and vision or hearing difficulties would be included here.
4. Does the child take any medication on a continuous basis? Are there

any behavioral effects of such medication? Some medications for allergies, for example, have a sedative effect, and the child may appear sleepy or inattentive. In such a case, it would be erroneous to assume that the child is not getting enough rest; it may merely be the effect of medication.

Language

This section is extremely crucial. Some information about the early language development of the child should be entered. Often parents cannot remember specific information (although many parents keep baby books), but they can recall whether the child's language appeared equal, better, or poorer, than other children. Parents can usually gauge the development of the child in relation to other children in the family. Some questions to be included are:

1. When did the child first speak words? Two- or three-word sentences?
2. In the parent's opinion (or teacher's) is the child's present vocabulary as good as most of his or her peers?
3. Does the child have considerable difficulty expressing needs, or describing things, or finding a word to name an object?
4. Does the child pronounce words adequately as compared to peers? Are some words or sounds always mispronounced? Teachers need to make a distinction here between immature speech, which is often found in children, and difficulties that go beyond "baby talk." For example, kindergarten children often have difficulty pronouncing some words, such as animal ("aminal"), elephant ("efelant"), and library ("libery"). These speech errors usually disappear and are no cause for concern.

School

School history is also crucial. As mentioned previously, frequent absences may have affected a child's learning. In some instances, a frequent change of teachers may have been an element. It is important for the teacher to remember that such factors may not be generally significant, but for the child who may have a propensity to learning problems, they may be significant indeed. This is the child who needed an optimal learning situation, not one with roadblocks in his path. The author had recent experience with a second grade child who had had seven substitute teachers during his first grade year. This may not have been a serious problem for other children in the class, but for this child with serious organizational problems, who could not adapt easily to new situations, it proved disastrous.

Teachers' comments, available in the child's folder, can give important clues. Johnny's reading problem may not have surfaced until third grade, but a careful reading of the file may indicate that even the kindergarten teacher noticed that Johnny was not attentive, was clumsy with scissors and crayons, and had great difficulty on the playground throwing, jumping, and skipping.

Typical questions that should be answered in this data collection are:

1. When did the child's learning problem first become apparent?
2. What steps, if any, were taken at the time to deal with the problem?
3. Has the child had any additional help, such as peer tutoring, extra help from the reading teacher, or remedial physical education?
4. Has the child moved frequently, or been changed from class to class?
5. What comments have his classroom teachers made about his learning problems or behaviors in prior years?

Social/Emotional

Such things in the child's life as the death of a grandparent, a new baby sister or brother, parents divorcing, or moving from one city to another, may influence how much energy a child is able to give to the learning situation. Again, while each of these events may not be traumatic in and of itself, for the child who is at risk they may prove harmful. Occasionally, the effects of social problems may not have been resolved; for example, the family may believe that the death of a grandparent was calmly accepted and understood, but the child may be harboring some residual concern that he or she was to blame. The teacher need not be a psychologist to understand that the child may have been preoccupied at school during that time, and the learning that everyone assumed was taking place did not occur.

Questions to be considered when looking into social/emotional background are:

1. How does the child get along with other children? Other adults? The family?
2. Does the child have friends?
3. Does he or she prefer to play primarily with older (or younger) children?
4. Is the child able to make new friends easily?
5. Does the child have a history of attention or behavior problems?

Previous Studies

A perusal of the child's folder for prior assessment or test data may give some insight into the nature and progression of the child's difficulty. In addition, if standardized testing is contemplated, it is important to see how recently such testing was done. The highly questionable results of standardized tests become even more questionable if there is a practice effect, that is, if the child took the same test only a short time before. In addition, there is no need to overtest, and if there is information in the child's folder that may be helpful, it may save time and energy on everyone's part.

These then are the elements of background information that are necessary for a thorough diagnostic assessment. It need not take a long time to compile this information. If the parent is available for an interview, a half-hour should be sufficient. If the assessor has an outline of what should be covered in the interview, short parent responses in each section should suffice. If the parent is not available, a questionnaire similar to that in Figure 3-7 may be used, although it will not be as satisfactory as a personal interview.

Figure 3-7.
Child History Questionnaire

Name: ______________________ Completed by: __________

Birthdate: __________ Age: ______yrs. ______mos. Relationship to child: ______

Referred by: ______________________ Date completed: __________

Instructions

Please answer the questions on this questionnaire as completely as possible. We will use the information to help make a thorough assessment of your child. If any questions are unclear, please place a question mark (?) next to the statement and we will review this area with you personally. Do not hesitate to add additional comments to clarify any areas that need explanation, or express criticism of this form. If any area of questioning is unclear, unreasonable, or too personal, please indicate. Where multiple choices are given, please underline, and place a star (*) in the margin for significant items.

Reason for referral: (Please list your child's problems in order of importance)

1. Family information

Family address ______________________Home phone __________

School ______________________Grade ________School phone __________

Father's name ____

Mother's name ____

Other children in the home

Name and age ____

Name and age ____

Name and age ____

Name and age ____

Other relatives or persons living in home ______________________________

____

Child is: natural ________ adopted ________

Family is: intact ________ separated ________

With whom does the child live? Both parents, mother, father, legal guardian, other

____

Does anyone take care of your child on a regular basis? No Yes

Child (disrupts, gets along with) family.

Child has mostly been a source of (pride, worry, friction) for family.

Parents (agree, disagree) on how to discipline child.

Discipline has been (strict, lenient, inconsistent, all of these).

Other children in the home have problems with (school behavior, grades, illness, emotional adjustment).

2. Birth history

A. This child was the (1, 2, 3, 4, 5, ___) in the family.

Birth was normal ________difficult ________ .

B. *Delivery:*

Place of birth: City ____________________State ____________

Birth weight: ____________________Length: ____________

Condition at birth: good poor

Any problems in nursery: No Yes

3. Child's development

At what age did your child sit up without support? ________months.

At what age did your child walk without support? ________months.

At what age did your child say 4 or 5 words? ________months.

At what age did your child speak in sentences? ________months.

How is your child's vocabulary now? Advanced, normal, poor.

Any speech problems? No Yes (explain) ______________________________

____

Rides a bike? Yes No at ________years.

(continued)

Figure 3-7 continued

Swims? Yes No at ________ years.

Stamina (endurance) OK? Yes No

Any large muscle coordination problems? Yes No

Any hand or eye coordination problems? Yes No

Does hearing seem normal? Yes No Hearing test recently? Yes No

Does vision seem normal? Yes No Eye exam recently? Yes No

4. School experience

Any nursery school experience? Yes No

Name of nursery school ____

Any problems in nursery school adjustment? No Yes

Explain ____

Current grade in school ________ Name of School ____________________

Name of current teacher ____

Days absent per year ________ Usual reason for absence ____________________

Describe any difficulties with academic work ____

____

When did you first notice school problems? ____

Since first grade, school personnel have reported: no serious problems, problems with behavior, speech, reading, writing, spelling, math.

Child has: been in special education class, failed a grade, been tutored, made satisfactory progress, ____.

School personnel have reported through the years that child: adjusts to other children, doesn't adjust, has some problems ____.

Child: likes school, hates school, is indifferent.

5. Behavior

Describe any behavior problems at school ____

____

Describe any behavior problems at home ____

____

Has your child expressed any of the following behavior frequently or intensively? (Check)

shy, timid ______	sleep problems ______	impulsiveness ______
withdrawal ______	laziness ______	destructiveness ______
defiance ______	unhappiness ______	can't concentrate ______
lack of confidence ______	clumsiness ______	depression ______
temper tantrums ______	crying episodes ______	other ______
unusual fears ______	memory loss ______	
fainting, falling ______	hyperactivity ______	

Family relationships: (Underline correct word)

Father: close, distant, little contact
Mother: close, distant, little contact
Brothers: good, poor, variable
Sisters: good, poor, variable
Child requires discipline: frequently, infrequently, never
Types of discipline: spanking, sent to room, restriction of privileges, other ____________
Discipline given by: father, mother, other
Response to discipline: good, poor, variable
Child cared for by other person(s)? ________ relationship ________

Self-care: Independent, dependent, sloppy, neat, forgetful.

Temperament/personality: moody, calm, easygoing, difficult, high-strung, whiney, demanding, leader, overactive, sensitive, lazy, aggressive, shy, irritable, quiet, active, easily excited, nervous, stubborn, impulsive, restless, confident, dreamer, pleasure for you, happy, immature, cocky, insecure, loving, impatient, forgetful, jealous, sassy.

Nonfamilial relationships

With other children: good poor
With adults outside of family: good poor

Play activities: Prefers own age, prefers older children, prefers younger children, no playmates, prefers to play by self, many friends, few friends, aggressive, shares well, enjoys outdoor play, prefers indoor play, "loner," always fighting.

Treatment: Has your child ever received treatment for psychological problems? Yes No

6. Personal/social

Sleep habits: Any difficulties in sleeping: Yes No

Energy level: Generally high Moderate Low
Any indication of hyperactivity? Yes No Explain ____________

____

7. Assessing child's strengths: (Underline appropriate word)

Physical: strength, speed, athletic ability, coordination ____________

Interests: sports, hobbies, arts, crafts, home ____________

Talents: speaking, drama, singing, music, dancing, art, fixing, cooking ____________

Experiences: travel, unusual history, summer ____________

Information: sports, home, current events, academic subjects, hobbies ____________

Modality: auditory, visual, tactile, motor ____________

Organizational skills: planning, negotiating, leading, supporting ____________

Athletic: bike, swim, baseball, ski, kickball, track ____________

Academic: verbal, special ability, creative, performance ____________

Personality: sense of humor, friendly, warm, independent, flexible, exploratory, tactful, truthful, likeable, energetic, dependable, organized ____________

____

(continued)

Figure 3-7 continued

8. Health/illness: (Note age and outcomes)

Serious illnesses ______________________________

Operations ______________________________

Accidents ______________________________

Hospitalization ______________________________

Allergic reactions ______________________________

List any medication regularly taken at present and in the past ______________________________

____

Please list anything else you think might be helpful in the space below. Thank you for your cooperation and patience.

____

____

____

____

____

____

____

____

____

____

____

____

____

In either event, the time devoted to complete this first section of the diagnostic assessment can save much needed time in the long run. A careful analysis of all the contributory factors can save the teacher from making wrong conclusions, and can hasten the development of a remedial program for the learning handicapped child.

Summary

The seriousness of a learning or behavior problem depends on at least five major factors. The problem can be defined in terms of the depth of the disorder and the number of areas that are involved. The seriousness of the problem increases when it cannot be explained by culture, language, or transitory circumstances; when it has been persistent over time;

and when it has resisted a number of remedial approaches. Thus, the more pervasive, long-lasting and resistant the problem, the greater the chance that it is serious and will require special attention.

Within the schools, nine domain areas define the most common areas of investigation. These areas include achievement, general behavior, perceptual-motor development, social skills, language development, adaptive behavior, vocational and career movement, general ability, and learning style. Information about domain areas can be developmental or current and can provide data that are useful in instructional planning.

Recording is an essential part of informal assessment. In order to be serviceable, recording procedures must be simple and accurate. Since a procedure that is burdensome will soon be discarded, the recording procedure is selected to fit the needs and style of the user. The record of assessment becomes the basis for further judgments and decisions. The degree to which it accurately represents the performance or behavior of the student determines, in part, the appropriateness of the plans and actions that follow.

The record format can guide the assessor and provide the outline of the areas to be investigated. Models provided in this chapter can help the assessor cover a range of important information. Some recording formats are narrowly focused and others are comprehensive in their coverage.

Bibliography

Dickinson, Donald J. "The Direct Assessment: An Alternative to Psychometric Testing." *Journal of Learning Disabilities* 13, no. 19 (1980): 8–12.

Dougherty, Edward H., and Dougherty, Anne. "The Daily Report Card: A Simplified and Flexible Package for Classroom Behavior Management." *Psychology in the Schools* 14, no. 2 (1977): 191–195.

Greenlee, William E. "A Natural System Approach." *Academic Therapy* 12, no. 3 (1977): 305–308.

Ingenkamp, Karlheinz. *Educational Assessment.* London: NFER Publishing Co. Ltd. Distributed by Humanities Press, Atlantic Highlands, New Jersey, 1977. See Chapter 6, "Interactions Between the System and Other Factors."

Kratochwill, Thomas R., and Green, Leslie M. "Process Assessment." *Academic Therapy* 13, no. 5 (1978): 563–568.

Salvia, John, and Ysseldyke, James E. *Assessment in Special and Remedial Education.* 2nd ed. Boston: Houghton Mifflin, 1978. See Chapter 3, "Considerations in Test Selection and Administration."

Stufflebeam, Daniel I., et al. *Educational Evaluation and Decision Making.* Bloomington, Ind.: Phi Delta Kappan, 1971. See Chapter 3, "Educational Decision Making."

TenBrink, Terry D. *Evaluation, A Practical Guide for Teachers.* New York: McGraw-Hill, 1974. See Chapter 6, "Obtaining, Analyzing and Recording Information."

Part Two

Techniques of Informal Assessment

Informal assessment encompasses a variety of methods and procedures. The selection of a method depends on the purpose of the assessment and the setting in which it takes place. Recording and reporting information is determined by the way in which the information is to be used.

Part Two considers these aspects of informal assessment, as well as the major methods of observation, interviewing, and questioning. Five observational procedures are described, the process of interviewing is examined, and the construction and uses of questionnaires are explored. The processes of judging the quality of information and of reporting the information either orally or in written form are examined in this part. Common errors in the interpretation and the reporting of information are also discussed.

Chapter 4
Methods of Observation

Observation is one assessment activity that teachers use every day. In the process of instruction the teacher is both a leader and a witness. What the teacher sees and hears creates a reservoir of information on which to base judgments. Yet, the skill of observation is largely overlooked in the training of teachers and other professionals who serve in the schools.

Casual, daily observation provides information of a general nature, and as long as learning and behavior progress normally this form of observation is sufficient. However, if the teacher wishes to increase teaching effectiveness, modify student behavior, or evaluate new teaching strategies, more analytic procedures are needed.

There are both direct and indirect methods of observation. Direct procedures require that behavior be viewed and recorded using a predetermined observational schema. The procedure is characterized by systematic recording, procedural controls, attention to purpose, and objective reporting. Indirect procedures rely heavily on memory and usually call for judgments and descriptions about the history of certain patterns of behavior. Indirect procedures are most often used to obtain an overview of behavior and to provide a generalized description of an individual.

Direct procedures are most useful for improving the instructional process. Table 4-1 compares the two procedures.

Table 4-1.
Major Differences Between Direct and Indirect Methods of Observation

	METHODS OF OBSERVATION	
AREAS OF DIFFERENCE	DIRECT	INDIRECT
Characteristics	Observational schema	Question format
	Direct view of the student's performance	Prior or ongoing experience with student
	Immediate record of observation	Report based on summary of prior experiences
Examples	Counting the numbers of times student is out of his or her seat	Completing a questionnaire about a pupil's behavior
	Writing an account of a sequence of behavior	Keeping a diary on student performance
	Recording the antecedents and unsequences of a behavior	Describing a student's behavior to another teacher
Uses	Describing specific behavior	Obtaining an overview of behavior
	Planned report on student performance	Unexpected need to report on behavior
	Measuring change	Communicating to other professionals about a broad spectrum of behavior
	Selecting target behaviors and intervention strategies	Searching for clues for appropriate intervention strategies

Of the two, direct observation is the more accurate and verifiable method of obtaining information. It involves preplanning and can be tailored to suit the needs of the teacher. It can provide reliable information about the impact of teaching methods and behavioral strategies. Indirect observation, on the other hand, is based on the casual accumulation of data and can provide a comprehensive overview of a student's behavior.

It allows the teacher to report impressions that are based on a history of experiences with a student. Indirect methods provide a general picture of the student and can suggest areas where more specific and direct data should be collected.

DIRECT OBSERVATION

The ultimate in direct, objective observation was described by Robert Heinlein in *Stranger in a Strange Land*. In Heinlein's science fiction society some persons were trained to act as neutral observers and could remember perfectly what occurred. The observer noticed and remembered even the most obscure detail. At some later date these "Fair Witnesses" could be counted on to give an accurate report of exactly what occurred. The Witness provided a living record of what had taken place. The report included no statements of judgment or interpretations.

This fictionalized role demonstrates several critical elements in the observational process. An observer needs to attend conscientiously to the details of the event. It is equally important to be able to recall data accurately. It is also helpful to suspend judgment and evaluation during the observation.

Characteristics

A written record of a direct observation should be made as near to the time of the event as possible. In this way ordinary mortals can approximate the perfect memory of the Witness. As the time between event and recording increases, forgetting and other memory distortions increase. In situations where the details of an event must be reconstructed from memory, it is helpful to focus on specific features that are clearly remembered and to expand the description through the recall of associated pieces of information. The accuracy of information arrived at through this method, however, is always open to question.

In technologically advanced school settings records may be made on videotape or auditory recorders and then viewed at a later time. The information from a recording should be reduced to a written record that catalogues, synthesizes, or summarizes the taped material. In this way the observation is analyzed and abstracted. The methods used to produce the written record are similar to those used in making other direct observations. The advantages of taped recordings are that they provide an exact reproduction of the event, they can be studied by several observers, and they can be analyzed and reviewed at a convenient time without the distortions caused by forgetting. The disadvantages lie in the loss of material outside the range of the electronic recorder, the dependency on the skill and flexibility of the operator and the equipment, and the time required to record and to view the recording.

Whether informal observations are made live or from prerecorded material, the content of the written record varies depending on the type of observation made. Written records can differ on several dimensions, depending on the type of subject selected, the time spent on the observation, the range of behavior included, and the form of notation used. In Table 4-2 several dimensions are listed, as well as the range of variations that can occur on each dimension.

Table 4-2.
Determinants of the Observational Record

DIMENSION	RANGE OF VARIATIONS		
Subject	Individual	⟶	Groups
Time	Seconds	⟶	Hours
Content	Single behavior	⟶	Multiple behaviors
Notation	Frequency count	⟶	Narrative report

An observation, for instance, can focus on a single individual, cover the first hour of each day, concentrate solely on out-of-seat behavior and be recorded by a frequency count. Observations can also trace a pupil throughout a sequence of behaviors and describe in narrative form the full range of activity that has occurred. In still another instance, an observation can focus on a group of students, cover twenty-minute periods on subsequent days, concentrate on ten categories of behavior, and record each occurrence within each category. The records of the different observations will differ significantly in both content and appearance.

The *procedural control* used in an observation will structure the manner in which data are collected. Each method requires some form of systematic data recording. The consistency in the manner in which data are collected and reported makes it possible to obtain comparable data at different times and in different settings. The use of a consistent procedural framework also assures the observer that similar data will be collected throughout the period of observation. Hence, if an observer establishes a clear definition of "talking out behavior" and then counts the occurrences at set intervals, there is some assurance that data drawn during different time periods are comparable and represent similar behavior.

The *purpose* for which observational data are collected will determine the method that is selected. For instance, if the teacher wishes to record a student's outbursts in class so the information can be discussed with a colleague, the method chosen will reflect the need for a detailed description that can be shared. If, however, the teacher wishes to test a procedure for reducing out-of-seat behavior, the method chosen for observation will need to include data collection periods before and after the intervention and some procedure for counting the occurrences or duration of the misbehavior. In yet another case the purpose may be to analyze the sequence of a behavior to help determine at what point the teacher should intervene. The method selected here will focus observations on three time periods: before, during, and after the behavior.

Objective reporting is critical to the accuracy of an observation. Earlier it was noted that Heinlein's Fair Witness made neither interpretation nor judgment. The teacher cannot indulge in this luxury because the teacher is responsible for each step: observation, decision, and action. The teacher can, however, suspend judgment while collecting the data. Observation methods are designed to curb observer bias and distortion. If a situation has been prejudged, the observer tends to bend data to fit expectations. If a truly significant appreciation and understanding of a behavior is to emerge from an observation, the observer needs to be ready to accept the results of the data and to reevaluate previous beliefs.

Occasionally, a teacher will need to seek assistance in order to confirm an observation or to ensure objectivity in reporting. The teacher can use a fellow teacher or other professional to repeat an observation or review the choice of methods. Third party observers, once informed on the procedure, can provide new insights about the behavior and can verify or correct teacher observations.

Methods

Four methods of observation are helpful in a variety of classroom situations. Each method involves taking samples of behavior and each has certain strengths and limitations. Each is designed to provide somewhat different information and to serve different needs.

Observational methods require taking samples of behavior, and the guidelines appropriate to other sampling studies are appropriate to classroom observation. Samples must be long enough and frequent enough to provide an accurate representation of a student's behavior. Some samples can be short, such as recording inappropriate behavior as students enter a classroom and go to their seats. However, most behavior tends to be intermittent, and in these cases an observation time of twenty minutes to one hour is more appropriate. When work samples are used, the number of items or occurrences needs to be large enough to rule out the chance of accident or irregular error or infraction. Three or more items provide a fairly good check on simple processes such as a sample of two-place addition, but fifteen or more items are often needed to establish a sufficiently large sample over a topic area such as the demonstration of skill in spelling or handwriting.

Samples of behavior need to be taken on four or five occasions before confidence can be established that a certain rate, pattern, or sequence of behavior is indeed characteristic of a student. The data that are collected before any change is introduced by the teacher are called *baseline data*. During the baseline period the student's regular pattern is recorded, and it is against these data that changes can be measured. It is important to recognize that any single observation may not adequately represent the behavior of a child or an adult. Multiple observations are one safeguard against an unrepresentative sample.

Four methods of observation are chronolog, frequency recording, sequence sample, and trait sample. In the chronolog a detailed narrative account is made of a continuous behavioral unit. The frequency recording of the numerical tabulation of targeted behaviors is a procedure that is often used in conjunction with the third and fourth methods. In a sequence sample the observer records a target behavior and then details the antecedent and consequent behavior. In trait sampling, observations are made and recorded according to predetermined categories of behavior.

Chronolog The chronolog is particularly useful when a detailed report of an event is needed. This form of observation is useful when a teacher is unable to identify the significant variables that surround the behavior of a student. The chronolog provides the most comprehensive report possible and includes all the elements that are seen or heard. The data obtained in this form of observation are easily reported to fellow teachers and other professionals and can provide them with the details needed to arrive at a comprehensive picture of the student's behavior.

The sample is made as follows. First, the teacher selects the particular type of event that he or she wishes to record. This could be, for example, an observation of a student during a social studies period to determine the student's actual behavior during a time when the assigned work is not completed. In another case it could be a narrative account of a student's role in a small-group assignment. The chronolog can also be used to record a teacher's activities during a particular period in order to determine the role of the teacher within a given instructional period.

The method of recording is narrative and objective. Written statements should be short, in plain language, and nonjudgmental. The following excerpt is an example of an objective observation.

John enters the room walking quickly and carrying his sweater in his hand.
He turns to the right and hangs his sweater in the coat area.
Walking toward his desk he pushes Jim from behind and laughs.
Jim hits back with his right hand and mumbles inaudibly.
John continues to his seat, stands next to his seat, looks around and calls to Mike, who is to his right and across the room.
"I told you I'd beat you!"
John sits down and Mary says, "Can I borrow your pencil?"

Words that evaluate, judge, draw conclusions, suggest intent, or imply purpose are avoided. Instead, clear descriptions of behavior should be used, as in the following examples.

Avoid	*Use*
He was happy.	He smiled and spoke with an elevated, quick voice.
He wanted the pen.	He said, "Jim, give me the pen."
Jim spoke. John became angry and wanted no more from Jim.	Jim spoke. John shouted "No" and shook his fist in Jim's face.
John was disinterested in the subject and did not listen to the teacher.	John left his book closed on his desk and looked toward the windows as the teacher spoke.

The time, setting, activity, and participants are identified and described briefly. The format shown in Figure 4-1 includes some of the relevant details that help describe the setting in which the event occurred.

Dialogue is recorded as completely as possible. Because many interactions occur quickly and words are delivered rapidly, intermittent statements should be recorded and the intervening comments reconstructed. Notations such as asterisks (*) allow the observer to indicate words that have been added from memory. The following dialogue was taken on a playyard where John (J) and Bill (B) were facing each other after Bill hit John.

J: Why did you do that?
B: What difference does it make to you?
J: I want to know.

B: You always butt in where it's not your business.
*J: I do not! You butt in!
B: You give me a pain, you jerk!
J: Leave me alone or I'll break your neck!
*J: Turns and walks away. Four other boys begin to move away. B is standing still.)
*B: You stay out of my way and you won't get hit!

Figure 4-1.
Form for Student Observation

Student Observation

Name ______________ Time ______________ Date ______________
Location ______________________ Activity ______________________
Students and adults present ____________________________________
____
Activity structure ____
Materials ____
Event ____
Observation: ____
____
____

Strengths: The strengths of the chronolog lie in the thoroughness of the report and fidelity to the individual student's style of behavior. Specifically,

1. It provides a comprehensive observation of all elements of the event.
2. It provides an accurate recording of the event.
3. It can easily be shared with the participants or a colleague.
4. It provides the basis for an analysis of behavior and can reveal the dynamics of an interaction.
5. It provides comprehensive data that can be reviewed, studied, and analyzed after the pressures that occur during the event have subsided.

Limitations: The limitations of the chronolog arise from the absence of specificity. That is, the very process that results in comprehensive and evaluation-free data also precludes categorization and selective analysis. The limitations are as follows:

1. The broad focus may tend to obscure significant or repetitive elements.
2. No easy system of analysis is available.
3. Reports tend to be long, and when several event descriptions are available, the volume of data is difficult to manage.
4. Information needs to be summarized if it is to be included in reports.

Frequency recording In order to assess the impact of a teacher's intervention on a student's behavior, it is necessary to count the behavior. Casual attention to behavior is not sufficiently accurate or perceptive enough to provide the information needed for appropriate and timely decisions. Counting the occurrence of a behavior is an easy and precise method for tracking the activity of a student and monitoring the influence of the teacher's strategies.

Frequency recording is a useful way to establish the characteristic patterns of specific behavior. For instance, by counting the times a student verbally interrupts, gets out of the seat, and/or strikes another student, the teacher identifies the rate at which these behaviors occur within a specified time. A later check will reveal whether the behavior has increased or decreased.

The method is relatively simple and data can be displayed in numerical or chart form. First, the observer selects a specific student behavior to record and change. Either single or multiple behaviors can be counted, but it is generally difficult to record more than five behaviors at the same time.

Behaviors must be observable and easily identified as simple actions. They can be either negative or positive actions, such as leaving the seat without permission, talking to a neighbor, shouting in the classroom, or completing items correctly, completing assignments on time, speaking in a quiet voice. Behaviors can also be observed as present or absent, such as:

Says "Good morning" ☐ yes ☐ no
Hangs up coat ☐ yes ☐ no
Brushes teeth ☐ yes ☐ no
Takes book out of desk ☐ yes ☐ no

A recorded frequency can represent either a single occurrence or an interval during which the behavior occurred. In this way a student's comment to a neighbor could count as one tally or a running conversation might receive a tally every fifteen seconds. Thus, a comment under ten seconds would count as one, while a conversation that lasted one minute would have a recorded frequency of four. The observer needs to establish the intervals of time that must lapse before a continuous event is scored a second, third, or more times.

Behaviors are tallied in a format that provides space for the name of the behavior, the observational period, and the frequency tally. Examples of formats are shown in Figures 4-2, 4-3, and 4-4.

In Figure 4-2 all behaviors were recorded for twenty minutes each day.

Figure 4-2.
Tally of Frequency of Behaviors Before and After Intervention

Joe
Name

Behaviors

Day / Time		Speaks out	Is out of seat	Taps pencil	Argues	Makes noises	
9-8 / 10:05	Tallies	IIII	IIII	II	I	II	Data Collected Before Intervention
9-9 / 10:10		卌I	III	I	II	III	
9-10 / 9:55		III	III	III	I	II	
9-11 / 10:06		IIII	IIII	I	I	II	
9-12 / 9:50		卌	II	II		III	
Total		23	16	9	5	12	
Average		5	3.4	1.8	1	2.4	
9-15 / 10:15	Tallies	I			I	III	Data Collected After Intervention
9-16 / 10:05			I	II	I		
9-17 / 10:00		I	I	I		III	
9-18 / 10:05		I				II	
9-19 / 9:55							
Total		3	2	3	2	8	
Average		.6	.8	.6	.2	1.8	

Length of each observation 20 min.

If a behavior was continuous it was given a tally every 15 seconds. Five days were recorded to establish a baseline. The second five days report on the behaviors after the teacher took action to correct them.

In Figure 4-3 a format is provided that can be used when only one occurrence of a behavior is possible. In this case the procedure is used on a child's at-home behavior. An X indicates an action taken without the need of an adult reminder.

Figure 4-3.
Record of Tasks Completed Without Adult Reminder over Fifteen-Day Period and with Two Different Adult Interventions

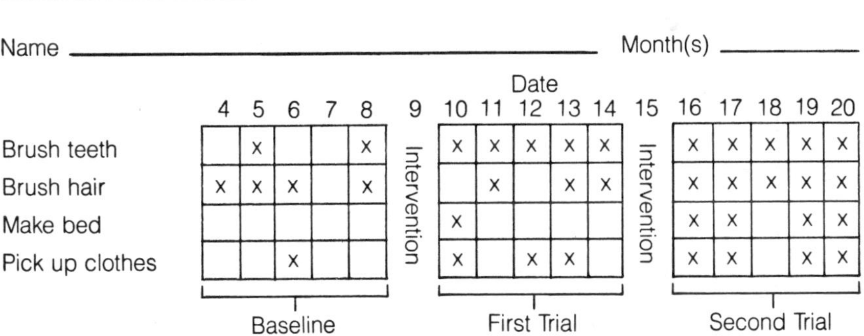

Name ______________________ Month(s) __________

	Date 4	5	6	7	8	9	10	11	12	13	14	15	16	17	18	19	20
Brush teeth		X			X	Intervention	X	X	X	X	X	Intervention	X	X	X	X	X
Brush hair	X	X	X		X			X		X	X		X	X	X	X	X
Make bed							X						X	X		X	X
Pick up clothes			X				X		X	X			X	X		X	X
	Baseline						First Trial						Second Trial				

In this example the first intervention is made after a five-day baseline period. A parent discussion with the child constituted the intervention, and some improvement in "brushing teeth" and "picking up clothes" is recorded. The second intervention involved the parents' introduction of a recording sheet on the behavior with the promise that five days of perfect behavior in two or more areas would result in a special treat. Significant improvement is recorded.

The example in Figure 4-4 plots a student's behavior and the average behavior of four peers. The baseline covers the first five days. The sixth day the teacher arranged a contract with the student to reduce speaking out in class. The contract was agreed upon early in the school day and speaking out was recorded on that day.

Strengths: The strengths of the frequency count rest in its clarity of focus and accuracy of reporting. Other strengths are as follows:

1. It gives quantitative data on the occurrence of a behavior.
2. It is an easy method by which to obtain pre and post samples of behavior.

Figure 4-4.
Frequency of Behavior by a Student and His Peers Before and After Intervention

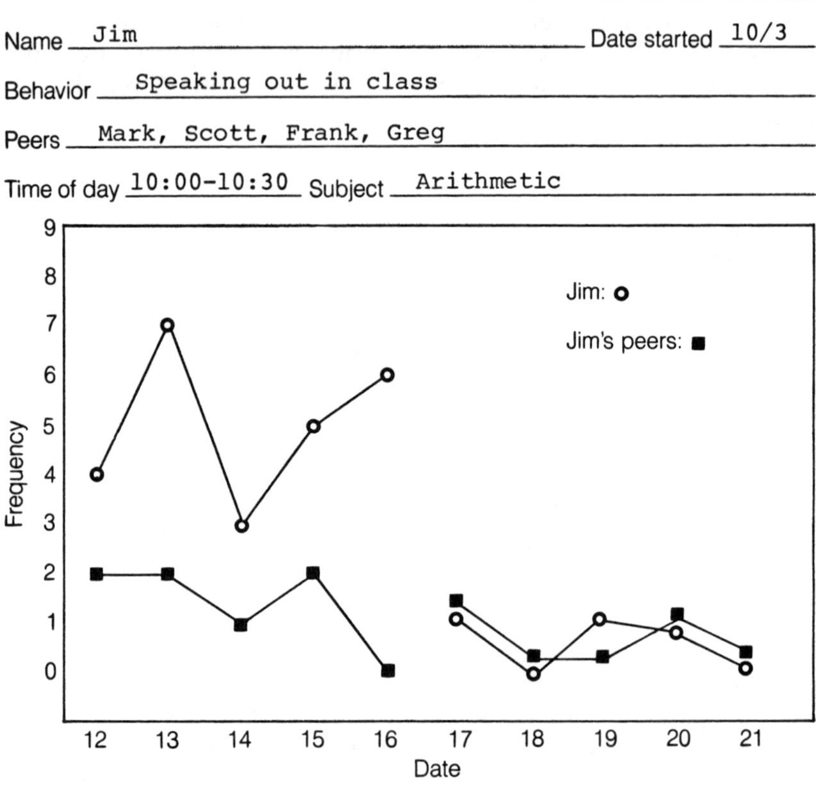

3. It forces the observer to select target behaviors.
4. It is clearly objective and common agreements can be reached as to what constitutes a behavior.
5. It can be used in connection with other methods of observation.

Limitations: This method restricts the attention of the observer to the identified areas of behavior and may neglect other important areas. In addition:

1. It provides no elaboration on the behavior.
2. It tends to be student-blaming since it does not take into account other forces in the environment.

3. It does not provide hints or guidance as to what intervention might be appropriate.

Sequence sample In the sequence sample the observer selects an incident that represents the problem the student is having. The observer carefully records the behavior at the moment of the problem and then records all that happens immediately after the problem. If a problem can be anticipated, a record is also made of the behavior that immediately precedes the incident. This antecedent behavior must be reconstructed from memory in cases where the incident cannot be anticipated. It is possible in this method to reconstruct entire incidents from memory. Observation is then used to verify, correct, and add to the record made from memory.

The sequence sample is especially useful in a classroom setting. An incident does not happen in isolation. It is part of an ongoing interaction between the student and the environment. A modification at any point in the sequence might change the student's behavior. In a classroom the teacher has the opportunity to influence antecedent behavior, the action itself, and the consequences of the action.

This assessment procedure includes three points of focus: antecedents (A), behavior (B), and consequences (C). The record format is shown in Figure 4-5.

Antecedents describe the situation immediately prior to the behavior. They include very brief descriptions of the type of activity, the time(s) and day(s), the location of participants, and the behavior of the teacher, student, and peers. The antecedents are the details of the setting just prior to the undesirable behavior.

Behavior is described in two different ways in two separate parts of the form in Figure 4-5. A description of the observed behavior is recorded under the column labeled "Behavior." The description can be brief, but it must be complete enough to tell what the student says and does in the incident. It is an objective description of the student's statement, action, or involvement. A description of the desired behavior is also recorded. This identifies what should be happening—the student behavior that is appropriate. It is the behavioral goal toward which student changes are directed. A clear statement helps to focus staff interventions and also allows for a review of the reasonableness of the expectation.

Consequences, or consequent behavior, immediately follow the undesirable behavior. Both the antecedent and consequent observations have temporal importance. They are observations of what happens just prior to and just after the behavior. Consequences tend to be people-oriented and include what the teacher does, what other students do, and what the problem student does.

Interventions can take place at point A, B, or C. The teacher can alter the antecedents so the setting is different. For instance, a student who is continually disruptive in a reading group can be separated for this activity. Or the behavior itself can be changed by using role playing and other behavior changing strategies. Consequences can also be arranged so that rewards (e.g., attention) are given for appropriate behavior rather than for misbehaviors.

Figure 4-5.
The Format for Recording Sequence Sample Data, Intervention Plans, and Actual Outcomes

Sequence Sample A B C

Name ____________ Location ____________ Date ____________

Problem description: ____

____

Antecedents | Behavior | Consequences

Desired behavior: ____

____

Intervention at *A B C*
(Circle one and describe intervention)

Outcomes
(What changes if any, occurred as a result of the intervention?)

Strengths: This is a thorough procedure for understanding the totality of a behavioral sequence. Other strengths are as follows:

1. It separates a behavior into its stimuli, action, and reward components.
2. It allows the teacher to select the focus point(s) for interventions.
3. It provides an opportunity for the teacher to observe the role that he or she plays in the student's performance.
4. It recognizes the influence of the environment and other students on the student's activity.
5. It provides information that is easy to collect and share with other professionals.

Limitations: Since the teacher constructs the sequence sample in a setting which he or she has created, it is possible for the teacher to overlook important elements. The best protection against this error is to review the sample with a fellow professional who is also familiar with the process. The reviewer should ask the observer about each detail in order to uncover what might have been omitted. Other limitations include the following:

1. Retrospective information, usually used in the antecedent section, is subject to the errors of forgetting or selective memory.
2. Stimuli (antecedent) are erroneously seen as causes for the behavior rather than as related events.
3. Other methods, such as frequency count, need to be included to provide accurate information on behavior change.

Trait sample The trait sample differs from the other three observational procedures in that the observation is recorded in predetermined behavioral categories. The observation is a closed system. Student behaviors are noted and coded according to the categorized procedure that has been chosen. Some systems lead from observation to prescription.

One of the most comprehensive observational systems is that developed by Spaulding (1980). He describes thirteen categories of "coping" behaviors, with six subcategories (Figure 4-6). When an individual student is to be observed, two other same-sex students are randomly selected and also observed in order to establish a base of "average" classroom behavior. A student is viewed for several seconds and the dominant behavior is noted and tallied in the appropriate category. The procedure is repeated for the second, then the third student. The cycle is repeated until at least twenty-four observations have been made on each student.

Figure 4-6.
Brief Form of the Categories of Student Behavior

1. *Aggressive behavior:*
Direct attack: grabbing, pushing, hitting, pulling, kicking; name-calling; destroying property: smashing, tearing, breaking.

2. *Negative (inappropriate) attention-getting behavior:*
Annoying, bothering, whining, loud talking (unnecessarily); attention-getting aversive noise-making; belittling, criticizing.

*3. *Manipulating, controlling, and directing others:*
Manipulating, bossing, commanding, directing, enforcing rules, conniving, wheedling, controlling.

4. *Resisting:*
Resisting, delaying; passive aggressive behavior; pretending to conform, conforming to the letter but not the spirit; defensive checking.

*5. *Self-directed activity:*
Productive working; reading, writing, constructing with interest; self-directed dramatic play (with high involvement).

*6. *Paying close attention; thinking, pondering:*
Listening attentively, watching carefully; concentrating on a story being told, a film being watched, a record played, thinking, pondering, reflecting.

*7. *Integrative sharing and helping:*
Contributing ideas, interests, materials, helping; responding by showing feelings (laughing, smiling, etc.) in audience situations; initiating conversation.

*8. *Integrative social interaction:*
Mutual give and take, cooperative behavior, integrative social behavior; studying or working together where participants are on a par.

*9. *Integrative seeking and receiving support, assistance, and information:* Bidding or asking teachers or significant peers for help, support, sympathy, affection, and so on; being helped; receiving assistance.

10. *Following directions passively and submissively:*
Doing assigned work without enthusiasm or great interest; submitting to requests; answering directed questions; waiting for instructions as directed.

SOURCE: R. L. Spaulding, *CASES Manual,* San Jose, Calif.: San Jose State University, 1980. Reproduced by permission of the author.

*Categories 3, 5, 6, 7, 8, and 9 are further coded as a or b in structured settings to indicate appropriate or inappropriate timing or location of activity (based on the teacher's expectations for the setting). Example: 5*a* would be recorded when a child was painting during art period (when painting was one of the expected activities). Painting during "story time" or in an academic setting would normally be coded 5*b*. The code *a* represents behaving in a certain coping category at the "right" time and place; *b* represents behaving in a certain coping category at the "wrong" time or place. What is "right" or "wrong" is based on the values and goals of the teacher or authority responsible in a given situation.

A child might be sharing with another child in an integrative manner (7) some bit of information the teacher regarded as highly inappropriate. It would be coded as 7*b* since it was an integrative act of sharing occurring at the "wrong" time in the "wrong" place, from the point of view of the teacher.

11. *Observing passively:*
    Visual wandering with short fixations; watching others work; checking on noises or movements; checking on activities of adults or peers.
12. *Responding to internal stimuli:*
    Daydreaming; sleeping; rocking or fidgeting; (not in transaction with external stimuli).
13. *Physical withdrawal or passive avoidance:*
    Moving away; hiding: avoiding transactions by movement away or around; physical wandering avoiding involvement in activities.

Table 4-3.
Eight Student Coping Styles from CASES

STYLE	FREQUENCY ITEMS		STYLE	FREQUENCY ITEMS	
A. Dominating,	1	____	E. Attentive,	6a	____
actively aggressive,	2	____	adult-oriented,	7a	____
bothering, controlling,	3b	____	compliant	9a	____
manipulating	9b	____	Total	E	____
Total	A	____			
			F. Assertive,	3a	____
B. Resistive, passive	4	____	socially integrative,	8a	____
aggressive, delaying,	5b	____	task-oriented		
peer-oriented,	7b	____			
off-task	8b	____	Total	F	____
Total	B	____			
			G. Appropriately task-oriented, independent, self-motivated	5a	____
C. Passive, withdrawn,	12	____			
avoidant, dreamy	13	____			
Total	C	____	Total	G	____
D. Peer-dependent,	6b	____	H. Conforming, passive, submissive to directions	10	____
distractible, off-task	11	____			
Total	D	____	Total	H	____

SOURCE: R. L. Spaulding, *CASES Manual,* San Jose, Calif., 1980. Reproduced with author-approved modifications.

Figure 4-7.
Frequency Count Recording Form for CASES

CASES Data Sheet Code name of subject ______________ Date ________

Setting ____________________ School ______________________________

Teacher (code) __________________ Observer ____________ Start ________

End ________

CASES Categories

Sample #	1	2	3a	3b	4	5a	5b	6a	6b	7a	7b	8a	8b	9a	9b	10	11	12	13
1																			
2																			
3																			
4																			
5																			
6																			
7																			
8																			
9																			
10																			
45																			
46																			
47																			
48																			
49																			
50																			
Totals																			
	1	2	3a	3b	4	5a	5b	6a	6b	7a	7b	8a	8b	9a	9b	10	11	12	13

SOURCE: R. L. Spaulding, *CASES Manual,* San Jose Calif.: San Jose State University, 1980. Adapted by permission of the author.

The tallies are totaled (Figure 4-7) and patterns of behavior determined. Spaulding has identified eight "coping styles" (Table 4-3) that represent singly or in some combination the behaviors exhibited by most students. When the style(s) has been established, teacher actions are tailored to effect student change. Treatment schedules for each style require the teacher to isolate, ignore, or reinforce student behavior so that appropriate behavior is encouraged and inappropriate behavior reduced.

Strengths: The trait sample provides a method for categorizing a full range of behaviors and for comparing student behaviors with a fair degree of objectivity. In addition:

1. It provides predetermined behavioral categories, thus reducing observer confusion.
2. It identifies behavioral styles or traits.
3. It can lead to prescription treatments for various behavioral styles.
4. It allows the teacher to monitor the impact treatments have on behavior.

Limitations: The trait sample is a time-consuming process and usually requires that a third party perform the observation. This procedure has the following additional limitations:

1. It provides mixed styles or traits that are difficult to interpret.
2. It tends to create the illusion that the child's behavior is independent of the teacher's style.
3. It limits the description of unique behaviors.

Each method of direct observation provides information that can be immediately acted upon. Each provides data on the progress of a student, on changes in behavior, and on the impact of instruction. Each provides basic information that is easily available to teachers in the classroom. When properly used these methods are the teacher's most effective assessment strategies.

INDIRECT OBSERVATION

While direct observation is based on viewing actual behavior, indirect observation is based on remembered behavior or perceived behavior. Indirect observation relies on memory and allows the viewer to aggregate his or her impressions. That is, the evaluation is based on an accumulation of experiences and observations. Such reports can vary greatly in their degree of objectivity. For instance, impressions gained over a long period of contact can provide a comprehensive description of student behavior and can be more reliable than occasional observations.

General impressions can also reflect the distortions and biases of the viewer. The negative qualities of a problem student, for example, tend to overshadow positive and appropriate behavior. Thus, a report based on data accumulated in memory may overlook positive or semiappropriate aspects of student behavior. Pervasive attitudes and expectations on the part of the observer will also significantly influence the opinions and beliefs that are held about a problem student. This can translate into distorted data. When indirect assessments are used, every effort must be made to represent the student's behavior accurately.

The two major procedures that are used to make indirect observations are the event recall and the rating scale. In the event recall, the observer is asked to reconstruct an event from memory. Experience has shown that there is a wealth of information stored in memory but not readily available to immediate recall. The second method, the rating scale, requires the observer to assign a rank, category, or description to the student. Five variations on the rating scale are described.

Event Recall

Often the only record of an event is in the memory of the observer. Although there are significant problems associated with data based on memory, such information can be very useful in assessment. The data usually need verification, but they can provide the tentative basis for action.

The central features and the major action in an event are usually remembered best. The attitudes and feelings of the observer are also easily recalled. It is the detail of an event that is "lost" from memory, and it is the detail that is most useful in assessment.

The procedure used to expand the amount of detail available from memory involves several steps. It can be accomplished alone or with the help of a patient colleague. It presupposes a willingness to review the event and discover the sequence and detail of what occurred. Memory is improved by an attitude of confidence and a willingness to "relive" an event. Any form of pressure or self-recrimination is counterproductive. The steps in event recall are as follows:

1. Elements that can be easily recalled should be established and noted.

2. The observer relaxes and reviews the event without feelings of pressure or harassment.
3. The observer attempts to "go back" in memory to the time of the event.
4. All participants, their roles, clothing, attitude, and activities are reviewed.
5. The event is redescribed and notes made of new elements.
6. The observer establishes her own action and that of other participants.
7. The observer attempts to remember what happened just before the event and what happened immediately after the event. All participants are included in this recall.
8. Each new memory or insight is gently pursued to open up new memories.
9. The observer is to feel comfortable with the effort and results of this review.

Hopefully, the information generated in this manner can provide details that can help in understanding and planning. To remember an event, however, is not necessarily to establish its authenticity; therefore, data generated in this manner must be acted upon cautiously and tentatively.

Strengths:

1. Sometimes it is the only method available to obtain information.
2. It is relatively easy to accomplish and can include all who were present at the time of the event.
3. It allows the observer to examine his or her role within the situation.
4. It uncovers little noticed details and provides the observer with clues as to information the observer may typically ignore.

Limitations:

1. It is not effective when the observer feels under pressure or scrutiny.
2. Data suffer from the distortions and biases that affect memory.
3. Information that was witnessed in a situation where the observer had not established an intent to be objective may be significantly limited by selective attention.
4. The opportunity to censor information is present.

Table 4-4.
Rating Scale Formats

TYPE OF SCALE	DESCRIPTION	RESPONSE FORMAT ITEM: "I LIKE SCHOOL"
Checklist	One of a variety of ways to simply check an item as appropriate.	Check one: _____ Yes _____ No
Category rating	Provides words that allow the respondent to select an answer that best characterizes the response to the item.	Select the answer (or item, adjective, etc.) that best completes the statement.
Numerical rating	Provides words and numerical representations that suggest equal intervals on a continuum. Can suggest comparability between items.	Circle one number: 1. No agreement 2. Low agreement 3. Medium agreement 4. High agreement 5. Total agreement
Graphic rating	A linear representation that suggests a continuum with equal intervals. One of the best procedures, combining words with space.	Check on the scale: |____|____|____|____| Very much / Some-what / Some / Not much / Very little
Forced-choice item	Requires the selection of a response from among a set of equally attractive, unpleasant, or otherwise similar choices.	Check one: Never Almost never Sometimes Almost always Always

Rating Scale

The rating scale is one of the simplest forms of observation. Scales are relatively easy to construct and to administer. The rater makes decisions about the subject on the basis of descriptions, categories, or topics, and assigns a numerical or qualitative description to the subject. The format makes such decisions easy to score and to aggregate. However, these instruments have many problems, including lack of validity, low stability of response, and overinterpretation.

The most useful rating scales are those that supply specific information about the rater. Information provided by students about their opinions, beliefs, attitudes, and understandings, for example, can have substantive value for program planning. Responses can let the teacher know the range of beliefs and attitudes that exist in the classroom. Student ratings about curricular units and teaching methods can help in the evaluation of the instructional program, and self-ratings by both teachers and students can lead to important instructional decisions.

Of lesser value to teachers are ratings that they complete on their students. These can be used in pre-post evaluations, but the teacher is better advised to use more performance-related methods, such as the frequency recording. Some indirect benefits, however, can accrue to the teacher who uses student rating scales. These scales occasionally provide insights about student behavior as a result of the way the information is displayed or summarized. They also have the effect of focusing attention on certain elements of behavior that might otherwise have been overlooked.

Five frequently used rating scales are: checklists, forced-choice items, category ratings, numerical ratings, and graphic ratings. Although each type reveals somewhat different information, the decision as to which type to use in a particular situation depends partly on the form that best suits the material and on the preference of the observer. A familiarity with each method will allow the observer to choose methods that provide the required information and are most appropriate for the subject matter. In Table 4-4 the five rating forms are briefly defined and illustrated.

Summary

Two forms of observation have been discussed, direct and indirect. The first requires the observation and recording of behavior while it is being performed or in detailed recall. The second is based on memory and reconstruction of behavior in order to provide a general picture of the student. Direct observation results in an exact description of student performance, while indirect observation provides a generalized description. Direct assessment is most helpful in making instructional and behavioral decisions; indirect assessment is best at giving a composite impression of behavior. The latter form allows for an overall description of the student.

The methods of direct observation range from the simple frequency count to the recording of predetermined behavioral characteristics. Each method has strengths and weaknesses and each can be used in combination with other methods. Exact records are necessary in order to determine consistency in behavior and changes in performance.

Indirect observation rests heavily on recall. Rating scales are the most common form of indirect observation and five formats have been briefly described. Each provides a general description of behavior and can be used to define the characteristic features of a student.

Bibliography

Cohen, Dorothy, and Stern, Virginia. *Observing and Recording the Behavior of Young Children.* New York: Teachers College Press, 1974.

Deshler, Donald D.; Ferrell, William R.; and Kass, Corrine E. "Error Monitoring of Schoolwork by Learning Disabled Adolescents." *Journal of Learning Disability* 11, no. 7 (1978): 401–414.

Epstein, Seymore. "The Stability of Behavior: II Implications for Psychological Research." *American Psychologist* 35, no. 9 (1980): 790–806.

Frick, Ted, and Semmel, Melvyn I. "Observer Agreement and Reliabilities of Classroom Observational Measures." *Review of Educational Research* 48, no. 1 (1978): 157–184.

Jones, Edward E.; Riggs, Janet M.; and Quattrone, George. "Observer Bias in Attitude Attribution Paradigm: Effect of Time and Information Order." *Journal of Personality and Social Psychology* 37, no. 7 (1979): 1230–1238.

Keefe, Francis J.; Kopel, Steve A.; and Gordon, Steven B. *A Practical Guide to Behavioral Assessment.* New York: Springer, 1978. See Chapter 2, "A Procedural Framework for Behavioral Assessment."

Moracco, John. "Field Observation and Recording Procedures for Elementary School Counselors." *Elementary School Guidance and Counseling* 12, no. 2 (1977): 127–132.

Murphy, Robert J., and Bryan, Ann J. "Multiple-baseline and Multiple-probe Designs: Practical Alternatives for Special Education Assessment and Evaluation." *The Journal of Special Education* 14, no. 3 (1980): 325–335.

Persons, W. Scott, and Brassell, William R. "A Practical Observational Procedure for Monitoring Four Behaviors Relevant to Classroom Management." *Psychology in the Schools* 13, no. 1 (1976): 64–71.

Riegle, Rodney P. "Classifying Classroom Questions." *Journal of Teacher Education* 27, no. 2 (1976): 156–161.

Rowley, Glenn L. "The Relationship of Reliability in Classroom Research to the Amount of Observation: An Extension of the Spearman-Brown Formula." *Journal of Educational Measurement* 15, no. 3 (1978): 165–180.

Rowley, Glenn L. "The Reliability of Observational Measures." *American Educational Research Journal* 13, no. 1 (1976): 51–59.

Scott, Myrtle. "Ecological Theory and Methods for Research in Special Education." *The Journal of Special Education* 14, no. 3 (1980): 279–294.

Spaulding, Robert L. *CASES Manual.* San Jose, Calif.: San Jose State University, 1980.

Chapter 5 Interview-Conferences and Questionnaires

Data collection is an important part of assessment. Two methods by which the teacher or other professional can collect data are the interview-conference and the questionnaire.

INTERVIEW-CONFERENCES

The interview ranks along with observation as one of the oldest forms of data collection. G. W. Allport, a famous psychologist, is quoted as saying, "If we want to know how people feel—what they experience and what they remember, what their emotions and motives are like, and the reasons for acting as they do—why not ask them?" The interview provides a gateway to private thoughts, emotions, and beliefs; it provides information that can greatly help a teacher to understand and predict behavior.

The *interview* is a form of conversation in which the interviewer—the teacher or other professional—seeks to elicit information. The conversation is purposeful and is guided by the interviewer. Often, information is exchanged in such a way that both parties increase their knowledge and understanding. However, the focus and course of the conversation is directed by the interviewer. The interviewer is responsible for the flow and movement of the exchange.

The *conference* is a meeting between two or more people for the purpose of a consultation or discussion. While the interview tends to be an inquiry, the conference is more clearly an exchange of information. The latter is a meeting for discussion and the former is a meeting for investigation. In actual practice in the school setting the two activities tend to blend together. That is, most teachers claim to hold conferences, but much of what occurs is information seeking, hence, interviewing. In this chapter the "interview" will refer to those parts of a conference where the teacher or professional seeks to obtain information.

Interviewing, in an informal sense, is a basic tool in teaching. Teachers continually find themselves talking with students and adults in an attempt to gather information, obtain clarification, determine positions, reconcile differences, probe for motivations, and a host of other data-generating verbal interactions. In a typical day a teacher may:

- Talk with a student in the morning to determine what can be done to increase her energy in the opening hours of class
- Discuss with a student ways to improve math performance
- Break up a fight and talk with each student separately and together
- Screen a potential class aide
- Discuss a student with a school nurse
- Talk with two students about their concerns for next year's class placement

In each exchange the teacher relies heavily on interview skills to generate information for decisions, agreements, and solutions.

The goal in each case differs and the data vary greatly, but common strategies of interviewing and discussion are employed throughout.

Advantages and Disadvantages

There are numerous positive aspects of the interview. During an interview a reluctant student or parent can be made to feel comfortable, and a high degree of candor achieved. A teacher can change the direction of the inquiry as the result of information generated during the exchange; he or she can also check on how well the interviewee understands questions or issues and can rephrase and clarify comments. A response can be reexamined and a question repeated in order to verify the dependability of a comment. All this can be accomplished in an informal, casual atmosphere and can occur either spontaneously or with advanced preparation. The interview format can be adapted so as to probe any problem or any consideration.

The negative aspects of the interview involve time requirements, interviewer bias, and response distortions. Conversations take time, especially when the purpose is an honest and thoughtful exchange. With adults, a few minutes of casual conversation are often needed to establish the rapport necessary for a free exchange of information. Children also respond to brief, casual introductory conversation. Their responses, their attention, and their patience tend to be shorter than that of the adult. In any event, listening and talking can require a considerable time commitment.

Because the data that flow from an interview are both elicited and screened by the interviewer, they are particularly vulnerable to interviewer bias. In an open interview, where the interviewer creates each question and sets the course of the conversation, predetermined opinions, judgments, and predictions can significantly influence the type of questions asked and the attitude that permeates the interview. Interviewee responses are both shaped by the form of the questions and subject to the distortions of the listener. Awareness of this potential problem and a willingness to listen and respond to the content and feeling of the interviewee can reduce the problem of bias in both questioning and listening. Several ways to achieve a more open and objective interview are the following:

1. Ask how the interviewee understands the problem or issue (e.g., "Pete, what do you think about the problem of talking in class?").
2. Acknowledge a response without judgment (e.g., "This seems to be how you feel.").
3. Rephrase a question that appears to upset or confuse the interviewee and accept responsibility for the upset or confusion (e.g., "I think I didn't say that very well. What I'm trying to ask is . . .").
4. Repeat an interviewee response as an indication that you have heard what the person has said (e.g., "You feel that other kids pick on you.").

The interviewee can distort information in several ways. First, he or she may not have access to the type of information the teacher or professional wants. Examples of this problem are apparent in the answers that children give when they are asked why they behaved the way they did. Children are often not aware of their motivation, and in an effort to escape the interrogation they create an answer. This problem can be reduced in several ways:

1. Ask questions only when there is reason to believe that the person can answer truthfully. For example, "Do you have any idea why you did that? What might it be?"
2. Allow the interviewee to decline to answer without fear of punishment or disapproval. For example, "Can you talk about it now? I'd like to hear, and it's OK if you want to wait."
3. Limit the use of "why" questions to subjects that are impersonal or nonthreatening. For example, "Why do you think people use drugs?" instead of "Why do you use drugs?" or "Let's look at what you can do to help at home" instead of "Why is it that Mary never comes to school with her homework completed?"

The interviewee will also distort answers in order to please or deceive the questioner. Both adults and children are aware of the process of conscious deception. The desire to please, however, has a more subtle influence, and responses of this nature often satisfy a need to be correct or accepted. Both problems can be reduced if the conversation or question is framed so that a "correct" response is not suggested and so that the interviewee does not stand to benefit or lose as a result of his or her answer. The following are suggestions for reducing or avoiding deception.

1. Allow for several responses to a question. For example, "What are a couple of things that happened just before the fight?" instead of "What caused the fight today?"
2. Avoid asking questions that incriminate the interviewee. State what is known. For example, "I noticed today that you took a pencil from Greg's desk. Let's talk about that." instead of "John, did you take a pencil from Greg's desk today?"
3. State the action you plan to take early in the interview so the student is not tempted to distort his or her response in an effort to influence a pending decision. For example, "This is what I want you to do today . . . ," "Now let's talk about how it can be prevented in the future."

Interview-Conference Process

In education most interviewing, aside from personnel selection, is unstructured. That is, there is no tightly organized format or series of fixed questions. The interaction tends to flow as it would in normal conversation. The record of the exchange is made after the interview, and therefore verbatim statements are included only to the extent that they can be remembered. The productivity of the interview greatly depends on the skill of the interviewer.

The process includes introduction, focus, queries or exchanges, and planning and conclusion (Figure 5-1). In spontaneous interviews that emerge from immediate situations there is little chance for preplanning. Many situations, however, can be predicted and for these the professional can be prepared. For example, disturbances on the yard can be anticipated and response patterns established and practiced. It is important that strategies that are to be used in times of stress be rehearsed so that they emerge smoothly and automatically. Prescheduled interviews lend themselves to preplanning and organization not possible in the spontaneous interview.

Figure 5-1.
The Process and Activities in an Interview-Conference

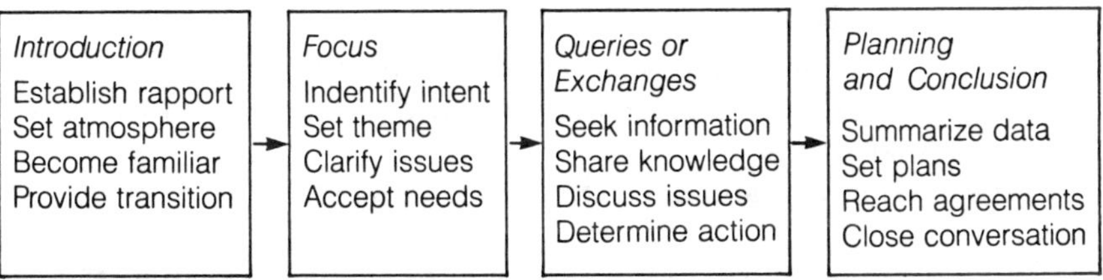

Introduction An introductory conversation is a legitimate and valuable part of the interview-conference process. It is especially important for people who are meeting for the first time or for those who meet infrequently. It provides time for each to become familiar with the other without interfering with the specific data collection process. Casual and trivial introductory conversation plays a critical role in the overall success of many interviews.

The introduction can bridge the gap between what occurred before the meeting and the more rigorous exchange that will follow. In this transition period both the interviewer and the interviewee get a glimpse at the style, speech pattern, and responsiveness of the other. The tone of the meeting can be set and the beginning of an exchange established.

The choice of subject matter in the introductory phase is a matter of personal style and preference. Generally a person talks about some neutral subject that is easy to discuss and is within the experience of both parties. The weather is often selected as the subject because it offends no one, is timely, and is a common experience for all. Comments about clothing, locating the room, general convenience, local sports, hobbies, or mood of the day are frequent choices for introductory topics. Reference to materials and projects in the classroom are also neutral introductory topics.

The form that introductory comments take determines, in part, the type of response that is given. Statements that express the teacher's ideas, beliefs, or opinions tend to make the teacher more familiar to the interviewee. And the use of questions allows the interviewee to express himself or herself. This combination of statements and questions can lead to an exchange. Comments in each format are illustrated in the following:

- "We have been working on projects all day and I hope you will excuse the condition of the room."
  (Statement and no conversational response expected.)
- "Hello, Mrs. Adult. Did you have any difficulty finding the room?"
  (Salutation and question calling for a short response.)
- "What do you think about all the roller skating that is going on lately?"
  (Question calling for an opinion.)
- "Windy days like today keep the children restless, and frankly I'm happy to see the end of the day. Does the weather affect you or your family that way?"
  (Mixed comment and question calling for a personal response.)

An introduction in which the teacher does all the talking may put the parent or child at ease but provides little information to the teacher and may set the pattern for a one-way discourse. On the other hand, an introduction built around questions can lead to a feeling of interrogation rather than an exchange. The mixed form of statements and questions is usually preferred in the school setting where the intent of the interview-conference is an exchange of information and where the desired result is a mutually agreed upon plan.

The introductory phase is brief when the parties are familiar with each other. Introductory talk in these situations is for pleasure rather than a prelude to the more businesslike interview. Some form of introduction, however, is almost always present. These statements illustrate opening statements by a teacher addressing a person he or she knows and sees regularly.

- "Hi, Mr. Friendly. I'm glad you could come. I could use some help."
- "Thank you for coming."
- "I think if we talk about this it will help."

- "Mrs. Parent, please sit down. I've looked forward to talking with you."
- "Are you free for a few minutes? I could use some information."

Each of these short introductory statements is used in lieu of a transition period. The statements are characteristic of opening comments used with a parent, with a psychologist or counselor who visits the teacher regularly, or with a student who is in daily contact with a teacher. Of course, transitory conversation may be needed even with persons with whom the interviewer is familiar. The alert interviewer watches closely to see if the interviewee makes the transition from before-meeting activities to a serious consideration of the subject at hand. If the interviewee has trouble responding to important questions or statements, the introductory phase should be reintroduced with phrases like:

- "Maybe you need a moment or two to collect your thoughts."
- "Would you like a little of the background on this?"
- "Is this a good time to discuss this?"
- "It seems as if you have something on your mind."
- "Let's sit somewhere more comfortable where we can concentrate."
- "Would you like to finish what you're doing before we start?"

In most situations the introductory period provides a preparatory phase for both parties. It need not be long or involved, but its presence is expected in most English-language communication. The interviewer selects a format that seems to best suit the situation and that allows him or her to be relaxed and natural. If the introduction flows easily and without strain, the interviewer has some assurance that a cooperative exchange will follow. Failure to establish a good exchange during this period, however, does not predict future problems. It does, though, alert the interviewer to an uneven beginning. The period of data collection has begun.

Focus The interviewer needs to have a clear perception of the purpose and intent of the interview. In many situations it is equally important to communicate these to the interviewee. It is also helpful to recognize that the purpose and intent of the interviewer are not necessarily the same as those of the interviewee. Clarity of purpose, shared intentions, and compatibility between the interviewer and the interviewee increase the success of the interview.

The purpose of an interview is the reason behind the meeting. A clear purpose allows the interviewer to concentrate the discussion on areas that are relevant to the issue(s). Lack of clarity creates confusion for both parties and results in a collection of data that, although often interesting, provide little help with the problem. When the purpose is clear the interviewer can prepare materials in advance and can plan an appropriate way to proceed.

The purpose of an interview in a school setting varies greatly. For the most part it is related to student behavior or achievement. It can, however, range from an interview with an administrator in order to clarify a directive to an interview with a prospective peer counselor who will assist in the classroom.

When the interviewee is clear as to the purpose of the discussion, it is relatively easy to focus the conversation. In many interviews the subject is uncertain as to the reason for the discussion and the result is confusion and suspicion. Brevity and clarity are the hallmark of effective statements of purpose. The following are good illustrations of statements of purpose:

- "John, I think it's time to talk about your math."
- "Mr. Smith, I'm curious about how this plan will be implemented."
- "I'm concerned about Mary's behavior on the yard."
- "I would like to ask you some questions about your background for this job."
- "We need to talk about what happened between the two of you at lunch."
- "I would like help on translating these results into practical activities."

In each of these examples the teacher or professional communicates the purpose of meeting to the party involved. Statements tend to be short, simple, and direct. In most cases this approach, following a sufficient introductory period, leads to a directed discussion.

Occasionally the teacher will choose to withhold a statement of purpose in order to let the interviewee express himself. This is clearly appropriate when the interviewee is eager to open the discussion. In this case the interviewee may hold a purpose common to the interviewer and an agreement can be achieved quickly. Here are a few comments that will encourage the interviewee to take the lead in the discussion.

- "I know you have some concerns. Would you like to start with what is important to you?"
- "That seems like a very important problem. I'd like to ask you some questions about it."
- "What is the thing about class that you would most like to change?"

- "Now that we have a few minutes would you like to tell me what it was you wanted to talk about earlier?"

In some instances the purposes of the interviewer and the interviewee differ significantly, and occasionally they are in direct conflict. In actuality the purposes of two individuals seldom coincide perfectly, so most interviews involve individuals whose reasons for participating vary somewhat. For example:

- A teacher may make an appointment with the principal in order to review an administrative decision, while the principal may keep that appointment in order to fulfill a commitment to be responsive to teacher needs.
- A teacher may discuss misbehavior with a student in order to resolve a problem, while the student may sit quietly and respond in order to avoid disapproval.
- A psychologist may be intent on illustrating the process a student uses to solve a problem, while the teacher who interviews the psychologist is interested in practical ways to improve the student's achievement.
- A teacher may seek a parent's assistance with a child, while the parent may be intent on pleasing the teacher without committing herself to any additional work at home.

Differences need not disrupt or thwart the professional's search for data and for problem resolution. Differences or conflicts require time to understand, to overcome, or to accommodate. They can be handled by acknowledging their existence and attempting to satisfy, at some level, the needs of both parties. Conflicts, on the other hand, require problem-solving strategies, and the conflict may or may not be resolved during the interview.

The resolution of differences cited in the previous list of examples might occur as follows. The principal's need might be satisfied if the teacher acknowledges the principal's willingness to set aside time to listen to the teacher's questions. The teacher, on the other hand, would still need to press the inquiry. In the case of the misbehaving child, attention directed to appropriate behavior could shift the focus from blame and disapproval to competency and positive action. The psychologist's interest in the child's thinking process, on the other hand, might be supported and verified if it coincides with the teacher's experience. The teacher meanwhile still needs information that could be used to assist the student immediately. In the situation with the parent, the teacher can acknowledge to the parent that this plan will be added work for the parent and then suggest that maybe the plan isn't reasonable or possible. If the parent is reluctant, a more acceptable plan can be sought or the teacher can decide that parent assistance is not to be expected at this time.

In each instance the difference in purpose is accepted. The teacher acknowledges, listens, and supports the needs of the interviewee. The teacher also makes clear his or her own needs and pursues the data that will be useful. To acknowledge a difference in needs is not to abandon the needs of either party. Instead, concern and understanding shown to the interviewee can open the door to a useful exchange of information.

Conflicts in purpose are more difficult to resolve. Conflicts occur when there are striking differences in beliefs, understanding, values, or priorities. Examples of some common conflicts that occur in school settings illustrate the wide range of polar positions that can exist.

- Beliefs:
  One party supports progressive teaching practices; the other wants traditional or conservative practices.
  One party believes in heavy homework assignments; the other has no faith in this procedure.
- Understanding:
  The teacher's information leads her to feel that she has been fair and lenient; the parents' information is that the teacher is unusually critical of their child.
  The principal has allocated materials based on district guidelines; the teacher has reason to believe that a large budget has been authorized for his type of class.
- Values:
  One person wants to have learning for enjoyment; the other prizes good grades.
  A trade (job) is respected by one person; a profession valued by another.
- Priorities:
  Little League practice is given priority over completion of homework assignments.
  Expenditures on household needs and recreation are given preference over adequate clothing and food for the child.

There are several options open to the interviewer when a conflict arises. The conflict can be ignored, explored, avoided, or resolved. A frequent strategy is to ignore the problem and proceed as if no difference exists. This form of self-deception can lead to misunderstandings based on faulty interpretation of available information. For example, parents who are opposed to homework may finally agree to a plan that involves homework but have no intention of carrying out their part of the agreement. In another case parents may agree that preparation in a trade is to be respected but still continue to push their adolescent into a profession for which he is ill suited.

A second approach to conflict involves exploring the point of view of the interviewer in an effort to identify possible solutions or compromises. In this approach differences are recognized, points of view exchanged, and some accommodations adopted. Shared points of view often increase understanding for both parties, and occasionally a point of view is changed. The old adage, however, generally prevails: A man convinced against his will is of the same opinion still. Respect for the opinions of others, as well as a clear expression of a point of view by the interviewer, often leads to some mutually agreeable compromise.

Avoidance is a choice available when the interviewer is aware that a conflict exists, and determines that the subject is not critical to the issue or is one that cannot be resolved, and, therefore, steers the discussion around the sensitive area. For instance, a teacher in a conference with a parent with strong feelings about book censorship may avoid introducing the subject of the class library rather than introduce a sensitive subject that is not relevant to the purpose of the meeting. The teacher may avoid an area of conflict in order to keep the interview on an agreeable or cooperative level; avoidance, however, skirts rather than resolves a problem.

In a more direct approach the interviewer can enter into problem-solving strategies in the hope of creating a satisfactory resolution. Again, acknowledgment of the conflict is basic and may create an opportunity to actively search for acceptable solutions. Problem-solving techniques essentially aim at arriving at a point of agreement. The following examples demonstrate expressions of acknowledgment, as well as attempts to open the conversation to possible solutions.

- "I know this is upsetting to you. Can we proceed with a few questions at a time? Stop me whenever you want."
- "I agree that homework doesn't work for some children, however, I would like to try it with Lisa. Is there some way we can do this so that it will be OK with you?"
- "The two of you don't look ready to talk yet. I'd like to spend some time with you today. When will be a good time to get together?"
- "I want to hear your ideas. I feel that if we can find a way to work together we can improve the classroom behavior."

It is possible for a conflict to remain unresolved. That is, during the interview ideas are expressed by both parties, data are gathered, and problem solving is attempted, and yet no resolution is found. The agreement is to disagree. This is a legitimate although disappointing outcome of an interview. Such a disagreement requires that the professional try other strategies to resolve the problem. Often the teacher is left to work out the problem with the student, without parental help.

Queries or exchanges At the heart of the interview are the questions or exchanges that provide the data sought by the interviewer. The form can be unstructured or structured. The interviewer, with clear purpose, directs the conversation so that it covers the major points needed to clarify the issue. For instance,

- After a fight in the schoolyard the teacher may question students to determine:
  How it began
  Who was involved
  Who was responsible
  What appropriate action should be taken
  What follow-up is needed
- During a discussion with a parent in an attempt to improve a student's classroom or homework assignments, the teacher may seek:
  Clarification of expectations
  Descriptions of home/school experiences
  Possible solutions
  Election of most acceptable plan
  Establishment of a follow-up
- In a discussion with a psychologist about the results of an evaluation, the teacher may seek:
  A description of specific reactions during testing
  The relevance of each finding to behavior and achievement
  Subsequent steps to be taken
  A determination as to who is responsible for each step
  A follow-up plan

The process of query or exchange in an interview is relatively simple. The question or statement is made, the response elicited, the answer is acknowledged, expansion is encouraged, data are recorded or remembered, and a new question or statement is introduced. Questions that are short and simply stated are more likely to be understood by both children and adults. The steps in the process are diagrammed in Figure 5-2.

Figure 5-2.
The Sequence of an Interview Query or Exchange

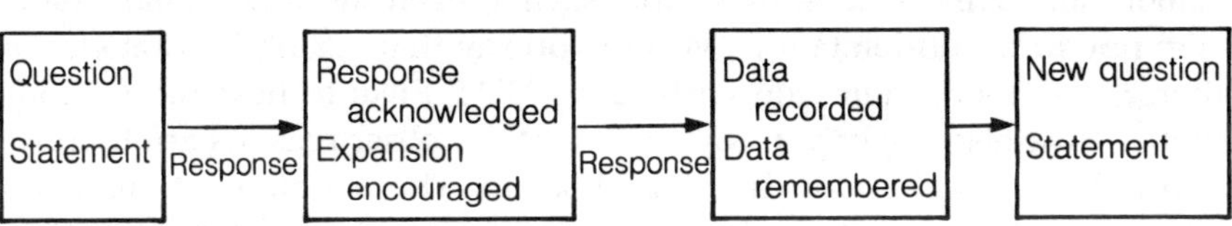

A key to the success of the query or statement is the ability to listen to the reply. Listening is a skill that requires training and practice. If the interviewer wishes to make a simple reply to a statement, it can be done with a "Thank you," a head nod, or some other casual sign of recognition. However, if the interviewer wishes to encourage more conversation, a more complete response is required. At one level the interviewer can make a brief restatement of the *verbal content* of the interviewee's comments. At a second level the interviewer can respond with an acknowledgment of the *feeling content* of the comments. At both levels the interviewer avoids making assumptions or interpretations. Acknowledgments are generally given to the last item expressed by the interviewee or to that item the interviewer wishes to have expanded.

The following are examples of these level acknowledgments:

1. The parent has explained how hard homework is to handle in their household—the upset it creates, the amount of time it takes, and the difficult nature of the assignments.
   Teacher acknowledges verbal content: "The homework is difficult."
   Teacher acknowledges feeling content: "The homework is upsetting to the family."
   Both acknowledgments: "The homework is hard to do and it upsets the family."
2. A student, very upset, is telling about a fight he had on the yard. He is telling what was said at the start of the fight and blaming the other student for starting it.
   Content acknowledgment: "The other boy was calling you names."
   Feeling acknowledgment: "You were very angry."
   Both acknowledgments: "You feel he started it and you were (are) very mad."

The acknowledgment of a statement frequently encourages further sharing. It communicates concern and understanding and yet allows for neutrality and disagreement. The major drawback is that careful listening takes time. But time spent at this point might eliminate later problems.

Another method used to encourage communication is the request for elaboration. This is done by simply saying, "Tell me more about that," "I'm not sure I understand," "Would you say that again?," "What else is there?," "Is there more you wish to say?," "I'd like to hear more about that," "How else might you say that?," "What other reasons are there?," "How do you feel about that?," and so on. These statements indicate interest on the part of the interviewer and lead the interviewee to further exploration and clarification.

Planning and conclusion The purpose of many interview-conferences is to arrive at a plan of action. That plan of action often requires either the active participation or the agreement of the student, the parent, or both—the plan cannot be achieved unilaterally. Cooperative discussion is essential to the success of the effort. The interviewer is responsible for leading the parties through the steps necessary to accomplish the purpose of the meeting.

The elements of cooperative planning include selecting the goal, strategies, areas of responsibility, time line, and follow-up procedures. The important tasks must be established, agreements reached, and commitments agreed upon. Once the goals and methods are determined, it is necessary to establish the areas of responsibility and the willingness and ability of the student or adult to carry out his or her part of the agreement.

Resistance must be acknowledged and addressed if a resolution is to be found. The following steps provide a guide to confronting and resolving an interview-conference obstacle: (1) acknowledge the problem, (2) restate the need, (3) establish steps, (4) reach agreement, (5) establish steps, (6) confirm new agreement. In the example that follows, a teacher becomes aware of an obstacle to the homework plan that is developing between the teacher (T) and the parent (P).

EXAMPLE	STEPS
T: "Doing homework in math must be difficult in your family."	Acknowledge obstacle
P: "It always ends in an argument."	
T: "If there was a way to get the homework done without a problem I think it would help his school work."	Restate need

EXAMPLE	STEPS
P: "We've tried several things and they never seem to work."	
T: "It's pretty difficult."	Listen
P: "Yes, I really don't like math myself."	
T: "Is there anyone in the family who can work with Jim without causing an upset?"	Alternative solution
P: "His older sister is pretty good."	
T: "Does he mind her helping?"	
P: "No, they get along well together."	
T: "Would it work if she helped him?"	
P: "It would, but she's pretty busy."	
T: "I could reduce the amount of work until he got better at it."	Alternative
P: "She would probably be willing to help."	Alternative
T: "His sister could help him."	Listen
P: "Yes, if it didn't take too long, like twenty minutes."	Agreement
T: "That would be fine. Do I need to talk with the sister? What would you suggest?"	Agreement
P: "I'll talk with her. If she needs to talk with you, I'll have her call or Jim will let you know."	Establish steps
T: "That's fine. I'd like to check in a week and see how the plan is going. What's the best way to do that?"	Establish steps
P: "Jim is pretty good at telling us how things are going. You could check with him."	
T: "Checking with Jim sounds fine. Do you think it will work? His sister and all?"	Confirmation
P: "I think it will."	Confirmation

Organizing the Interview-Conference

In a scheduled interview the professional has the option of working from a semistructured format. The major advantage to structure is that it helps to ensure that all important elements are included in the interview-conference. Without structure, the professional must rely on memory to cover all that is important. The major drawbacks are that structure, tightly followed, can hamper a free exchange of information and can create a formal atmosphere.

Figure 5-3.
Suggested Preplanning and Conference Form to Be Used When a Student Problem Exists

Interview-Conference Form
(Problem)

Student		Parent-Guardian-Profession	
Date	Birthdate	Place	Interviewer

Reason for interview-conference: ______

Special notations: ______

School information/observations: ______

Interview questions: ______

Possible plans: ______

Actual plans: ______

Follow-up plans and results: ______

In scheduled interview-conferences some form of outline will help the teacher organize material and provide a place for recording the results of the meeting. Interview organizing strategies are shown in Figures 5-3 and 5-4. The first is a form to use with interviews that are undertaken because a problem exists and there is a need for planning and problem resolution. Figure 5-4 is a basic format that may be used for periodic parent conferences where the purpose is to report pupil progress and share information.

Figure 5-4.
Suggested Preplanning and Conference Format to Be Used in Periodic Conferences

Parent Conference Outline (Periodic)

Room and Material Arrangement
- Display
- Seating
- Handouts

Greeting and Seating

Academic and/or Grade Presentation
- Example materials
- Verbal descriptions
- Demonstration materials
- Unique pupil characteristics

Parent responses
- Questions
- Comments
- Concerns

Discussion of Problem Solutions (if any)
- Exchange of observations
- Possible solutions
- Strategy agreements
- Role responsibilities

Future Instructional Plans
- Materials to be introduced
- Projects and/or field trips
- Pupil and parent role

Closing
- Appreciation for participation
- Future meetings

An interview-conference notice can provide the interviewee with a preview of the purpose and content of the conference and allow him or her the opportunity to plan questions or comments. The parent conference notice shown in Figure 5-5 indicates to the parent the content of the meeting and informs him of ways the conference can be used to his advantage. Examples of possible questions are given to encourage the parent to participate actively in the meeting. Space is provided to encourage the interviewee to plan questions in advance of the meeting.

Figure 5-5.
A Parent Conference Notice That Helps Parents Prepare for the Conference

Parent Conference Notice

Dear ________________________,

A parent conference has been scheduled for ___(name)___ in room ___(room)___, at ___(school)___ school on ___(date)___ at ___(time)___. If this day or time is not convenient for you, please call ___(phone no.)___ and arrange for another appointment.

Parent conferences are formally held twice a year and can be arranged at other times as needed. At the conference you are encouraged to ask questions, share information, and make comments. Examples of typical questions are given below. Space is provided on this sheet so you can make notes about what you would like to discuss.

I look forward to seeing you.

Sincerely,

Example questions or comments:	Your questions or comments:
How is Cheryl doing in reading?	
What can be done to improve Terri's spelling?	
What are Lisa's strengths?	
I think Greg is good at math. Does it show up in class?	
How does Scott get along with others?	

The referral supplement in Figure 5-6 combines information giving with specific inquiries. In the contemporary school, the teacher often has access to other professional specialists such as an academic specialist (e.g., reading), counselor, nurse, psychologist, special education teacher, and speech and language specialists. Each specialist often has a referral form specially designed to provide data to him or her. The referral supplement, however, is initiated by the teacher and provides the specialist with the problems and questions the teacher wants answered. In this

Figure 5-6.
A Referral Form Designed So the Teacher Can Direct Inquiries to the Support Staff

Referral Supplement

From: ______________________ To: ______________________

______	______	______	______
Pupil	Birth date	Grade	Date

______	______	______
School	Room	Preferred conference times

Brief school history and current performance:

Particular areas of concern:

Questions I would like answered:

way the teacher is able to communicate a concern and prepare the specialist for the subsequent inquiry with the student.

The interview-conference can take many forms. It can be spontaneous or preplanned. Almost always, the teacher or professional is seeking information. It is advantageous to be prepared in advance with a mental or written format. Rehearsed responses and procedures can help in crisis situations. Also, thoughtful preparation can ensure the success of an interview. And a prepared interviewee can enhance the quality of an interview-conference.

QUESTIONNAIRES

The questionnaire is an interview in written form. It allows the questioner to gather responses from many persons simultaneously without investing a great deal of time. It also makes no demands on the professional for interview skills since the forms are self-administered. The uniform nature of the format allows data to be compared and provides data on both group tendencies and unique characteristics.

Need

Questionnaires are constructed in several steps, beginning with a determination of what information is needed. Involved in this step is the identification of the purpose of the inquiry and an examination as to how the information is to be used. Answers to these inquiries will help determine the content of the questionnaire and the form in which the data will be most useful. The need expressed in the statement, "I wish to know how children feel about the field trips" is not sufficient to provide a solid basis for questionnaire construction. In addition, it is necessary to answer the questions: What is the purpose of this inquiry? and How will the data be used? Clear answers to these two questions will help guide the test constructor through the rest of the steps.

Questions

Writing the questions is the second step in the construction of a questionnaire. The questions should be clear, concise, and unambiguous. Short statements are preferred over long statements. TenBrink (1974) identifies ten types of questions that are useful in teaching situations. They provide a useful analysis of oral as well as written questions:

1. Leading questions: "What do you think about open book exams?"
2. Comparative questions: "Which do you prefer, arithmetic or history?"
3. Recall-of-past-event questions: "What did you like best about the first day in class?"
4. Recall-of-past-respondent-behavior questions: "What did you do when someone called you a name?"
5. Feeling questions: "How do you feel about the rules in this class?"
6. Cause-effect questions: "What makes it hard for you to complete assignments?"
7. What-was-(is)-there-about-it questions: "What upsets you most about the fight on the yard?"

8. "Would" questions: "If you were the teacher, what would you do to improve this classroom?"
9. "Should" questions: "How should someone act when he is talking and is interrupted?"
10. "Why" questions: "Why do you think schools teach math?"

One problem with the questionnaire is that questions can be misinterpreted, and there is no easy way to check on the responder's level of understanding. The fixed format also limits response variations and may lead to conclusions that are artifacts of the questions rather than characteristics of the responder. The following are examples of common errors:

EXAMPLES	RESPONSE PROBLEMS
Questions that call for memory not readily available, such as the age at which a child took his first step.	Guessing
Questions that are subject to different interpretations, such as those with imprecise words or complex sentence structure.	Misinterpretation
Lengthy questionnaires or those that appear to be of little value.	Random response
Single question on a topic.	Unreliable

Format

The questionnaire includes the directions, the questions, and the response made. Directions need to be simple and short, seldom involving more than one or two sentences. They introduce the form and occur whenever a response change occurs. Questions are clear statements that probe for a targeted content. The response made includes the form of the question and an answer trailer. A variety of modes are possible.

The original list of questions provides the content area to be examined but not necessarily the format for that examination. Therefore, in the third step of writing the questionnaire, questions are refined and rewritten so they communicate clearly to the respondent and at the same time report information that can be organized and interpreted by the questioner. Such factors as the age, maturation, fluency, and number of respondents limits what can be asked, how it can be asked, and how much can be asked. At the same time, the questionnaire writer needs to be aware of the volume of data he or she can process and the form the data must take if they are to be useful.

A number of questionnaire formats are available. Items can be checked, ranked, rated, or answered.

Checking Checking is one of the fastest response forms, and when combined with comment sections it provides both open (personal reply) and closed (forced choice) response structures. The following are examples of these combined forms:

	Item	*Response* Yes	No
EXAMPLE 1.	Your child has had:		
	Loss of hearing	____	____
	High fever	____	____
	Physical limitations	____	____
	If answer is yes, please comment: ______________		

EXAMPLE 2. Please check times when you might be available to help in the classroom:

On special occasions	____
Monthly	____
Weekly (1 or more hours)	____
Daily (1 or more hours)	____
Other times	____
Not available to help	____

EXAMPLE 3. I find it easiest to study when:

Alone ____	With others ____	Other ____
Quiet ____	Some noise ____	Other ____
At desk ____	On floor ____	Other ____
Morning ____	Early afternoon ____	Other ____
Late afternoon ____	Evening ____	Other ____

Ranking Ranking is a procedure that allows the responder to compare one alternative to another and to determine the relative value of each item. Its major weakness is the assumption that there are relative differences where none may actually exist in the mind of the respondent. The following are examples of ranking; the first is a forced choice.

EXAMPLE 1. Please rank the following choices for field trips being from 1 to 5, with 1 being the most desirable and 5 the least desirable:

Place	*Rank*
Superior Court Session	____
Central Police Station	____
Tax Collector's Office	____
Mayor and Administrator's Offices	____
City Council Session	____

EXAMPLE 2. How would you rank the major events of the last month:

Item	*Rank*
______________________	*1*
______________________	*2*
______________________	*3*

Rating The rating of questionnaire items allows the respondent to place a value on the item without having to compare it to other items. Ratings are generally easy for the respondent to complete, and the results are easily tallied. Weaknesses of this format include: (1) the assumption that the respondent has an opinion on the subject and (2) the assumption that the points on the scale have the same significance to each respondent. Following are examples of rating scales. The first example assumes that all items can be answered using the same answer descriptors. The second example uses answer items that are tailored to the questions. Responses could be more specific, but then the questionnaires would take longer to read and complete.

EXAMPLE 1. Indicate the amount of learning this semester.

Item	*High level*		*Average level*		*Low level*
English	1	2	3	4	5
Social studies	1	2	3	4	5
Math	1	2	3	4	5
Economics	1	2	3	4	5
Physical education	1	2	3	4	5

Item	*High level*		*Average level*		*Low level*
Shop or homemaking	1	2	3	4	5
Business	1	2	3	4	5

EXAMPLE 2. 1. How would you rate the student's general attitude toward school:

1	2	3	4	5
Hates school	Poor attitude	About average	Very good	Loves school

2. How well is the student liked and accepted by other children:

1	2	3	4	5
Extremely unpopular	Unpopular	About average	Very popular	Extremely popular

Answering Questions that leave the response open to the unique answer of the respondent give the maximum amount of response latitude and, at the same time, are the most difficult to tabulate or summarize. Such questionnaires are most manageable when the group of respondents is small and are nearly impossible to handle when the group is very large. Questionnaires like these can be designed along several formats. Two common procedures are provided in the examples.

EXAMPLE 1.
1. I could improve my school work if I ______________.
2. I get upset when ______________.
3. When I go on the schoolyard, I ______________.
4. Most kids think that I ______________.

EXAMPLE 2. I would like information on how to improve service to you and the special education pupil in your room. Please take a moment and jot down your ideas:

1. <u>Strengths of the program</u> <u>Program limitations</u>

____

____

____

____

____

2. Areas of concern where assistance might be helpful
   a. Academic areas

   b. Nonacademic areas

   c. Social areas

3. Comments on the type of assistance that has been most useful in the past

The questionnaire is a relatively simple way to gather information quickly and in a manageable form. The stability of the data is influenced by the length of the questionnaire and by the subect under consideration. In general, the more items that focus on a particular subject, the more likely it is that test results will be stable. At the same time, subjects such as personal opinions fluctuate and change over time.

Questionnaires with carefully selected questions, with pretested items, and with follow-up interviews to verify results can be a valuable assessment procedure. They can be constructed by teachers and other student support personnel and can be used to examine almost any activity, skill, belief, or attitude. They tend to be inexpensive and require little time, and can provide timely and relevant information.

Summary

The teacher is frequently involved in interviewing. Much of the information the teacher uses in decision making results from data gathered in conversations with students, parents, and fellow professionals. The skill of interviewing is seldom developed in teacher training or in the training of other school-related professionals. Skillful use of interviewing strategies can significantly improve the quality of the information that is generated in this way.

A successful interview calls for a clear purpose and direction. The skills of listening and problem solving greatly facilitate the process, which leads to plans and agreements. From beginning to end, the interview is designed to elicit information; to convey concern, understanding, and information; and to arrive at a plan or achieve closure.

The questionnaire is the written form of the interview. It can generate information from large numbers of respondents, can cover a broad range of topics, and can provide anonymity. A variety of formats are available and include those that permit respondents to answer freely and in their own words and those that restrict responses to predetermined categories. The questionnaire, like the interview-conference, is a vehicle for gathering data. This method, however, usually solicits rather than dispenses information and does not allow for an information exchange.

Together, the interview-conference and the questionnaire provide methods for the ongoing collection of timely information.

Bibliography

Berdie, Douglas R., and Anderson, John F. *Questionnaires: Design and Use.* Metuchen, N.J.: Scarecrow Press, 1974.

Black, Kathryn N. "The Teacher and the Parent Conference." *Contemporary Education* 50, no. 3 (1979): 162–165.

Brown, Duane; Wyne, Marvin D.; Blackburn, Jack E.; Powell, W. Conrad. *Consultation: Strategy for Improving Education.* Boston: Allyn and Bacon, 1979. See Chapter 8, "Parental Consultation and Education."

Burke, Joy P., and DeMero, Stephen. "A Paradigm for Evaluating Assessment Interviewing Techniques." *Psychology in the Schools* 16, no. 1 (1979): 51–60.

Egan, Gerard. *The Skillful Helper—A Model for Systematic Helping and Interpersonal Relations.* Monterey, Calif.: Brooks/Cole, 1975.

Evans, Joyce. *School/Home Observation and Referral System.* Teachers' Guide. Monterey, Calif.: CTB/McGraw-Hill, 1978.

Freund, Judith H.; Bradley, Robert H.; and Caldwell, Bettye M. "The Home Environment in the Assessment of Learning Disabilities." *Learning Disabilities Quarterly* 2, no. 4 (1979): 39–51.

Friedman, Robert. "Using the Family School in the Treatment of Learning Disabilities." *Journal of Learning Disabilities* 11, no. 6 (1978): 378–382.

Glaser, Barbara, and Kirschenbaum, Marty. "Using Values Clarification in Counseling Settings." *The Personnel and Guidance Journal* 58, no. 9 (1980): 569–575.

Gorden, Raymond L. *Interviewing Strategy, Techniques and Tactics.* Homewood, Ill.: Dorsey Press, 1980.

Gordon, Thomas. *Teacher Effectiveness Training.* New York: Peter H. Wyden, Publisher, 1974.

Keefe, Francis J.; Kopel, Steven A.; and Gordon, Steven B. *A Practical Guide to Behavioral Assessment.* New York: Springer, 1978.

Loven, Michael D. "Four Alternative Approaches to the Family/School Liaison Role." *Psychology in the Schools* 15, no. 4 (1978): 553–559.

Molyneaux, Dorothy, and Lane, Vera W. *Effective Interviewing: Techniques and Analysis.* Boston: Allyn and Bacon, 1982.

Moreno-Milne, Nidia. "Effective Parent-Teacher Conferences—Some Basic Tips." *Academic Therapy* 16, no. 6 (1980): 219–221.

TenBrink, Terry D. *Evaluation: A Practical Guide for Teachers.* New York: McGraw-Hill, 1974.

Chapter 6
Reporting Assessment Information

The type of report used in informal assessment depends on the person for whom it is intended. Most frequently, assessment information is gathered for the teacher's own use and follows the simple process of moving from recording to analysis to use. Assessment data that provide self-assessment information for teachers or students also require little in the way of formal reporting. Assessment information intended for parents or professionals requires more elaborate and detailed treatment. The degree of formality and sophistication required depends on who is to read or use the report.

The most casual reporting methods are those used when teachers report to themselves. Shorthand records, idiosyncratic notations, and private symbols do not interfere with the use of this material over short time periods. However, the more time that lapses between the casual recording and the use of assessment data, the greater the loss in detail and accuracy. Precise and readable analysis and reporting is always recommended and is essential to an accurate report.

When assessment data are to be used to make important classroom decisions, the notations and computations, translations and analysis need to be carefully recorded. A profile of the data or some other method of display can be helpful to the teacher who must sort through large amounts of information (see Figure 6-1). Relevant records are easier to retrieve and are more likely to be used if they are held in a single location, such as a student file or folder. Stored data are also more likely to be revised and updated if space is provided for new data and entries can be made easily.

Data gathered and used by teachers and students can be recorded simply and do not require a written report. Both groups are familiar with the background and the context of the assessment, and therefore do not generally need the elaboration and interpretation a third party would require. When a teacher makes an oral report, he or she may find the type of data outline shown in Figure 6-1 sufficient to support a cogent presentation.

When a teacher or other assessor presents data to a person outside the assessor-student dyad, enough information must be given so that the problem or situation can be clearly understood. The information provided to parents will differ significantly from that provided to other professionals because the parent is a partner in the experiences of the student, holds information about the student, has a vested and concerned interest in the student, and is neither interested in nor equipped to deal with highly technical aspects of instruction.

Items that are most relevant to the parent are:

1. Present skill level of behavior of the student
2. An understanding of expected or average performance at the student's age and developmental level
3. Samples of the current work or performance
4. Plans that will help to improve the situation
5. Strong as well as weak points in skills and performance
6. Feedback on assistance that parents have been providing
7. Guidance in help parents can provide

ORAL REPORTS

Reports to parents are generally presented orally even when a written one is also provided. The parent should be given time to discuss, question, and challenge what is presented. Only the briefest comments are given on the telephone—and no negative information is given in this manner.

Figure 6-1.
Teacher Profile of Formal and Informal Data

Student Bob Clark Grade 6.3 Date 11/18

Area of assessment	Type of assessment	Date	Subject	Results
Achievement	Group test (formal)	9/16	Math.	
			Comp.	5.3 grade level
			Reas.	4.9 " "
			Reading	
			Voc.	3.8 " "
			Comp.	4.1 " "
			Lang.	
			Gram.	5.8 " "
			Spell.	6.0 " "
	Criterion	9/20	Math. Reading	Not available Not available
	Observation	9/20–9/25	Math	½ assignments completed 20% error rate
	Content analysis	9/20	Reading	Likes reading sports page and other sports information (e.g., magazines). Reports well written but soc. studies assignments late and sparse (2 and 3 points of information per report). Creative language paper 7 pgs., information report 2 pgs. Reading required in soc. sc. and information reports; not required in creative report.
Behavior	Observation	8/8–11/18		Friendly and cooperative student. Busy at his desk 95% of the time. Quiet and soft spoken. Good in sports, liked by classmates and chosen first or second in both class and yard activities. Other students help him with assignments willingly.

The assessor needs to have reports, samples of work, and suggested material or strategies available at the time of the conference. Material that is present at the discussion must be open for inspection and provided in a form that is clear and neat. A detailed data format ensures that all important information is included in the conference. A flexible discussion format allows the assessor to adapt to the needs of the parent. Student work samples, which are often the easiest materials for the parent to understand, can be an introduction to more complicated assessment data. Lengthy attention to detail, however, can confuse and distract a parent to the point where critical elements in the report are missed.

Reports to other professionals are presented either orally or in written form. If the presentation is oral, a summary written carefully beforehand provides some insurance against a disorganized delivery. The written summary requires a careful examination of information and a systematic review of the data. This process helps the assessor prepare for the oral presentation and discussion. Oral presentations vary in formality, interaction, and time limits. The well-prepared participant, however, is the most likely to be heard and understood.

The following suggestions can help improve an oral presentation:

1. Write a summary of important information.
   If a written summary is not possible, an outline of the presentation is highly desirable. Data should be organized under domain areas and the order of presentation established.

2. Include background data and information on the present situation.
   The more knowledgeable the presenter, the more likely it is that information will be accepted and used in decision making. Information credibility is in part a function of the authority of the presenter, the completeness of the data, and the manner of the delivery. Clear, concise, objective information that adequately covers the case is the goal of assessment reporting.

3. State problems in behavioral terms.
   The most objective and verifiable comments about human performance tend to be those based on the observation of behavior. Comments about the cognitive, affective, and motivational elements of performance tend to be based on data obtained less directly, and are subject to errors in interpretation, conjecture, and speculation. Statements about behavior address the action of the student and provide the observable indices of the condition(s) under consideration. Changes in these indices provide evidence that the action taken to bring about change is effective. Once the problem has been

clearly stated in behavioral terms, information that is related to skill level, attitudes, motivation, and so on will help to suggest the direction for special assistance. Several examples of brief behavioral descriptions follow.

> Mary cries an average of two times a day. This happens only when she is in a game or a project with other children. She either walks off by herself or puts her head down on her desk and cries.
>
> John has not completed a written language assignment in over a month. His group test scores show him to be a year below his grade level in spelling, grammar, and punctuation. He talks to students on either side of him about 50 percent of the time during writing assignments.
>
> My third period class spends the first fifteen minutes of each period getting ready to work and the last ten minutes getting ready to leave. During these times I am busy answering questions; at least ten of the twenty-five students are talking, and three to four are out of their seats.

4. Include samples of work or clearly stated examples of behavior. Assessment data and summaries often do not include language precise enough for the listener to picture the actual behavior of the student. A teacher has access to many behavior examples and work samples that illustrate exactly what the student does. These can be drawn from the classroom, the yard, or from the test situation. Behavior drawn from unusual settings such as testing should, however, be verified in other, more natural settings. Brief illustrations not only create a more real understanding of the individual, but they also suggest the subtle coping mechanisms used by the student. These illustrations help the listener understand facets of the student that otherwise might go undetected. The following are illustrations:

> When John yells out in class he always turns to his right, shouts over his shoulder, and then holds that position as if waiting for a reply, which he sometimes gets.
>
> I have watched Greg in the English period and noticed that instead of writing his assignments he writes notes, which he passes to Ralph or Scott. When not writing notes he draws pictures of cars, makes complicated doodles, or traces drawings from the book. (Assessor shows drawings.)

Jo is always first to the reading circle. She smiles often and appears to follow along in her book, reading the word slowly when she is called upon. However, she is unable to tell what she has read.

5. Data that can be quantified should be converted to that form. Numerical statements should be made whenever possible. This improves the preciseness of the language in stating the problem, collecting data, analyzing, summarizing, reporting, and planning. Most descriptive words that express quantity, volume, or distance can be replaced by numbers. It is allowable to say "John fights a lot" in ordinary conversation, but in assessment more precision is demanded. The frequency, as well as other aspects of fighting, must be described. A more acceptable problem statement is: "John averages one fight a day during school hours." The following is a partial list of words for which numbers can be substituted:

about	almost	limited
considerable	fairly	frequently
few	greater	higher
just about	many	moderately
more	multitude	increase
nearly	numerous	often
practically	rather	scant
several	some	somewhat
sort of	sparse, tend	variety
various	very	voluminous

WRITTEN REPORTS

Written reports are the most formal assessment presentations. There are two basic types of reports. One is limited in scope and reports on a particular subject area or a single domain. This report is useful when the analysis and discussions are to be narrowly focused, such as might occur in examining problems in math computations, reviewing interest areas, investigating fighting on the schoolyard, and so on. The second type of written report is the diagnostic or comprehensive report. This report occurs when the assessment covers a range of behaviors, or multiple domains. It may also be used when a single domain area, such as language, has been subjected to an exhaustive examination, such as might occur when a speech therapist makes a thorough evaluation.

The single area or single domain report tends to focus on one problem or a cluster of highly related problems. It is, therefore, appropriate to specify the exact goal or problem in the report. A brief background, directly related to the problem, should be provided, followed by formal and informal test and observational data. Baseline or entry skill levels should be identified and a summary of the information and the outcome or plan of action given. A suggested format is shown in Figure 6-2.

Figure 6-2.
Content Outline for Limited Report

I. Identifying data
  A. Name
  B. Age
  C. Grade
  D. Assessor
  E. Date of report
II. Background
  A. Behaviorally stated problem
  B. Problem history
  C. Current status
III. Assessment information
  A. Name test(s) or procedure(s)
  B. Report results for each
  C. Provide synthesis of information
IV. Summary
  A. Brief restatement of information
  B. Recommendations

The diagnostic assessment report is more global in scope than the single area report. It includes a more thorough statement of student performance, appearance, and background. It makes a general statement about the problem or skill under consideration, and lists the goals and objectives of the study. Tests or strategies are named either after the opening, identifying data or within each domain section. Formal and informal information is given in transformed or tabulated form when possible and interpretations are provided for each set of data. A summary section reviews important information and synthesizes the information from the various domains. A recommendation section includes statements that follow logically from the assessment information. A suggested format is shown in Figure 6-3.

Figure 6-3.
Content Outline for Diagnostic Report

- I. Identifying data
  - A. Name
  - B. Age
  - C. Grade
  - D. School
  - E. Location
  - F. Assessor
  - G. Teacher
  - H. Date of report
- II. Assessment administered (testing)
  - A. Formal tests by name
  - B. Informal tests or strategies by name: for example, interview, observations criterion tests, situation analysis
- III. Observations and history
  - A. Student characteristics and description
  - B. General statement of problem
  - C. History relevant to problem
- IV. Results of assessment
  - A. Domain area: for example, achievement
    - 1. Observations
    - 2. Data synthesis
  - B. Domain area: for example, behavior
    - 1. Test results
    - 2. Data synthesis
  - C. Domain area (etc.)
- V. Summary
  - A. Synthesis of important information within each domain area
  - B. Interrelationships of data from different domain areas
- VI. Recommendations
  - A. Behavioral statement in temporal sequence
  - B. Plan given if necessary

JUDGMENTS, DECISIONS, AND APPLICATIONS

Once the assessment data have been analyzed, judgments are made about the value, importance, accuracy, and usefulness of the information. Collected data must be evaluated carefully. Some information may be untrustworthy, inappropriate, tangential, or misleading. Answers to the following questions will help improve the quality of judgments made about data:

1. Are you confident about the reliability of the source of the data?
2. Are you confident about the appropriateness of the method used to gather the information?

3. Is the information stated in objective or appropriately qualified terms?
4. Is the information appropriate for the problem?
5. Is there evidence to support the interpretation of the data?
6. Do the data provide new information on the subject?
7. Are you reasonably sure that the data are fairly representative of the subject?
8. Are there any circumstances that would cast doubt on the accuracy of the information?

At times the assessor is in a position to review or accept the judgment statements made by others. Statements such as: "This is a good remedial program," "John has low motivation," "The special class is the best placement for Mary," and "He will continue to fail as long as he can't read" are all statements of judgment and have significant implications for the student and for instructional planning. The careful assessor examines and checks all statements of judgment with inquiries such as: "What leads you to that opinion?," "What evidence is there to support that?," "Is there a way that it won't be true?," "Let's review the information again and see if there is another conclusion," "I would like to study the problem further," and "That may be true in this situation but what evidence is there that it is a general problem?" Judgments are opinions and as such are open to examination and reconsideration.

Decision making is defined as consideration that leads to a conclusion or a determination. It is a process that, according to Stufflebeam et al. (1972), "includes four stages: (1) becoming aware that a decision is needed, (2) designing the decision situation, (3) choosing among alternatives, and (4) acting upon the chosen alternative" (p. 50). Decisions are made at every step in informal assessment, beginning with a decision that the problem requires investigation and culminating with the evaluation of the plan that has been implemented. Between these two points there is the selection of a target behavior, the choice of assessment methods, and the report with a summary and recommendation of action.

The selection of the target behavior is a critical decision that influences all the steps that follow. The decision is based on a series of considerations. The first is a clear statement of the problem and a description in behavioral terms. In the following example each paragraph opens with a general statement followed by a behavioral description. Two domains under consideration are behavior and academic performance.

Rosa is a behavior problem in class and in the yard. She has a loud voice and talks to neighbors about 19 percent of class time unless tightly monitored. She hits classmates at least once a day and when angry (once a day), she swears at children and "calls them names." Classmates complain that she won't let them work and she is out of her seat at least twice an hour.

School production is low and skill in reading is two years below grade level. She turns in one assignment out of three in social studies and language. Papers are short (less than a page) and misspellings occur in one out of five words. Math achievement is at grade level.

The history of the problem(s) suggests its resistance to change, and the number of domains involved establishes the range of the problem(s). This information, in turn, suggests whether the assessor will make a limited or comprehensive assessment. In Rosa's case, for instance, it was determined that in the primary grades she was quiet, withdrawn, and unfriendly. During the past two years she had become more outgoing and aggressive. At least two domain areas were involved, and the problem was affecting Rosa, her classmates, and the teacher. The overall scope and impact of the problem was substantial and a comprehensive assessment was clearly warranted. The disruption caused by the behavior problem, however, was so severe that the immediate need was for behavior control, and the initial assessment choice was limited to that aspect of the problem. The academic investigation started as soon as Rosa became manageable in class.

Rosa's case illustrates the basic steps in determining the focus of assessment. That choice is based upon:

1. A description of the problem
2. A scope and history of the problem
3. The priorities identified in the situation

The choice of methods or instruments depends on the type of information needed. When stated as a question it becomes: "What information do I need to understand or solve this problem?" That question is followed by "How can I develop that information?" That is, the question might be answered in part or wholly by an interview, an observation, a review, a test, or some other method of assessment.

The decision on the choice of assessment procedure becomes one of selecting the method that both delivers the required information and satisfies the needs of the situation. It combines what is desirable with what is possible. The decision involves the following considerations:

1. Assessment methods available
2. Appropriateness to the situation
3. Appropriateness to the student

4. Usefulness of outcome data
5. Reliability and validity
6. Time and cost vs. expected usefulness

The decision on reporting method is relatively easy. That choice is determined by the expected use of the information. If information is to be used only by the teacher, scoring and analysis are generally sufficient. Organization and synthesis of the data are desirable at the teacher level, but they become critical when data must be reported to parents or other professionals.

A balance between economy and sufficiency is the key when deciding how much to include in a report. The relevance of data is not a sufficient guide because in some cases it would lead to an overly long and complicated report. Common practice provides some limits on the length and complexity of a report. The overriding considerations are included in the dictum: Include information that bears directly on the problem, is not provided in other reports, allows the reader to make an independent decision, and provides the documentation that leads to the recommendations.

Good reporting depends ultimately on whether or not the assessor is willing to devote the time required to prepare a complete representation of the data. The assessor's job is eased if there is a standard format that can be modified to account for unique variations. The format provides a guide for organization and a familiar sequence for reporting. Reporting usually becomes easier with experience.

Recommendations are based on the data that have been developed but they should also include an element of what "can be" or "should be" accomplished. Recommendations are strongly tied to goals and focus on what the student, teacher, or parent must do to achieve more satisfactory levels of performance. Decisions as to what needs to be done for the student are relatively direct outcomes of the assessment.

A more difficult type of recommendation addresses how a particular goal or objective can be implemented. Such a recommendation implies that the assessor has translated the assessment information into action. The "how to" recommendation requires an understanding of a variety of options in teaching or behavioral strategies, including those that are most appropriate for the student and those that best fit the instructional setting. Decisions of this type require a broad understanding of situational and instructional factors. Such recommendations are warranted when the assessor is familiar with the instructional setting and is knowledgeable about the wide variety of options available in instruction and behavior management.

COMMON ERRORS IN INTERPRETATION AND DATA REPORTING

Errors occur during the process of assessment, reporting, and recommending. Since most assessment is based on some sampling procedure, there is an inherent possibility that the sample will not be truly representative of the student's behavior. Also, the test might be inappropriate or an invalid measure of the area under consideration. Assuming, however, that the assessment procedure is appropriate and reliable, a number of other possible problems remain.

Recording and Computation

Errors in recording and computation are to be expected. All computations need to be checked for accuracy. If a result is unexpected or does not seem to match ordinary observation, the recording and computation should be reviewed. Anytime a result varies markedly from previous results the method of recording, computation, and any transformations should be checked. Behavior usually does not change dramatically, and reports that suggest such a change should be suspect and subjected to careful scrutiny.

Overlooked Information

Overlooked basic developmental information also leads to errors in assessment. In a comprehensive assessment a thorough knowledge of the developmental history is critical to the interpretation of current information. For instance, if a student has been absent from school for several months during the last few years, it could explain a natural gap in learning that might otherwise be seen as a learning disability. In another case poor coordination in primary grades might explain a student's reluctance to play sports in a higher grade, even when the original developmental lag is no longer present.

Situational Factors

Situational factors can lead to errors in assessment. The impact of the current situation is not always apparent when assessing a student. A change in the home, antagonism with other students, and dislike of the teacher are but a few of the situational factors that can influence skill development or performance. The easiest way to avoid overlooking a situational problem is to review the history of the student's development in the problem area. A long-term problem is more likely to be related to a student characteristic than a situational condition. (Bilingual or culturally different children are an exception to this rule.) A newly emerging problem, however, requires that particular attention be paid to the current situation. A problem may be related to new demands placed on the learning skill of the student or to factors outside the immediate learning task. A review of current conditions in the instructional, school, home, and community setting can uncover significant influences not directly related to instruction. At issue is whether changes in the student or changes in the setting will have the greatest impact on behavior and learning.

Extension of Implications

A class of errors occurs when the assessor extends the implications of the data beyond what is justified and overgeneralizes, overinterprets, or overrecommends. Assessment data are samples of behavior and are limited by that fact to a rather narrow band of implications. For instance, almost all data should include an implicit warning, cautioning the user that the data were gathered at a particular time and within a particular context. To make statements about behavior outside that context and without collaborating evidence is highly speculative and should be so indicated. Thus, a statement about a student's grade level in reading can be quite accurate outside school in those situations that closely approximate the classroom task. The same information, however, might give a very misleading prediction of the success of the individual on a responsible job that requires little reading. Similarly, behavior in a classroom does not give a clear indication of the student's behavior at home or among his peers outside of school.

Interpretation error occurs most often when the data are used to suggest the cause of a behavior. It is seldom possible in assessment to establish a clear cause-and-effect relationship. For instance, the statement "Mary's parents are getting a divorce and it has affected her school work" is a cause-and-effect statement; it is most likely oversimplified or inaccurate, and it does little to improve Mary's condition. A more accurate assessment of the problem might determine that Mary has been unable to complete homework at home and no longer has the help her father once gave her in her assignments. The critical questions to ask of an interpretation are: Do the data and evidence lead to this conclusion? and Does the conclusion assist in planning for the student?

Overrecommending occurs when the data presented do not support the recommendation. The assessor often deals with two levels of recommendation: that based on concrete evidence and that based on speculation. Speculation is acceptable and, at times, provides the impetus to creative planning and problem solving. The error occurs, however, when both levels are reported as if they had equal amounts of supporting documentation. Qualifying phrases such as the following will help to indicate a suggestion based on less than solid evidence:

It is possible that . . .

The following might be tried . . .

Another avenue of approach might be . . .

There is some suggestion that . . .

Although not clearly indicated it may be that . . .

An overall impression leads to . . .

Untested Solutions

A fifth type of error occurs when untested solutions are proposed. In most school-related problems no one-to-one correlation between problem and remedial teaching method exists. There is, therefore, a fair degree of speculation whenever a particular method or plan is recommended. Ideally, the student is pretested for the solution, as well as tested for the problem. Until the solution is tried there is no assurance it will be helpful. When assessment and methods become more sophisticated, this may no longer be a problem. At the present level of understanding, however, a recommendation is a suggestion to try a solution. This is not too critical when recommendations are for teaching methods or behavioral strategies; each can be easily modified or rescinded. It becomes critical, however, when the recommendation calls for a radical change in the student's environment, such as enrollment in a special class or retention at a grade level. These latter recommendations require careful consideration because they have permanent and long-lasting effects on the student.

Such serious recommendations also have long-term implications that are often overlooked at the time of the initial decision. Retaining a student a second time in the elementary grades (putting him two years below his age level), for example, not only delays entrance into junior and senior high school where he might find more appropriate classes and a larger choice of friends but advances the age of high school graduation to a point when it becomes an unlikely goal. Important recommendations often have both short-term and long-term effects, and since pretesting the impact of the solution is not possible, every attempt must be made to anticipate long-term effects.

The assessor has now completed the cycle that began with the suspicion of a problem. The suspicion led to the determination of a problem, then to an analysis, which in turn resulted in a report and in recommendations. Assessor judgments were made at each step and the results hopefully lead to improved student performance or behavior.

Summary

When data are to be used by someone other than the person who gathers the information, some reporting format is necessary. Information that is merely "passed forward" has very little impact. The usefulness of information depends on how it is organized, presented, and summarized. There are traditional formats that help in the reporting process. Informally gathered information requires the same thoughtful organization and clear presentation that is accorded formal information. The form of the report depends on whether the presentation is oral or written.

It is critically important to make judgments about the accuracy and usefulness of the information that has been gathered. Assessment information is then translated into decisions about the action to be taken by the professional, the student, or the parent. Caution must be used to avoid common errors that occur in the interpretation and reporting of data.

Bibliography

Hollis, Joseph W., and Donn, Patsy A. *Psychological Report Writing: Theory and Practice.* Muncie, Ind.: Accelerated Development, 1973.

Meyering, Ralph A. *Uses of Test Data in Counseling.* Boston: Houghton Mifflin, 1968.

Rockowitz, Ruth J., and Davidson, Phillip W. "Discussing Diagnostic Findings with Parents." *Journal of Learning Disabilities* 12, no. 1 (1979): 11–16.

Roundtree, Derek. *Assessing Students: How Shall We Know Them?* New York: Harper and Row, 1977. See Chapter 6, "How to Interpret and How to Respond."

Sax, Gilbert. *Principles of Educational Measurement and Evaluation.* Belmont, Calif.: Wadsworth, 1974. See Chapter 17, "Disseminating and Reporting Test Information and Data."

Schenck, Susan J. "The Diagnostic/Instructional Link in Individualized Educational Programs." *The Journal of Special Education* 14, no. 3 (1980): 337–345.

Stufflebeam, Daniel L., et al. *Educational Evaluation and Decision Making.* Bloomington, Ind.: Phi Delta Kappa, 1972.

Sundberg, Norman D. *Assessment of Persons.* Englewood Cliffs, N.J.: Prentice-Hall, 1977. See Chapter 11, "Integrating and Communicating Assessment Information."

Tallent, Norman. *Psychological Report Writing.* Englewood Cliffs, N.J.: Prentice-Hall, 1976.

Woody, Robert H., and Woody, Jane D. *Clinical Assessment in Counseling and Psychotherapy.* New York: Appleton-Century-Crofts, 1972.

Part Three
Assessment of Performance

A bias that has seriously hindered our understanding of how to achieve success with children is the belief that the fault lies with the student—that is, "Something is wrong with Billy." In fact, however, when they look carefully at the problems, most teachers will agree that there are more similarities than differences between the learning handicapped child and "normal" children. The difficulty is more likely to be the fact that current teaching methods are inappropriate to the learning style of the child.

A thorough knowledge by the teacher of how children learn can eliminate this deficiency. Teachers then can identify the discrepancy and modify the instruction appropriately. Some difficulties a child may be experiencing are serious and will significantly alter the way the child learns in the classroom. Such children may require the services of the resource specialist or other special education teacher. Other difficulties, however, may be minor and entirely acceptable, being within the range of unique differences expected among all individuals; these will require only a minor modification in instruction to ensure that the child will progress more satisfactorily.

The important thing is for the teacher to know enough to make this distinction. Minor problems, if left undetected and unattended, can become serious ones in just a few years. Early identification of these areas of potential difficulty is crucial. The child who, in first grade, is performing five or six months behind other children may be over two years behind by the time he or she is in fourth grade. Even though the child is learning, the learning may be at a slower rate and each year the child falls further behind. For the slow learner this can be anticipated and planned for accordingly. For learning disabled children, it may be totally unnecessary. Much of the curriculum in the early grades depends on a good foundation, and if fundamentals are not well understood the child continues to fall behind. Corrective teaching at an early age, then, becomes very significant. The important role for the teacher becomes one of assessing in which area the child is failing to progress so that timely interventions can be made.

The regular teacher, as well as the special education teacher, needs to have a thorough grounding in child development, for the regular classroom teacher is usually the first to become aware of a child's learning problem and must be the first to provide assistance to the child as well as seek help if it is needed.

Many factors contribute to the ability of a child to learn as he or she grows from infancy to adulthood. Early development depends greatly on *physical* factors, on the child's motor development and on his awareness, through the senses, of the world around him. The child's perceptions of the environment and the interrelationship of the elements in it contribute to his concept development, and are the basis for the language he uses. This *cognitive* awareness continues as the child grows, and becomes more refined as he learns an increasingly sophisticated language to describe his concepts. Even while he matures physically and cognitively the child responds emotionally to his environment, and his experiences increase his ability to relate to an ever-enlarging world. This *affective* component provides motivation, social expression, and the emotional responses with which he will interact with other children, teachers, his family, and the other important people in his life.

In Part Three we look at these three areas: the *physical, cognitive,* and *affective.* Chapter 7, "Sensorimotor Development," discusses the importance of the child's physical development. Chapter 8, "Thinking and Language," considers the child's cognitive development. Chapters 9 and 10 discuss the development of the skill concepts involved with spelling and handwriting and reading and arithmetic. Chapter 11, "Student Behavior," is concerned with affective development. All three components—physical, cognitive, and affective—are necessary to the development of a healthy mind and body.

If a careful diagnostic assessment is performed, a picture should emerge of how a child learns. The teacher should then understand how the child functions and how he is likely to continue to function. Years of previous attempts to correct weaknesses or deficits have generally been filled with frustration, and the efforts were largely unsuccessful. What is now required is not, "Something is wrong with Billy," but "Something is wrong with the curriculum" that made it difficult for Billy to learn. Perhaps the "teaching style" is not consonant with Billy's "learning style."

Two steps remain on the road to successful learning. One is a task analysis of the subject being taught and a matching of each step with Billy's ability to learn it. The second is a change from tasks in which there is a poor match to other teaching materials or other methods that will be more suited to the manner in which the child processes information.

Chapter 7
Sensorimotor Development

Developmental Approach
Survey Assessment
Diagnostic Evaluation
Case Study of a Child with Motor and Organizational Difficulties

Motor learning is the first learning of the human organism. While recent literature seems to suggest that a newborn infant can see and hear earlier than previously believed, the information that a baby gains from his sense of motion (rocking, being carried), touch (warmth, holding, closeness of his mother's body), and form (handling objects, hardness, softness) seems to be the basis for his first learning. It has always been understood that lack of ability to move, such as is found in the cerebral palsied child, will affect a child's awareness of his or her environment or ability to play, but it was not until research was done by Swiss psychologist Jean Piaget (1955) that a greater appreciation of the significance of motor development to intellectual (cognitive) and language development emerged. Previous to that time, physical development was considered one facet of the child's development, but its relationship to affective and cognitive development was not fully understood.

DEVELOPMENTAL APPROACH

When the work of Piaget was finally translated and distributed in English-speaking countries, researchers found that it suggested a new understanding of the development of thinking and cognition. This "developmental" approach appears to be more productive than the "problem"-oriented approach often taken by teachers and other professionals faced with the child who is not achieving. It allows the teacher to focus on the similarities, rather than the differences, displayed by the child to the normally expected sequence. It also allows for a greater appreciation of the importance and interrelationship of sensory and motor development to school activities, such as reading and arithmetic, and even more, to thinking and language.

Although motor activities play an important part throughout childhood, and even beyond, in the development of an individual, it is in this first period of his or her life—Piaget's sensorimotor period—that motor and sensory development is most important. Piaget theorizes that it is the child's perceptions and his integration of those perceptions into his cognitive framework that are the beginnings of intellectual thought. Perceptions are obtained through the developing senses, beginning first with kinesthetic and motor, and then expanding to include visual and auditory. What a child perceives is what he knows, and as time progresses, what he talks about. The quality of those perceptions, therefore, is very important to the developing child.

Sensorimotor development is a comprehensive description of the information obtained by the individual through the senses (hearing, sight, taste, smell, touch, and body movement). In the normally developing child, information is transmitted to the brain primarily through the three major senses: movement, hearing, and sight.

Since the brain controls all the activities of the body, the information it receives is central to the child's learning. The brain must first receive information, then it must integrate and process the information, and finally it must direct movement, language, thinking, or any other behavioral expression of the individual. Each sensory channel provides information through a separate series of nerves and muscles, all of which are integrated in the brain. The child who has a sensory handicap, such as the child who is hard of hearing, visually handicapped, or cerebral palsied, will not obtain information through the senses in the same way as other children. Learning, for these children, must be stimulated in order for them to achieve in the academic areas included in the school curriculum.

Figure 7-1 is a diagrammatic description of the developmental sequences of these principal sensory areas. According to most authorities, each area of a child's development begins at birth and continues until it is fully developed, at approximately the age shown on the chart. Age levels are given as indicators of approximate periods and cannot be interpreted strictly; individual children may vary widely. As we can see by the heavy

Developmental Sequences

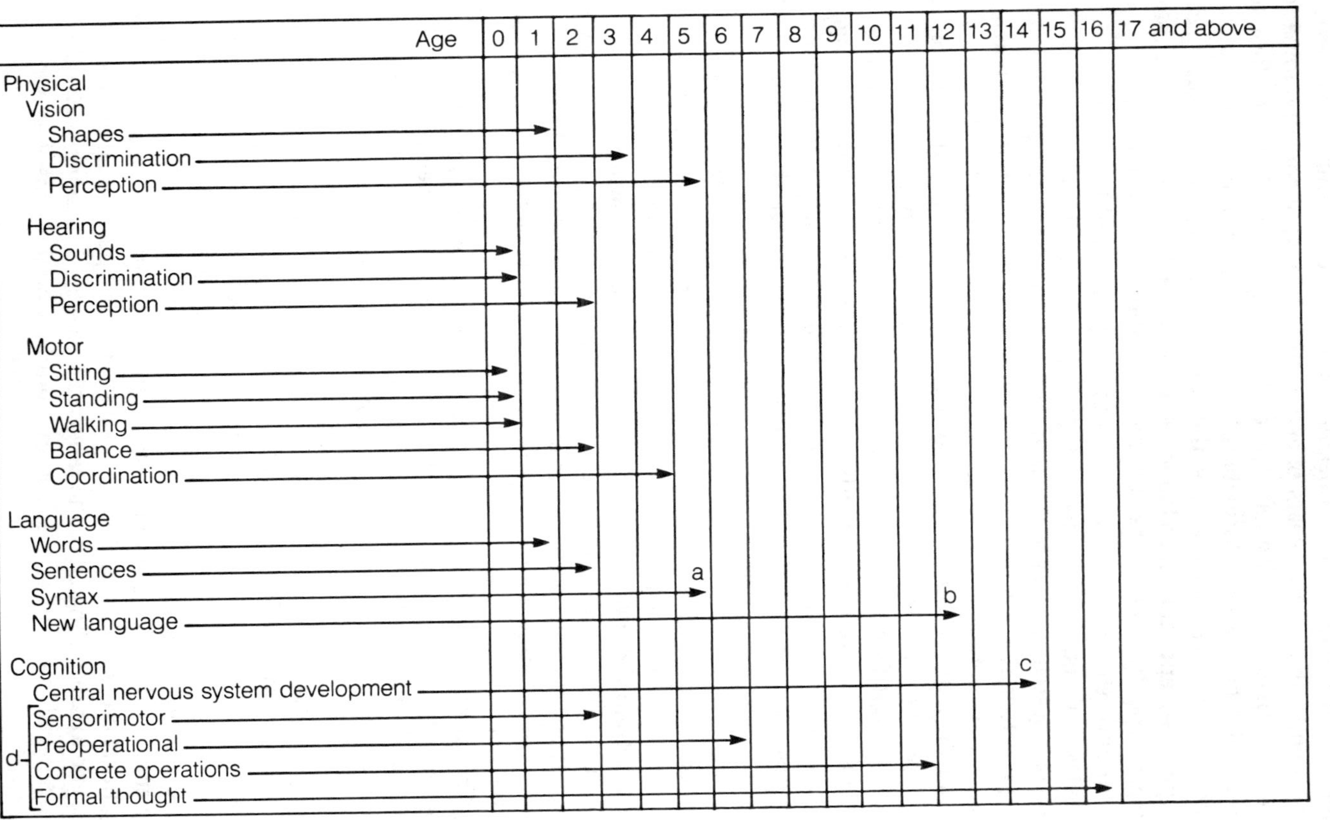

lines, most sensory abilities become well developed during the period between birth and two years of age, a period roughly corresponding to Piaget's sensorimotor period. The child is apparently able, therefore, to obtain the necessary information for concept development during this period. It is important to see the interrelationship among biological sequences, and the correlation of each with Piaget's developmental stages. Only by such an examination can the complexity of the human brain and what it must possess in order for the child to be able to do what we call reading, writing, and spelling be comprehended. The central nervous system, or the brain itself, according to Hebb (1966), continues to grow, together with the body, until the child reaches puberty, usually somewhere between twelve and fifteen. Hebb points out that this growth is not only the result of chronological development but that the brain also increases in size and weight as the result of active use in thinking and concept formation. The development of the child's cognitive and language functioning depends on adequate sensory input. In many instances a student may have difficulty learning abstractions simply because, due to perceptual or sensory deficits, he or she has not had adequate experience for developing concepts.

Some researchers have suggested that if a child has missed, and therefore not developed, basic concepts such as distance, because of lack of sensory or perceptual experiences, the correct remedial approach would be to retrain the individual in the "missed" skills (Delacato, 1963). However, understanding of the developmental levels in the maturing child would seem to negate this approach. While providing missed early experiences might appear logical, the brain of the child has continued to grow as he matures, and there is no "going back."

Several rationales for this position can be made. First, the brain has continued to grow and develop. It is unlikely that this development could be erased and begun anew, as if unraveling wool and reknitting it. All other facets of the child's development have also continued to progress, and it does not seem possible to retrace and begin again.

Second, the development of the child's brain has been cumulative; that is, many interrelated and integrated factors have influenced its development. In this instance two and two do not necessarily make four; two and two may very well make five, or even six. Every bit of knowledge a child obtains is not simply added to information already gained; it has a spreading effect and makes previously obtained bits of information more meaningful. Therefore, attempting to retrain a specific perceptual area would also mean unraveling all of the tangential effects—but since such effects are generally unknown, this action would be neither possible nor productive.

Third, the child has matured emotionally and socially during his lifetime, and the tasks by which the teacher attempts to retrain deficit areas must be ones that are meaningful, relevant, and motivating to the child at this point in his life. An eight-year-old child is not motivated for long by tasks performed by a much younger child, and considerable effort must be expended by adults to keep him on task.

For all of these reasons the task of teaching skills that are identified as missing is probably not possible. Therefore, in assessing the students sensorimotor performance, it is necessary to identify areas that are deficient—not for the purpose of teaching or retraining them—but in order to determine what corrective or remedial measures are necessary to make the child successful at the specific tasks in reading, writing, or arithmetic that are required.

For example, seven-year-old Susan is having great difficulty with handwriting. Her pencil grip is awkward, letters are poorly formed, and writing is slow and laborious. Assessment may identify several deficient areas: motor-planning, position-in-space, and directionality. The end result in terms of classroom performance is poor writing, and very little, if any, classroom production in subjects that require writing.

The seven-year-old, however, is still developing her sensory system. Susan may be having more difficulty than other children in her class, but all seven-year-olds are still in the process of establishing their sensory systems. Exercises designed to help improve her perceptual-motor skills, such as position-in-space, might be helpful for Susan. Because of the level of Susan's physical and sensory development, perceptual exercises such as throwing bean bags or balls at a target or tracing geometric shapes may have some success, or they may at least increase Susan's spatial awareness, which can, in turn, improve her handwriting.

John, on the other hand, is seventeen years old, and exhibits exactly the same problems evidenced by Susan. John's sensory system is already fully developed, and the teacher can assume that additional training in spatial relationships, and possibly even in handwriting, are not going to produce the desired result. John's remedial program may well include developing alternative approaches to the required task, so that his written language development is not affected by the fact that he has difficulty in handwriting. For John, a typewriter would be the best teaching tool, and little, if any, time should be spent on handwriting or related activities. Certainly perceptual-motor training, as it is understood today, would not be efficient in teaching John.

Perceptual training may not help John in terms of his academic performance, but it is highly likely that John is having difficulty in other areas of his life that involve motor performance. His ability on the sports field, for example, may be affecting his social/emotional/affective relationships. Thus it may be useful to have John learn specific motor skills that will increase his functioning in this area; however, the focus and intent of the program would be entirely different than it would be for Susan.

SURVEY ASSESSMENT

It is unlikely that the teacher will find a student deficient in sensorimotor development without its being noticeable in some academic area such as arithmetic, spelling, or handwriting. Occasionally, however, a kindergarten or primary age child appears to be unduly clumsy but has no other obvious symptoms. Since it is unusual for young child to have gross-motor difficulties and good fine-motor skills, (thus, fewer activities in the early grades require the degree of coordination expected in handwriting or reading), closer scrutiny may be in order. Problems in cognitive skills that require good motor performance can be expected if both gross- and fine-motor abilities are delayed.

Table 7-1 provides a checklist that can be used by the teacher to determine whether a student is experiencing difficulties. In this checklist regular classmates are the models for comparison; the teacher merely checks in the appropriate space how the individual child compares. When the total number of points checked is tallied, any score over 50 should be scrutinized, and any score over 65 indicates that the student needs a more thorough evaluation.

Table 7-1.
Sensorimotor Screening

	ABOVE AVERAGE SCORE 0	AVERAGE SCORE 1	BELOW AVERAGE SCORE 2
I. Gross motor			
1. Throws a ball	______	______	______
2. Participates in sports	______	______	______
3. Posture	______	______	______
4. Running/rhythm	______	______	______
5. Balance	______	______	______
6. Energy	______	______	______

SOURCE: Developed by Arlee S. Maier. Copyright © 1980 by Arlee S. Maier.

	ABOVE AVERAGE SCORE 0	AVERAGE SCORE 1	BELOW AVERAGE SCORE 2
7. Reaction time	______	______	______
8. Strength	______	______	______
9. Endurance	______	______	______
II. Visual/motor—auditory/motor			
10. Draws or writes without erasures	______	______	______
11. Enjoys arts and crafts	______	______	______
12. Handwriting	______	______	______
13. Pencil grip	______	______	______
14. Papers are neat	______	______	______
15. Can "read" pictures	______	______	______
16. Hand dexterity	______	______	______
17. Draws well	______	______	______
18. Uses punctuation	______	______	______
19. Ignores distracting noise	______	______	______
20. Articulates	______	______	______
III. Organization			
21. Keeps desk neat	______	______	______
22. Turns papers in on time	______	______	______
23. Begins work promptly	______	______	______
24. Enjoys table games	______	______	______
25. On time to school	______	______	______
26. Follows directions	______	______	______
27. Helps organize class activities	______	______	______
IV. Study skills			
28. Papers are complete	______	______	______
29. Works independently	______	______	______
30. Can tell time	______	______	______
31. Attention	______	______	______
32. Reaction to substitute teachers	______	______	______
33. Reaction to unexpected change of schedule	______	______	______

(continued)

Table 7-1 *continued*

	ABOVE AVERAGE SCORE 0	AVERAGE SCORE 1	BELOW AVERAGE SCORE 2
V. Social skills			
34. Chosen for team in sports	______	______	______
35. Converses well	______	______	______
36. Is well groomed	______	______	______
37. Interprets gestures and body language	______	______	______
38. Has friends in class	______	______	______
39. Plays with class at recess	______	______	______
40. Not easily upset	______	______	______
41. Good listener	______	______	______
42. Reacts to noise	______	______	______
Total	______	______	______

Figure 7-2. Sensorimotor Checklist

A. Gross-motor development
   1. Basic
      a. Rolling
      b. Sitting
      c. Crawling
      d. Walking
      e. Running
   2. Advanced
      a. Throwing
         (1) Two hands
         (2) One hand
      b. Jumping
         (1) Two feet
         (2) One foot
      c. Skipping
      d. Dancing
   3. Coordination
B. Fine-motor development
   1. Finger movement
   2. Handling objects
   3. Tracing
   4. Coloring
   5. Cutting
   6. Geometric forms
   7. Pictures
   8. Handwriting
   9. Motor-planning
   10. Laterality
      a. Hand
      b. Foot
      c. Eye
      d. Right/left orientation
         (1) Self
         (2) Other
         (3) Position-in-space
      e. Left-to-right progression (directionality)
         (1) reading
         (2) Writing
   11. Organization
C. Auditory development
   1. Nonverbal
      a. Hearing
      b. Localization
      c. Perception
      d. Figure-ground identification

2. Verbal
   a. Auditory discrimination
   b. Auditory closure
   c. Auditory memory
      (1) Numbers
      (2) Words
      (3) Sentences
      (4) Directions
   d. Auditory sequencing
      (1) Sounds
      (2) Sound blending

D. Visual development
   1. Perception
      a. Multiple-choice
      b. Copying
   2. Speed of perception
   3. Figure-ground discrimination
   4. Visual discrimination
      a. Nonverbal
      b. Verbal
   5. Visual memory
      a. Color
      b. Designs
      c. Letters
      d. Words
   6. Form constancy
   7. Spatial relations
      a. Position-in-space
      b. Size
      c. Relationship

SOURCE: Developed by Arlee S. Maier. Copyright © 1980 by Arlee S. Maier.

DIAGNOSTIC EVALUATION

Figure 7-2 (section II of the diagnostic checklist given in Figure 3-6) is an outline for the diagnostic assessment of sensorimotor performance. The checklist provides an outline for the teacher to use in assessing the student's skills, and enables the teacher to determine to what extent school performance is affected. In each section skills are arranged in sequence. The teacher may assume that if a child is able to perform a higher function satisfactorily it will not be necessary to evaluate the lower; it can be assumed that the skill is at least at a functional level. Each skill requires competence with the one previous. Comments should be entered in the appropriate section so that information can be organized.

A description of each skill to be observed in the assessment follows:

A. Gross-motor development
   1. Basic
      a. Rolling: Ability to roll over evenly without allowing limbs to flop over.
      b. Sitting: Sitting erect on the floor with legs extended, or on a chair without falling to the side.
      c. Crawling: Crawling with alternative right and left movements of hands and feet; good bilateral coordination between right and left sides.
      d. Walking: Coordinated walking with relatively even steps, arms swinging in opposition to the foot stepping forward.

e. Running: Running smoothly with relatively even pace, arms bent slightly, and moving in opposition to the feet.

2. Advanced
   a. Throwing
      (1) Throwing a ball accurately with two hands at least 15 feet.
      (2) Throwing a small ball with one hand approximately 25 feet.
   b. Jumping
      (1) Two feet: Standing jump of approximately 2 feet in distance without losing balance or falling to the side.
      (2) One foot: Hopping on right or left foot without losing balance; covering approximately 1 to 1½ feet in distance.
   c. Skipping: Skipping right and left feet alternately with good rhythm, and with hands moving in opposition to feet.
   d. Dancing: Not a measure of the child's dancing ability; the skill being assessed is the youngster's ability to move in rhythm and time with the music.
3. Coordination: Good coordination in gross-motor activities with children of same age in games, sports, or other recreational activities.

B. Fine-motor development
   1. Finger movement: Ability to do things with the fingers, such as picking up small objects or pointing; demonstrates good pincer and hand grasp.
   2. Handling objects: Grasping a box, block, paper, or other small object with dexterity, positioning the fingers to provide maximum support for the objects handled. A good measure of this ability is to ask the child to assemble a series of nesting blocks or nuts and bolts, thus giving the teacher an opportunity to see him handle objects and work with two hands in opposition.
   3. Tracing: Tracing a drawing or design; allows assessment of the child's ability to keep the pencil on the line, following an S curve, changing direction appropriately, and using efficient methods of tracing, progressing from left to right and top to bottom.
   4. Coloring: Coloring a simple design, staying within the lines, and pressing with an even hand on the crayon or chalk.

5. Cutting: Handling scissors is often difficult, particularly when cutting a curve or an S curve, since the blades of the scissors must be aligned properly with the paper. The child should use appropriate scissors, that is, a left-handed child should use left-handed scissors since the blades are aligned properly for the child.
6. Geometric form: Copying simple geometric forms: Cross, circle, triangle, square, and rectangle; keeping them approximately the same size as the design provided.
7. Pictures: By asking the student to draw a picture of a person, the teacher can observe child's ability to identify body parts and draw them in relationship to one another, as well as his ability to compose a picture; artistic ability is not being assessed—merely youngster's ability to control pencil on paper.
8. Handwriting: The child's ability to keep letters on the line, evenly spaced, and correctly formed. (A more thorough evaluation of handwriting is described in Chapter 9.) A small handwriting sample is often sufficient to identify motor difficulty.
9. Motor-planning: Assesses the youngster's ability to determine how to proceed on a task and can be observed in almost any task the teacher desires; child must determine how to follow a sequence of activities that will reach a particular goal. A task such as following directions to make a small object, such as a Christmas tree ornament, will allow the teacher to observe the child's ability to plan the necessary steps to achieve even a simple task that has not been sequenced for him.
10. Laterality
    a. Hand: Which hand is preferred. Occasionally the teacher will observe that the child will use one hand for writing, and the other for such activities as cutting, drawing, or eating.
    b. Foot: Which foot is preferred. An easy way to assess this is to ask the child to stand with feet together and take one step forward or ask the child to kick a ball. The foot the child uses to step out on in walking or uses to kick with is usually the preferred foot.
    c. Eye: The dominant eye can be identified by asking the child to look at a distant object through a paper tube. The child will place the tube on the dominant eye. There has been much discussion about the significance of crossed dominance, that is, the child who is right-handed but left-footed,

or left-eyed. Crossed dominance is probably of little importance in ordinary school activities. It does not appear to have any significant effect on academic tasks such as reading and writing. It may play a role, however, when the child is aiming at a target. In those instances, the aim will be slightly off and the child must learn to compensate for this.

d. Right/left orientation
   (1) Self: Can identify own right shoulder, left foot, right eye, and so on.
   (2) Other: Ability to transpose right and left on a person facing him or her; can point to the right shoulder, left leg, right hand, of the teacher or other person.
   (3) Position-in-space: Ability to follow series of directions such as turn right, walk three steps to the left, or draw an X in the upper right-hand corner of the page; can be assessed informally by giving child a series of similar directions. This ability is important to such things as reading maps, following directions, and setting up paper-and-pencil tasks. Use of a map is sometimes a motivating way of assessing a student's right/left orientation. A child can be asked to draw a small map showing how he or she travels home from school, or gets to the principal's office from the classroom. The child can use a commercially produced map to show how an automobile would travel from one locale to another.

e. Left-to-right progression (directionality): Poor directionality is occasionally observed as children read. They frequently lose their place and must return to the beginning of the line to continue with the sentence or paragraph. This can be more readily observed in oral reading since it is more apparent when the child is floundering. Monitoring eye movements as child is reading silently is more difficult.
   (1) Reading: Left-to-right progression is customary in the English language. If left-to-right progression is not well established it becomes most apparent in nonverbal activities, that is, in "reading" a series of pictures or assembling a sequence of unattached cartoons. The teacher may give the student a typewritten paragraph and ask him or her to cross out one letter of the alphabet,

such as all the As. If the material is nonmeaningful, that is, if it is not words, the child may progress from right to left or in a random fashion. Left-to-right progression is the most efficient method of scanning a page, and students who do not do so usually work slowly.

(2) Writing: Letters should be formed correctly. Occasionally children do not automatically return to the extreme left margin when writing several lines.

11. Organization: Organization is closely related to motor-planning. It is the ability to plan how to do something and do it without great effort. The child who knows how to proceed on a simple task, such as setting up a paper to perform an arithmetic assignment, also seems to know how to proceed to obtain library books, take notes, outline, and write a report to be presented in class. Organizational difficulties are often first noticed as youngsters become older and the requirements for performance are increased. Some children do not appear to have learning disabilities until they reach the fourth or fifth grade, when written reports are requested more frequently.

The activities listed thus far, in sections A and B, are sequential in nature. In order to observe where difficulty begins and at what point compensatory techniques or intervention will be necessary, it is often helpful for the teacher to present the tasks listed in reverse order. Organizational difficulties will be apparent in many school subjects other than written language, notably handwriting, spelling, and arithmetic.

C. Auditory development

1. Nonverbal

a. Hearing: A hearing screening should be performed by an audiologist for any youngster having difficulty with listening, following directions, spelling, or remembering. Most of the time no deficit is identified, but occasionally and unrevealed loss is observed. For some of these children, once assistance is offered through more favorable seating, techniques the speech therapist or audiologist may provide, or, if necessary, a hearing aid, learning problems may disappear.

b. Localization: Ability to determine direction and distance of sound. In classroom activities, the teacher is able to observe that the child turns toward the sound of someone speaking or calling to him.

c. Perception: Identifying a sound such as coughing, humming, whistling, hand clapping, or finger snapping. The teacher may ask the student to identify sounds in the environment such as an airplane, a typewriter, or a door closing.

d. Figure-ground identification: Ability to listen only to sounds one wishes to listen to and ignore sounds not relevant to tasks at hand. This can easily be identified by observing how attentive the child is to a particular task despite what may appear to be distracting noises. The child who is able to study while listening to the television or music is an excellent example of a youngster who has successful figure-ground discrimination. This youngster is able to "tune out" distracting noises.

2. Verbal

a. Auditory discrimination: Ability to discriminate between sounds, and ability to detect differences between words that may appear similar, such as *vie-thy, beam-ream,* or *fix-fish.* The child who has spelling errors or misunderstands directions may have auditory discrimination difficulties. Many children who have satisfactory hearing do not develop good discrimination during early language development; this problem eventually interferes with school progress. Dialect may be a contributing factor to difficulties with standard English. For example, one of the manifestations of Black English is the reduction or loss of final consonant sounds. A child who is accustomed to speaking and hearing Black English may think that *fold* and *bowl* rhyme. The teacher needs to be aware that this is a dialect differential and not an auditory discrimination problem.

b. Auditory closure: Ability to identify words that are presented in an incomplete, confused, or distorted manner. Words are often not articulated clearly in speech, so the listener's ability to hear and identify an incomplete word such as *acaroni/macaroni* or *dress/dresser* is important.

c. Auditory memory: Most of the research indicates that the auditory function most related to reading is memory. While the ability to recall long series of words is not necessarily relevant, the child must be able to hold sufficient information in memory to complete a sentence or a thought without losing meaning.

(1) Numbers: The youngster's ability to remember sounds or numbers in sequence can be assessed by giving him a series of numbers or letters and asking him to repeat them. Most children can recall a series of four or five. This skill is important in order to develop the ability to blend sounds into words.

(2) Words: The child's ability to remember words presented in isolation can be measured by presenting him with a list of ten or fifteen unrelated words and asking him to repeat as many as possible. The procedure can be repeated several times. A youngster in first through third grade should be able to remember at least half of a list of fifteen words, and those in the upper grades should be able to remember the entire list after four or five presentations.

(3) Sentences: Sentences with six to eight syllables can be presented first; then the number of syllables can be increased to twenty-five or thirty. A child should be able to repeat a sentence more readily than a list of unrelated words, since he or she is more apt to recall the sequence from context.

(4) Directions: Children must be able to follow a series of three or four sequential directions without forgetting. This ability can easily be assessed by giving a series of directions and noting how many the child recalls in proper sequence.

d. Auditory sequencing

(1) Sounds: Auditory sequencing is related to auditory memory except that it requires the student to remember correct order. This ability can be tested by tapping a series of patterns (i.e., soft-hard-soft-soft-hard) on the table, and asking the child to imitate them. Series can be presented in increasing length.

(2) Sound blending: A task of auditory sequencing using meaningful material can be given informally by presenting the child with a sequence of sounds and asking him to indicate the word they comprise (i.e., *d-e-s-k/desk,* or *e-l-e-p-h-a-n-t/elephant*).

D. Visual development

1. Perception: Ability to perceive a visual stimulus and identify it correctly.
   a. Multiple-choice: Ability to search for an object, design, or letter similar to the one shown by the teacher. Many readiness workbooks have pages with such tasks, and these are readily adapted to this purpose.
   b. Copying: Ability to copy a form or part of one exactly. The teacher may present the child with a series of geometric shapes or designs and ask the child to (1) complete a design that has been started to make it like the stimulus design, or (2) to copy the design exactly as shown. Several formal tests, such as the Bender Visual Motor Gestalt Test and the Beery-Buktenica Developmental Test of Visual-Motor Integration, include this task. However, formal means of assessment are not necessary. If a student is not able to function appropriately on this task, the teacher must determine if he does not see or perceive the design, or if he has motor difficulties and is therefore unable to plan the necessary movements to reproduce the design accurately.
2. Speed of perception: How rapidly a youngster can identify a particular form and match it to a similar form. If a child takes considerable time to perform this task, it is reasonable to assume that he or she will have difficulty identifying letters rapidly enough to read in a functional manner.
3. Figure-ground discrimination: Ability to discriminate a particular shape, letter, or form from other shapes on a page. A child with poor figure-ground discrimination will become confused by a visually crowded page. Many textbooks, in an effort to be interesting or cheerful, are very colorful and include many diagrams and pictures. This can be particularly confusing for the child with poor figure-ground discrimination who is then unable to locate and focus on the desired word.

   Teachers can assess figure-ground discrimination by typing a ten-line "paragraph" using letters in random order with no content. They then ask the child to cross out all instances of a particular letter—for example, all D's—in the "paragraph." Most primary age children will make 10-15 percent errors. Older children will make none. This task also helps identify a directionality problem.

4. Visual discrimination
   a. Nonverbal: A series of pictures or designs taken from readiness materials or magazines can be shown and the child asked to identify some that are similar or different from the one or ones presented earlier by the teacher.
   b. Verbal: The child is asked to identify letters or words that are similar or different from ones presented. Visual discrimination for letters is extremely important to basic reading. Letters and words often vary little. For example, the difference between *h* and *n* is only a short elevation of the initial stem of the letter.
5. Visual memory: Visual memory has been noted in the research to be the visual task most closely related to reading. The child's ability to see a shape, letter, or word, and to recall it is essential to adequate reading skills. The teacher can assess visual memory in a number of ways.
   a. Color: A series of color chips can be placed on a table in front of the student and then removed. The teacher then asks the child to reproduce the design presented, using colored chips he has in his possession.
   b. Designs: A similar task can be constructed using geometric shapes or numerals.
   c. Letters: Letters can be shown briefly, and the child asked to reproduce them.
   d. Words: A word can be shown for three seconds and then the student asked to write it. Visual memory is best assessed if the teacher uses words that are not within the student's sight vocabulary, so that meaning will not be used as a memory device.
6. Form constancy: Ability to identify a letter or word regardless of the form in which it is presented. Thus, the word *book* written in manuscript is as easily identified as the same word presented in cursive or print. The child's ability to visually identify and perceive the printed symbol as meaningful regardless of its size, shape, or means of presentation is a basic and important task in reading.
7. Spatial relations
   a. Position-in-space: Spatial relations are important in visually scanning a picture or page. The student needs to be able to

look at a picture and identify where objects or people are in relation to others in the picture—for example, where the table is in relation to the chair.

b. Size: Ability to appreciate the relative size of objects. For example, a house may occupy only a square inch on the page, but the child understands that it represents something large. The ability to identify size in a picture is related closely to the ability to perceive depth and perspective. Small objects are perceived to be in the distance, and those that appear large are known to be in the foreground.

c. Relationship: Ability to identify whether one object is larger than another based on the relationship of objects in the environment. In a drawing of any size, a child perceives a car to be an object that is larger than he is and one into which he may enter, whereas he perceives a cup, which may appear larger than the car, to be a smaller object.

The checklist and outline provide the framework for assessing the level of the child's integration of sensory and motor functions. By referring to the developmental sequences chart (Figure 7-1), the teacher can determine that remedial techniques may be appropriate for the young child, whereas for the older student they may be reserved for compensatory techniques that are used as "cues" in performing specific tasks. The information obtained through the use of the checklist should not be used to develop activities for each of the abilities mentioned, instead it should be incorporated into teaching. That is, the student who experiences difficulty in an area should be given more attention when that specific skill is required in learning an academic task.

CASE STUDY OF A CHILD WITH MOTOR AND ORGANIZATIONAL DIFFICULTIES

Billy, 10½ years old, was in the fifth grade at the time he was referred for special education services. The presenting problem was described by his physician:

> Billy has difficulty in school getting along with other children. He becomes easily angry at home, but his anger problems are worse at school. He complains he can't do his school work and asks for constant help. His teacher tries to help him with work and then Billy becomes very angry. He yells or swears in class. When asked to leave the classroom, he refuses to do so. When angry at home, he yells and jumps about the house. Despite his temper control problem, Billy is

> popular at school and in the neighborhood. He is reported to be very skilled at sports. He has no serious learning problem, although math is his most difficult subject. He appears to read at fourth grade level according to his mother, but she is not sure about his comprehension or memory. Cursive writing is terrible; he prefers to print, and prints poorly. He has been sent home from school on two occasions this year. On one occasion he threw a bat during a ball game in a fit of temper.

Billy was seen by the school psychologist, who gave him a Weschler Intelligence Scale for Children—Revised (WISC-R) and found him to have a verbal IQ of 102, a performance IQ of 74, and a full-scale IQ of 87. In addition, the psychologist found that Billy had many feelings of anger and hostility toward adult authority figures, as well as very low self-esteem. Billy saw himself as a "loser." He was unhappy about his inability to perform satisfactorily in school and his inability to meet his parents' and his own expectations. The psychologist felt the 28-point difference between the verbal and performance scale scores on the WISC-R to be statistically significant. He referred Billy for an evaluation with the learning disability specialist.

The learning disability specialist went through Billy's school records. She found the following information.

Billy attended playschool at age four. He liked it at first but refused to attend in the second semester. Kindergarten found him a reluctant participant in games. Billy's mother agreed with his feeling that kindergarten activities were boring. The first grade teacher found that academic progress was average. Billy's mother noticed reading problems, but the teacher did not agree and refused to refer him to a reading specialist. In second grade, Billy was referred to the reading specialist and received remedial help in phonics using DISTAR (Englemann and Bruner, 1969). The teacher reported that he made good progress with this approach. Third grade was remembered by both Billy and his mother as a disaster. Billy was in constant conflict with the teacher, challenging her, and laying traps for her. He refused to do work in his workbooks. In fourth grade Billy was placed with a teacher who had a reputation for being able to handle problem children. The mother reported this teacher got more out of Billy than previous teachers, but behavior problems persisted, and his attitude toward the teacher took a turn for the worse during the second semester when Billy claims that she, the teacher, had changed.

The learning disability specialist spent some time assessing Billy. Evaluation revealed that he was working at the 6.5 grade level in reading recognition and comprehension. Arithmetic comprehension was at the 4.5 grade level; however, arithmetic performance was at the second to third grade level. On a multiple-choice spelling test in which Billy was allowed to choose the correct word from a series, Billy's performance was at fifth grade level; however, on a spelling test in which he was asked to write the word to be spelled, his performance dropped to the 3.5 grade level. Billy was unable to produce a written paragraph. His handwriting was very poor, and he had difficulty getting what he wanted to say down on paper. He commented to the specialist that he didn't like to write and didn't do much of it.

Coincidentally, Billy's fifth grade teacher happened to be involved in after-school sports, and he had filmed the children in his class playing a soccer game; the psychologist and learning disability specialist were able, therefore, to see Billy on film playing in a soccer game. What the film revealed was that in a game like soccer, Billy, who was a large and strong child, was able to run down the field hitting the ball with various parts of his body, literally "pushing" his way to the goal. To those watching the film it seemed that other children "got out of his way." It appeared that the requirements of a game like soccer were such that Billy was not required to be careful or precise in his movements in order to be successful. It was obvious that he enjoyed and was good at soccer.

When questioned about other sports activities, Billy's teacher revealed that he wasn't particularly good at activities that required coordination. In team sports, like football, kickball, or baseball, Billy was often not chosen to be part of a team because he was unable to make good judgments as far as team activities were concerned.

The therapist determined that Billy's greatest difficulties were in areas requiring motor performance, such as handwriting, organization of papers, putting answers in workbooks, and initiating and completing assignments. The only part of the picture that had not originally appeared to fit the pattern of motor difficulties was the report that he was good at sports. But after seeing the film and talking with the teacher, the therapist noted that his performance now appeared consistent with his other organizational problems.

The learning disability specialist determined that Billy was a strong visual learner, but that he had difficulty with motor and organizational activities. A teaching program was planned for him that would allow him to progress at his expected level in areas that required reading, thinking, and oral language skills; tasks that required writing, however, would be adjusted so that Billy could complete them. Billy was permitted to make some class reports orally instead of in writing; questions on tests were constructed so that he could select the correct answer rather than write complete sentences and paragraphs. In some instances where answers were required, he was permitted to provide them in single words or short phrases.

Billy has motor problems. He can't move rapidly. He has difficulty organizing activities; he doesn't know which way to proceed even if he does know what he wishes to do. His handwriting is poor and slow, and therefore he is not satisfied with the end product of his attempts at written language. Looking at the history in Billy's cumulative folder, it could be seen that clues were provided as early as kindergarten. At that time, Billy refused or was reluctant to participate in games. He prospered with the phonetic approach to the teaching of reading, but had difficulty with workbooks and with any tasks that required writing.

Billy's difficulty in school progressed as he got older and the requirements for performance in school were increased. This is a fairly common occurrence with children who have motor and organizational difficulties.

With minor modifications in requirements for written work, Billy was accommodated comfortably in a classroom. His behavior problems improved considerably. The need for additional psychological counseling was not completely eliminated, as Billy had reached fifth grade with a history of difficulty in school and with the poor self-image that results from such a history. It is possible and probable, however, that with improved performance in the classroom as a result of changes in the instructional program, counseling can be successful much more rapidly than expected. Billy's future looks much more promising.

Summary

Sensorimotor experiences are the basis for all physical, emotional, and cognitive development. Only fairly recently has the relationship of physical and sensory development to thinking and learning been relatively well understood. Prior to this time, age-level scales were used to indicate the developmental sequences through which a child passes to reach physical maturation. The work of Piaget pointed out the strong relationship between physical and cognitive development. Piaget's theories, based on the premise that learning takes place through the interaction of the child with his or her environment, have been supported by the findings of many others, including Hebb and Bruner et al.

The importance of rich and varied sensory experiences during the early years of a child's life cannot be overemphasized. The child who has not had the opportunity for these experiences, either because of motor or physical handicaps, or because of limited opportunity, may evidence difficulty in learning when presented with academic tasks in school. It seems unlikely that experiences missed in a child's life can be re-created, since he or she has continued to grow and develop. Through informal assessment, however, teachers can identify areas in which the child may not have fully developed skills. The teacher may then use teaching techniques to point out features that the child may not discriminate independently, or to modify the learning task so it uses materials and methods that capitalize on the skills the child does possess.

A sensorimotor screening is provided to help the teacher determine if the child needs more extensive evaluation, and a detailed structured series of observations is described in the event a diagnostic assessment is desired. Examples of tasks the teacher may observe naturally in the classroom or develop using simple materials are given.

Finally, a case study of a child with motor difficulties was presented to show how teachers and other professionals can be misled by failing to analyze carefully the basic elements that may be contributing to either academic or behavioral problems.

Bibliography

Beery, K. E., and Buktenica, N. *Beery-Buktenica Developmental Test of Visual-Motor Integration.* Chicago: Follett, 1967.

Bender, Lauretta. *The Bender Visual Motor Gestalt Test.* New York: American Orthopsychiatric Association, 1938.

Bruner, J.; Oliver, R. R.; and Greenfield, P. M. *Studies in Cognitive Growth.* New York: John Wiley, 1966.

Delacato, Carl H. *The Diagnosis and Treatment of Speech and Reading Problems.* Springfield, Ill.: Charles C Thomas, 1963.

Eisenson, Jon. *Aphasia in Children.* New York: Harper and Row, 1972.

Englemann, S., and Bruner, F. C. *DISTAR: An Instructional System for Reading Instruction.* Chicago: Science Research Associates, 1969.

Harrow, A. J. *A Taxonomy of the Psychomotor Domain.* New York: David McKay, 1972.

Hebb, D. O. *A Textbook on Psychology.* 2nd ed. Philadelphia: W. B. Saunders, 1966.

Lenneberg, E. H. *Biological Foundations of Language.* New York: John Wiley, 1967.

Money, John. *Reading Disabilities: Progress and Research Needs in Dyslexia.* Baltimore: Johns Hopkins University Press, 1962.

Munsinger, H. *Fundamentals of Child Development.* New York: Holt, Rinehart and Winston, 1971.

Piaget, Jean. *The Origins of Intelligence in Children.* New York: International University Press, 1955.

Weschler, David. *Weschler Intelligence Scales for Children—Revised.* New York: The Psychological Corporation, 1974.

Chapter 8
Thinking and Language

Parents, teachers, and others who work with children generally use the term *thinking* to refer to those functions related to cognitive or concept development. When speaking of children, the terms *intellectual ability, mental ability,* and *reasoning ability* can be used interchangeably. All these terms imply the child's innate ability to learn and profit by school experiences. Children who do not grow at the same rate, or to the same level as most of their peers, are thought to be retarded; those who are much advanced are often labeled "gifted." While one can obviously distinguish among children, overgeneralizations can be most harmful, particularly to those who fall at the lower end of the scale, with all its adverse social and legal implications.

RELATIONSHIP BETWEEN THINKING AND LANGUAGE

A more analytical definition of *cognition* or *concept development* may be: the *acquisition, processing, storage, and retrieval of information obtained by a person through his senses, perceptions, and experiences.*

Thinking, then, can be considered as the *use* of this cognitive ability, and the instrument of this use, the human brain, can be likened to an elaborate and sophisticated computer with almost unlimited capacity. It is through language that we are able to communicate what this computer is processing. We talk about what we are thinking.

The ability to use language is a major difference between humans and other animals. It is the means by which people communicate facts, as well as thoughts, ideas, feelings and desires to one another. Language enhances the ability to socialize and allows it to occur. Most importantly, language allows one generation to transmit its culture to the next. Parents and teachers teach children values through the spoken word; in this way, they teach them manners and ways of behaving, as well as the difference between right and wrong. Societal values are transmitted through the use of language in books, movies, television, and theater.

The relationship between thinking and language has been discussed and debated for years; the debate is reminiscent of the age-old question: Which comes first, the chicken, or the egg? In this case, the following questions are asked: "Does the child need to think in order to develop language?" or "Must he have language in order to develop logical thinking?"

Authorities have differing views. Piaget (1955) believed that children develop concepts from their personal experiences, and that they do not need to describe them in order to understand them. Vygotsky (1962), on the other hand, believed that language stimulated concept growth and that children needed to have adults provide them with language models to describe what was happening to them. Many others, (Carroll, 1964; Bruner et al., 1966) take a middle ground, and feel that while children need to explore the universe and discover "truths" for themselves, providing them with words to describe their explorations helps them make more discoveries.

Most authorities do agree that there is a close relationship between the development of language and the development of intellectual growth, and that while there are important differences, there are equally important similarities. Even theorists like Piaget and Vygotsky move toward a more central position in their later writings. All agree that children usually follow a sequence in both cognitive and language development. Some describe an age-related sequence (Gessel, 1949) and some a scale of norms based on age (Weschler, 1974). Before possible deviance can be discussed, it is important that this developmental sequence be understood. In this way areas in which the child under assessment appears to have a "developmental lag" can be inspected, and measures necessary to help him reach that stage or compensate for the lack of it can be taken.

The degree to which this lag is observed in the evaluation of a child may well determine the seriousness of his difficulty. If the differences noted are relatively minor, the child may be considered mildly disabled, and the difficulty could be approached by a method or technique that would assist him in a specific skill; if the difficulty noted appears to be more serious or pervasive, however—that is, if it covers several areas of his development—then it will require more intensive remediation.

Although age-level taxonomies have been useful, children do not always develop at the same rate, and therefore greater flexibility in what is to be expected is needed. The stages identified by Piaget are more flexible, and help provide the framework by which behavior may be examined. By using this method the child will not necessarily be penalized if he has not achieved a certain ability at a specified chronological age.

PIAGET'S DEVELOPMENTAL STAGES

The belief that all learning is based on an individual's ability to relate that learning to prior experience is central to Piaget's theory. Piaget views this as an active process; that is, the child develops understandings or concepts based on his or her active experiencing of the environment. According to Piaget, this interaction between active experience and the child's thinking processes is a necessary factor in cognitive growth. A child's most active interaction with the environment generally occurs during the first period of his life as he moves, sees, hears, holds, or handles objects in the environment. Examples of this include an infant's need to handle, shake, or throw a toy; the child even bites or licks it in his effort to understand exactly what it is.

Piaget believes that normal intellectual growth depends on three factors: (1) the *continuing* development and growth of the central nervous system—if an impairment prevented the brain from maturing normally, some delay in the development of cognitive functioning would probably occur; (2) the child's physical and active *interaction* with the environment; and (3) the process of "equilibrium," that is, the *integration* of information obtained by the child through his interaction with the environment. Information is integrated by two means. The first is assimilation, the child's ability to incorporate new ideas or experiences into previously acquired experience; the second is accommodation, which allows the youngster to modify and change his or her conceptions and respond in a new way to the information now integrated into his scheme of thinking. This process of constant mental readjustment is the factor Piaget feels moves the child from one stage of cognitive development into another. He names four clearly defined stages of cognitive development: the sensorimotor stage (birth to approximately age two), the preoperational stage (approximately ages two to seven), the concrete operations stage (ages seven to eleven), and the formal operations stage (age eleven and above) (see Figure 8-1).

Figure 8-1.
The Piaget Model

Formal operations (Perceptual reorganization): 11 to 15 years

Hypothetical-deductive logic
A → X
A + B + X?
B → X
Propositional thinking (mammals feed on milk; whales are mammals)
Reversibility (10 × 5 = ?; 50 : 5 = ?)
Symbolic functioning (area = length × width)

Concrete operations: 7 to 11 years

Groupings of logical relationships (ducks, birds, animals)
Arithmetic groups and measurement (sets, etc.)
Simple classification (color, shape)

Preoperational thought: 2 to 7 years

Intuitional abstractions (animistic thinking), 5 to 7 years
Simple irreversible representations (water-level problems), 4 to 5½ years
Beginning representations (egocentric interpretations), 2 to 4 years

Sensorimotor stages (Beginning of time, causality, space, object permanence, play assimilation, imitation): birth to 2 years

Invention of new means through mental combinations (pushes doll carriage away from wall), 18 months
Discovery of new means through active experimentation (moves pillows to obtain covered watch), 12 to 18 months
Coordination of schemata and first intentional behaviors (places mother's hand on music box), 8 to 12 months
Motor recognition and procedures for making interesting sights last (shakes head when moving object stops), 4 to 8 months
First acquired adaptations and sensorimotor responses (grasps toys when presented), 1 to 4 months
Use of reflexes (sucking and assimilation), birth to 1 month

SOURCE: R. E. Valett, *Developing Cognitive Abilities: Teaching Children to Think* (St. Louis: C. V. Mosby, 1978), p. 33. Used by permission of the author and publisher.

Sensorimotor Period

The sensorimotor period is the shortest, but it is the one in which the greatest learning takes place; and as the basis for further cognitive development, it is of primary significance. Generally, in his first few months an infant interacts with his environment reflexively. His early moves are based on his need for food—on making sucking movements and noises and searching for the offered food. In every activity he moves and interacts in a way that primarily relates to his own body. In later months the infant's behavior and interest goes beyond his own body to contact with the environment, and he may grasp, look, or move in an effort to reach out and obtain what he desires. As he approaches the age of one year, the youngster learns to interact with objects; that is, he can search for something hidden from view. He clearly expects certain objects within his immediate vicinity to remain there, and to return once removed from view. During the last part of the sensorimotor period the youngster attempts to problem solve in a new and different way. For example, if an object with which he has been playing is removed from his immediate view, he may search for it under pillows, behind boxes, or under cupboards, even though he has never seen any of those specific activities demonstrated previously. He also attempts to imitate people, both in their actions and in the sounds they make. He is beginning to develop the ability to communicate.

Piaget stresses the importance of providing an opportunity throughout the sensorimotor period for the child to explore and interact with all the objects and people in his environment. The child who has a rich environment, who is provided with many different opportunities for experience, will undoubtedly progress through this period more rapidly and with greater cognitive development. During this period the process of assimilation and accommodation begin to develop, so that as each new experience occurs and is understood, the child's way of reacting changes and he no longer responds in the same way. It is through this process that his physical and social interaction is incorporated into his emerging cognitive development.

Preoperational Period

The preoperational period is sometimes divided into two stages since it covers such great development and a long period of the child's life. The development of symbolic functions is experienced in the period between two to four years. During this period the child achieves the capacity to form a mental symbol for objects or experiences in his or her environment. He is able to think about things with which he has had immediate and personal experience, and he is also able to remember or think about things that are no longer immediately present. It is during this period that the child begins to use words, not as an adult uses them, but as a means for attaching meanings to the concepts he has developed.

During the second half of the preoperational stage the child thinks about or acts upon objects or events but is still dealing only with experiences with which he has personally been involved. There are certain limitations to his thinking; that is, he is not able to rearrange or reinterpret experiences that he has had. He is developing basic concepts of classification and conservation—the ability to understand that the quantity or event is the same and does not change merely because it appears in a different shape, design, or sequence—but all thinking is still dominated by his immediate environment and activity. The preoperational child is not able to understand fully the concepts of quantity, weight, measurement, and volume.

During this period, too, object perceptions are developed; the child proceeds from the level of nondifferentiation between himself and the world to a greater understanding of his relationship to the environment through observation, movement, or direct contact. Piaget has indicated that perceptual activity is an intimate part of the sensorimotor period and sensorimotor intelligence, but that cognitive thought does not come about until the child can free himself from the immediacies of perceptual and motor activity, to then concentrate on activities of higher mental processes.

Concrete Operations Period

During the third period, concrete operations, the child begins to think about things that are removed from his immediate experience or presence. He or she is still able, however, to think only about things that are related to, or only slightly removed from, personal experiences; thus, the child is unable to infer, deduct, or predict the outcome of certain behaviors. He is, however, able to associate things that go together, and he understands cause and effect and why certain things occur, particularly those things with which he has personal experience.

Formal Operations Period

The fourth stage, the formal operations period, is the period of suppositional thought. The child is now able to think about things that might happen; this ability is based on combining ideas in a systematic manner and developing some predictive ability. His thinking changes from, "This is true, then . . ." to "If this were true, then. . . ." At this stage of thinking, the child is able to check all possible combinations. In other words, a concrete thinker sees each link as independent of the others, but the formal thinker sees each link in relation to one another.

IMPLICATIONS OF PIAGET'S STAGES

There are a number of factors educators need to understand in this developmental sequence of cognition that have important implications for our assessment of children experiencing learning problems.

1. The young child thinks about things differently from the adult. He is unable to learn some things, since all of his learning is based only on his own previous experiences. It is important for the teacher to understand that he cannot think about something with which he has had, as yet, no experience. The child under seven or eight thinks about events based on limited information. He is egocentric in his thinking, that is, he thinks only about things that are related to him or his immediate environment.

2. The young child's use of language is different from the adult's. Words may not have the same meaning for a young child as for the adult. Just because the child has learned the name or label for an object does not mean that he has assimilated that meaning into his own mental structure.

3. The young child does not learn in the same way an adult learns. Learning takes place primarily from observation and interactions, that is, physical activity. Therefore, a young child below the level of formal operations will not learn very well from such things as reading or listening to a lecture about experiences far beyond his range.

4. Piaget's concept of assimilation and accommodation requires that an experience be *moderately* novel. If an experience is radically different, the child will be unable to assimilate it into his current cognitive structure. The child can accommodate new experiences more readily if they are only *somewhat* novel or new.

5. Piaget points out that intellectual development is progressive. It seems to follow a particular sequence, a sequence that appears to be universal. A young child is incapable of learning concepts that are too advanced for his particular stage of development. Although experience can be enhanced through stimulation, experiments, and activities, the teacher must recognize that even if a child knows the proper phrases to use to describe an event, there is a good possibility that the event is not

yet fully integrated into his cognitive functioning. Piaget's clinical method shows that, for this reason, a child's initial verbal response is often superficial and may not be a true indication of his real understanding of these subjects. Thus, testing results are often open to question, a fact which is the basis for our suggestion that several observations and/or experiences are necessary to obtain a true picture of a child's functioning.

Since Piaget indicates that cognitive growth depends on interaction, social interaction (discussed in Chapter 11) is important in developing mental ability. Interaction with other people—talking, being in groups, playing together—provides experiences and information that is incorporated into the child's thinking. As Ginsberg and Opper (1969) point out, "social experience not only helps people to adjust to others at an emotional level, it also serves to clarify a person's thinking, and helps him to become, in some ways more coherent and logical" (p. 228). They further state that Piaget points out that "conversation and the clash of opinion is often beneficial for mental growth" (p. 230)—again emphasizing the relationship of language and intellectual growth.

COGNITIVE SKILLS

In the process of developing logical thought the child explores his universe and develops an understanding about it. Even before he can talk, he must have something to think about. In other words, the child cannot just develop a vocabulary; he needs something to think about to which the vocabulary may be attached. It is actually this "inner language," or comprehension, that we call thinking, and it too follows a developmental hierarchy (Table 8-1). In order to comprehend the child must:

1. Observe and perceive objects and events in his environment
2. Classify, categorize and associate information according to similarities, common attributes, life cycle, cause and effect, sequence, time, and the relationship of objects to one another
3. Store information in memory
4. Analyze and relate new information received to the stored information in order to make comparisons
5. Develop theories and principles based on information received, analyzed, and stored
6. Make judgments and evaluations based on obtained information
7. Infer or predict future events based on a series of related experiences

Table 8-1.
Cognitive Skills Taxonomy

COGNITIVE OBJECTIVES	SENSORIMOTOR ADAPTATIONS (BIRTH–2 YEARS)	PREOPERATIONAL INTUITIONS (2–7 YEARS)	CONCRETE MANIPULATIONS (7–11 YEARS)	FORMAL REVERSIBLE OPERATIONS (11 YEARS AND OLDER)
Knowledge: Conditioned response, terms, facts, conventions, methods, classes, and relations	Reflective assimilations, visual-motor accommodations, schematic organizations and coordinations	Perceptual-representative judgment, irreversibility, intuitional abstractions	Receptive vocabulary, general information, number concepts	
Comprehension: Elements, rules, translation, interpretation, extrapolation	Experimental discovery	Single property classification, correspondence sets, visual generalizations, simple seriation	Seriation of pictures and patterns, quantitative seriation, conservation of quantity and space, arithmetic computation, multiple classification, reading vocabulary, general comprehension	Time, reversibility

(continued)

SOURCE: R. E. Valett, *Developing Cognitive Abilities: Teaching Children to Think* (St. Louis: C. V. Mosby, 1978), p. 50. Used by permission of the author and publisher.

Table 8-1. *continued*

COGNITIVE OBJECTIVES	SENSORIMOTOR ADAPTATIONS (BIRTH–2 YEARS)	PREOPERATIONAL INTUITIONS (2–7 YEARS)	CONCRETE MANIPULATIONS (7–11 YEARS)	FORMAL REVERSIBLE OPERATIONS (11 YEARS AND OLDER)
Application: Semantic, figural, symbolic, behavioral	Invention	Manual expression, perceptual-motor coordination, visual-motor memory	Mathematical reasoning, language mechanics, expressive vocabulary	Reality problem solving, creative divergency, social competency
Analysis: Units, relationships, organizational, principles	Listening and attending, visual organization, and closure		Auditory-vocal sequential memory, word attack skills, spelling, reference skills	Propositional thinking
Synthesis: Integration, planning, originality, theorizing	Motor planning, visual-motor patterns, visual-motor integration		Sensory integration, auditory vocal closure, reading comprehension similarities	Figure-symbolic abstractions and relationships
Evaluation: Self-criticism, external validation, implications	Self-awareness		Analogies, social interpretation, self-correction	Hypothetical-deductive reasoning, self-actualization

Myklebust (1954) divides language into three categories: receptive, inner, and expressive. In an informal assessment, it is the area of *inner language,* or concept attainment, that we must analyze in order to determine the child's ability to process information in the important areas of: (1) classification and categorization, (2) association, (3) size, (4) body parts identification, (5) sequencing, (6) time, (7) problem solving, (8) making inferences, and (9) predicting outcomes.

Because thinking and language are closely related, and because the teacher is not required to make the fine distinction between the processing of language symbols and the basic cognitive skills required to process, inner language has been included in informal assessment along with receptive and expressive language skills. If the teacher finds the child does not understand oral as well as written language, then a more thorough assessment should probably be done by a specialist in speech and language.

LANGUAGE DEVELOPMENT

The cognitive processes that are used to process the child's inner language were described earlier. Figure 8-2 illustrates the relationship of inner language to the other two parts of the language process: receptive and expressive language. Figure 8-3 illustrates the modality, or neurophysiological, processes that are required for the development of that language. If the brain is thought of as a computer, then these physiological or modality processes are the *input.* The senses provide that input. Although information is received to some extent through the senses of taste and smell, it is received primarily through the kinesthetic or motor, the auditory, and the visual senses. Sensory input is interpreted and perceived as meaningful by the brain, and is then incorporated into the child's cognitive framework in order to develop concepts of inner language, that is, the child's comprehension of what has been received.

Neurophysiological development is important in developing language, but so too are the psychological or cognitive implications inherent in *listening, speaking, reading,* and *writing.* Psycholinguistics, the study of how language is acquired, looks at both of these elements and how they interact.

The study of psycholinguistics gained importance with the publication of Noam Chomsky's *Syntactic Structures* (1957) and gained impetus as more and more psychologists became interested in how children develop language. As Figure 8-2 indicates, receptive language develops first. Following this, the internalization process takes place, that is, concepts are

Figure 8-2.
The Language Process

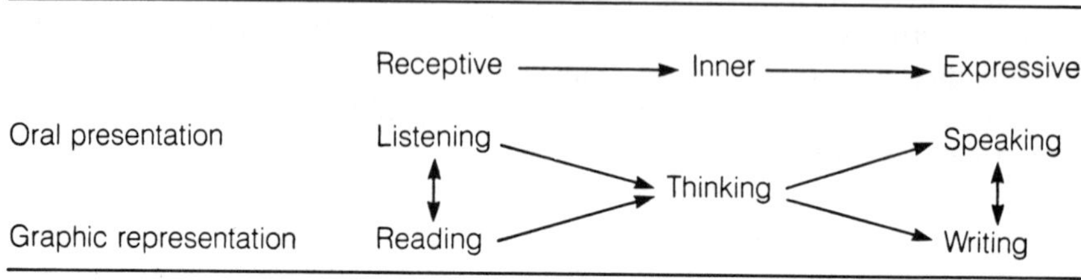

Figure 8-3.
Modality Processes Required for Language

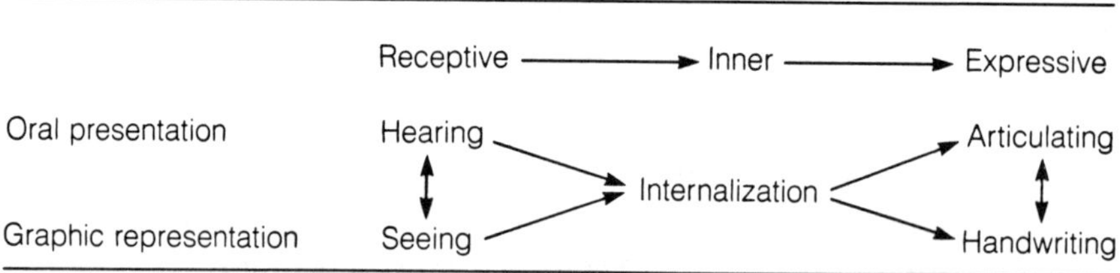

developed from the child's own experience. Finally, expressive language develops as the child internalizes and is able to communicate what he has received. Tables 8-2 and 8-3 show the progression of the child's physical ability to reproduce sounds and his pyschological ability to understand and use words in spoken language.

Language is generally thought of as having four components: phonology, morphology, syntax, and semantics.

Phonology

Phonology is the sound system of the language. The child's ability to perceive and reproduce sounds is the basis for his or her ability to reproduce speech. Table 8-2 describes the phonological system a child is expected to develop. Basic to the child's ability to develop a phonological system is his ability to hear sounds accurately; in addition, he must have sufficient control of his mouth, tongue, and breath to reproduce the sounds. Notice that the sound system is fairly complete before the child enters school. Although there may be some variation in the age at which each child develops the phonological system, the teacher should refer to the speech therapist any child who seems markedly delayed.

Table 8-2.
Pattern of Normal Language Development in Articulation and General Intelligibility

AGE (YR.)	ARTICULATION	GENERAL INTELLIGIBILITY
1–2	Uses all vowels and consonants *m, b, p, k, g, w, h, n, t, d.* Omits most final consonants, some initial. Substitutes consonants above for more difficult. Much unintelligible jargon around 18 mo. Good inflection, rate.	Words used may be no more than 25% intelligible to unfamiliar listener. Jargon near 18 mo. almost 100% unintelligible. Improvement noticeable between 21 and 24 mo.
2–3	Continues all sounds above with vowels but use is inconsistent. Tries many new sounds, but poor mastery. Much substitution. Omission of final consonants. Articulation lags behind vocabulary.	Words about 65% intelligible by 2 yrs.; 70–80% intelligible in context by 3. Many individual sounds faulty but total context generally understood. Some incomprehensibility because of faulty sentence structure.
3–4	Masters *b, t, d, k, g,* and tries many others including *f, v, th, s, z,* and consonant combinations *tr, bl, pr, gr, dr,* but *r* and *l* may be faulty, so substitutes *w* or omits. Speech almost intelligible. Uses *th* inconsistently.	Speech usually 90–100% intelligible in context. Individual sounds still faulty and some trouble with sentence structure.
4–5	Masters *f* and *v* and many consonant combinations. Should be little omission of initial and final consonants. Fewer substitutes but may be some. May distort *r, l, s, z, sh, ch, j, th.* No trouble with multisyllabled words.	Speech is unintelligible in context even though some sounds are still faulty.
5–6	Masters *r, l, th,* and such blends as *tl, gr, bl, br, pr,* etc. May not master these sounds until age 7½.	Good

SOURCE: Herold Lillywhite, "Doctor's Manual of Speech Disorders," *Journal of the American Medical Association* 167 (1958): 850–858.

Morphology

Until the publication of Chomsky's *Syntactic Structures,* most linguists assumed that children learned to use language by imitating their parents or others in their environment. What Chomsky discovered was that children appear to learn rules for language development. He pointed out that children were able to say sentences they had never heard and still put them into a correct syntactical and morphological structure. For example, assume a child has never heard the past tense for *buy,* but understands that *ed* added to a verb connotates the past tense. The fact that he says *buyed* instead of *bought* only serves to demonstrate that he is using the rule (even though in this case it is erroneously applied) instead of repeating something he has heard.

Morphology is the use of words or parts of words to give meaning to the language. Inflection, root words, suffixes and prefixes, and even punctuation, are all morphological components of words. For example, *walk* indicates the action of a person, whereas *walked* indicates both the action of a person *and* that it already happened. Similarly, the word *girl* is one morphological unit; *girl's* has two morphological units: the concept of girl, as well as the concept of possessing; the word *girls'* has three morphological components: girl, plural, and possession. Children use morphological clues in language to derive meaning from spoken language. A good understanding of morphology is invaluable in word analysis and developing reading for comprehension.

Syntax

Syntax is the use of proper word order to make sense and the ability to have different words in the sentence agree in such things as tense, gender, and number. For example, the words "Tied their tree bicycles the boys to the" has the same number of words as "The boys tied their bicycles to the tree," but the words in the first phrase need to be rearranged to make sense. In addition, the fact that the subject of the sentence is *boys* means that the pronoun must be *their* to denote plural, and so must *bicycles.* Children develop this linguistic competence, learn the proper combination of words to make sense from their experience, and usually come to school with this ability. Eisenson (1972) points out that children who have reached the ag eof 5 years, 8 months, or achieved a mental age roughly equivalent to this age, have usually developed the ability to use the basics of the English language. Therefore, we can assume that most children entering school have a basic oral syntactic ability on which the teacher may build the corresponding graphic ability. (See Table 8-3).

Semantics

Semantics is the understanding of words and their meaning as used in sentences and paragraphs. Children need to learn a large and varied vocabulary. Words may have a surface meaning, that is, definition, but used in certain combinations they may also have a deeper meaning. An example is the use of the word *head* (meaning actually "mind") in "He has a good head on his shoulders."

Table 8-3.
Pattern of Normal Language Development in Expressive Speech and Comprehension of Speech

AGE (YR.)	ARTICULATION	GENERAL INTELLIGIBILITY
1–2	Uses 1 to 3 words at 12 mo., 10 to 15 at 15 mo., 15 to 20 at 18 mo., about 100–200 by 2 yr. Knows names of most objects he uses. Names few people, uses verbs but not correctly with subjects. Jargon and echolalia. Names 1 to 3 pictures.	Begins to relate symbol and object meaning. Adjusts to comments. Inhibits on command. Responds correctly to "give me that," "sit down," "stand up" with gestures. Puts watch to ear on command. Understands simple questions. Recognizes 120–275 words.
2–3	Vocabulary increases to 300–500 words. Says "where kitty," "ball all gone," "want cookie," "go bye bye car." Jargon mostly gone. Vocalizing increases. Has fluency trouble. Speech not adequate for communication needs.	Rapid increase in comprehension vocabulary to 400 at 1½, 800 at 3. Responds to commands using "on," "under," "up," "down," "over there," "by," "run," "walk," "jump up," "throw," "run fast," "be quiet," and commands containing two related actions.
3–4	Uses 600–1,000 words, becomes conscious of speech. 3–4 words per speech response. Personal pronouns, some adjectives, adverbs, and prepositions appear. Mostly simple sentences, but some complex. Speech more useful.	Understands up to 1,500 words by age 4. Recognizes plurals, sex difference, pronouns, adjectives. Comprehends complex and compound sentences. Answers simple questions.

(continued)

SOURCE: Herold Lillywhite, "Doctor's Manual of Speech Disorders," *Journal of the American Medical Association* 167 (1958): 850–858. Copyright © 1958, American Medical Association. Used by permission.

Table 8-3. *continued*

AGE (YR.)	ARTICULATION	GENERAL INTELLIGIBILITY
4–5	Increase in vocabulary to 1,100–1,600 words. More 3–4 syllable words. More adjectives, adverbs, prepositions, and conjunctions. Articles appear. 4, 5, 6 word sentences, syntax quite good. Uses plurals. Fluency improves. Proper nouns decrease, pronouns increase.	Comprehends from 1,500 to 2,000 words. Carries out more complex commands, with 2–3 actions. Understands dependent clause, "if," "because," "when," "why."
5–6	Increase in vocabulary to 1,500–2,100 words. Complete 5–6 word sentences, compound, complex, with some dependent clauses. Syntax near normal. Quite fluent. More multisyllable words.	Understands vocabulary of 2,500–2,800 words. Responds correctly to more complicated sentences but is still confused at times by involved sentences.

SURVEY ASSESSMENT

We must distinguish here between speech and language. Speech is the ability to produce sounds, beginning with noises such as the babbling produced by an infant, and leading to complete and well-formed sentences. Language is the use of speech to understand and communicate ideas. A child who has difficulty producing intelligible words or forming grammatical sentences—that is, difficulty in speech—probably needs the services of a trained speech therapist. The teacher who identifies such difficulties should refer the child for these services.

Language is involved in nearly every subject the child will encounter in school. It is crucial that this aspect of the child's development be assessed. Language problems are difficult to identify, and the teacher must carefully evaluate the child who is encountering problems in reading comprehension or in writing. Usually the child who is having difficulty with spoken language will evidence even greater problems in writing. For that reason, the language screening given here is for spoken language. If the child's problem is limited only to written language, a screening will not clearly identify the problems, and a more thorough evaluation of samples of written work should be made.

In order to screen language performance, the teacher should check each of the items in Table 8-4. A score of 28 or more should be carefully scrutinized; a score of 36 indicates that a more thorough evaluation needs to be performed. If the child obtains a score of 12 or more on any one of the three sections on the screening, a more thorough evaluation by the teacher or the speech therapist is also indicated.

Table 8-4.
Spoken Language Screening

CATEGORY	ABOVE AVERAGE 0	AVERAGE 1	BELOW AVERAGE 2
I. Receptive Language			
1. Volume of voice	______	______	______
2. Understands gestures	______	______	______
3. Remembers directions	______	______	______
4. "Reads" picture stories	______	______	______
5. Response time to questions or direction	______	______	______
6. Listening vocabulary	______	______	______
7. Enjoys listening to books	______	______	______
8. Interprets anger or teasing from others	______	______	______
II. Inner Language			
9. Amount of general knowledge	______	______	______
10. Gets "point" of story or discussion	______	______	______
11. Understands directions or demonstrations	______	______	______
12. Sense of humor	______	______	______
13. Sticks to topic	______	______	______

(continued)

Table 8-4. *continued*

CATEGORY	ABOVE AVERAGE 0	AVERAGE 1	BELOW AVERAGE 2
14. Can predict what will happen next	______	______	______
15. Can summarize story	______	______	______
16. Can do simple mental arithmetic	______	______	______
III. Expressive Language			
17. Pronunciation	______	______	______
18. Speed of speech	______	______	______
19. Speaks in complete sentences	______	______	______
20. Uses words in correct order	______	______	______
21. Uses correct word in conversation	______	______	______
22. Ability to recall names for objects or people	______	______	______
23. Can repeat a story	______	______	______
24. Participates in class discussions	______	______	______

Score:

27 or less	Satisfactory performance.
28–35	Child should be watched and language abilities checked on a periodic basis.
36 or more	Thorough evaluation needed.

DIAGNOSTIC EVALUATION

Figure 8-4 (section III of the diagnostic checklist given in Figure 3-6) is the checklist of abilities for the diagnostic assessment of language. Since many of the items can be entered from observation of the child's performance in the classroom, the checklist should be kept available so that the teacher can make entries during the school day. Checklist items are described in the following section to give the teacher an idea of what to

Figure 8-4.
Language/Cognition Checklist

A. Inner language
   1. Categorization
      a. Pictures
      b. Words
      c. Similarities and differences
      d. Common characteristics
   2. Play behavior
   3. Associations
      a. Nonverbal
         (1) Picture opposites
         (2) Picture associations
         (3) Picture interpretation
         (4) Picture absurdities
      b. Verbal
         (1) Opposites
         (2) Reasoning (syllogisms)
         (3) Associations
         (4) Inferences
         (5) Outcomes
   4. Size
   5. Body parts identification
      a. Point
      b. Name
   6. Sequence
      a. Pictures
      b. Verbal
      c. Abstract
         (1) Visual
         (2) Verbal
      d. Predicting outcomes
   7. Time concepts
      a. Social
      b. Automatic
         (1) Days
         (2) Months
         (3) Seasons
      c. Clock
         (1) Set
         (2) Read
   8. Problem solving
      a. Visual
         (1) Searching for details
         (2) Finding hidden objects
         (3) Answering questions
      b. Verbal
         (1) Recalling details
         (2) Resolving situations
      c. Abstraction
         (1) Determining design sequence
         (2) Determining number sequence

B. Receptive language
   1. Nonverbal
      a. Response to gestures
      b. Identification of pictures
      c. Identification of function of objects
      d. Identification of actions in pictures
      e. Identification of noises made by persons
      f. Identification of environmental noises
      g. "Reads" picture story
      h. "Reads" maps
      i. "Reads" graphs
      j. "Reads" diagrams
   2. Verbal
      a. Listening
         (1) Auditory closure
         (2) Vocabulary
         (3) Prepositions (location)
         (4) Adverbs (sequence)
         (5) Conversation
         (6) Speed of listening
      b. Comprehension
         (1) Words
         (2) Sentences
         (3) Paragraphs
         (4) Understanding sequence
         (5) Recalling details
         (6) Getting the main idea
         (7) Drawing conclusions
         (8) Making inferences
         (9) Critical listening

C. Expressive Language
   1. Nonverbal gestures
   2. Verbal
      a. Articulation
      b. Voice

(continued)

Figure 8-4 continued

- c. Intonation
- d. Fluency
3. Word finding
   - a. Conversation
   - b. Description
     - (1) Objects
     - (2) Pictures
     - (3) Stories
     - (4) Directions
4. Sentence formation
   - a. Conversation
     - (1) Participates with group
     - (2) Adjusts language to social situations
   - b. Description
     - (1) Communication
     - (2) Oral reports
   - c. Creative expression
5. Written language
   - a. Productivity
   - b. Sentence structure
   - c. Punctuation
   - d. Form
     - (1) Creative writing
     - (2) Paragraphing
     - (3) Written reports
     - (4) Correspondence
   - e. Ability to abstract
     - (1) Use of vocabulary
     - (2) Development
     - (3) Elaborations
     - (4) Developing major theme
     - (5) Developing minor points
     - (6) Use of summation, conclusion, prediction
     - (7) Constructing plot
     - (8) Figurative language
   - f. Spelling
   - g. Handwriting
   - h. Self-correction

SOURCE: Developed by Arlee S. Maier.

look for in each area, and so that the opportunity to observe the child's performance can be created if none occurs naturally. If possible, more than one observation should be entered on the checklist to avoid error and to help the teacher obtain an accurate picture of the child's behavior. Within any category the skills are listed in order of increasing difficulty. If a child can perform a higher skill, the teacher may assume he or she can successfully do all those that lead up to it. Only a few examples are necessary to indicate that the child possesses the skill.

A. Inner language
   1. Categorization: Ability to put objects, pictures, and words into categories that go together; ability to classify according to color, form, or function.
      - a. Pictures: The teacher can cut pictures from a magazine or mail-order catalog, and ask the child to sort them according to categories. The child may be asked to generate his own categories, or they may be provided for him. The older child should be able to generate categories according to his own criteria. Any reasonable categorization should be accepted.
      - b. Words: The child can be given a list of words and asked to

organize them into categories, such as (1) things that make music, (2) objects larger than an automobile, (3) things used in the kitchen. Since language is being measured, the child should either be able to read the words himself or they should be read to him, and his answers recorded.

c. Similarities and differences: Pictures and words can be arranged according to which ones are alike and which are different.

d. Common characteristics: Pictures, designs, and words can be organized into groups with common characteristics. If the child is able to generate groups, he can be asked to reorganize according to new criteria; for example, oranges, bananas, berries, pears, lemons, and apples are all fruit, but they can be recategorized into (1) fruit that can be eaten directly and (2) fruit that must be peeled.

2. Play behavior: Ability to play appropriately, that is, follow rules, communicate with others, or put equipment away. This ability can inform the teacher how aware the child is of his environment and interpersonal relationships. If the child *behaves* as if he understands how things go, he has the necessary concepts.

3. Associations
   a. Nonverbal
      (1) Picture opposites: The child can sort pictures into opposites such as (1) a person going upstairs/a person going downstairs; (2) hot liquid/cold liquid; (3) coat on/coat off.
      (2) Picture associations: The child can pair things that go together, for example, shoes/socks, knife/fork.
      (3) Picture interpretation—The teacher can show the child a picture or a cartoon series and ask what is happening or what story it tells.
      (4) Picture absurdities: The child is asked to tell what is "funny" or absurd about a picture, such as a picture of an elephant in a barnyard. Old workbooks or children's magazines often have such pictures and they can be clipped out.
   b. Verbal
      (1) Opposites: The child can be asked to give a synonym or antonym for a word provided by the teacher.
      (2) Reasoning (syllogisms): Social or absurd situations are presented to the child and he is asked to indicate what should have occurred.
      (3) Associations: The child is asked to indicate what comes next or what follows according to climate, time, growth, or life cycle.

(4) Inferences: The child is asked to indicate what came before or what will follow in cause-and-effect types of situations.
(5) Outcomes: The child is able to predict what might occur given a circumstance and set of facts.

4. Size: The child is asked to sort out a series of objects according to size, both increasing and decreasing. A more difficult skill is to have the child indicate size differences of objects in pictures that are not reproduced according to scale.

5. Body parts identification: In drawing a picture of himself or other human figure no major body parts are omitted or distorted.
   a. Point: The child is asked to point to himself to show body parts named by the teacher.
   b. Name: When parts of the body are indicated by the teacher on a person or picture, the child is able to name them.

6. Sequence
   a. Pictures: The child is asked to arrange pictures cut from magazines, workbooks, or books to "tell a story."
   b. Verbal: The child can tell a simple story, describe how to make something, or describe how to get somewhere, such as to the public library from school.
   c. Abstract
      (1) Visual: Given a series of geometric designs arranged in a pattern, the child can complete the sequence, for example, □◇□◇□◇□◇
      (2) Verbal: Given a pattern of taps on the table, or a sequence of musical notes, the child can reproduce them up to a series of five or six.
   d. Predicting outcomes—The child is asked to observe a series of pictures or listen to a sequence of words, and indicate the next few items in the sequence.

7. Time concepts
   a. Social: The child is asked to indicate that he understands the uses of time in our culture. He may be asked:

      What is longer, a day or an hour?
      What is shorter, a second or a minute?
      Which is longer, a minute or an hour?
      Which is shorter, a day or a week?
      What do we use to tell time?
      How old will you be on your next birthday?
      What grade will you be in next year?

What did you do last summer?
Where is your mother now?
When is your birthday?
How soon will it be Christmas?

b. Automatic
   (1) Days: The child can name the day of the week and can answer questions like "What day comes after Wednesday?"
   (2) Months: The child is able to name the months of the year and answer questions like "What month comes before January? What month does Thanksgiving come in?"
   (3) Seasons: The child can name the seasons, and put them in order.
c. Clock
   (1) Set: Using a small cardboard clock with movable hands, the teacher asks the child to set the clock for:

   12:30
   5:00
   3:45
   7:15

   (2) Read: Using the cardboard clock, the teacher sets the hands and asks the child to read:

   9:25
   6:00
   4:30
   10:45

8. Problem solving: This is related to associations (section A.3) and information gained in either section may be useful. If the teacher feels that the child was able to perform easily on associations, this section may be omitted.
   a. Visual: The child is able to use visual clues to solve problems. This may include:
      (1) Searching for details in a picture to solve a "riddle."
      (2) Finding a hidden object in the room, or in a picture.
      (3) Using a sequence of pictures to answer a question, such as "Why do you think Sam was hiding under the bed?"
   b. Verbal: The child is able to listen to a story or passage for verbal clues to solve a problem. This may include:
      (1) Recalling details to solve a riddle.
      (2) Listening to a social situation such as "What would you do if you found a small child walking on the street crying?" and indicating how to resolve it.

c. Abstraction: The child is able to use nonmeaningful information and develop strategy for solving a problem. An example would be:

(1) Looking at a series of designs involving more than one criteria and determining which would come next; for example,

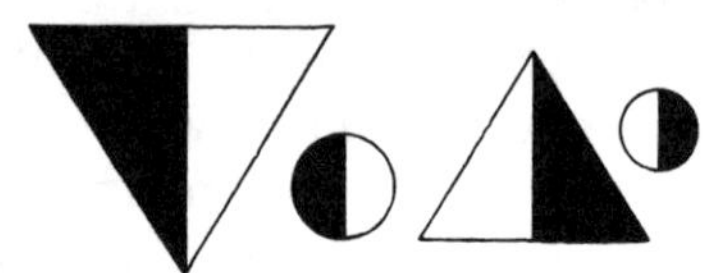

(2) Looking at a series of numbers and determining which would follow; for example,

1 3 5 7 9 ?

2 5 9 14 20 ?

B. Receptive language

1. Nonverbal

a. Response to gestures: The teacher can make gestures to the child, moving his or her hands to indicate things such as "come here," "stop," "sssh" (fingers in front of mouth); or the teacher can show the child pictures of faces and ask him to identify if the person is sad, happy, angry, and so on. The *Peabody Language Development Kit* (Dunn and Smith, 1966) is a good source of such pictures.

b. Identification of pictures: The child is asked to identify objects and people in pictures.

c. Identification of function of objects—The child is able to identify an object's use: broom/to sweep, telephone/to talk, suitcase/to carry clothes.

d. Identification of actions in pictures: The child is asked to identify from a photograph or illustration what a person is doing: jumping, running, sleeping, swimming, cutting the grass, and so on.

e. Identification of noises made by persons: The child is asked to close his eyes and identify sounds such as humming, whistling, clapping, finger snapping, and foot scraping.

f. Identification of environmental noises: The child is asked to listen and identify noises in the environment, such as voices talking, typewriter, cars in the street, airplanes overhead, air-conditioning, pencils scratching as others write, and so on.

g. "Reads" picture story: The child is able to tell the story indicated by a sequence of pictures without words; for example, (1) picking corn in a field, (2) husking the corn, (3) cooking corn in the kitchen, (4) family sitting at the table eating corn. This task can sometimes be done simultaneously with picture sequencing.

h. "Reads" maps: The child is able to tell how to get from one place to another by looking at the map; he is able to identify mountains, cities, oceans, rivers, and so on, and is able to use the key to identify symbols.

i. "Reads" graphs: The child is able to explain what a line graph and bar graph indicate. He understands what the axes mean.

j. "Reads" diagrams: The child is able to follow directions or construct something such as a simple car-model that is explained by diagram.

2. Verbal
   a. Listening
      (1) Auditory closure: The child is able to identify words that are distorted, spoken with a foreign accent, or partially pronounced. This can most often be observed in daily activities, and no formal task need be constructed.
      (2) Vocabulary: The teacher determines if the child understands words spoken by most children his age.
      (3) Prepositions (location): The teacher determines if the child understands location words such as *under, next to, over, behind, in front of,* and so on.
      (4) Adverbs (sequence): The teacher determines if the child understands words indicating sequence, such as *later, then, first, before, after,* and so on.
      (5) Conversation: The teacher observes if the child understands most of the words used in general conversation with peers, teachers, and others in his environment.
      (6) Speed of listening: Ability to receive and process information rapidly enough to integrate it. When language functions are slow, the child has difficulty keeping up with the teacher's explanation. Often children "tune-out" because they cannot absorb information rapidly. The teacher needs to observe this and note the child who may require longer to process. Short sentences, spoken somewhat more slowly, may be all that is necessary. These concepts apply to both oral (lis-

tening) and graphic (reading) language. Both need to be assessed.

b. Comprehension
   (1) Words: Similar to vocabulary. Does the child understand the words used in classroom activities at his grade level?
   (2) Sentences: The child's ability to understand the meaning of sentences used in his academic program. Literal comprehension for syntax and information needs to be assessed here.
   (3) Paragraphs: The teacher needs to assess whether the child understands the content of a paragraph, and whether he understands that the sentences within the paragraph all relate to the same general topic.
   (4) Understanding sequence: Ability to comprehend the order of activity or logic presented in classroom activities. The teacher may ask the child to list the sequence in order, or may ask the child specific questions to determine that it was understood.
   (5) Recalling details: The teacher must determine if enough detail is retained from what is heard or read that the child is able to answer specific factual questions posed by the teacher.
   (6) Getting the main idea: The child is able to paraphrase the intent of a selection, and point out the salient feature or features. In a written selection he may be able to underline the topic sentence.
   (7) Drawing conclusions: After hearing information, the child is able to infer the major themes from his understanding of the important ideas. He is able to make judgments about what he has heard or read.
   (8) Making inferences: The child is asked to predict or project outcomes other than the one presented to him. He may be asked to anticipate what will occur next.
   (9) Critical listening: The child is able to absorb the information presented; then, based on the conclusions and inferences he makes, he forms a value judgment as to the bias, fairness, or importance of what he has heard. Critical listening (or reading) requires that the child relate the new information to something already known and then make a value judgment.

C. Expressive language
   1. Nonverbal: Gestures—Ability to communicate using gestures and facial movement.

2. Verbal
   a. Articulation: The teacher should assess if the child is able to pronounce words intelligibly. By the time they are seven, most children pronounce words well.
   b. Voice: The teacher needs to assess if the loudness or softness of the child's vocal quality is satisfactory for good communication.
   c. Intonation: The teacher determines if the child uses inflection or speaks with expression. Intonation makes language colorful and interesting to hear.
   d. Fluency: Ability to speak clearly, with adequate speed, and with proper syntax in order to be well understood. Automatic usage of language in terms of verb forms, comparisons, and superlatives is included here.
3. Word finding: The child's ability to find the right word to use in order to be descriptive, precise, and accurate. Everyone is occasionally at a loss for words. Frequent difficulty, however, may signal a problem.
   a. Conversation: The teacher should note if word finding is frequent or prolonged in general conversation.
   b. Description: Ability to find the correct word to be descriptive and exact when describing an event or an object.
      (1) Objects: The child's ability to find the correct word to be precise in describing an object.
      (2) Pictures: Ability to find the correct words to describe a picture. The use of a picture should help the child who has difficulty in spontaneous conversation.
      (3) Stories: Ability to use varied descriptions and a wide vocabulary in story telling.
      (4) Directions: Ability to give directions clearly and accurately. The child needs to have a large enough vocabulary at his command to perform this task.
4. Sentence formation
   a. Conversation: This skill is related to word finding, but the teacher needs to assess the child's use of full sentences in conversation, rather than the use of particular words and phrases.
      (1) Participates with group: The child's ability to engage in conversation freely and fully.
      (2) Adjusts language to social group: The teacher needs to assess whether the child speaks more simply when speaking to a younger child, uses current slang (or dialect) in speaking to peers, and/or uses more formal and polite language in speaking to adults or authority figures. It is important to see

if an older child uses more formal speech in formal situations, such as in giving reports or conducting a meeting.

b. Description: Related to word finding, but broader and related to the child's active intent to enrich his vocabulary.
   (1) Communication: The teacher should note if the child uses a wide variety of words in general conversation, or whether he uses the same words and phrases repeatedly.
   (2) Oral reports: The child's ability to use a broad vocabulary and interesting sentence structure in giving oral reports to the class.
c. Creative expression: The creative use of language to create a mood, influence emotions, motivate others, and so on. The teacher needs to assess how effectively the child uses language to influence, create impressions, or motivate others to action. This is particularly important as the child grows older.

5. Written language: Many of the elements that are important for spoken language may also be assessed as the student uses written language to communicate.
   a. Productivity: The teacher needs to assess the quantity of written work to see if it is satisfactory for the student's age and grade level. Such things as the number of words, sentences, and words per sentence should be evaluated.
   b. Sentence structure: The teacher should determine if the student uses well-formulated sentences. Particular note needs to be made of (1) subject and predicate agreement, (2) complexity of sentences, (3) run-on sentences, (4) word order, (5) word omissions, (6) agreement in tense, number and gender, (7) variety in sentence structure, and (8) amount of information in a sentence.
   c. Punctuation: Punctuation is more carefully evaluated in Chapter 9, on spelling. In this section a general impression of the adequacy of the child's use of punctuation should be made.
   d. Form: The child's ability to shift writing style depending on the need.
      (1) Creative writing: Use of paragraphs, quotations, and chapters for full expression.
      (2) Paragraphing: The child's understanding of the fact that all sentences in one paragraph are related, and that a new idea requires a new paragraph.
      (3) Written reports: The student's ability to set up a format to report information so that it is clear, sequential, and logically developed. The ability to outline should be evaluated here.
      (4) Correspondence: The ability to use letters for friendly com-

munication, for making inquiries or complaints, and for conducting business.

e. Ability to abstract: Here the teacher needs to evaluate how the child transfers his concepts of oral language into written format. Particularly important to assess are:
   (1) Creative and varied use of vocabulary
   (2) The logical or coherent development of the paper
   (3) The elaborations used by the student to support or explain his point
   (4) How the student points out his major theme
   (5) How the student develops minor points
   (6) Use of summation, conclusions, and predictions
   (7) Ability to construct a plot
   (8) Use of allegory, metaphor, and other figurative language
f. Spelling: Is spelling adequate for good communication (covered more thoroughly in Chapter 9)?
g. Handwriting: Is handwriting legible (covered in Chapter 9)?
h. Self-correction: Ability to monitor and proofread written work, to correct errors. Most students should write a draft and correct it before final preparation. Adequate time needs to be allotted for this.

After making several observations of the child in the classroom, or, in some instances, performing on teacher-made tasks, the teacher will be able to see a pattern of the child's strengths and weaknesses emerge. Usually a child will not be able to use a higher level skill before the lower level one is well developed. Thus, it is unlikely that the child who has poor listening skills will develop great proficiency in reading, or that the child who has poor oral language will be able to write well. Language skills are hierarchical, and remedial and corrective activities must be modeled on this premise.

Summary

Thinking and language are generally felt to be closely related, as children use words to describe what they are thinking and teachers and parents use words to teach and explain about the world to them.

Thinking refers to the activity of the child's brain as it reacts to live experiences; it is the process by which learning, or concept formation, takes place.

In the early period of a child's life, all of this activity is related to information perceived through the senses. As new experiences occur, the child's concepts change and become refined. A developmental sequence occurs; this sequence is loosely related to age levels, but it permits greater flexibility in achieving stages for each individual.

The work of Piaget describes this developmental sequence through which all children progress.

Early researchers felt that a child's language development was modeled on that of the adults around him, but Chomsky's research revealed that children learn language patterns or rules that they can apply even in new situations. Most children are able to use language adequately by the time they enter school; thus, the learning of the graphic forms of language, reading, and writing can be built on this foundation.

The survey assessment is designed to identify if a child is having difficulty with linguistic structure or language, or if his difficulty is in identifying the graphic code (letters and words) used to express language. If the difficulty is related to the spoken language, the correct remediation may consist of an enriched oral language program. The survey assessment can also be used to identify if the child is experiencing difficulty in receptive language (listening to and understanding spoken words and sentences), inner language (processing the information received) or in expressive language (speaking and communicating).

The diagnostic assessment is a series of structured observations of the various components of the three language processes. By this means the teacher hopes to identify if the child (1) does not understand and interpret sounds, pictures, gestures, words, and sentences; (2) does not relate those sounds, pictures, and words to previous experiences, and thus is unable to store them in memory and retrieve them when needed; and (3) is not able to express himself using words and sentences in order to communicate ideas with others, both orally and in written form.

Language skills are hierarchical. A child who cannot understand, cannot read and comprehend; a child who cannot speak and communicate orally, cannot express his thoughts in writing.

Bibliography

Bruner, J.; Oliver, R. R.; and Greenfield, P. M. *Studies in Cognitive Growth.* New York: John Wiley, 1966.

Carroll, J. B. *Language and Thought.* Englewood Cliffs, N.J.: Prentice-Hall, 1964.

Chomsky, Noam. *Syntactic Structures.* The Hague: Mouton, 1957.

Dale, P. S. *Language Development: Structure and Form.* 2d ed. New York: Holt, Rinehart and Winston, 1976.

Dunn, L., and Smith, J. O. *Peabody Language Development Kit.* Circle Pines, Minn.: American Guidance Service, 1966.

Eisenson, Jon. *Aphasia in Children.* New York: Harper and Row, 1972.

Gessell, A. *Gessell Developmental Schedules.* New York: The Psychological Corporation, 1949.

Ginsberg, H., and Opper, S. *Piaget's Theory of Intellectual Development.* Englewood Cliffs, N.J.: Prentice-Hall, 1969.

McNeil, David. *The Acquisition of Language: The Study of Developmental Psycholinguistics.* New York: Harper and Row, 1970.

Myklebust, Helmer. *Auditory Disorders in Children.* New York: Grune and Stratton, 1954.

Pflaum-Connor, Suzanne. *The Development of Language and Reading in Young Children.* 2d ed. Columbus, Ohio: Charles E. Merrill, 1978.

Piaget, Jean. *The Origins of Intelligence in Children.* New York: International University Press, 1955.

Valett, Robert E. *Developing Cognitive Abilities: Teaching Children to Think.* St. Louis: C. V. Mosby, 1978.

Vygotsky, L. *Thought and Language.* Cambridge, Mass.: MIT Press, 1962.

Weschler, David. *Weschler Intelligence Scale for Children—Revised.* New York: The Psychological Corporation, 1974.

Chapter 9
Spelling and Handwriting

Spelling and handwriting are basic skills needed by any student who wants to be successful in using written language. This chapter discusses the development of these skills and presents methods for assessing them. After the assessment, the teacher is better able to complete the match between the analysis of the student's abilities and a task analysis of the skill required. Performance objectives can then be projected for realistic and attainable goals.

SPELLING

Spelling is a subject that creates great difficulties for students, but it is least understood and attended to by teachers. Poor spelling usually contributes to poor performance in nearly every other subject, and for this reason poor spellers are often thought to be poor learners, an overgeneralization that does not appear to be supported by fact. Because spelling is such a complex skill, requiring the integration of language, auditory, visual, and motor abilities, it is one of the most difficult for children to learn; and learning disabled (LD) students usually have more difficulty with spelling and written language than with any other subject. Just why this is so has never been clearly understood; however, it may be related to the fact that LD students are often more poorly organized, and therefore do not integrate skills as effectively.

Originally, spelling was presented orally. The "spelling bee," an institution not often used today, was employed in classrooms all over the country to encourage and enhance the development of good spelling skills. In reality, the spelling bee is remembered fondly by students who did well, but remembered as humiliating and degrading by those who found spelling difficult and were usually eliminated early in the contest.

The Nature of Spelling

Spelling is one of the major subjects taught in school about which very little is known. Cronbach (1969) points out that most teachers employ a teaching style that is almost identical to the way they were taught as children. This is particularly true of spelling. Most teachers confirm that spelling is taught by providing a list of words on Monday and having a test on Friday. Words are studied by reciting orally to a friend or parent, or by "writing each word five times."

Spelling as a subject first appeared in the late 1700s. Words at that time were often spelled several different ways, and it was not until the appearance of the first dictionaries that a single, accepted form was identified for most words in the English language. Early spelling lists were made up by each teacher. Around the beginning of the twentieth century, word lists began to appear; these were based on the words used by children in their reading and/or writing assignments. About 1910 the first spelling demon list appeared, beginning the practice of studying difficult words and mastering a common spelling of them using a variety of techniques, most of which were developed by teachers to fit their teaching styles. For many years "write each word five times" was the accepted assignment, and, fortunately for most children, it seemed adequate for their needs. The poor spellers didn't learn by any method, and ten or even fifteen repetitions made no difference.

Researchers generally have been uninterested in spelling. The little research that has been done has not resulted in clear information. Triggs and Robbins (1944) did a study of adults who were poor spellers and came up with five major characteristics usually exhibited by this group:

1. They do not proofread or check their writing.
2. They commonly mispronounce the words they misspell, and have a tendency toward unclear articulation.

3. They substitute other words for those they cannot spell, instead of trying to learn new spellings.
4. They are poor in language skills generally, including reading.
5. They are poor in penmanship, and careless in forming letters.

This study identified many correlating difficulties, but did not establish consistent relationships between spelling and language, cognitive functioning, or perceptual/motor functioning.

A study conducted in Sweden in 1964 and reported by Barsch (1974) delineated five characteristics of good spellers:

1. They have good language ability, including a general familiarity with words, their structure, and use.
2. They have good knowledge of sequential probability.
3. They have good immediate memory for visual materials.
4. They reason inductively rather than deductively.
5. They have high interest in reading.

Again, several of the elements appear to have little apparent relationship. A survey of significant research on spelling provides little definitive information. Most available material has been confined to "how to teach" rather than "what is the problem." One slim volume containing thirty articles on spelling had several articles claiming to be the only sure approach, and several others exhorting the reader to try an auditory, visual, written, artistic (finger painting), or movement approach. The reader is left to choose which method is the most appropriate. Most readers probably end up choosing that which more closely approaches their own previous experience in spelling instruction.

A Task Analysis of Spelling

Spelling is generally thought to be the skill of identifying a word, either because it is needed in writing or dictated by someone, and then generating the proper sequence of letters needed to produce that word by naming or writing them. Naming, or spelling orally, is usually only required in school or on those occasions when it is necessary to spell out a word, often a name, for greater clarity. In everyday use, spelling is a written task, as is required in correspondence, notes, reports, and other school or work-related activities. A hierarchy of skills is required for success in spelling.

Spelling as a Linguistic Skill

Depending on the authority cited, the sounds of the English language consist of either forty-four or forty-five phonemes or sounds; written language, however, uses only twenty-six letters. It is necessary for the speller to know what particular combination of letters will produce each phoneme, including the many different possibilities for the same sound. For example, cinder, cymbal, sitter, and symbol, all begin with the same phoneme. In addition, these same letters are often used to identify a different phoneme—for example, cipher, cyclone, silo, not to mention sight, and psychology. Another example can be found in the wide variety of letter combinations used to produce the final sound in: few, blue, too, shoe, and through. There are many such examples—so numerous that it is difficult, if not impossible, to develop a system by which there can be direct sound/symbol correspondence. In order to spell these words correctly, the speller needs to be familiar with the word. It is, therefore, necessary for most successful spellers to be able to recognize the word as a meaningful unit. In order for this to occur, the speller must hear and understand the word; it must be in either his or her listening or reading vocabulary.

The fact that it is important for the speller to understand the meaning of the word to be spelled may seem obvious. Yet, it cannot be assumed that a student fully understands a word simply because he can repeat it, or even if he can spell it. Particularly in the early elementary grades, or whenever a student first learns to read, the teacher must be sure to determine that the word, including all its meanings, is in the student's speaking vocabulary. Although most words in a spelling lesson are known to the student, others may be spelled without meaning, by memorizing a sequence of phonemes or letters. A student who understands a word is able to distinguish between (1) homonyms, words that sound alike but are spelled differently, such as *red-read, flour-flower, stake-steak;* and (2) homographs, words that are spelled similarly but have different meanings and pronunciations, such as *read, sow, polish.* Sometimes both the sound and the spelling are the same. Only from context can the speller differentiate, for example, between the different meanings of the word *bow:* to bend the body from the waist, an instrument used to shoot an arrow, or a piece of ribbon. *Fair* can be a description of equality, a comment about the weather, or a gathering of people to display their wares.

The English language is a combination of both phonological (sound) and morphological (form) elements. It is not arbitrary. The person well acquainted with his or her language can attempt first to sound out a new word, and where phonetic analysis falters, morphological analysis can fill the gaps. In this way the linguistic competency of the student can help fill in the necessary letters. At the basic level, students know the regular sound/symbol system of words that both fit into a regular pattern and can be spelled readily. At this level, patterns of sound/letter combinations such as *met, let, pet, set* can be learned and extended to produce any number of words, or syllables of multisyllable words. At a more advanced level, however, although such words as *read, thread, lead, tread,* and *spread,* can be grouped together, it now becomes necessary for the student to visualize the word, as the regular phonetic patterns of words do not apply consistently.

The misconception that words can be "sounded out" has probably contributed to more poor spellers than any other factor. Even in sounding out such simple words as those just listed (*thread, lead,* etc.) the child must know the meaning of the word. *Thread* is uncomplicated. Even though it has at least two meanings (as a noun and as a verb), the word is pronounced and spelled similarly in both instances. But *lead* can be confusing. It can be spelled in two ways (*led, lead*) depending on how it is used in context, and pronounced in two ways (rhyming with *fed* or *feed*), depending on the context. The English language is clearly not phonetic; a simple sound/symbol correspondence is often not possible.

Carol Chomsky (1972) and others who study the phonology of the English language point out that there is, however, much greater regularity than the casual observer recognizes. Chomsky found that the conventional spelling of words in English corresponds closely to an underlying abstract level or representation within the sound system of the language. It is, for instance, the vowel sounds that are frequently misspelled. Vowel sounds are usually identified according to the stress placement of the vowel, and in other instances according to what is called "vowel reduction," which results in the "schwa" sound. An example of this would be the word *courage.* If attempted by itself, the schwa (unstressed mid-central) vowel (spelled with an *a* in this case) could be almost any vowel, but if the word is studied in combination with other words having the same root, the vowel becomes clear: *courageous.*

Consonants are subject to the same type of analysis. With such a system, words like *medicine* and *medicate* could be more readily understood and correctly spelled. In addition to the phonological (sound) elements that can be understood from a morphological (form) and lexical (base word) analysis, an understanding of such elements as root words, prefixes, suffixes, accent, and syllabication can help the speller develop greater facility with the written word. For example, although the sound of the final phoneme of *washed* is *t,* knowledge of verb endings make it clear to the speller that the past tense usually ends in *ed.*

In Chapter 8 we defined language as existing on two levels, the oral and the graphic (Figure 8-2). Since spelling is a written task, it occurs at the graphic level; that is, the person is required to write the word to be spelled. In order to produce a graphic symbol, the student must also be able to identify the graphic symbol; that is, he or she must be able to read the word. Spelling, then, can only be learned in conjunction with, or subsequent to, learning to read.

Spelling as a Visual Skill

Spelling a word requires that the proper sequence of letters be produced. The student needs to recall or think about the graphic symbol for each of those letters and then recite their names aloud. Or, he must picture the proper combination of letters, and produce them on paper with pencil or pen. In either case, the child must visualize the word as it will finally be written. Many of us have had experience with a child who has memorized a spelling list to perfection the evening before a test, but who has entirely forgotten all the words the next day. We conjecture that this occurs because of two circumstances. The first is that the words were memorized as a sequence of sounds, by the letter names, but not as a blend of sounds. In other words, the act of oral spelling requires that the word be analyzed into separate sounds and the sequence memorized. At this point the child is relying on his auditory memory, a skill that may be poor. Since the memory is of a sequence of separate letters, the child must rely on the number of letters he can remember, rather than generalizing them into a whole.

Most good spellers remember the spelling of a word by writing it. When the speller cannot remember the exact spelling, he will write it several ways and choose the one that *looks* the best. This is the reverse of the oral process. The letters are being synthesized into a whole, and the student is being asked to remember the general configuration of the word to be spelled. Since the two processes are dissimilar, one method cannot be used to learn how to do the other.

Spelling as a Motor Skill

The third component in analyzing our definition is the fact that the ability to write is required in order to spell on paper. If the student is to produce the proper sequence of letters, he or she must be able to produce the word as it is mentally pictured. He must have either the necessary motor ability or the mechanical means, such as a typewriter, to produce the letters. A child with motor difficulties is busy trying to remember how to form the letters; he is often then not able to devote the necessary energy to visualizing how the word is sequenced as a whole.

Motor skill completes the list of necessary elements. In summary, we see that in order to spell the child must be able to:

1. Understand the word to be spelled as a meaningful word.
2. Read the word.
3. Visualize the word.
4. Have the ability to write the letters and the word.

If any individual or combination of these elements is poorly developed, the student will encounter difficulty in spelling. The degree of disability is determined by the severity of the limitation in the four areas.

Strategies for Assessing Spelling Skills

The assessment of spelling skills is usually undertaken for the following purposes:

1. Placement in the appropriate book or instructional materials
2. Analysis of problem areas in order to plan appropriate remedial instruction
3. Ongoing measure of the progress made as a result of instruction.

Placement The question of class placement in spelling is rarely considered by the classroom teacher. As a rule, performance in spelling will not affect whether the student will be promoted or retained, and deficiency in spelling alone is not usually considered cause for referral for special services. Instead, the general practice is for the teacher to follow one of two courses of action. Some teachers will assign the same spelling list to all students in the class and a few children will simply receive a poor score on this list week after week. Most spelling series have a review lesson after every six or eight weeks so the student has an opportunity to review the words missed on the weekly tests. The review lesson, however, presents a formidable number of words and may overwhelm the poor student. The second practice is to assign only a limited number of words to the poor speller, thereby enabling him to experience some success each week. Of the two, the last method is preferable, since it provides an opportunity for positive reinforcement, and reduces the possibility of complete failure.

In both approaches, words are generally drawn from the spelling book used by all children in the class, the only modification being a reduction in the number of words to be learned. Most classes have a modest range of workbooks, so that a student in a typical fifth grade class may be assigned words from a fourth or even a third grade speller. Spelling tests are used primarily for the purpose of determining the level of book from which the spelling lesson will be taken. This is a quick procedure that takes only a few minutes. The objective is to obtain a grade level for instructional purposes.

A more desirable method of determining placement is to develop a word list related to the reading and other lessons in which the student is involved. In this procedure the words selected for study are the words used in written and spoken language; the words included in the spelling lessons are closely connected to the words the student needs to write.

Analysis of problem areas for instructional purposes A detailed analysis of the child's spelling errors is made in order to define areas of need and to determine an instructional approach. This error analysis provides, in part, the data base of a comprehensive diagnostic evaluation of a child. Information recorded in this fashion forms the basis for developing instructional strategies, and aids in developing performance objectives. Information gleaned from informal measures is at the heart of a good spelling instruction.

If a screening is needed to determine grade level or to document that a child has a spelling problem, a quick test, such as the diagnostic spelling test in Figure 9-1 is entirely satisfactory. There is no need to overdiagnose. To plan a specific remedial program, however, a more extensive sample is necessary. Such a sample requires at least 100 words (Spache, 1976). These words need to be drawn from a comprehensive spelling list rather than collected from 100 words in the student's writing. The latter is likely to result in important information being omitted, since a student normally avoids using words he cannot spell.

The teacher dictates a list of words for the student to write, assuring him that the results will be used to develop a spelling program, and not to grade. An example of the list that may be used is presented in Figure 9-2. This list, taken from Spache (1976), contains words in which only one error is likely to occur. The most likely error appears immediately after the correct spelling, although other errors are possible.

Figure 9-3 provides a matrix on which errors can be recorded and analyzed. An analysis of individual errors gives specific information; a matrix is a format that highlights areas of general difficulty. Errors are tallied on the matrix according to the skill areas required in spelling. Each error is recorded only once, and in the case of several possible explanations the *most likely* should be chosen. Computation of the percentage scores for all cells of the matrix is necessary for careful analysis. A cal-

Figure 9-1.
Diagnostic Spelling Test

Directions: Dictate the following list of eighty words, first alone, put in a sentence, and again alone. The words are listed by grade level, ten words to each level. The first group is for grade 1, the second for grade 2, etc. Dictate until six consecutive errors are made at any one level. The level on which a student misspells two or more words is considered the student's spelling instructional level.

1. a
2. the
3. go
4. it
5. not
6. see
7. will
8. please
9. he
10. like
11. about
12. brother
13. chair
14. lion
15. name
16. next
17. room
18. were
19. where
20. your
21. thought
22. basket
23. knew
24. could
25. string
26. farther
27. over
28. please
29. space
30. piece
31. figure
32. until
33. hungry
34. people
35. saving
36. medicine
37. friend
38. cloth
39. thin
40. watch
41. umbrella
42. position
43. kitchen
44. whether
45. author
46. smoothly
47. niece
48. unite
49. babies
50. tenth
51. latter
52. monument
53. replied
54. revenge
55. ashamed
56. difference
57. battery
58. advertise
59. diamond
60. orphan
61. knowledge
62. reign
63. industrious
64. league
65. familiar
66. museum
67. gossip
68. acquaintance
69. stationary
70. caution
71. bachelor
72. presence
73. dawn
74. spherical
75. establishment
76. variety
77. leisure
78. disgusting
79. appropriate
80. essay

Figure 9-2.
Spelling Errors Test for Grades 2 to 8

Grades 2 to 4

1. bite–bit
2. and–an
3. arrow–arow
4. almost–allmost
5. dark–darck
6. ankle–ankel
7. bead–beed
8. bush–buch
9. flies–flys
10. bare–bear
11. bags–bogs
12. bottom–botton
13. boxes–boxs
14. bridge–brige
15. asleep–aslep
16. also–allso
17. negro–negrow
18. ate–aet
19. creep–creap
20. buzz–buss

SOURCE: G. D. Spache, *Diagnosing and Correcting Reading Disabilities* (Boston: Allyn and Bacon, 1976), pp. 240–244.

21. bull–bool
22. four–for
23. pail–pale
24. bump–bunp
25. fasten–fasen
26. farther–father
27. bigger–biger
28. later–latter
29. plank–planck
30. born–bron

31. cotton–cotten
32. cave–kave
33. gain–gane
34. here–hear
35. did–ded
36. him–hin
37. breast–brest
38. hatch–hach
39. cutting–cuting
40. lose–loose

41. rent–reant
42. giant–gaint
43. caught–cought
44. fishing–fiching
45. laughing–lafing
46. buy–by
47. flew–flow
48. am–an
49. comes–coms
50. bound–bond

51. broom–brom
52. melon–mellon
53. so–sow
54. drum–durm
55. dollars–dollers
56. lace–lase
57. looked–lookt
58. deer–dear
59. he–hi
60. jumping–junping

61. cookies–cookes
62. march–mach
63. dropped–droped
64. until–untill
65. books–bookes
66. girl–gril
67. hall–holl
68. mice–mise
69. paw–por
70. eight–ate

71. her–har
72. rich–rick
73. match–mach
74. crack–crak
75. glass–glas
76. welcome–wellcome
77. coming–comeing
78. field–feild
79. ton–tun
80. often–offen

81. though–thow
82. bake–back
83. hoe–how
84. lamp–lanp
85. alone–alon
86. starve–stave
87. hammer–hamer
88. lily–lilly
89. hop–hope
90. nickel–nickle

91. obey–obay
92. pony–pone
93. babies–babys
94. meat–meet
95. hot–hat
96. room–roon
97. awhile–awile
98. street–steet
99. begged–beged
100. hoped–hopped

101. an–and
102. patch–pacth
103. cellar–celler
104. recite–resite
105. parties–partys
106. rake–rack
107. let–lat
108. seem–seen
109. cracker–craker
110. studying–studing

111. bonnet–bonet
112. already–allready
113. grab–grabe
114. piece–peice
115. heap–heep
116. slice–slise
117. aim–ame
118. pear–pair
119. red–rad
120. bedroom–bedroon

Grades 5 and 6

1. basement–basment
2. barley–barly
3. address–addres, adress
4. already–allready
5. fever–feaver
6. angel–angle
7. creek–creak
8. advice–advise
9. accept–except
10. birth–berth
11. hoe–how
12. bedroom–bedroon
13. beast–best
14. capture–capure
15. arrest–arest
16. chose–choose
17. fled–flead
18. chief–cheif
19. beef–beaf
20. base–bace
21. compare–compair
22. deer–dear
23. reward–reword
24. improved–enproved
25. cleaning–clening
26. governor–govenor
27. account–acount
28. chosen–choosen
29. chest–cheast
30. candle–candel

(continued)

Figure 9-2 continued

31. celebrate–celabrate
32. advice–advise
33. mere–mear
34. eight–ate
35. stump–stomp
36. kindergarten–kindargarden
37. wrist–rist
38. carrying–carring
39. appear–apear
40. handful–handfull

41. export–exsport
42. freight–frieght
43. harbor–harber
44. crash–crach
45. parties–partys
46. fare–fair
47. flew–flow
48. themselves–themselfs
49. earnest–ernest
50. forward–foward

51. approve–aprove
52. helpful–helpfull
53. forty–fourty
54. giant–gaint
55. beggar–begger
56. decided–desided
57. aid–ade
58. fought–fort
59. tip–tep
60. thinking–thinging

61. hope–hop
62. government–goverment
63. allow–alow
64. hoped–hopped
65. tar–tare
66. deceive–decieve
67. destroy–distroy
68. blaze–blase
69. claim–clame
70. due–dew

71. cost–cast
72. jumping–junping
73. knitting–nitting
74. dodge–doge
75. canned–caned
76. proper–propper
77. using–useing
78. hose–hoes
79. honor–honer
80. deuce–deuse

81. aim–ame
82. groan–grown
83. pump–pomp
84. import–inport
85. bruise–bruse
86. pumpkin–punkin
87. beginning–begining
88. dining–dinning
89. closing–closeing
90. niece–neice

91. conductor–conducter
92. practice–practise
93. babies–babys
94. herd–heard
95. slip–slep
96. gross–grose
97. buying–bying
98. quarter–quater
99. finally–finaly
100. fearful–fearfull

101. ninth–nineth
102. puzzle–puzzel
103. earliest–earlyest
104. prize–prise
105. underwear–underware
106. loan–lone
107. stir–ster
108. attack–attach
109. failed–faled
110. stitch–stich

111. bluff–bluf
112. lining–linning
113. giving–giveing
114. shield–sheild
115. fragrant–fragrent
116. reduce–reduse
117. phone–fone
118. loss–lose
119. step–stap
120. lamp–lanp

Grades 7 and 8

1. completely–completly
2. adjust–ajust
3. accommodate–accomodate
4. administration–addministration
5. construction–construcktion
6. angle–angel
7. ballot–ballet
8. response–responce
9. accepted–excepted
10. pause–paws
11. stump–stomp
12. congratulate–congradulate
13. condemn–condem
14. boundary–boundry
15. afford–aford
16. amendment–ammendment
17. complexion–complextion
18. chapel–chaple
19. accordance–accordence
20. selected–celected
21. companies–companys
22. principle–principal
23. reward–reword
24. gratitude–graditude
25. acquire–acuire
26. breadth–breath
27. addressed–adressed
28. control–controll
29. completed–compleated
30. Christian–Christain
31. basis–bases
32. type–tipe
33. grateful–greatful
34. choir–quire
35. cost–cast
36. attack–attach
37. affectionately–affectionatly
38. badge–bage
39. affair–afair
40. compel–compell
41. exist–exsist
42. guardian–guardain
43. compliment–complement
44. absence–absense
45. hereafter–hearafter
46. clause–claws
47. flew–flow
48. gross–grose
49. approach–approch
50. delicious–delicous
51. affection–afection
52. arise–arrise
53. regret–regreat
54. label–lable
55. affect–effect
56. anticipate–antisipate
57. duties–dutys
58. coarse–course
59. Sabbath–Sabboth
60. import–inport

(continued)

Figure 9-2 continued

61. autumn–autum
62. official–offical
63. connect–conect
64. arouse–arrouse
65. owing–oweing
66. receiving–recieving
67. celebration–celabration
68. underwear–underware
69. concern–consern
70. council–counsel

71. stir–ster
72. improved–inproved
73. arrangement–arrangment
74. substitute–subsitute
75. correct–corect
76. limited–limitted
77. pleasing–pleaseing
78. ruffle–ruffel
79. benefit–benifit
80. concert–consert

81. compare–compair
82. capitol–capital
83. pump–pomp
84. thinking–thinging
85. clothe–cloth
86. quantity–quanity
87. commission–commision
88. occasion–occassion
89. refer–refere
90. seize–sieze

91. calendar–calender
92. hence–hense
93. niece–neice
94. border–boarder
95. slip–slep
96. themselves–themselfs
97. cocoa–coco
98. temptation–temtation
99. communicate–comunicate
100. rebel–rebell

101. regard–reguard
102. siege–seige
103. applied–applyed
104. extension–extention
105. claim–clame
106. desert–dessert
107. fell–fill
108. kindergarten–kindergarden
109. courtesy–curtesy
110. appropriate–appropiate

111. disappoint–disapoint
112. remit–remitt
113. remembrance–rememberance
114. villain–villian
115. approval–approvel
116. discussed–discusted
117. phone–fone
118. formerly–formally
119. hoe–how
120. line–lime

---

culator can help the teacher make the necessary computations. Although this is a time-consuming task, the insight gained is worth the effort.

A score of 25 percent or less on any cell of the matrix indicates that the area is only of minor concern. The student is able to function at a minimal level at least, and spelling instruction to correct those problems may be conducted as incidental information during reading or language instruction. Areas where the score is 26 percent or more indicate that the

Figure 9-3.
Spelling Error Analysis Matrix

Skill	Substitutions	Omissions	Additions	Sequencing	Total
Phonetic ability					$T =$
	$t =$ $\frac{t}{T} =$ %	$t =$ $\frac{t}{T} =$ %	$t =$ $\frac{t}{T} =$ %	$t =$ $\frac{t}{T} =$ %	$\frac{T}{RS} =$ %
Visualization					$T =$
	$t =$ $\frac{t}{T} =$ %	$t =$ $\frac{t}{T} =$ %	$t =$ $\frac{t}{T} =$ %	$t =$ $\frac{t}{T} =$ %	$\frac{T}{RS} =$ %
Linguistic performance					$T =$
	$t =$ $\frac{t}{T} =$ %	$t =$ $\frac{t}{T} =$ %	$t =$ $\frac{t}{T} =$ %	$t =$ $\frac{t}{T} =$ %	$\frac{T}{RS} =$ %
Total	$T =$ $\frac{T}{RS} =$ %	$T =$ $\frac{T}{RS} =$ %	$T =$ $\frac{T}{RS} =$ %	$T =$ $\frac{T}{RS} =$ %	$T = T = T = RS$ $RS =$

$$\frac{\textit{Total Errors (TE)}}{\textit{Words Given (W)}} = \textit{Error Rate (ER)}$$

$ER =$

SOURCE: Developed by Arlee S. Maier. Copyright © 1980 by Arlee S. Maier.

child is more seriously disabled and that instruction in curriculum areas requiring writing will be seriously hampered and should be avoided for a while.

The use of the matrix allows the teacher to analyze the area of difficulty in the skill areas of phonetic ability, visualization, and linguistic performance, and by the type of error such as substitutions, omissions, additions, and sequencing. Errors are tallied on the matrix according to these definitions:

	DEFINITIONS	EXAMPLE	
PHONETIC ABILITY		HEARD	WRITTEN
PS	Substitutions: placing another sound or syllable in place of the sound in the word	match nation	mach nashun
PO	Omissions: leaving out a sound or syllable from the word	grateful temperature	graful tempature
PA	Additions: Adding a sound or syllable to the original	purchase importance	purchasing importantance
PSe	Sequencing: putting sounds or syllables in the wrong order	animal elephant	aminal efelant
VISUALIZATION		HEARD	WRITTEN
VS	Substitutions: substitution of a vowel or consonant for those in the given word	him chapel	hin chaple
VO	Omissions: leaving out a vowel, or consonant, or syllable from those in the given word	allow beginning	alow begining

	DEFINITIONS	EXAMPLE	
PHONETIC ABILITY		HEARD	WRITTEN
VA	Additions: adding a vowel, consonant, or syllable to those in the given word	welcome fragrant	wellcome fragerant
VSe	Sequencing: putting letters or syllables in the wrong order	guardian pilot	guardain pliot
LINGUISTIC PERFORMANCE		HEARD	WRITTEN
LS	Substitution: substitution of a word for another having somewhat the same meaning	ring house	bell home
	Substitution: substituting another word due to different language structure (teacher judgment)	came ate	come et
	Substitution: substitution of a completely different word	pear polish	pair collage
LO	Omissions: omitting word endings or prefixes, suffixes	pushed unhelpful	pusht helpful
LA	Additions: adding endings, prefixes, suffixes	cry forget	crys forgetting
LSe	Sequencing: reversing syllables	discussed disappoint	discusted dispapoint

Figure 9-4.
Sample Analysis of Spelling Errors

Skill	Substitutions	Omissions	Additions	Sequencing	Total
Phonetic ability	𝍸 |||	𝍸	|	𝍸	$T = 19$
	$t = 8$ $\frac{t}{T} = 42$ %	$t = 5$ $\frac{t}{T} = 26$ %	$t = 1$ $\frac{t}{T} = 5$ %	$t = 5$ $\frac{t}{T} = 26$ %	$\frac{T}{RS} = 28$ %
Visualization	𝍸 |||	||	𝍸 𝍸 ||	||||	$T = 26$
	$t = 8$ $\frac{t}{T} = 29$ %	$t = 2$ $\frac{t}{T} = 7$ %	$t = 12$ $\frac{t}{T} = 43$ %	$t = 4$ $\frac{t}{T} = 14$ %	$\frac{T}{RS} = 42$ %
Linguistic performance	𝍸 𝍸 𝍸 𝍸				$T = 20$
	$t = 20$ $\frac{t}{T} = 100$ %	$t =$ $\frac{t}{T} = 0$ %	$t =$ $\frac{t}{T} = 0$ %	$t =$ $\frac{t}{T} = 0$ %	$\frac{T}{RS} = 30$ %
Total	$T = 36$ $\frac{T}{RS} = 55$ %	$T = 7$ $\frac{T}{RS} = 10$ %	$T = 13$ $\frac{T}{RS} = 19$ %	$T = 9$ $\frac{T}{RS} = 13$ %	$T = T = T = RS$ $RS = 67$

$$\frac{\text{Total Errors (TE)}}{\text{Words Given (W)}} = \text{Error Rate (ER)}$$

$ER = 56\%$

Table 9-1 illustrates the use of error analysis. An example of the entire sample is not included here. Figure 9-4 is the matrix developed from the completed sample.

Table 9-1.
Sample Error Analysis of a Student's Spelling (Grades 5 and 6)

5. fevery	PA	Addition of additional vowel sound at end of word
	(VA)	Possible addition of letter due to faulty visual memory
6. angle	PS	Substitution of *g* for *k* sound
9. actseip	PA	Addition of first *t*
	PO	Omission of *t* sound at end
	VA	Addition of extra vowel
14. captcher	PS	Poor visual recall, substitution of phonic approximation
17. flead	VA	Poor visual recall, substitution of *ea* for *e*
18. chife	VSe	Poor visual recall, letters in wrong sequence
26. compaire	VS	Poor visual recall, confusion as to which rule to apply
32. advice	VA	Poor visual recall, additional *d*
33. mineir	LS	Probably unknown word; poor phonic attack
36. kidengarden	PO	Omission of first *n* phoneme
	PS	Substitution of *n* for *r*
	(PSc)	Possible sequence difficulty
41. exspot	PO	Omission of *r*
42. fraient	(LS)	Possibly unknown word
	VO	Poor visual recall
44. casrh	VSe	Poor visual recall, wrong sequence
	PSe	Reversed auditory sequence
45. prettys	LS	Substitution of another word
48. themself	PO	Omission of final *s*
	(LS)	Possible misunderstood word
53. fourtt	LS	Probably misunderstood word for *fourth*
	PO	Omitted final sound *y*
54. gaint	PSe	Poor auditory sequence
	(VSe)	Poor visual recall for sequence

(continued)

Table 9-1 *continued*

68. blazize	(LS)	Possibly misunderstood word
	PA	Added extra phoneme
73. nemmenting	LS	Misunderstood word
	(PSe)	Poor auditory sequence
77. useing	VA	Poor visual recall, extra *e*
78. huose	VS	Poor visual recall, extra *u*
86. pumkien	VO	Poor visual recall, omitted *p*
	VA	Poor visual recall, extra *e*
87. begiaining	PSe	Poor auditory sequence
88. dinneing	VA	Poor visual recall, extra *n* and *e*
90. neace	VS	Poor visual recall, substituted *ea* for ie
98. quaiter	LS	Probably misunderstood word
	PO	Omitted *r* sound
99. finelly	VS	Poor visual recall, substituted *e* for *a*
100. freially	LS	Probably misunderstood word, perseverated on previous word
103. orlistesy	LS	Probably misunderstood word
	PSe	Poor auditory sequence
104. prizzizes	VA	Poor visual recall, addition of extra letters
	(LS)	May have misunderstood word
113. givving	VA	Poor visual recall, additional letters
114. sheald	VS	Poor visual recall, substitutes *ea* for *ie*
115. fragreat	PO	Poor auditory recall, omitted *n* phoneme

The sample indicates that this child's spelling exceeds the 50 percent level for functional use, so that one can conclude that it presents a serious hindrance to the development of written language.

Further analysis indicates the possibility that this student frequently (30 percent of the time) misunderstands the words to be spelled. His greatest difficulty is in the visual areas, particularly in recall and in the sequencing of letters. While phonetics is an area of relative strength, it, too, is close to the 30 percent level and does not suggest a clear avenue for remedial teaching, particularly since linguistic skills are not strong.

In addition, there is some indication that this student does not "shift gears" readily. There is one clear bit of evidence of perseveration (fixating on a prior activity)—example 100—and one or two other possible examples—notably examples 103 and 104.

Based on this analysis, several implications for instruction can be made:

1. Emphasis should be on word meaning. No words that are not clearly understood by the child should be included in spelling.
2. Words chosen for spelling should come from the child's written work.
3. A multimodal approach to learning may be most successful. The *trace—say—write* method should be used.
4. Emphasis should be placed on visualization, that is, closing the eyes and "seeing" the word, along with writing the word from memory. Proofreading should be employed as a monitoring device; this should also help to increase visualization.

Ongoing measure of instructional gains After the error analysis has been completed, it is likely that a pattern will emerge, indicating those areas in which the child has the greatest difficulty, and those areas in which he is strongest. Based on the assumption that a child will learn more efficiently and rapidly if his natural inclinations are encouraged, a spelling program should be developed that takes into account the child's strengths and avoids, initially at least, words he is likely to confuse. Recalling Piaget's principle of introducing only *moderately* novel experiences, only one or two words that touch on a problem area should be introduced at a time. Spelling words chosen from a variety of sources are entered in the "Word" column on the spelling word chart (Figure 9-5). Success with a word is recorded by placing the date at the appropriate level: "Recognition," "Recall," "Use in Writing" or "It's Mine!" Recognition is tested by flashcard or by a correct choice made from a list of similar words on two separate occasions, at least one day apart. Recall involves writing the word from dictation on three separate occasions, at least one day apart. The last, and most important phase is use. To successfully complete this phase, the student must have used the word in classroom activities on three separate occasions. Finally, a colored sticker or dot is place on "Mine" at the end of the line to indicate that the child has completed RRUM; Recognize, Recall, Use, It's Mine!

The spelling word chart is an example of a criterion measure or recording device that allows ongoing assessment. It is particularly suited for self-recording by the student. Whenever possible, the teacher needs to select a recording procedure that both monitors growth and provides a current assessment of the skill. In this way, more elaborate diagnostic procedures such as error analysis will be required only infrequently.

Figure 9-5.
Spelling Word Chart (RRUM)

Name ______________________

Word	Recognize			Recall			Use in Writing			It's Mine!
	Date	Date	Date	Date	Date	Date	Date	Date	Date	

HANDWRITING

In Chapter 8 we discussed oral and written language, primarily as they are related to content. In this section consideration is given to the *form* of written language, that is, the technical factors involved with producing language. Three areas need to be assessed: handwriting, capitalization and punctuation, and organization or format.

The Nature of Handwriting

Historically, handwriting, or penmanship, was a means of identifying the educated or cultured person in society. Before the introduction of the printing press all manuscripts were done by hand, and even after the invention of the typewriter most correspondence and formal reports were handwritten. As late as 1920, "good form" required handwritten letters. As a result, great emphasis was placed on handwriting in school. Until shortly before World War II, handwriting was a major curriculum area, and children spent anywhere from twenty minutes to an hour each day perfecting this important skill. Great emphasis was placed on a uniform product, and handwriting scales, against which each child's product could be compared, were provided for each grade level. Early scales were very complex (Zaner-Bloser, 1968), particularly the capital letters. Current handwriting texts employ a simplified version, but capital letters are still quite formal.

With the increased use of the typewriter for business, the importance of handwriting diminished. At the same time, classes were introduced to teach typewriting. In recent years less emphasis has been placed on the necessity for children to develop uniform production. Legibility is the main criterion, and children are freer to develop greater individuality.

Simultaneous with the decline in standards in handwriting was the introduction of manuscript printing for children in the primary grades. The rationale for this was that it would be easier for children to make the transfer from printed letters, as found in books, to cursive handwriting by means of an intermediate handwriting system that more closely approximated print, as well as allowing for the relatively less developed motor skills of the young child. While the former may be true, the latter often is not, and it is particularly the child with poor motor skills who has the most difficulty with manuscript printing as well as cursive writing.

A Task Analysis of Handwriting

Handwriting is an automatic motor skill involving finger dexterity, motor-planning, and visual-motor coordination. Unlike spelling, handwriting is primarily a kinesthetic skill. The writer does not visualize the formation of each letter; the hand seems to reproduce it automatically. Only in the learning stage is the child aware of the details of the letters. As skill develops, this process becomes automatic and the student is free to concentrate on spelling or on the message being written. For this reason early handwriting instruction begins with large letters, to better provide kinesthetic input to the brain.

Finger dexterity Finger dexterity requires that the child have an adequate pincer grasp to hold the pencil, and proper coordination to balance it between thumb and finger at the proper angle in order to make an impression on the paper.

Motor-planning Motor-planning requires that the child learn the sequence of motor activities made by the fingers and hand to produce the letters. It involves good directionality, knowing which way to form the round letters (counterclockwise), and which way to form the loops on tall letters or letters that drop below the line (*l, j, t*). The amount of pressure to place on the pencil to produce a satisfactory image (not too light or too dark) and to avoid breaking the pencil point is also a motor-planning (tactile) skill. According to Piaget's principle of *active* learning, this skill can be developed only through practice. For the child who has directionality or motor-planning difficulties, cursive writing might be better since it allows for fewer mistakes, as the child keeps the pencil on the paper and need not decide which way to proceed with each new letter.

Visual-motor coordination The visual-motor coordination required for handwriting involves monitoring the letters to see that they correspond with the image in memory. It also involves seeing that the letters are placed on the line, that proper spaces are left between letters and words, and that, when the end of a line is approaching, the correct decision is made as to whether to complete the word, hyphenate it, or move to the next line. This skill requires spatial ability and judgment.

These three skills are also part of the assessment of sensorimotor factors. If assessment of the child in that analysis indicates that these skills are poor, it is to be expected that handwriting will be poor. If the problem is severe, if there seems to be a physical basis for the problem, or, as in the case of an adolescent, if repeated remedial activities in handwriting have not produced much improvement, then typewriting may be indicated in order to allow written language expression to develop.

Assessing Handwriting

Screening handwriting performance is done simply. If the handwriting is legible and easily read, further evaluation is usually not necessary. In some instances it is only the capital letters that are difficult for the child, and a simplified handwriting system (Figure 9-6) can be introduced.

If the student's handwriting is a serious handicap to performance in school, Figure 9-7 will help the teacher make an error analysis. Each section should be evaluated diagnostically by the teacher so that proper remedial instruction or compensatory techniques can be introduced. If the total score on the analysis is over 83, written performance is probably being seriously hampered, and alternative ways of allowing the student to demonstrate language will need to be developed until writing performance is improved.

Figure 9-6.
A Simplified Alphabet: Printed Capitals and Cursive Lower Case

ABCDEFGHIJ
KLMNOPQRS
TUVWXYZ

abcdefghi
jklmnopqr
stuvwxyz

Figure 9-7.
Analysis of Handwriting Errors

Directions: Analysis of handwriting should be made on a sample of the student's written work, not from a carefully produced sample. Evaluate each task and mark in the appropriate column. Score each task "satisfactory" (1) or "unsatisfactory" (2).

I. Letter formation

A. Capitals (score each letter 1 or 2)

A ____	G ____	M ____	S ____	Y ____
B ____	H ____	N ____	T ____	Z ____
C ____	I ____	O ____	U ____	
D ____	J ____	P ____	V ____	
E ____	K ____	Q ____	W ____	
F ____	L ____	R ____	X ____	

Total ____

B. Lowercase (score by groups)	Score (1 or 2)
1. Round letters	
a. Counterclockwise *a, c, d, g, o, q*	____
b. Clockwise *k, p*	____
2. Looped letters	
a. Above line *b, d, e, f, h, k, l*	____
b. Below line *f, g, j, p, q, y*	____
3. Retraced letters *i, u, t, u, w, y*	____
4. Humped letters *h, m, n, v, x, z*	____
5. Others *r, s, b*	____

C. Numerals (score each number 1 or 2)

1 _____	4 _____	7 _____	10–20 _____
2 _____	5 _____	8 _____	21–99 _____
3 _____	6 _____	9 _____	100–1,000 _____
			Total _____

II. Spatial relationships

	Score (1 or 2)
A. Alignment (letters on line)	_____
B. Uniform slant	_____
C. Size of letters	
1. To each other	_____
2. To available space	_____
D. Space between letters	_____
E. Space between words	_____
F. Anticipation of end of line (hyphenates, moves to next line)	_____
Total	_____

III. Rate of writing (letters per minute)

Score (1 or 2)

Grade 1: 20
2: 30
3: 35
4: 45
5: 55
6: 65
7 and above: 75 _____

Scoring

	Satisfactory	*Questionable*	*Poor*
I. Letter formation			
A. Capitals	26	39	40+
B. Lowercase	7	10	11+
C. Numerals	12	18	19+
II. *Spatial relationships*	7	10	11+
III. *Rate of writing*	1	2	6

Capitalization and Punctuation

Capitalization is necessary to help delineate the beginning of thought patterns and to help convey meaning in written language. Punctuation is the graphic correspondence to the inflection and stress used in spoken language. Both are important to reading and writing with full comprehension and fluency. The first part of the checklist in Figure 9-8 will provide the teacher with a method of informally assessing the student's use of these skills. While the sophisticated writer has a thorough knowledge of capitalization and punctuation, the student who is not anticipating going to college or entering the clerical field may not need to have functional use of the more sophisticated levels of usage. Each section of the checklist has been divided into a basic level and an advanced level to permit the teacher to make this determination.

Figure 9-8.
Analysis of Punctuation and Format

Directions: Score each item "satisfactory" (1) or "unsatisfactory" (2).

I. Capitalization
   A. Basic level
      1. First word of a sentence ______
      2. The word I ______
      3. Proper nouns; words used as proper nouns (George, Georgian, Spain, Spanish) ______
      4. Names of peoples, races, tribes, languages (Chinese, Caucasian, Iroquois, Latin) ______
      5. Titles (Queen Elizabeth, President Washington, Senator Johnson) ______
      6. Names of government bodies or documents (The World Bank, The Constitution of the United States) ______
      7. Holidays, months of the year, days of the week ______
      8. Names of planets, specific plants, geographic entities (Saturn, Rose, Asia—not sun, earth, moon) ______
      9. Titles of books, plays, magazines (except prepositions) (The Taming of the Shrew, Crime and Punishment) ______
   B. Advanced level
      1. First line of verse ______
      2. Names for the Bible and parts of it, nouns that refer to the Deity (Scriptures, Old Testament, Supreme Being) ______

SOURCE: *Webster's New Collegiate Dictionary,* 8th ed. (Springfield, Mass.: G. & C. Merriam, Co., 1979).

3. Names of various treaties, acts, period, important events (Versailles Treaty, the Crusades, Prehistoric age) ________
4. General geographic terms that are part of a specific name (San Francisco Bay, Canal Boulevard, Middle West) ________
5. General political terms that are part of a specific name (Holy Roman Empire, State of Ohio, the Third Republic) ________
6. Names of registered trademarks (Coca-Cola, Chevrolet) ________

II. Punctuation
- A. Basic level
  1. Period
     a. End of sentence ________
     b. After an abbreviation ________
     c. Between dollars and cents, before a decimal ________
     d. After numbers or letters preceding a list ________
  2. Comma
     a. To separate independent phrases joined by a coordinating conjunction ________
     b. To separate words in a list ________
     c. Between cities and states, date and year ________
     d. To separate a quotation from the rest of the sentence ________
     e. After the salutation and closing in a letter ________
     f. After *yes* or *no* when it begins a sentence ________
     g. In numbers to separate hundreds, thousands, and millions ________
  3. Question mark
     a. At the end of a question ________
     b. After a question that is part of a quotation ________
  4. Colon
     a. To indicate that a list will follow ________
     b. To separate the hour and minutes ________
  5. Exclamation point
     a. After an exclamation ________
  6. Quotation marks
     a. To indicate the exact words of a speaker ________
     b. To indicate the title of part of a book, a lecture, painting, or ship ________
  7. Apostrophe
     a. To indicate possession ________
     b. In a contraction ________
  8. Hyphen
     a. To separate syllables in a word at the end of a line ________
  9. Underline
     a. To indicate that the word or words are a book title ________

(continued)

Figure 9-8 continued

B. Advanced level
   1. Period
      a. After headings in outlines, lists, displays ______
      b. At end of line of verse ______
      c. To indicate intentional omission or interrupted sentence (So I told her . . . come on time.) ______
   2. Comma
      a. Words placed out of natural position (He came into the room and, after wiping his feet, sat down.) ______
      b. Before of in indicating residence or position (Senator John Boyd, of Indiana) ______
      c. To separate modifying phrases (In the first place, he will tell a story.) ______
      d. Inverted names in a bibliographic list (Holmes, Oliver Wendell) ______
      e. Separate two or more names or titles in succession (Carl Somers, Ph.D., M.D., President) ______
      f. After the name of a person when it introduces a quote ("John, come over here!") ______
   3. Question mark
      a. In parentheses at the end of a word, phrase, or date to indicate uncertainty (Omar Khayham (? – 1123?)) ______
   4. Semicolon
      a. To separate the clauses of compound sentences in the absence of a conjunction or if the clauses are oppositional (Make no terms; resist to the last.) ______
      b. Before an illustrative phrase (It was a good idea; for example, it worked on Friday.) ______
   5. Colon
      a. After the salutation in a business letter (Dear Sir:) ______
      b. To introduce a formal direct quote (Abbot said: The troops came directly from Paris.) ______
      c. To separate points of numerical ratios (24:31) ______
      d. Between chapter and verse in a biblical quote, or volume and page number in a bibliographic quote (Corinthians 13:4–13; *Journ. of Admin.*, 17:31–35) ______
   6. Dash
      a. To mark an abrupt change in the sense ("If you will listen, I will explain—but perhaps you do not care.") ______
      b. To indicate omission of letters or words (Mr. M—— of New York; yelling ——— loudly.) ______
      c. To indicate *to* in dates or places (1980–1983, Lisbon–New York) ______

7. Parentheses
   a. To set off a work or comment by way of explanation (That is the truth (enough for him to know).) ________
8. Quotation marks
   a. To indicate a quotation within a quotation ("I heard him say, 'Don't be late,' and then he closed the door.") ________
   b. To enclose technical terms (This is a "permanent press" shirt.) ________
9. Hyphen
   a. In a compound word when the second element is capitalized (pro-American) ________
   b. To indicate a relationship between words (one-to-one) ________
   c. In a compound word when the first element is *self* (self-inflicted) ________
   d. To avoid doubling a vowel if it will be confusing (anti-establishment) ________
10. Underline
   a. To indicate italics ________

III. Format
   A. Basic level
      1. Narrative writing
         a. Indenting paragraphs ________
         b. Quotations as separate paragraphs ________
         c. Titles ________
      2. Plays
         a. Dialogue ________
      3. Letters
         a. Personal
            (1) Date ________
            (2) Salutation ________
            (3) Body ________
            (4) Closing ________
         b. Business
            (1) Internal address ________
            (2) Addressing envelopes ________
      4. Study skills
         a. Heading ________
         b. Outlining ________
         c. Lists ________
         d. Reports
            (1) Introduction ________
            (2) Body ________
            (3) Summary ________
            (4) Conclusions ________

(continued)

Figure 9-8 continued

B. Advanced level ______
   1. Narrative writing
      a. Chapters ______
      b. Subtopics ______
   2. Plays
      a. Stage direction ______
      b. Set direction ______
   3. Poetry ______
   4. Letters
      a. Business
         (1) Requests ______
         (2) Invoices ______
         (3) Announcements ______
         (4) Invitations ______
   5. Study skills
      a. Reports
         (1) Note taking ______
         (2) Annotation ______
         (3) References/Bibliography ______
         (4) Scientific reports ______
         (5) Graphs ______
         (6) Tables ______

Organization and Format

The successful writer is able to adjust the format of his writing to the purpose for which the writing is performed. Certain conventions need to be observed by the student in organizing written material so that it is easily read by the writer or conforms to the rules observed in the business world. Creative writing is in paragraph form, but reports may be in outline, and letters either in friendly or business format. Addresses on envelopes, lists, invitations, tables, charts, diagrams, and so on, all require familiarity with formats, and communication is hindered if the student does not use them. The second part of Figure 9-8 is a list of the formats with which the student should be familiar. Those necessary for simple or general use are contained in the "basic level" sections, and those required for advanced academic or business use are listed in the "advanced level" sections. The teacher assesses the level of the student's performance on the basis of his or her understanding of the student's need.

Summary

Spelling is probably one of the most misunderstood subjects taught in school. Very little research that sheds any light on the question of why some people are good spellers and others are not has been conducted.

In this chapter a task analysis of spelling as a linguistic skill is made, showing that while many English words may not be phonetic, that is, may not be analyzed using the traditional "sounding out" method, there are phonological and morphological regularities that make the relationship of the letters to sounds understandable.

While many children study spelling orally, spelling is used in life primarily as a written skill. The writer most often relies on his or her visual memory of how the word should look in order to spell it correctly. It is suggested that the most common method of studying and the skill required for success in spelling do not complement one another, and that a method of learning emphasizing writing would be more satisfactory. Such an emphasis would also require the student to have the ability to write the letters and words correctly on paper.

A quick screening test is given to help the teacher place a child at the proper level of spelling study. A more thorough sample, using at least 100 words as recommended by Spache (1976), is given to help the teacher assess which areas in the task analysis—(1) phonetic, (2) visual, or (3) linguistic—are preventing the child from being successful in spelling. A method of error analysis is illustrated so that the teacher may identify the specific difficulty and plan a teaching strategy accordingly. Scores using a percentage of errors help the teacher identify if the problem warrants concern.

A criterion method (RRUM) that allows the student as well as the teacher to monitor progress in learning his own misspelled words is given. Watching his own progress helps motivate the student, and enables the teacher to keep a record showing the student's use of the words in written work.

The use of a pencil or pen to produce written letters and words requires fine finger dexterity, good motor-planning, and good hand-eye coordination. Each of these is discussed more thoroughly in Chapter 7. Handwriting samples can often be used to assess these abilities. This method of assessment requires that the teacher watch how the child produces the letters. Letters may look adequately formed, but they may be executed backwards or extremely slowly, indicating that the child is drawing rather than writing easily. Handwriting produced this way may be extremely fatiguing and frustrating for the child, and may trigger many behavioral problems that at first glance do not appear to be related.

For the teacher who wants to assess the quality of a student's handwriting, and the use of punctuation in written work, two scales are presented that help in recording this information. In addition, the format used in written work may need to be assessed. A section on this aspect of writing is included here since content is not the prime consideration. Teachers need to determine that a student is able to present information in acceptable format—for social or business use (letters, notes) or in study skills (note taking, report writing). The checklist provides a method whereby the progress an individual makes in learning these skills can be recorded as the skills are taught and mastered.

Bibliography

Barsch, Ray. . . . *and Sometimes Y.* Canoga Park, Calif.: Ray Barsch Center for Learning, 1974.

Chalfant, J. C., and Scheffelin, M. A. *Central Processing Dysfunctions in Children.* Bethesda, Md.: National Institute of Health, 1969.

Chomsky, Carol. "Reading, Writing, and Phonology." *Harvard Educational Review* 40 (1970): 287–309.

Chomsky, Carol. "Stages in Language Development and Reading Exposure." *Harvard Educational Review* 42 (1972): 1–33.

Cronbach, L. J., and Snow, R. E. *Individual Differences in Learning Ability as a Function of Instructional Variables.* U.S.D.E. Final Report, Contract number OEC-4-6-06129-1217. Stanford, Calif.: Stanford University Press, 1969.

Fernald, Grace. *Remedial Techniques in Basic School Subjects.* New York: McGraw-Hill, 1943.

Hanna, P. R.; Hodges, R. E.; and Hanna, J. S. *Spelling Structure and Strategies.* Boston: Houghton Mifflin, 1971.

Johnson, D. J., and Myklebust, H. R. *Learning Disabilities: Educational Principles and Practices.* New York: Grune and Stratton, 1967.

Markoff, A. M. *Teaching Low Achieving Children Reading, Spelling, and Handwriting.* Springfield, Ill.: Charles E. Thomas, 1976.

Spache, G. D. *Diagnosing and Correcting Reading Disabilities.* Boston: Allyn and Bacon, 1976.

Triggs, F., and Robbins, E. W. *Improve Your Spelling.* New York: Holt, Rinehart and Winston, 1944.

Zaner-Bloser. *Evaluation Scale.* Columbus, Ohio: Zaner-Bloser, 1968.

Chapter 10
Reading and Arithmetic

Reading and arithmetic are complex skills whose development is important to students, particularly in today's world. This chapter discusses each of these and presents methods for assessing them.

READING

Everyone has a different definition of reading. If the question, "What is reading?" is asked of a room of students, parents, teachers, and administrators the answers will vary greatly:

- Reading is recognizing letters that make words.
- Reading is sounding out a sequence of sounds to make words.
- Reading is recognizing symbols that have meaning.
- Reading is recognizing words that, put together, make sentences that convey ideas.

- Reading is identifying words and understanding what they mean.
- Reading is understanding what the author is trying to say.

The list is endless. Each of these definitions is correct, but none is complete. Each includes one important facet of reading, but reading is all of them combined, and more. Johnson and Myklebust (1967) give a more comprehensive definition: Reading is "a visual symbol system superimposed upon a previously acquired language system" (p. 15). Harris and Sipay (1971) suggest that reading is:

1. Sensing: Focusing eyes on symbols that are transmitted to the brain
2. Perceiving: Recognizing the symbols as being a word that, based on previous experience, has meaning
3. Achieving meaning: Understanding the meaning of a series of words presented in a sequence to create an idea
4. Reacting: Thinking about the idea presented and reacting physically, emotionally, or cognitively
5. Learning: Having an experience that enriches and changes previously acquired concepts to increase knowledge

This definition goes far beyond those listed at the beginning, and points out the close interrelationship between reading, thinking, and language. The correlation between Harris and Sipay's five steps and Piaget's sequence of development is readily apparent. Now reading is defined as a complex and integrative function, and therefore must be assessed as a total function. If the teacher assesses only splinter skills, such as the component parts of decoding, the information obtained will be a list of the skills the student can or cannot perform, but it will not assess how well the child is able to *read.* Figure 10-1 outlines the many facets of the Harris and Sipay reading program, which encompasses three broad goals. Several of these facets may be covered in one reading activity; the teacher must be aware, therefore, of the scope of the skills included.

This concept of reading as an integrative skill probably explains why there is so much contradictory research (Cook and Welch, 1980) regarding the effect of training in various skills on children's ability to learn to read. Cook and Welch point out that research has failed to show that specific instruction in such things as auditory memory, visual discrimination, or initial consonant blends enhances the student's learning of the reading act.

In this text, reading is defined as the *meaningful interpretation of the graphic (or printed) symbols representing verbal language and concepts.*

Figure 10-1.
Total Reading Program

- I. Developmental reading
  - A. The mechanics of reading
    - 1. Development of a large sight vocabulary
    - 2. Development of skill in identifying unfamiliar words through the use of
      - a. Context
      - b. Phonics
      - c. Structural analysis
      - d. Dictionary
    - 3. Development of good eye-movement habits
    - 4. Development of good postural habits while reading
    - 5. Development of oral reading skills
      - a. Phrasing and expression
      - b. Volume, pitch, and enunciation
    - 6. Development of speed and fluency in silent reading
  - B. Reading comprehension
    - 1. Acquisition of a rich, extensive, and accurate vocabulary
    - 2. Learning to interpret thought units of increasing size
      - a. The phrase
      - b. The sentence
      - c. The paragraph
      - d. The story
    - 3. Learning to read for specific purposes
      - a. Finding and understanding main ideas
      - b. Locating answers to specific questions
      - c. Noting and recalling details
      - d. Grasping the sequence of events
      - e. Anticipating outcomes
      - f. Making inferences
      - g. Following directions
      - h. Grasping the author's plan and intent
      - i. Evaluating and criticizing what one reads
      - j. Remembering what one reads
- II. Functional reading
  - A. Learning to locate information
    - 1. Mastering alphabetical order
    - 2. Using an index
    - 3. Using an encyclopedia
    - 4. Using other reference works
  - B. Developing functional comprehension skills
    - 1. Learning specialized vocabularies

(continued)

SOURCE: Albert J. Harris and Edward R. Sipay, *Effective Teaching of Reading*, 2nd ed. (New York: Longman, 1971), pp. 18–20. Copyright © 1971 by Longman, Inc. Reprinted by permission of Longman, Inc., New York.

Figure 10-1 continued

2. Applying comprehension skills in content subjects
   a. Learning to read textbooks in content subjects
   b. Learning to read independently in content subjects
3. Developing specialized reading skills needed by special subject matter, e.g.,
   a. Reading arithmetical problems
   b. Interpreting maps, charts, graphs, and diagrams
   c. Reading about scientific experiments
4. Learning to organize and record what one reads
   a. Outlining
   b. Summarizing
   c. Note taking
5. Learning to remember what one reads
   a. Previewing
   b. Reciting to oneself
   c. Reviewing

III. Recreational reading
   A. Development of interest in reading
      1. Enjoyment of reading as a voluntary leisure-time activity
      2. Skill in selecting appropriate reading matter for oneself
      3. Satisfaction of present interests and tastes through reading
   B. Improvement and refinement of reading interests
      1. Development of more varied reading interests
      2. Development of more mature reading interests
      3. Achievement of personal development through reading
   C. Refinement of literary judgment and taste
      1. Establishment of differential criteria for fiction and nonfiction, prose and poetry, and drama
      2. Development of appreciation for style and beauty of language
      3. Learning to seek for deeper symbolic meanings

Reading as a Language Skill

Sensorimotor abilities are necessary in order for the child to sense and perceive. The child needs concepts of space and form in order to distinguish between *A* and *H*; and concepts of soft/loud, high/low in order to distinguish between the sound of *book* and *took.* The handicapped child may have difficulty interacting with his or her environment and therefore may have difficulty in learning concepts as easily as the child who is able to move, hear, see and perceive easily and rapidly; he may also be hampered in his acquisition of cognitive and language skills.

Since reading is the interpretation of a written symbol system (letters and words) representing verbal symbols (sounds and spoken words), success in reading depends on adequate oral language ability. In Chapter 8 we discussed the sequence of skills identified as inner, receptive, and expressive language. If the lingustic system is not well established, difficulty in reading can be anticipated, even expected, and no teaching in sound blending or manuscript printing will make any significant difference. Language skills must exist and be well developed in order for the integrative function of reading to take place.

Figures 10-2 and 10-3 illustrate what actually occurs in the act of decoding a word and understanding what it means. The beginning reader follows several steps in order to identify a word (Figure 10-2). Children who learn by the whole-word (visual) approach follow a sequence of five steps, while those who follow the sound-blending (auditory) method follow eight. In either case the end result is the same. Once past the basics of decoding, the integrative function of reading assumes greater importance. The advanced or *efficient* reader looks at the word and translates it immediately into meaning (see Figure 10-3). He no longer even needs to know how to pronounce the word. In the future, the only occasions on which this reader will need to use all the steps in Figure 10-2 are when he comes upon an unfamiliar word that cannot be deciphered from context.

Reading as a Cognitive Skill

Many researchers have reported that success in reading is related to intelligence. Children who exhibit better reasoning skills in dealing with their environment or in listening and speaking will develop better reading comprehension. Figure 8-2 gives the taxonomy of cognitive skills we measure in thinking. The same hierarchy can be applied to the student's comprehension of reading material. If the child cannot think about something, he cannot understand it when he reads it. Kaluger and Kolson (1978) describe learning expectancy levels (LEL) to indicate the level of reading with comprehension a child can be expected to achieve. LEL's are computed on the mental age of the child. A child with a mental age of six should be reading at the first grade level. Each subsequent year is computed accordingly (Kaluger and Kolson, 1978, p. 138):

GRADE	MENTAL AGE
1	6
2	7
3	8
4	9
12	17

Figure 10-2.
The Beginning Reader: Task Analysis of Steps in Reading for Meaning

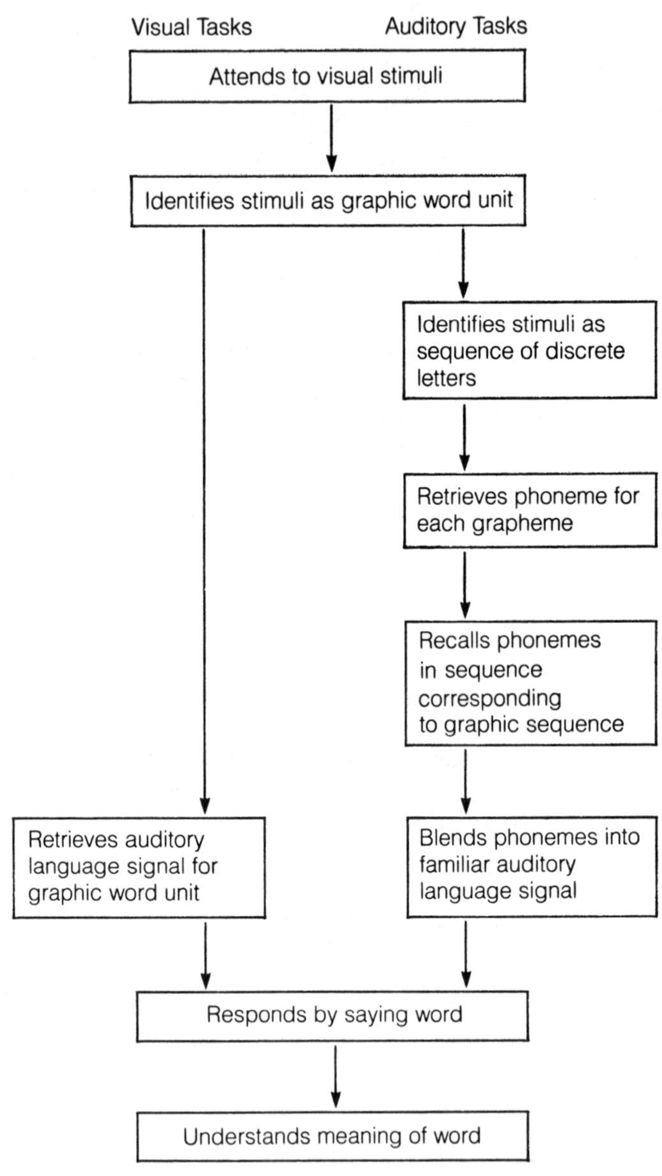

Figure 10-3.
The Advanced Reader: Task Analysis of Steps in Reading for Meaning

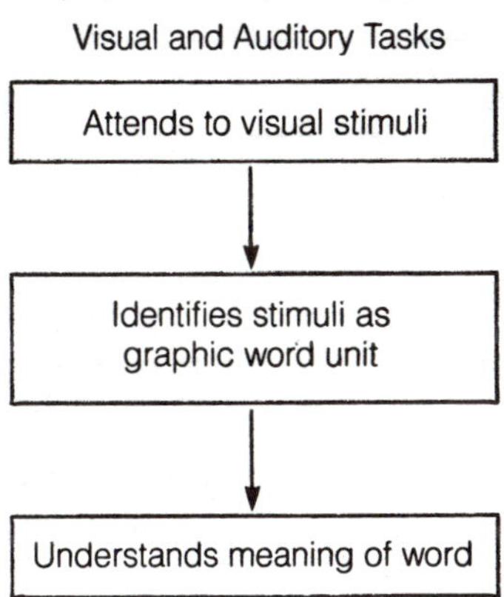

The sequence of reading skills leading to comprehension and reading for a specific purpose are displayed in Table 10-1. Comparison to the hierarchy of cognitive skills given in Table 8-1 points up the close relationship between reading and thinking and between spoken language and thinking. Any assessment of reading problems experienced by a child must be considered in this relationship.

Reading Assessment

Reading performance is assessed using a survey or a diagnostic evaluation format. The survey format is used primarily when a child performing below expectations must be identified for the purpose of providing specific remedial instruction. In this instance, it is necessary merely to identify that the child is performing below grade level, and to identify in what general area there is difficulty. The severity of the difficulty becomes the determining factor.

The diagnostic evaluation includes a thorough appraisal of the child's functioning; it indicates what may be the basis for the difficulty, and usually results in a plan for remedial teaching.

Survey assessment If a survey assessment is indicated by the answers to the questions in Chapter 2, it will consist of a listing of the skills needed to perform in the classroom, and a listing of the areas in which the child is deficient. Since the survey is *curriculum*-oriented, it should

Table 10-1.
Relationship of Hierarchy of Cognitive Skills to Reading Skills

COGNITIVE SKILL	READING SKILL
Knowledge	*Literal Comprehension*
Understands specific information, facts, rules, classes, and relations	Understands words, sentences, and paragraphs. Can recall details Can recall sequence Can remember what is read
Comprehension	*Interpretation*
Understands differences, can interpret and apply to other situations	Can make generalizations Can identify main idea Can analyze characters Increases amount and diversity of vocabulary Can come to conclusions Can predict outcomes
Application	*Functional Use*
Can apply information to new situations and behaviors	Can read in informal settings such as menus, dictionary, telephone directory, or newspapers Can read for specific purpose Develops fluency and speed
Analysis	*Study Skills*
Can understand how things go together Can reorganize ideas	Can locate information Can take notes Can outline
Synthesis	*Study Skills*
Can integrate information Can plan a new activity Can develop theories	Can do research Can use specific study skills, such as for science or mathematics
Evaluation	*Critical Evaluation*
Can be critical of situations, of self, or of other people Can make objective evaluation of situation Can assess implications	Develops interest in reading Can read for recreation Discriminates good literature Evaluates propaganda or bias

SOURCE: Adapted from B. S. Bloom, *Taxonomy of Educational Objectives* (New York: Longmans, Green & Co., 1956).

include the components of the reading program normally expected by children at the current grade level. No one sequence of skills is taught in the reading program, but most children are taught using a similar sequence. A sample list such as that given in Table 10-2 may provide sufficient information, or the teacher may choose to use the list that accompanies the reading series currently being used by the class.

Table 10-2.
Curriculum Sequence Chart: Reading

GRADE	SKILLS ACQUIRED
Kindergarten	Identify sounds and pictures Express ideas in complete verbal sentences Understand meaning of words such as *above* and *far*. Understand concepts of size, small, etc. Recognize and identify colors Organize objects into groups Match forms Understands beginning concepts of number
Grade 1	Recognize letters of alphabet; can write and give sound Auditory and visual perception and discrimination of initial and final consonants Observe left to right progression Recall what has been read Aware of medial consonants, consonant blends, digraphs Recognize long sound of vowels; root words; plural forms; verb endings *-s, -ed, -d, -ing;* opposites; pronouns *he, she* Understand concept of synonyms, homonyms, antonyms Understand simple compound words Copy simple sentences, fill-ins
Grade 2	Comprehension and analysis of what has been read Identify vowel digraphs Understand varient sounds of *y* Identify medial vowels Identify diphthongs Understand influence of *r* on preceding vowel Identify three-letter blends Understand use of suffix *-er* Understand verb endings (for example, *stop, stopped*)

(continued)

Table 10-2 continued

Grade 3	Recognize multiple sounds of long *a* as in *ei, ei, ay, ey* Understand silent *e* in *-le* endings Understand use of suffix *-est* Know how to change *y* to *i* before adding *er, est* Understand comparative and superlative forms of adjectives Understand possessive form using *s* Use contractions Identify syllabic breaks
Grade 4	Recognize main and subordinate parts Recognize unknown words using configuration and other word attack skills Identify various sounds of *ch* Recognize various phonetic values of *gh* Identify rounded *o* sound formed by *au, aw, al* Use and interpret diacritical markings Discriminate among multiple meaning of words
Grade 5	Read critically to evaluate Identify diagraphs *gn, mb, bt* Recognize that *augh* and *ough* may have round *o* sound Recognize and pronounce muted vowels in *el, al, le* Recognize secondary and primary accents Use of apostrophe Understand suffixes *-al, -hand, -ship, -ist, -ling, -an, -ian, -dom, -ern* Understand use of figures of speech: metaphor, simile Ability to paraphrase main idea Know ways paragraphs are developed Outline using two or three main heads and subheadings Use graphic material
Grade 6	Develop ability for critical analysis Recognize and use Latin, Greek roots, such as *photo, tele, graph, geo, auto* Develop generalization that some suffixes can change part of speech, such as *-ure* changing an adjective to noun (*moist-moisture*) Understand meaning and pronunciation of homographs Develop awareness of shifting accents

Minor differences or gaps in a child's performance will probably require only minor modification of lessons, or additional explanation and practice in problem areas. If the child is performing poorly in more than one or two areas, the teacher may determine that the diagnostic evaluation, the *child*-oriented assessment, is more appropriate.

Diagnostic evaluation The diagnostic evaluation of a child's performance can best be performed by the classroom teacher if time is available, or, if not, by the reading specialist. The teacher has observed the child's performance and knows what should be expected of him based on his level of language and cognitive skills. The diagnostic evaluation is an effort to document the extent of the disability, and to identify the severity of the problem in order to determine what intervention is needed. Even if the remedial program is instituted in the child's own classroom, it is necessary to obtain documentation in order to be able to measure progress.

There are several points the teacher needs to remember in performing a diagnostic evaluation:

1. Reading is *based on language.* The child cannot read with greater comprehension than he can listen.
2. Reading is an *integrative* skill. While some analysis of word attack skills can be made, analysis of isolated skills is primarily useful for recording progress in teaching.
3. Reading is a means of *communicating ideas.* If the message is transmitted, the child's reading skill is satisfactory.
4. Reading requires at least average *speed* in order to be efficient. If a child reads too slowly or laboriously comprehension is lessened.

Figure 10-4 provides a checklist for the diagnostic evaluation. In order to be fully comprehensive, the information obtained should be correlated, where there is an overlap, with language and sensorimotor areas. The teacher should note in the checklist areas in which the child is deficient. Most entries can be made from informal observation in the classroom. The following are descriptions of areas that will require individual assessment.

I. Reading level

A. Listening comprehension level

Listening comprehension may be assessed by reading to the child selections from basal readers of increasing grade levels, and then asking the child six questions about the selection. If possible, two

Figure 10-4.
Checklist of Reading Abilities

I. Reading level
   A. Listening comprehension level ____________
      1. Independent ____________
      2. Instructional ____________
   B. Silent reading level ____________
      1. Independent ____________
      2. Instructional ____________
   C. Oral reading level ____________
      1. Independent ____________
      2. Instructional ____________

II. Reading rate
   A. Oral: ________wpm
      1. Mispronunciations
         a. Whole words ____________
         b. Word parts ____________
      2. Words pronounced by teacher (after 5 secs) ____________
      3. Omissions
         a. Words ____________
         b. Word parts ____________
      4. Substitutions
         a. Easy words ____________
         b. Common word parts ____________
      5. Insertions ____________
      6. Reversals ____________
      7. Word-by-word reading ____________
      8. Repetitions
         a. Phrases ____________
         b. Word parts ____________
         c. Whole words ____________
      9. Punctuation ignored ____________
      10. Self-corrections ____________
   B. Silent
      1. Can adjust rate to purpose of reading ____________
      2. Average rate
         a. 1st grade (80 wpm) ____________
         b. 2nd grade (115 wpm) ____________
         c. 4th grade (158 wpm) ____________
         d. 6th grade (185 wpm) ____________

e. High school/average adult (200 wpm) ______
f. College student (280 wpm) ______
g. Speed reader (500+ wpm) ______

III. Word attack skills
A. Phonetic patterns
1. Consonant sounds ______
(*p, b, m, wh, w, sh, f, v, t, ch, s, d, l, r*)
2. Beginning blends ______
(*bl, cl, fl, gl, pl, sl, br, cr, dr, fr, gr, pr, tr, thr, sc*)
3. Rhyming elements ______
(*ack, ake, all, an, ark, at, ate, ay, ell, en, ef, ight, ill, ing, it, old, ook, at, own, an*)
4. Vowel sounds ______
(long, short, plus *r*, dipthongs, *oo*, *a* plus *l* or *w*)
5. Vowel rules
a. Short vowel clue ______
b. Silent *e* ______
c. Two vowels together ______
d. Final vowel ______
B. Structural patterns
1. Known endings (*-s*, *-ed*, *-ing*) ______
2. Compounds ______
3. Contractions ______
4. Changing structure
a. When adding endings (*-s*, *-ed*, *-ing*) ______
b. Doubling consonant ______
c. *y* to *i* ______
d. Dropping *e* ______
5. Prefixes ______
6. Suffixes ______
C. Syllabication patterns
1. Polysyllabic words ______
2. Syllabication rules ______
3. Accent ______
4. One vowel sound per syllable ______
5. The schwa ______
D. Motor patterns
1. Left-to-right eye movements ______
2. Pointing with finger ______
3. Moves lips in silent reading ______

(continued)

Figure 10-4 continued

IV. Comprehension
- A. Literal
  1. Matches words and pictures ____________
  2. Understands vocabulary
     - a. Recognizes synonyms ____________
     - b. Recognizes antonyms ____________
     - c. Recognizes homonyms ____________
  3. Understands meaning of
     - a. Sentence ____________
     - b. Paragraph ____________
     - c. Chapter ____________
     - d. Book ____________
  4. Recognizes sequence ____________
  5. Uses context clues ____________
  6. Follows oral directions ____________
  7. Follows written directions ____________
- B. Interpretive
  1. Recognizes main idea ____________
  2. Recalls supporting detail ____________
  3. Makes generalizations ____________
  4. Makes conclusions ____________
  5. Predicts outcomes ____________
  6. Recognizes cause and effect ____________
  7. Makes deductions ____________
  8. Relates reading to prior knowledge ____________
- C. Critical
  1. Recognizes difference between fact and opinion ____________
  2. Recognizes author's purpose ____________
  3. Recognizes mood of story (poem, article) ____________
  4. Understands figurative language ____________
  5. Reads for verification ____________
  6. Explores alternative sources ____________
  7. Reads newspaper (magazines, books) ____________
  8. Enjoys reading ____________

V. Functional reading
- A. Study skills
  1. Can alphabetize ____________
  2. Uses table of contents ____________
  3. Uses index ____________
  4. Can read abbreviations ____________

5. Interprets symbols ______
6. Can use maps ______
7. Can identify topic sentences ______
8. Can take notes ______
9. Can summarize information from several sources ______
10. Can outline ______

B. Library skills
1. Has a public library card ______
2. Uses library from 1 to 4 times per month ______
3. Uses dictionary ______
4. Uses glossary ______
5. Uses card catalog ______
6. Can use an atlas ______
7. Can use an encyclopedia ______
8. Can use *Reader's Guide* ______
9. Can use abstracts ______

C. Life skills
1. Can use telephone directory ______
2. Can use bus (train, air) schedules ______
3. Can read menus ______
4. Can read road signs ______
5. Can locate information in newspaper ______
6. Can read job applications ______
7. Understands advertisements ______

SOURCE: Developed by Arlee S. Maier. Copyright © 1980 by Arlee S. Maier.

or three questions should be factual, and two or three interpretive. Basal readers should be used because the vocabulary contains words and concepts that are usually understood by children of the appropriate age. Five correct answers indicates that the child understands enough to work independently at that level. Four correct means that the level is appropriate for instruction, and three or fewer correct means the selection is too difficult. Listening comprehension is the best quick indicator of reading expectancy level. If a child understands an oral presentation of a selection, he or she can probably learn to read at that level.

The teacher should choose materials in current use in the classroom, and select a 50- to 100-word passage at random. The level at which five out of six questions are answered correctly is the *independent level.* Four correct indicates the *instructional level.*

B. Silent reading level

Since reading is an activity by which meaning is transmitted, the most important measure of silent reading is comprehension. A cloze test as described by Bormuth (1969) is the best means of doing this. This technique involves

1. Selecting a passage
2. Deleting words (but not proper names or the first word of a sentence)
   a. Every tenth word for fact-laden material
   b. In narratives, every fifth word for grades 7 and above, every sixth word for grades 5 and 6, every seventh word for grades 3 and 4, every eighth word for grades 1 and 2
3. Keeping the first and last sentence intact
4. Scoring
   a. 44 percent of the items correct would indicate the instructional level
   b. 57 percent of the items correct would indicate the independent level

Figure 10-5 is an example of the cloze technique, which may be used to assess silent reading levels.

C. Oral reading level

The teacher should select 100-word passages from basal readers of increasing grade levels. A typewritten copy on which the teacher can write is a great convenience, although a record of errors can be kept by reading another copy of the book. The number of errors is tallied and the total recorded. Ninety-five percent of the words—that is, 95 of the 100 words—should be read correctly in order to consider the grade level appropriate for independent reading. Ninety words read correctly indicates the instructional level. If the child makes more than ten errors in reading the 100-word passage, the level is too difficult.

II. Reading rate

The teacher can make an informal assessment of the child's reading as he or she performs in the classroom.

There are no expected word-per-minute rates for oral reading, as some people speak more rapidly than others. The teacher must make a subjective assessment of whether the child reads at an acceptable

Figure 10-5.
Cloze Test: The Red Flyer (Grade 2—Every 8th Word)

Directions: Before you write anything, read the whole story to yourself one or two times. Then put the word you think fits best into each space with a number.

Nick and Chris were twins. Tony was their (1) __________ friend. The three boys stood in front (2) __________ the big store. They could not stop (3) __________ at the red bike in the store (4) __________. "The Red Flyer! That's the bike I (5) __________," said Chris. "So do I!" said his (6) __________. Tony said nothing. He just looked at (7) __________ bike in the window for a long (8) __________.

When it was time to go, the (9) __________ walked with Tony to the bus stop. Then (10) __________ twins walked home.

All the way home, (11) __________ talked about the Red Flyer. That night, (12) __________ twins had a long talk with their (13) __________. They told about the bike in the (14) __________. Whitewall tires! Big headlights! A real car horn! "If (15) __________ can save the money," said Nick, "may (16) __________ buy two Red Flyers?"

"Why, Nick," said (17) __________ Peters. "You will need one hundred dollars for (18) __________bikes like that! How can two boys (19) __________ so much money?"

"We will work," said Chris. "We (20) __________ to work on Saturdays and holidays. When (21) __________ closes, we can work every day. And (22) __________ will save all the money we make."

Nick (23) __________ Chris looked at each other. "It will (24) __________ us five months," said Nick. "It's March (25) __________. We can get the bikes in July."

Nick (26) __________ Chris surprised everyone. They took every job (27) __________ could get. They asked the storekeepers for (28) __________. They cut grass in front yards and (29) __________ yards. They were baby sitters too.

They (30) __________ all the money they made to the (31) __________. A man at the bank gave them (32) __________ little green bankbook. The boys liked to (33) __________ out the bankbook to look at it (34) __________ and over again.

It seemed a long (35) __________ before they had ten dollars. It seemed (36) __________ longer before they had twenty dollars. The (37) __________ worked and worked. March and April went (38) __________. The bankbook showed only thirty dollars.

"We (39) __________ buy one bike yet," said Chris. But the twins (40) __________ not give up. They went on working. May (41) __________ and then June. They had forty dollars. Then fifty (42) __________.

The school was over for the summer. "Now we can get more jobs," they said. And (43) __________ did. Soon they had saved sixty dollars. Then (44) __________ dollars. Then eighty. Then ninety. At last (45) __________ the big day. The boys looked at (46) __________ bankbook. There it was—one hundred dollars. "We did it! We did it!" they shouted.

Nick (48) __________ the bankbook up high. "Now we can (49) __________ two Flyers!" he cried.

All at once Chris (50) __________ down. "Yes," he said slowly. "We can (51) __________ two bikes. But what about our friend Tony?" "Say, (52) __________ right," said Nick. "What about Tony?" Nick (53) __________ at Chris. Chris looked at Nick. "That Red Flyer (54) __________ so wonderful," said Nick. "We saw a (55) __________ bike for $33."

(continued)

Figure 10-5 continued

"What good are whitewall (56) __________ anyway?" Chris said. "What's going on here?" (57) __________ Mr. Peters in surprise. "Well," Nick told (58) __________, "if we get just two bikes, Tony (59) __________ ride with us. Then the three of (60) __________ can't do things together any more."

"You (61) __________," Chris put in. "Tony has to work (62) __________ the farm for his father. It takes (63) __________ longer to save money."

"I see," said Mr. Peters.

"So (64) __________ is what we want to do," Nick (65) __________. "We want to get three bikes for (66) __________ money. Tony will pay us back when he (67) __________."

"What do you think, Mother?" asked Chris. "Father, (68) __________ do you think?" Mr. and Mrs. Peters (69) __________ at each other.

"We are proud of (70) __________ way you saved your money," said Mrs. Peters. "But we are even more proud of the fine way you are going to spend it."

1. best	2. of	3. looking	4. window	5. want
6. brother	7. the	8. time	9. twins	10. the
11. they	12. the	13. parents	14. window	15. we
16. we	17. Mr.	18. two	19. save	20. want
21. school	22. we	23. and	24. take	25. now
26. and	27. they	28. jobs	29. back	30. took
31. bank	32. a	33. take	34. over	35. time
36. even	37. boys	38. by	39. can't	40. did
41. passed	42. dollars	43. they	44. seventy	45. came
46. their	47. did	48. held	49. get	50. sat
51. get	52. that's	53. looked	54. isn't	55. good
56. tires	57. asked	58. him	59. can't	60. us
61. see	62. on	63. him	64. this	65. said
66. the	67. can	68. what	69. looked	70. the

Key

100% = 70 correct
44% = 31 correct (instructional level)
57% = 36 correct (independent level)

speed, with satisfactory fluency and expression. An error analysis can be made, and specific errors pointed out on the checklist. This error analysis will help the teacher assess the frequency of specific errors the child makes and pinpoint remedial tasks to be developed. It does not indicate *why* the child makes errors. Some errors are due to carelessness and need only to be pointed out to the child. Others may be due to auditory, visual, motor, or linguistic factors as described in Chapters 7 and 8, and the underlying cause should be taken into account in developing a remediation program.

Silent reading can be evaluated by timing a child for five minutes and dividing the number of words read by 5. The average number of words per minute that is given on the checklist is intended as a guide. Some variance is to be expected and is entirely normal.

The good reader adjusts his or her reading rate to the difficulty of the material being read. For example, a selection filled with facts or technical information must be read slowly and carefully; a short story or a novel can be read more rapidly; and a newspaper or magazine article is often skimmed very rapidly.

III. Word attack skills

While, as mentioned earlier in this chapter, an analysis of word attack skills is most useful in developing the *teaching* program, it is necessary to identify a child's specific problem areas in order to develop the teaching sequence at the appropriate level. The teacher can refer to Table 10-2 to identify the correct level. If the difficulties concern only a few specific points, these can then be taught individually; a major modification of the reading program is not required.

IV. Comprehension

The three levels of comprehension—literal, interpretive, and critical—are delineated, so that the teacher may evaluate the level of the child's cognition of reading material. A careful evaluation of the findings can be made by referring to Table 10-1.

V. Functional reading

This section of the checklist can be completed by indicating what the child *does* in the classroom or in the community. This application of reading skills is perhaps the most important to evaluate, since the goal of any school program is to prepare the student to use reading skills for some practical goal.

The reading checklist cannot be evaluated by the use of a numerical score. Once the checklist has been completed, the teacher will see a pattern emerge of areas where the child has particular difficulty. This pattern, or profile, needs to be evaluated in conjunction with the assessment of the child's thinking, language, and sensorimotor skills. A teaching program can then be planned that will combine remedial teaching with curriculum adaptation, so that the child will experience success while learning.

ARITHMETIC

Little research has been done on children who experience difficulty in working with numbers. The reason for this is perhaps that more children have problems with language arts (such as reading, spelling, and writing), or perhaps that parents and teachers are not as unhappy when a child is not doing well in arithmetic. A parent may even tell the teacher, "I didn't do well in arithmetic either. I guess Johnny is a chip off the old block!"

In many instances the implied meaning of this comment is true. That is, people do manage to finish school and get a job with poor math skills. But it is probably less true now than previously, due to the increased technology required in business and the increased use of computers in many areas of everyday life. Youngsters having difficulty with arithmetic today will probably be more seriously handicapped in their adult lives than their parents were with the same degree of disability.

A problem teachers often encounter in trying to help children in this subject is that they themselves are uncomfortable with arithmetic. In addition, arithmetic has generally been presented in a highly sequenced curriculum, and children progress through it according to grade level. In some instances they simply do not progress beyond a certain point if a teacher assumes that earlier skills have not been mastered; for example, a teacher may not teach division if he or she assumes that the child does not know his multiplication tables, feeling that the child, in this case, would not be able to master division. Chalfant and Schefflin (1969) feel that one of the reasons so little research has been done in this area is that arithmetic and mathematics do not require the same skills. They point out that, "*Mathematics* is the abstract science of space and number which deals with space configuration, interrelations, and abstractions of number. *Arithmetic* is the branch of mathematics that deals with real numbers and their computations" (p. 119). Chalfant and Schefflin go on to say:

> The concrete nature of arithmetic and the abstractness of mathematics not only suggests that different cognitive abilities may be involved but that they might be disordered in several different ways. In mathematics, for example, children might experience difficulty in handling the operations, interrelations, and abstractions of number, or the structure, measurement, and transformation of space configurations. Difficulty in arithmetic might include such things as reading or writing isolated numerals or a series of numerals, reading and writing numbers whose names are not written the way they are spoken (twenty one = 21, not 201), recognizing the categorical structure of numbers (units, tens, hundreds, thousands), and doing computational operations. (p. 119)

This important distinction between mathematics and arithmetic needs to be well understood by the classroom teacher before he or she attempts any evaluation of a child's weaknesses in number concepts. While an extensive analysis is not within the purview of this book, a brief discussion will provide some background to help teachers make the distinction.

The Nature of Mathematics

Most researchers agree that mathematical readiness comprises several basic abilities (Hammill and Bartel, 1975; Chalfant and Schefflin, 1969).

General intelligence There seems to be some correlation between the general intelligence of the individual and his or her ability to use mathematical concepts (Barakat, 1951). This correlation may arise because intelligence is commonly considered to be the ability to solve problems, and mathematics requires that skill in great degree. In Chapter 8 we discussed Piaget's concept of developing cognition, which may be one approach to understanding what is meant by the relationship of intelligence to number concepts. Mathematical readiness requires that the child have established the basic concepts of: spatial representation, classification, one-to-one correspondence, seriation, flexibility or reversibility, conservation, and the necessary language to describe those concepts. Brownell and Moser (1949) studied the foundations necessary for the development of higher level mathematical concepts. They found that without these "basic concepts" the child may learn to compute, but will not develop the conceptual or cognitive base that will allow him to "use" number theory.

Tables 10-3, 10-4, and 10-5 indicate the importance of each of these basic skills in the developing cognitive framework of the child, according to Piaget. The relationship of Piaget's early stages to the development of language and thinking skills has already been described. An evaluation of the child's ability in these areas is far more meaningful than an arbitrary IQ score and will allow us to predict the child's ability to develop math skills based on his "readiness." What is commonly called problem solving is probably the ability to abstract concepts of numerical quantity as they are related to all of the factors listed in Tables 10-3, 10-4, and 10-5. These concepts are well developed in most children who have reached the mental age of 11 or 12, the end of Piaget's period of concrete operations. The period of higher mathematics begins at the age of 11 or 12, the period of formal operations. This coincides with the time the youngster enters junior high school.

Table 10-3.
Mathematical Readiness According to Piaget's Sensorimotor Period (Birth to 2 Years)

COGNITIVE CONCEPT	READINESS OF CHILD
Spatial Relations	
The ability to perceive and compare spatial forms and patterns accurately. The ability to visualize size, depth, and distance.	Can perceive objects and distinguish one from another. Kinesthetic information if obtained through motor activity: handling, holding, moving.
Object permanence	Can perceive and remember objects even when partially hidden from view.
Size	Cannot distinguish unless differences are great.
Distance	Cannot think about. Developing concepts through exploration and movement.
Time	Can relate only to own basic physical needs—hunger, fatigue.
Classification	
The ability to group objects according to certain defined characteristics.	Most often cannot classify because child forgets the characteristic to identify the class.
One-to-One Correspondence	
The child's ability to understand that one object is *one*, regardless of its characteristics and that the number concept of one child is the same as one apple. The ability to count meaningfully is related to this concept.	Cannot do.
Seriation	
The ability to order objects in relation to one or more of the characteristics, i.e., length, weight, or volume.	Cannot do.

COGNITIVE CONCEPT	READINESS OF CHILD
Reversibility	
The ability to recognize that objects, when changed and rearranged can return to their original condition.	Cannot do.
Conservation	
The ability to recognize that number, size, weight, and volume remain the same regardless of the arrangement or shape of the object or objects.	Cannot do.
Language	
The ability to use words describing the concepts of number, comparing, contrasting, and problem solving.	Understands concepts big/little, more/less, but does not use words.

Table 10-6 illustrates how each one of these basic concepts forms the basis for understanding the principles of mathematics and the skills directly related to each concept.

Other factors Several things that may be related to difficulty in mathematics are not basic mathematical concepts. Such factors include the following:

1. Inability to identify and remember correctly numerals, words, and symbols, such as 6, 21, thirty-six, or +, −, ÷, %, $, used for computation. This inability may indicate a problem not in mathematics but in reading, and it should be treated in the same way as any other inability to identify a symbol with meaning. Although this problem is not common, it does occur and is related to dyslexia. The teacher must be sure that the problem is a real one and that the child is not merely confused about what the symbol means.
2. Lack of practice for higher level processes. The confusion of words or symbols may be related to lack of practice. Children need sufficient time to practice a new skill before they can be considered to have learned it. A child may understand a new concept and appear

Table 10-4.
Mathematical Readiness According to Piaget's Preoperations Period (2 to 7 Years)

	READINESS OF CHILD	
COGNITIVE CONCEPT	STAGE I (2 to 5 YEARS)	STAGE II (5 to 7 YEARS)
Spatial Relations		
The ability to perceive and compare spatial forms and patterns accurately.	Can discriminate between similar objects, if distinction is obvious.	Can discriminate difference in pattern if shape is similar.
The ability to visualize size, depth, and distance.		
Object permanence	Well established.	Well established.
Size	Can distinguish differences.	Can begin to discriminate using two characteristics. Can recall differences from own experiences.
Distance	Knows distance within own experience.	Can think about distance using concrete experiences.
Time	Remembers what comes first. Can wait according to own daily activities. Understands: today, tomorrow, morning, afternoon.	Can anticipate and plan on the basis of own experiences. Understands relative length of "minute," "hour," "day." Realizes birthdays are repeated, and how old will be on next birthday. Can tell time to hour.
Classification		
The ability to group objects according to certain defined characteristics.	Most often cannot classify because child forgets the characteristic to identify the class.	Can classify using some definite property, i.e., redness, but cannot put into more general category because does not understand the concept of inclusion: i.e., bananas, apples, and oranges are all fruit.

One-to-One Correspondence The child's ability to understand that one object is *one*, regardless of its characteristics and that the number concept of *one* child is the same as *one* apple. The ability to count meaningfully is related to this concept.	Rarely understands. Can count by rote, but is usually reciting a memorized list of words and will skip items or "count" when no object is present.	Can do with some assistance. Spatial concepts are not well developed, so child will have tendency to assume that other characteristics influence numerosity. Has difficulty with such games as Musical Chairs.
Seriation The ability to order objects in relation to one or more of the characteristics, i.e., length, weight, or volume.	Cannot do, because cannot consider all the characteristics of an object.	Can do with objects that are equally separate from each other, i.e., line up sticks that are one inch, two inches, three inches, etc., but has more difficulty with such items as stones that are of random shapes and weights.
Reversability The ability to recognize that objects, when changed and rearranged can return to their original condition.	Cannot do.	Cannot do. Can perform an experiment such as pouring water from two beakers back into one larger one to prove the same amount of water is present, but does not understand concept.
Conservation The ability to recognize that number, size, weight, and volume remain the same regardless of the arrangement or shape of the object or objects.	Cannot do. Concentrates on only characteristics and centers on how object "looks."	Can do with some help. If shown that there are equal number of cups to saucers, will remember even when they are separated and rearranged. Understands conservation of quantity.
Language The ability to use words describing the concepts of number, comparing, contrasting, and problem solving.	Uses names for size, although there is some confusion, i.e., "big" for "tall" or "larger."	Uses words correctly to describe size, weight, depth, distance. Increasing vocabulary to correspond to increasing ability to classify. Can easily identify and label "biggest," "littlest."

Table 10-5.
Mathematical Readiness According to Piaget's Concrete Operations Level (7 to 11 Years)

COGNITIVE CONCEPT	READINESS OF CHILD
Spatial Relations	
The ability to perceive and compare spatial forms and patterns accurately.	Can identify and remember patterns and symbols.
The ability to visualize size, depth, and distance.	
Object permanence	Well established.
Size	Can identify and recall from own experiences. Can relate similarities to things in own experience. Can order using more than one characteristic.
Distance	Can think about experiences. Not always necessary to have manipulative present.
Time	Can sequence days, months, and seasons. Can estimate how long has elapsed, or anticipate how long something may take. Can tell time to minutes.
Classification	
The ability to group objects according to certain defined characteristics.	Can think of several characteristics at once and classify according to class inclusions: i.e., for a small, yellow flower, dandelion and daffodil fit all characteristics, but daisy, sunflower, and lemon do not. Child understands subclasses.
One-to-One Correspondence	
The child's ability to understand that one object is *one*, regardless of its characteristics and that the number concept of one child is the same as one apple. The ability to count meaningfully is related to this concept.	Does understand, and can isolate characteristic to be considered from others, i.e., can understand that six houses are equivalent in number to six pencils. Can place each one of separate-pairs groups into pairs.

COGNITIVE CONCEPT	READINESS OF CHILD
Seriation	
The ability to order objects in relation to one or more of the characteristics, i.e., length, weight, or volume.	Can order according to size, weight, or volume.
Reversability	
The ability to recognize that objects, when changed and rearranged can return to their original condition.	Child can perform, and does so frequently to firmly establish concepts of conservation.
Conservation	
The ability to recognize that number, size, weight, and volume remain the same regardless of the arrangement or shape of the object or objects.	Achieves understanding of conservation of weight at 9 or 10 years. (Conservation of volume is not fully understood until 11 or 12 years.)
Language	
The ability to use words describing the concepts of number, comparing, contrasting, and problem solving.	Can change vocabulary as indicated in problem solving. Reflects greater understanding of class inclusion.

to be able to apply it, but may need additional drill before the skill is sufficiently internalized to be automatic. In order to do arithmetic with ease, basic skills must be performed automatically and without careful analysis each time, so that speed can be developed. Children who are inattentive and distractable often do not get sufficient drill experience. They accomplish only one-third of the drill that others perform, and they may need additional time and creative methods for additional experience.

3. Inadequate development of fundamentals. Because of absence, inattention, or poor understanding of instruction, a child may not have developed the proper sequence of skills needed to provide a basis for higher level performance. Arithmetic is a sequential task. Each skill depends on good learning of a prior one. If the sequence is not followed, a weak "link" may cause the entire "chain" to come apart.

Table 10-6.
The Cognitive Foundation for Mathematical Concepts

COGNITIVE CONCEPT	MATHEMATICAL CONCEPT
Spatial Relations	
Objects and object performance	Visualization of geometric shapes: circle, square, triangle, rectangle
Form constancy	Horizontal and vertical notation
Distance	Measurement
Weight	Measurement
Depth	Measurement
Volume	Measurement; geometry
Size	Measurement; estimation
Classification	Sets: identical, equivalent, equal, unequal
One-to-One Correspondence	Zero Counting: cardinal and ordinal numeration
Seriation	Counting: cardinal and ordinal numeration Counting by twos, threes, fives, tens Number line
Reversability	Commutative property Associative property Inverse functions: addition/subtraction, multiplication/division
Conservation	Problem solving
Quantity	Place value Clustering/visualization
Weight	Measurement
Volume	Measurement

4. Inability to read with comprehension. Word problems require that the child understand what he or she is reading. Heddens and Smith (1964) found that most arithmetic textbooks have a higher level of reading than a reading text of the same grade level. The child who is a poor reader may simply not be able to read directions or the facts of a problem. Given the same material orally he may be able to perform adequately. Vocabulary may be a problem if a known word is used in a different context. Such words as *prime, base,* and *power* are used in an entirely different way in mathematics than in reading.
5. Inability to estimate as an informal means of monitoring the correctness of an answer. The inability to estimate hinders the child from checking to see whether the answer obtained is reasonable. Of all the skills listed in this section, the ability to estimate is most closely associated with understanding mathematical concepts, but children often do not learn this skill. Their only method of checking is to thumb to the answer key or to perform some "checking" function, such as multiplying a division problem, to see if it was worked correctly. Children need to learn the strategy of monitoring each step of computation so they can develop an understanding of where an error occurs.

The remaining two items of this list are closely related to sensorimotor functioning. If, in assessing motor performance, such problems are noted, the teacher can anticipate difficulties in mathematics and arithmetic.

6. Inability to plan or organize a sequence of steps. The inability to plan or organize a sequence of steps is related to motor planning and is sometimes evidenced early when a child is unable to perform simple tasks such as unscrewing a lid. Knowing how to go about doing something is a basic organizational skill (discussed in Chapter 7). In arithmetic computation, the child needs to remember the sequence of steps to be followed in order to resolve the problem. Following steps learned by rote often results in errors. In order to remediate this difficulty the child will need instruction in organization, not necessarily in mathematics.
7. Inability to write a neat and legible paper. The inability to arrange the symbols on the paper efficiently or to write the numerals legibly and neatly is also related to motor difficulties. This problem can create many errors for the child who does know his mathematics. A number 7 that ends up looking like a 2 will produce a wrong answer, as will an 8 placed in the tens column instead of the

hundreds column. Here too, the problem is not poor understanding of qualitative concepts, but one of handwriting and organization. Remedial measures will need to be planned accordingly.

Survey Assessment

Since arithmetic is a sequentially arranged activity, it is relatively easy for a teacher to assess where in the sequence of skills a child appears to have difficulty. The instructor's manual of almost any arithmetic series lists the sequence of skills introduced at various grade levels that can be used as a guide for an informal assessment. Table 10-7 is an example of a curriculum sequence that can be used for this purpose.

Table 10-7.
Curriculum Sequence Chart: Mathematics

GRADE	SKILLS ACQUIRED
Kindergarten	Rote counting to 10 Use whole numbers in serial order Begin cardinal numbers, ordinal numbers Begin reading numerals One-to-one matching Addition as joining of sets
Grade 1: First Half	Rote counting to 100 Read and write whole numbers through 50 Place value at tens place Equivalent/nonequivalent sets Know meaning of signs −, +, and = Addition and subtraction as inverse functions Solving missing addend problems Using 0 in subtraction
Grade 1: Second Half	Rote counting beyond 100 Counting by fives, twos, tens Odd and even numbers Signs (&) Read and write to 99 Begin fractions ½ , ⅓, ¼ Addition combinations through 19 Addition of two-digit numbers with 2 or 3 addends through 99 (no carrying) Subtract two-digit numbers to minuends of 19 or less Multiples of 10 (2 tens = 20, 3 tens = 30)

GRADE	SKILLS ACQUIRED
Grade 2: First Half	Place value to hundredth place Addition two-digit numerals with 3 or 4 addends with sums less than 100 (no carrying) Subtract two-digit numerals (no borrowing) Understand division as separation of set into equivalent sets
Grade 2: Second Half	Count by ones, twos, fives, tens, hundreds, through 999 Odd-even numbers Read and write numerals through 999 Write numerals in expanded notation Introduce carrying (regrouping) Subtraction involving borrowing at the tens, hundreds places with numerals including 0 Begin combination of multiples of 2, 3, 4, and 5 with products of 0–25. Know meaning of x and y Begin division problem with same facts as above.
Grade 3: First Half	Count and write to 1,000 Place value for thousands Equivalent fractions for ½, ¼, ⅓ Roman numerals to XII Addition of three-digit numerals with carrying Subtraction facts with combinations of 0–19 Introduce $\sqrt{\ }$ for division
Grade 3: Second Half	Read and write numerals with dollars and cents Rounding of numbers Fractions ⅙, ⅛ Roman numerals through XXX Addition up to seven digits Begin addition of fractions with like denominators, with sums less than 1 Subtraction of 4–7 digits with borrowing Multiplication through 9 × 9 Multiplication of two- or three-digit factors by one factor with or without carrying Division with combination through 9 × 9
Grade 4: First Half	Read and write whole numbers to 9,999 Roman numerals through C Understand concepts of ½, ¼, ⅓ as equivalent sets of groups of objects, as well as congruent parts of a whole

(continued)

Table 10-7 *continued*

GRADE	SKILLS ACQUIRED
Grade 4: Second Half	Read and write numerals to million Place value for million Learn names *numerator* and *denominator* Multiplication of two-digit numeral by two-digit multipliers Division with two-digit divisor Fractional parts, fifths, sevenths, ninths
Grade 5: First Half	Relationship between improper fractions and mixed fractions Write improper and mixed fractions Add three- and four-digit numbers of 2–6 addends Add fractions with like denominators Subtract like and mixed fractions with like denominators Multiply three-digit numbers by two-digit multipliers Two-digit divisors with 5–9 in one's place
Grade 5: Second Half	Decimals and place value Add decimal fractions Add fractions with unlike denominators Subtract five-digit numerals, fractional numbers, mixed numbers from whole numbers Multiplication with multiples of 100
Grade 6: First Half	Learn to express numbers by using exponents Vocabulary: *power, squared, cubed* Add and subtract fractions with unlike denominators Multiplication with three-digit multipliers Multiplication of fractional numbers with proper fractions, whole numbers, and improper fractions Division of fractional numbers
Grade 6: Second Half	Relate percent to ratio, fractions, and decimals Add positive and negative numbers Multiplication with decimals and decimal fractions Division of decimal fractions

The teacher can give the student a few problems of each type to compute and then see where in the sequence he or she begins having difficulty. One technique teachers often use is to take several old workbooks and let the student go through them, working a few problems on each page at his own pace. When the student begins to have difficulty, a more specific analysis of his errors can be made.

The teacher needs to identify if the problems are specific in nature, are related only to the child's ability to perform *arithmetic* functions, or if there is a basic lack of understanding. If the child's mathematical concepts are satisfactory but there is difficulty in computation, remedial procedures can be carried out in the classroom with the aid of a peer tutor or with some additional assistance from the teacher.

Diagnostic Evaluation

Sometimes the teacher is not able to determine easily if a student's difficulty is with concept formation or with computation. In this event an error analysis needs to be performed to help make that determination.

Figure 10-6 is an example of the kind of specific analysis that the teacher will make of the errors made by the child. Each problem must be carefully examined to identify exactly what the child was thinking while performing the computation. In some instances it may be necessary to ask the child, "What did you do here?" or "What were you thinking when you did this?"

After a specific analysis of the child's errors, a checklist of arithmetic skills (see Table 10-8) can be used to make a profile of the student's strengths and weaknesses. The teacher should put a checkmark in the appropriate column—"above average," "average," or "below average"—for each skill the child should be able to perform. No score is entered for skills that are above the child's expected age or grade level.

When the checklist is completed, the following interpretation can be made:

- Above average: The total score obtained is *less* than the number of skills checked.
- Average: The total score obtained is *equal* to the number of skills checked.
- Below average: The total score obtained is *one and one-half* the number of skills checked.
- Deficit area: The total score obtained is *twice* the number of skills checked.

If the child is old enough to have completed the entire checklist, the scoring key can be used to record the problem areas. It is important to remember, however, that the score is not important. Rather, it is important for the teacher to evaluate each skill area to determine where the problem is, and then develop a plan for working with the child that will approach the root of the difficulty. Only in this way will the teacher develop a program that will provide the child with a firm mathematical foundation and help him avoid further problems as he progresses through school.

Figure 10-6.
Common Arithmetic Errors

Analysis	*Example*
1. Lacks mastery of basic addition facts.	$\begin{array}{rr} 3 & 2 \\ +4 & 3 \\ \hline 7 & 4 \end{array}$
2. Lacks mastery of basic subtraction facts.	$\begin{array}{rr} 3 & 8 \\ -2 & 5 \\ \hline 1 & 2 \end{array}$
3. Lacks mastery of basic multiplication facts.	$\begin{array}{r} 32 \\ \times\ 3 \\ \hline 86 \end{array}$
4. Lacks mastery of basic division facts.	$35 \div 5 = 6$ $\begin{array}{r} 6 \\ 9\overline{)56} \\ -56 \\ \hline 0 \end{array}$
5. Subtracts incorrectly within the division algorithm.	$\begin{array}{rl} & 3)\ 73 \text{ rem } 1 \\ & 70) \\ 3\overline{)230} & \\ -21 & \\ \hline 10 & \\ -9 & \\ \hline 1 & \end{array}$

SOURCE: F. K. Reisman, *A Guide to the Diagnostic Teaching of Arithmetic*, 2nd ed. (Columbus, Ohio: Charles E. Merrill, 1978). Copyright © 1978 by Bell & Howell. Reprinted by permission.

Analysis	*Example*
6. Error in addition of partial product.	432 ×57 3 0 24 21 6 0 24 0 24
7. Does not complete addition: a. Does not write renamed number.	85 +43 28
b. Leaves out numbers in column addition.	4 8 2 ← +3 15
8. Rewrites a numeral without computing.	↘ 72 +15 → 77 → 32 × 3 → 36
9. Does not complete subtraction.	582 − 35 47
10. Does not complete division because of incompleted subtraction.	1) 41 40) 7/3 9 7 −2 8 0 7 7
11. Fails to complete division; stops at first partial quotient.	50 7/ 370 350

(continued)

Figure 10-6 (continued)

Analysis	*Example*
12. Fails to complete division; leaves remainder equal to or greater than divisor.	80 rem 9 9/ 729 720 ——— 9
13. Does not complete multiplication within division algorithm.	1) 201 rem 3 200) 3/ 603 600 ——— 3
14. Does not add by bridging endings—should think 5 + 9 = 14, so 35 + 9 = 44.	35 +9 —— 33
15. Lacks additive identity concept in addition.	35 +20 —— 50
16. Confuses multiplicative identity within addition operation.	71 +13 —— 73
17. Lacks additive identity concept in subtraction.	43 −20 —— 20
18. Confuses role of zero in subtraction with role of zero in multiplication.	37 −20 —— 10
19. Subtracts top digit from bottom digit whenever regrouping is involved with zero in minuend.	30 −18 —— 28
20. Confuses role of zero in multiplication with multiplicative identity.	7 × 0 = 7

Analysis	*Example*
21. Confuses place value of quotient by adding extra zero.	20 30/ 60
22. Omits zero in quotient.	30 rem 3 4/ 1203 1200 ——— 3
23. Lacks facility with addition algorithm: a. Adds units to units *and* tens;	37 + 2 ——— 59
b. Adds tens to tens *and* hundreds;	342 + 36 ——— 678
c. Adds units to tens *and* hundreds;	132 + 6 ——— 798
d. Is unable to add horizontally: Thinks: 3 + 7 + 1 = 11; writes 1 4 + 3 = 7 (+ 1 carried) 5 = 5 May add zero to make sum greater than largest addend: 1850.	345 + 7 + 13 = 185 8 5 ——— 185
24. Does not regroup units to tens.	37 + 25 ——— 52
25. Does not regroup tens to hundreds (or hundreds to thousands).	973 +862 ——— 735
26. Regroups when unnecessary.	43 + 24 ——— 77

(continued)

Figure 10-6 (continued)

Analysis	*Example*
27. Writes regrouped tens digit in units place, carries units digit (writes the 1 and carries the 2 from "12").	(2) 35 + 7 51
28. When there are fewer digits in subtrahend: a. subtracts units from units *and* from tens (*and* hundreds);	783 −2 561
b. subtracts tens from tens *and* hundreds.	783 − 23 560
29. Does not rename tens digit after regrouping.	54 − 9 55
30. Does not rename hundreds digit after regrouping.	532 −181 451
31. Does not rename hundreds or tens when renaming units.	906 −238 778
32. Does not rename tens when zero is in tens place, although hundreds are renamed.	803 −478 335
33. When there are two zeroes in minuend, renames hundreds twice but does not rename tens.	5 6 11 700 −326 284
34. Decreases hundreds digit by one when unnecessary.	3 7 1 −1 3 4 1 3 7

Analysis	Example
35. Uses units place factor as addend.	$\begin{array}{r} 32 \\ \times\ 4 \\ \hline 126 \end{array}$
36. Adds regrouped number to tens but does not multiply. * 7 × 5 = 35; 30 + 30 = 60	$\begin{array}{r} 35 \\ \times\ 7 \\ \hline 65^{*} \end{array}$
37. Multiplies digits within one factor. * 4 × 1 = 4; 1 × 30 = 30	$\begin{array}{r} 31 \\ \times\ 4 \\ \hline 34^{*} \end{array}$
38. Multiplies by only one number.	$\begin{array}{r} 457 \\ \times\ 12 \\ \hline 914 \end{array}$
39. "Carries" wrong number.	$\begin{array}{r} 8\ \ \\ 67 \\ \times\ 40 \\ \hline 3220 \end{array}$
40. Does not multiply units times tens.	$\begin{array}{r} 32 \\ \times\ 24 \\ \hline 648 \end{array}$
41. Reverses divisor with dividend. * Thinks 6 ÷ 3 instead of 30 ÷ 6	$6\overline{)30}$ = 2 *
42. Does not regroup; treats each column as separate addition example.	$\begin{array}{r} 23 \\ +\ 8 \\ \hline 211 \end{array}$

(continued)

Figure 10-6 (continued)

Analysis	*Example*
43. Subtracts smaller digit from larger at all times to avoid renaming.	273 −639 ——— 446
44. Does not add regrouped number.	37 × 7 ——— 219
45. Confuses place value in division:	
a. Considers thousands divided by units as hundreds divided by units;	1) 200) 201 3 /6003 6000 ——— 3 3 ———
b. records partial quotient as tens instead of units;	50) 100) 150 7 / 735 −700 ——— 35 35 ———
c. omits zero needed to show no units in quotient.	2 rem 1 3/ 61 6 ——— 1
46. Ignores remainder because: a. does not complete subtraction; b. does not *see* need for further computation; c. does not know what to do with "2" if subtraction occurs, so does not compute further.	80 7 / 562 560 ———

Table 10-8.
Checklist of Arithmetic Skills

SKILL AREA	ABOVE AVERAGE 0	AVERAGE 1	BELOW AVERAGE 2
I. Basic Concept: *Vocabulary*			
1. Add/plus, subtract/minus			
2. Multiply/divide			
3. Odd/even			
4. Open/closed			
5. Base, factors, prime			
6. Symbols: =, −, +, −, ÷,			
7. Set(s)			
8. Zero			
II. Basic Computation			
Addition			
9. Addition facts			
10. Horizontal notation/no carrying			
11. Vertical notation/no carrying			
12. Vertical notation/with carrying			
13. Column addition			
14. Decimals			
Subtraction			
15. Subtraction facts			
16. Horizontal notation/no regrouping			
17. Vertical notation/no regrouping			
18. Vertical notation/with regrouping			
19. Borrowing from zero			
20. Decimals			

(continued)

Table 10-8 *continued*

SKILL AREA	ABOVE AVERAGE 0	AVERAGE 1	BELOW AVERAGE 2
Multiplication			
21. Tables 1–5	_______	_______	_______
22. Tables 6–10	_______	_______	_______
23. One-place multiplication	_______	_______	_______
24. Two-place multiplication	_______	_______	_______
25. Three-or-more-place multiplication	_______	_______	_______
26. Use of zero as a place-holder	_______	_______	_______
27. Multiplying by 10, 100, 1,000	_______	_______	_______
28. Decimals	_______	_______	_______
Division			
29. Tables 1–5	_______	_______	_______
30. Tables 6-10	_______	_______	_______
31. Short division	_______	_______	_______
32. Long division/subtractive method	_______	_______	_______
33. Long division/regular notation	_______	_______	_______
34. Use of zero as a place-holder	_______	_______	_______
35. Dividing by 10, 100, 1,000	_______	_______	_______
36. Decimals	_______	_______	_______
37. Conversion of fractions to decimals	_______	_______	_______
III. Fractions			
Concepts			
38. Common fractions: ½, ⅓, ¼, ¾	_______	_______	_______
39. Fractions as part of a whole	_______	_______	_______
40. Fractions as part of a set	_______	_______	_______

SKILL AREA	ABOVE AVERAGE 0	AVERAGE 1	BELOW AVERAGE 2
41. Common denominator	______	______	______
42. Lowest common denominator	______	______	______
Addition			
43. Addition of like fractions	______	______	______
44. Addition of unlike fractions	______	______	______
45. Addition of mixed fractions	______	______	______
Subtraction			
46. Subtraction of like fractions	______	______	______
47. Subtraction of unlike fractions	______	______	______
48. Subtraction of mixed fractions	______	______	______
Multiplication			
49. Multiplication of like fractions	______	______	______
50. Multiplication of unlike fractions	______	______	______
51. Multiplication of mixed fractions	______	______	______
Division			
52. Division of like fractions	______	______	______
53. Division of unlike fractions	______	______	______
54. Division of mixed fractions	______	______	______
IV. Measurement			
Length			
55. Vocabulary	______	______	______
56. Computation/English	______	______	______
57. Computation/metric	______	______	______

(continued)

Table 10-8 *continued*

SKILL AREA	ABOVE AVERAGE 0	AVERAGE 1	BELOW AVERAGE 2
Area			
58. Vocabulary	_______	_______	_______
59. Computation/English	_______	_______	_______
60. Computation/metric	_______	_______	_______
Liquid measure			
61. Vocabulary	_______	_______	_______
62. Computation/English	_______	_______	_______
63. Computation/metric	_______	_______	_______
Dry measure			
64. Vocabulary	_______	_______	_______
65. Computation/English	_______	_______	_______
66. Computation/metric	_______	_______	_______
Temperature			
67. Fahrenheit	_______	_______	_______
68. Celsius	_______	_______	_______
Time			
69. Clock/to the hour	_______	_______	_______
70. Clock/to the half-hour and quarter-hour	_______	_______	_______
71. Clock/to the minute	_______	_______	_______
72. A.M./P.M.	_______	_______	_______
73. Twenty-four-hour clock	_______	_______	_______
74. Calendar: days	_______	_______	_______
75. Calendar: months, years	_______	_______	_______
Money			
76. Identification of coins, bills	_______	_______	_______
77. Computation using money	_______	_______	_______

SKILL AREA	ABOVE AVERAGE 0	AVERAGE 1	BELOW AVERAGE 2
V. Geometry			
Identification/Definition			
78. Basic shapes: circle, square, triangle, rectangle, oval	______	______	______
79. Geometric shapes: parallelogram, pentagon, hexagon, octagon	______	______	______
80. Three-dimensional shapes: cube, sphere, pyramid, cylinder, cone	______	______	______
81. Elements: point, line, segment, angle	______	______	______
Computation			
82. Two-dimensional: radius, diameter, circumference, angle	______	______	______
83. Three-dimensional shapes	______	______	______
VI. Word Problems			
84. Isolating relevant information	______	______	______
85. Determining process to be used	______	______	______
86. Understanding "unknown"	______	______	______
87. One-step problem: construction of equation (number sentence)	______	______	______
88. Two-step problem: construction of equations (number sentences)	______	______	______
89. Estimating as means of checking	______	______	______

(continued)

Scoring Key: Checklist of Arithmetic Skills

SKILL AREA	ABOVE AVERAGE	AVERAGE	BELOW AVERAGE	DEFICIT AREA
I. Basic Concepts: Vocabulary	4	8	12	16
II. Basic Computation				
Addition	3	6	9	12
Subtraction	3	6	9	12
Multiplication	4	8	9	16
Division	5	9	12	18
III. Fractions	8	17	25	34
IV. Measurement	11	23	34	46
V. Geometry	3	6	9	12
VI. Word Problems	3	6	9	12
Total	44	89	128	178

Summary

Reading is a complex skill that requires the reader not only to decode the words, but also to understand the author's meaning. The child's ability to read depends, therefore, on his competence with oral language. The child who is able to decode, but whose experience and ability to understand are limited, will not be able to learn to read satisfactorily beyond his own linguistic level. An analysis of the relationship between reading and general cognitive levels, as described by Bloom, is provided so that teachers may first assess the child's level of language and cognition as described in Chapter 8, and then estimate the level of comprehension that can be expected in reading. A child who exhibits difficulty in comprehension may need classroom activities related to oral language as his or her primary remedial activity.

The survey assessment using an illustrative sequence of skills at various grade levels helps the teacher develop a better understanding of how far the child has progressed. Such a method may be helpful in choosing materials or in pinpointing a specific skill that needs to be taught. It is also useful in keeping records of an individual student's progress.

A checklist is provided for evaluating a child's mastery of reading mechanics. First an assessment of the oral, silent, and comprehension reading levels are made. Problems relating to rate are assessed in order to evaluate the extent to which motor performance may be contributing to reading difficulty, and to evaluate the student's ability to adjust the speed of silent reading to the purpose of the reading. Next, word attack skills are analyzed in a highly structured sequence.

Three levels of comprehension are assessed: literal (i.e., understanding the meaning of words, sentences, and paragraphs), interpretive (i.e., generalizing, reasoning about prior and future events, making predictions), and critical (i.e., evaluating what is read in terms of bias, literary merit, or logical presentation).

In functional reading, the necessary study and library skills the child needs to be successful in school subjects such as history and science, as well as in life skills such as using directories, maps, following directions, and locating information, are evaluated. Since the goal of any school program is to provide the student with the ability to use the skills obtained, it is important to assess the extent to which this has been accomplished. This is particularly important for secondary school students who may be nearing the end of their school careers.

The section on arithmetic distinguishes between mathematics and arithmetic. Mathematical ability is the ability to abstract, using space and number relationships and configurations, while ability in arithmetic is the computation of real numbers to demonstrate and illustrate those abstractions.

In earlier chapters of this book the importance of sensory and motor learning to language and cognitive skills was emphasized. Here an analysis of Piaget's concepts of spatial organization and number abstraction is given, and the relationship to problem solving and the developing intellect of the child can be seen. Although it is not necessary to attach an intelligence score to a child's ability to conceptualize, each of these early concepts is directly related to what we call "mathematical readiness."

When a student encounters difficulty in arithmetic, areas not involving direct mathematical concepts must also be examined. Difficulty with language, for example, may contribute to difficulties with arithmetic, since the ability to understand verbal expressions is necessary to perform the mental manipulations involved in computing. Problems in reading also contribute to difficulties in arithmetic, since word problems, as well as the highly abstract symbol system used, are an integral part of any arithmetic curriculum above the third grade. Motor skills, particularly those relating to the proper placement of numerals on the page (spatial relations), and organization (motor-planning) also contribute to difficulty in arithmetic. Once an error analysis identifies problem areas, a detailed examination of each may contribute significantly to the teacher's understanding.

The survey assessment uses a suggested sequence of skills to estimate grade placement for a child, and to provide a mechanism for recording progress as teaching and learning occur.

The diagnostic evaluation consists primarily of an error analysis, designed to pinpoint the nature of the child's difficulty. This analysis provides a percentage-based score that allows the teacher to evaluate the significance of any difficulty encountered by the child. The remedial program can then be developed for a specific area.

Bibliography

Barakat, M. K. "A Factorial Study of Mathematical Abilities." *British Journal of Psychology* 4 (1951): 137–156.

Bloom, B. S. *Taxonomy of Educational Objectives.* New York: Longmans, Green, 1956.

Bormuth, J. R. "Factory Validity of Cloze Tests as Measures of Reading Comprehension Ability." *Reading Research Quarterly* 4, no. 3 (1969): 358–365.

Brownell, W. A., and Moser, A. G. *Meaningful Versus Mechanical Learning: A Study in Grade Three Subtraction.* Duke University Research Studies in Education, no. 8. Durham, N.C.: Duke University Press, 1949.

Chalfant, J. C., and Scheffelin, M. A. *Central Processing Dysfunctions in Children.* Bethesda, Md.: National Institute of Health, 1969.

Chall, Jeanne. *Learning to Read: The Great Debate.* New York: McGraw-Hill, 1967.

Cook, J. M., and Welch, M. W. "Reading as a Function of Visual and Auditory Process Training." *Learning Disability Quarterly* 3, no. 3 (1980): 76–87.

Fries, C. C. *Linguistics and Reading.* New York: Holt, Rinehart and Winston, 1962.

Gibson, E. J., and Levin, H. *The Psychology of Reading.* Cambridge, Mass.: MIT Press, 1975.

Goodman, K. S., ed., *Miscue Analysis: Applications to Reading Instruction.* ERIC. Urbana, Ill.: National Council of Teachers of English, 1973.

Hammill, D. D., and Bartel, N. R. *Teaching Children with Learning and Behavior Problems.* Boston: Allyn and Bacon, 1975.

Harris, A. J., and Sipay, E. R. *Effective Teaching of Reading.* 2d ed. New York: Longmans, 1971.

Heddins, J. W., and Smith, K. J. "The Readability of Elementary Mathematics Books." *Arithmetic Teacher* 10 (1964): 466–484.

Johnson, D. J., and Myklebust, H. R. *Learning Disabilities: Educational Principles and Practices.* New York: Grune and Stratton, 1967.

Kaluger, G., and Kolson, C. J. *Reading and Learning Disabilities.* 2d ed. Columbus, Mo.: Charles E. Merrill, 1978.

Lovell, K. *The Growth of Understanding in Mathematics.* New York: Holt, Rinehart and Winston, 1971.

Piaget, Jean. *The Child's Conception of Number.* New York: W. W. Norton, 1965.

Chapter 11
Student Behavior

Assessments of student behavior can be roughly separated into two categories: analyses that have direct application to behavior change and those that provide information for understanding behavior. The first type tends to provide data relevant to a specific student action; the second generates information that is more global and may represent a class of behaviors in a student or group of students. A well-defined target behavior is more appropriately the subject of the first type of assessment, while class attitudes, for example, or a lack of confidence in a student may be effectively understood using the second type of assessment strategies.

DIRECT APPLICATION

The first four methods described in this chapter on behavior assessment are expansions of methods presented in Chapter 4. The options log and environmental inventory are added in order to provide a broader understanding of student behavior. Each can be effectively used in a behavior management program. In fact, even if other assessment methods are used to collect background information, one of the six observation methods may still be used to verify or monitor change. For instance, attitudinal information gained in a self-evaluation procedure may help a teacher choose a strategy for behavior change, but once the strategy is in place it may be monitored by a frequency count.

Chronolog

It is often desirable to determine the entire sequence of events that occurs in an episode of a student's behavior. For instance, a teacher may wish to discover the exact interaction that occurs between a student and her peers during periods of assigned seat work. A teacher may also wish to determine the role that his own interaction plays in the behavior of a student. In order to accomplish these tasks, a careful record must be kept of the movement, interactions, and work activity of the student, teacher, and peers during the target period. The following is an example of a chronolog; it is followed by a brief examination of possible teacher actions:

> *Setting, 10:45:* The teacher, standing before the class, asks the students to begin their arithmetic assignment. She points to the assignments written on the chalk board and asks if everyone knows what they are do to. There are no student questions. Students move about: some get materials from their desks, others go to the paper storage area, two are at the pencil sharpener, one stands at the teacher's desk, and another two are at a book storage area. Talking is low and between pairs of students.
>
> *Focus:* Fred is at his desk, getting out his materials and a book. He looks around as he sorts through his books and materials. He turns to the girl at the desk to his right, and he stops preparing his desk for work.
> He says something in a low, inaudible voice and attends to her response.
> She answers in a low, inaudible voice. She returns to her work.
> Fred continues to arrange his book and papers on his desk top.
> *10:47:* Fred leaves his desk and goes to the paper area.
> He stands while two other students select paper.
> He taps lightly on the back of one student, and the boy moves slightly without stepping aside.
> In a low voice Fred speaks to one of those standing at the paper cabinet.
> The boy responds to him with a short statement and a smile.
> When the students leave, Fred selects a sheet of paper.
> He turns but continues to stand, with sheet in his hand, and watches two boys talking at a nearby desk.

10:49: Fred continues to stand and watches others in the class, including the teacher, who is at her desk.
The teacher looks up from her desk and asks the two students standing at a desk to "Get to work." She asks Fred to sit down.
10:50: Fred walks slowly back to his desk, stopping two times, each time silently watching a student work. Each time the student at the desk looks up, says nothing, and then goes back to work.
10:52: Arriving at his desk Fred sits slowly; he opens his book and begins to finger through the pages.
10:54: He continues to finger through the pages; he appears busy.
10:58: He stops turning pages and writes his name on his paper.
10:59: He watches the student at the next desk work.
11:00: He stands and goes to the teacher's desk and asks what he is to do. She opens her copy of the book and shows him.
11:01: He returns slowly to his desk, stopping at a boy's desk and asking in a soft voice what he is doing. The boy points at the work and says he's trying to do what he was supposed to complete the previous day.
11:03: Fred returns to his desk, sits and looks around.
11:05: He has opened his book and fingers through the pages.
11:08: He stands up, takes the paper that he had written his name on, crumples it, takes it over to a wastepaper basket, and drops it in.
11:09: He walks over to the paper cabinet and selects another sheet. On his way back to his desk he again stops at a student's desk, saying nothing, and watches what the student is doing.
11:12: The teacher tells Fred to return to his desk and begin working. He moves immediately but slowly to his desk.
11:13: Now in his seat, he slowly writes his name on his new sheet of paper.
He begins to leaf through the book.
He finally stops at a page and looks at it while he chews on the eraser on his pencil.
11:15: He copies the first problem on his paper.

The chronolog provides insight into the delaying tactics Fred uses on a math seat-work assignment. Thirty minutes lapsed between the time he was given an assignment and the time he started.

The chronolog is analyzed by breaking the episode into activity units. In Fred's chronolog the entire episode centered around a period of seat work. Fred's activities included:

- Preparing for the assignment (in seat)
- Getting paper (out of seat)
- Talking, touching, or observing other students

- Communicating with the teacher
- Beginning the assignment

This information can help the teacher understand the student's actual behavior and can help her decide where she will place her emphasis. Assuming the student is able to do the work he has been assigned, the teacher might select any one of a number of methods to help Fred start more quickly and maintain his productivity. She could talk with him about starting his work on time, arrange a contract, provide a schedule of reinforcement, put him with a more conscientious student, monitor him more closely, and so on. In Fred's case he is not completing his work because he isn't beginning it soon enough to be able to finish.

Frequency Count

The frequency count is a basic instrument of assessment. Its simplicity allows it to be used in almost any situation, with any behavior, and with comparative ease. It is the most direct and representative method for determining the occurrence of a behavior and for monitoring change or lack of change. Two examples will illustrate its application in assessing and tracking student problems.

Example A: A classroom teacher has noticed that his third-period class is considerably more talkative and less productive than any of his other classes. One behavior that has come to his attention is an almost constant need for the students to ask for help and seek his attention. He decides to keep a count on how many questions are asked of him during the first fiteen minutes of the class.

After several days (baseline) of counting and recording this behavior, he determines that he receives an average of seventy-five questions, statements, and comments during that fifteen-minute time period each day. He assumes that the count is reliable because the class behavior during the baseline period was similar to what he usually experienced. He decides to change the interaction pattern by encouraging the class to work more independently, and he tells the students that he will allow only three questions during the first fifteen minutes of that period.

A week later, his average count is three questions during the first fifteen minutes and five in the subsequent forty minutes. His assignment book reveals that the time needed to complete an assignment in class has been cut in half. If the questioning behavior had continued, his count would have immediately alerted him to both the failure of his intervention and the need to select a new plan.

Example B: A student in a classroom is frequently out of his seat. Standard admonitions have not changed this behavior, and the teacher plans a new approach to the problem. She first selects a ten-minute period of time after recess for her frequency count and, every half minute, notes whether the student is seated. The counting is maintained for five days to establish the baseline.

At the end of the week the teacher discusses the frequency count with the student and by mutual agreement arrange a contract that calls for in-seat behavior. She continues the frequency count and after three days determines that there is no change in behavior. She then chooses a second intervention.

During a time when the class is empty, the teacher has the student rehearse in-seat behavior, including raising his hand and working with materials at his desk. She also makes positive comments to the student while he is in his seat. The frequency count is continued for a week, and the teacher finds that the student remains in his seat during all but one day. On that day (the third), he is out of his seat at only one observation point.

In both this case and the preceding one, the teacher chose the frequency count as a way to establish the rate of occurrence prior to an intervention. The count was continued until the teacher was confident that a means had been developed to reach and sustain the desired level of behavior. Once the improvement was established, the counting was discontinued.

Sequence Sample

In the sequence sample, the observation is focused on a specific incident in behavior. The time involved may be no more than a minute or two. The critical elements are: (1) a brief behavioral statement of the student's action at the point of the problem, (2) a list of all the conditions operating immediately before the problem, and (3) those conditions that immediately follow the problem.

Table 11-1 describes a single but representative incident of behavior for John, a junior high school student. John is often upsetting to the class, and one of the more upsetting things he does is make mouth noises.

Data provided in the sequence sample allow the teacher or other professionals to determine at which one of three points in the sequence an intervention might be most appropriate. Any behavior can be influenced at any one of the three stages, and the sequence sample clearly provides behavioral data at each point. John's case can be used to illustrate the

Table 11-1.
Sequence Sample

ANTECEDENTS	BEHAVIOR	CONSEQUENCES
Seat work, language assignment beginning, writing sentences required	Student makes a mouth noise.	One student tells John to stop. He does not acknowledge the comment and continues.
11:00 A.M.; whole class is in a similar assignment; teacher is at another student's desk.		Teacher ignores for approximately three minutes.
		Teacher says, "John, let's be quiet."
Talking among students is permitted and is low and generally task-related		John looks up and stops noise.
		Four minutes later he is making the noise again.

Other related information:

Mouth noises are made only during seat work.

John is capable of doing the work he has been assigned.

Teacher has tried ignoring the behavior, but that didn't help.

When John makes noises, the general level of talking in the room increases.

Goal: To extinguish John's inappropriate noises during the language period.

variety of interventions possible at the antecedent, behavior, or consequence points.

A selection of possible intervention strategies that might influence the antecedents to John's behavior include: isolation during seat work, changing the time of the activity, rearranging the room during seat work, giving John special directions for seat work, or creating a moratorium on seat work for John. Some of the strategies that might influence John's choice of behavior during seat work are: discussing with John his behavior, contracting for appropriate behavior, role playing appropriate behavior, providing visualization activities around seat work, or introducing self-talk activities designed to increase self-control.

Some of the modifications that would act on the consequences of John's behavior include: making positive comments about silent, productive time; providing a check sheet on silence, with an ultimate reward; instituting a class plan to ignore John's problem; setting a time out arrangement for misbehavior; selecting a self-rewarding plan; or providing for immediate removal from class for continued noise making.

The ultimate choice of interventions depends on the preference of the teacher, the flexibility available in the setting, and the likelihood of positive results. An intervention that includes planning contributions from John and that results in an agreement between the teacher and John has the best chance for success. If a plan fails, another strategy, which can focus on one of the other points in the sequence, can be chosen.

Trait Sample

One trait sample procedure described in Chapter 4 was that designed by Spaulding (1980). In his assessment, the student and two randomly chosen classmates are observed and behavior is recorded in nineteen descriptive categories. When the counts in each category are totaled at the end of the observation, they describe the student along eight behavioral styles. Figure 4-9 provides the clusters of scoring categories within each style.

Spaulding's (1980) treatments for each style rely on changing the consequences of behavior. The basic procedure is to selectively isolate, ignore, or reinforce specific categories of behavior. For example, the following is the treatment schedule for style A behavior:

1. Set strict, narrow limits (set specific routine to follow). Give no choices, set specific concrete academic tasks.
2. Assign to specific work station (to work alone).
3. Instruct individually or in groups of six or fewer.
4. Supervise closely (do not leave child unattended).
5. Punish *all* unacceptable behavior immediately by social isolation (time-out from reinforcement).
6. Reinforce *all* emerging desirable behavior (100 percent schedule).
7. Ignore visual wandering (*11*) and daydreaming (*12*).
8. Ignore 3b (manipulation) when directed toward teacher.

The exact item treatment for a student with a dominant style A profile would be to:

- Isolate behaviors in categories: 1, 2, 3b
- Ignore behavior in categories: 4, 5b, 7b, 8b, 11, 12, 13
- Reinforce behavior in categories: 3a, 5a, 6, 7a, 8a, 9a, 10

The advantage of a trait sample like Spaulding's is that teachers' actions can be designed to affect specific student behaviors. The analysis of the student's behavior in the classroom is multidimensional, and the teacher is provided not only with a clear description of the behavior but direct suggestions as to what teacher behavior will lead to more appropriate student behavior.

Options Log

In analyzing behavior, one aspect that is often overlooked is the alternative behaviors available to the student. There is usually more than one correct way to act, and there are an infinite number of acceptable individual variations. It is often important to determine the range of behaviors that a student has in his total repertoire of actions. Some students do not change their behavior because they do not have acceptable alternatives. Strange as that may seem, many actions are performed because no other is immediately available to the individual. This individual has no choice but to act as he or she acted before.

The options log is an examination of the behaviors individuals knowingly have available to them. The log can include behavior that is described verbally or demonstrated physically. The first gives the range of alternatives that the individual recognizes as possible. The latter provides some assurance that the individual can act out a behavior.

Because most logs are developed in reference to specific behavior problems, the focus of the inquiry is directed toward concrete alternatives under specific conditions. For instance, a student who does not complete homework assignments might be asked to describe the various ways the assignments can be completed. A class that is discussing drug use might itemize the ways people can go to sleep without using a sleeping pill. In both cases the teacher or other professional can suggest methods that have not been offered by the individual or the group. Some active student response, however, will be needed so the adult will know how the student(s) understands the teacher's alternative(s).

Even when a student has verbally described a behavioral option, the assessor cannot be sure that the student can act on the option. The use of role playing, behavior rehearsal, or some other demonstration method is required if the log is to include options that can be acted upon. A complete option log includes both statements of the possible behaviors that can be used in a situation and the evidence that the behavior can actually be performed by the individual or the group. A brief record of the process will allow the assessor to analyze the options and determine if all the reasonable alternatives have been considered. A format for the option log is provided in Figure 11-1.

Environmental Inventory

Another method of direct assessment of behavioral activity is the environmental inventory. This inventory details the current conditions for learning and behavior, and attempts to predict or project an anticipated level of student behavior in a new setting. The effectiveness of the procedure is based on the premise that common conditions in two settings should produce similar results and that transfer of learning occurs where stimulus and reinforcement conditions remain relatively constant.

Figure 11-1.
Format for An Options Log

Statement of the situation: ____________________

Possible student actions	Anticipated reactions	Evidence of student skill
1.		
2.		
3.		
Other		

There are several situations in which this assessment procedure is useful.

One use of the environmental inventory is in the prediction of how a student in one setting will perform in a second setting. This procedure, which is in its infancy, is far from perfected. It works best where the environment of the present location has provided a wide variety of training experiences. For instance, a student in a special program may have experienced instruction in groups of one, two, six, twelve, and fifteen students. A brief description of the student's ability to learn in each setting, the content and conditions of successful instruction in each, and the special nature of supervision can supply clues about how the student might learn best in another location. A similar check of behavior management experiences in each setting will help staff in other locations anticipate what supervision might be necessary in their setting. Figure 11-2 illustrates an environmental inventory on Mary, a special education student who is being considered for a move from one program to another.

Figure 11-2
Example of an Environmental Inventory

Name: Mary School: Brentwood Class: Special
Age: 7 yrs. 2 mos. Birth Date: 1-18-75 Teacher: Lee
Reason for Review: Possible move to new location
Request: Environmental Inventory of Current Situation

Class Members: Eight students from 5 years to 8½ years of age.

Adult Supervision: One teacher and one paid aide.

Class Activities: Beginning reading, manipulative math, physical education, language and writing, socialization, music, and art.

Teaching Situation: Instruction in skills is one-to-one or one teacher to two students; Mary is successful and attentive in group situation in P.E., snack time, sharing, and easily completed activities like "clean up."

Large-Group Instruction and Activities: Mary talks and annoys other students when work is at a level (above age 5) where she cannot be successful. Behavior can become unruly and physically abusive to other children.

New Learning: All new tasks must be introduced in one-to-one or two-to-one instruction. Reinforcements in the form of checks, food, and praise are effective. Time outs are effective in the control of misbehavior.

General Behavior: Mary will behave most of the time when in successful activities. She responds positively to praise and support from adults; she is unaffected by comments from other children.

In Mary's case the staff at the new situation will need to consider whether they have the staff members available to parallel the current program. If not, they need to determine other ways they might manage her behavior in large groups and give her enough attention to produce effective learning.

The second use of the inventory is to determine the conditions under which instruction should take place so that it most closely approximates the "natural" conditions in which learning will be applied. In this case the study is made of the natural setting in order to determine the most likely way for appropriate skills and behavior to be triggered, reinforced, and evaluated. The procedure is relevant to all subject areas where the student is expected to apply in the "real world" what is learned in school. Vocational training programs, for instance, are often designed to be small replicas of actual work situations. Also, regular and special class programs can be modified to present the student with experiences that are much like those he or she will encounter in another type of class or in an out-of-class situation. In these cases the inventory is used to describe those other settings accurately so they can be duplicated in the classroom.

INDIRECT ANALYSIS

Indirect analysis of behavior is based on self-reporting procedures. Attitudes, beliefs, feelings, and preferences are not always available to the assessor through direct observation of behavior, and yet knowledge about these conditions can help the professional choose an appropriate course of action. Methods that can be most helpful are attitude surveys, sociograms, projective techniques, and self-assessments. The first two have been described briefly in previous chapters.

Attitude Survey

Examples of *attitude survey* questions were given in the questionnaire section of Chapter 5. Questions such as "What do you think about open book exams?" and "How do you feel about the rules of this class?" and "I get upset when ________" tend to elicit statements of feelings and emotions. Attitude surveys uncover the personal feelings and beliefs of students. This information can help teachers decide on behavioral interventions and instructional programming. For instance, a direct observation of behavior may determine that certain materials have low interest value for students. It may, however, take an interest inventory to determine the types of materials that are more likely to appeal to the individual or to a group of students.

Direct analysis may be used to determine behavior at a given time, but indirect methods provide clues as to why that behavior occurred and what alternative behaviors might be possible. Such stem phrases as "How do you feel about . . . ?", "Tell me what you like best and least about . . .", "What is more important to you . . . ?", "Name some of your interests," "Do you believe that . . .?", and "What should you do when . . .?" allow students to express their attitudes, beliefs, feelings, and interests. Both group and individual information can be solicited either orally or in written form.

The reliability of this information can be improved by asking a cluster of questions around the same topic, by asking similar questions in several different settings, or by aggregating the responses of many students to several questions. A cluster of questions related to subject preference might include these:

- What is your favorite subject?
- What subject would you like to discuss in class?
- What do you like to read or write about?
- What school work do you like to do in the morning?
- When you have free time, what school subject do you choose for extra work?
- Why do you like your favorite subject?

When oral questions are asked of a group, answers tend to reflect the feelings of dominant members of that group. Speakers can be swayed by forceful or high prestige members, and individual variations can be lost in silence. Although group questioning is useful when a consensus is desired or variations need to be examined, the same procedure can give a distorted impression of individual beliefs and feelings. When the group approach is used efforts should be made to elicit honest, individual contributions. Individual and small-group interviews provide an effective alternative where group interaction is not needed.

Sociogram

The *sociogram* is used to determine the degree of attraction between various members of a group. Usually the data are obtained by asking students to nominate or rate their peers in a given situation. They can be asked to select a single student for a given nomination or asked to rate their first, second, and third choice. In the sociogram in Figure 11-3, the students were asked to select their first, second, and third choices as work partners in a social studies project. Different situations invariably produce different choices. Areas under examination can be adapted to fit the circumstances. The following are representative of a variety of possible sociogram topic areas:

- Lunch partner
- Math partner
- Roommate
- Project leader
- Baseball teammate
- Crossing guard
- Cleanup assistant
- Co-chairperson (socials)

The results can also be tabulated as they are in Figure 3-2, and this will provide information on the frequency of choice. Data can also be graphically displayed so as to reveal the actual choice patterns. The graphic in Figure 11-3 takes the material in Chapter 2 and highlights individual choices. In this example Frank receives no choices and is an "isolate" in this group structure. Lisa and Cheryl receive four choices each and are the "stars." Mutual choices occur between Lisa and Peter, Gary and Cheryl, and Joy and Susan.

The sociogram reveals positive boy-girl choices in this group of ten students. The two highly selected students are connected by a student who chooses both "stars." The possibility for friction exists at points where the "stars" choose students who, in turn, prefer the other "star"; for example, in the case of Bill and Ann. If Frank is to feel a part of the group it will probably be best to place him in a subgroup that contains Frank's first or second choice. This sociogram identifies two student clusters and an isolate.

The sociogram can have potentially harmful side effects. No matter how carefully the questions are worded and how well the results are hidden, the participants can look upon the procedure as a popularity contest. The traditional identification of "stars" and "isolates" can be viewed as paralleling the winner and loser categories of a contest. Any action that supports this comparison can have negative effects on the feelings of participants. Sociograms are constructed to refer to specific activities; the data, therefore, have a narrow focus and are often relevant for only a short period of time. The narrow focus coupled with the potentially harmful impact on individuals' feelings limits the use of sociograms as a behavioral assessment strategy. When it is used, the data should be gathered infrequently, kept confidential, and interpreted narrowly.

Figure 11-3.
Sociogram of Students' First and Second Choices in a Social Studies Project

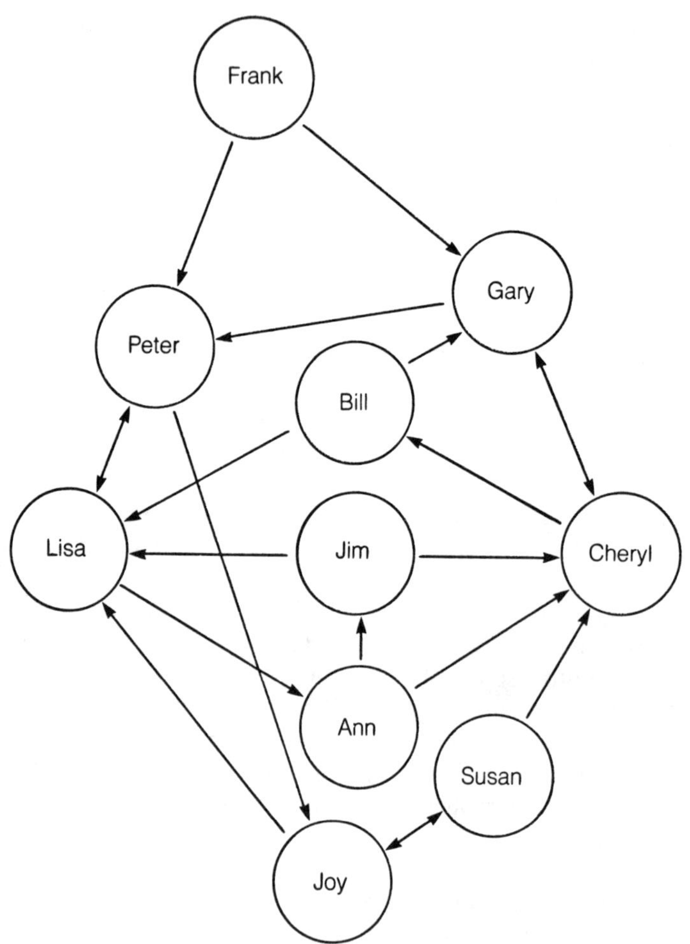

Projective Techniques

Projective techniques are a third type of indirect assessment. The procedure involves presenting the student with an ambiguous, unstructured stimulus, and then recording and interpreting the responses. The limitation of the technique has always rested with the interpretation. Ideally a student's responses will give clues as to his or her attitudes, beliefs, needs, and inner conflicts. The responses, however, can be influenced by many factors unrelated to the inner state of the student. The physical environment, the "mind set" aroused in the school setting, the examiner's appearance and attitude, and the experiences preceding the testing are but a few of the uncontrolled variables that can help shape the student's responses. The wise assessor approaches projective data with a full awareness of these basic interferences and with a recognition of the limits of interpretation. At best this procedure gives clues and tentative insights, both of which require verification before they can be acted upon.

The most widely used projective method is sentence completion; however, pictures, drawings, role playing, "three wishes," fairy tales, and other imaginative and loosely structured stimuli can also give rise to student projections. These activities are usually seen as "fun" and are less testlike than most other methods. They also tap the fantasy and creative part of a student. Figure 11-4 gives examples of common items that are used in sentence completion tests.

Figure 11-4.
Common Stems Used in Sentence Completion Tests

Incomplete Sentences

1. I am happy when ________________.
2. I like ________________.
3. I am sad when ________________.
4. What I like best at school is ________________.
5. I would like to know ________________.
6. I think that ________________.
7. I wish that ________________.
8. In sports I ________________.
9. On the school yard ________________.
10. I get mad when ________________.
11. In school I ________________.
12. The teacher ________________.
13. I worry about ________________.
14. My biggest wish is ________________.
15. In my family ________________.

(continued)

Figure 11-4 continued

16. When I get mad I ______________________.
17. My friends at school ______________________.
18. My mother ______________________.
19. When I have work to do I ______________________.
20. Kids at school ______________________.
21. When I go home I ______________________.
22. I think that ______________________.
23. My father ______________________.
24. The subject I don't like is ______________________.
25. Happiness is ______________________.

The degree of structure in a projective measure will partially determine the form and content of the student's response. If the assessor asks a student to respond to a blank picture or to produce an original skit, the assessor will have less control over the response than if she asks the student to tell what is happening in a picture that depicts a teacher talking with a student or if she asks the student to produce a skit in which a parent talks with a son or daughter. The more unstructured the task, the more the assessor's purpose is hidden and the more unpredictable the response. Increasing the structure makes the assessor's purpose more apparent, but it also helps the student to focus his comments on the areas under consideration.

Projective information should be interpreted cautiously and tentatively. Literal interpretations are difficult enough, but generalized statements are even more tenuous. The following is a list of some of the common themes to emerge from projective information:

- Interpersonal perceptions of respondent towards: parents, friends, opposite sex, teachers, authorities, enemies, etc.
- Emotional feelings about persons, activities, success, failure, prior or anticipated events, etc.
- Attitudes and beliefs of characters toward others, events, duties, roles, work, etc.
- The content, role, and outcome of action or inaction.
- Coping strategies related to interpersonal relations, conflicts, affection, problems, tension, etc.
- Identification with characters including sympathy, support, antagonism, confusion, disdain, worship, etc.

These themes can be used as a general guide in analyzing projective data. The assessor, however, is seldom sure whether the respondent is portraying his or her own feelings or actions, those seen in others, or those created for the test.

Self-assessment

Student *self-assessment* can occur in a number of ways. One common example is when a student, caught in the act of misbehavior or confronted with a previous misdeed, is asked "Why did you do that?" The question usually contains both the elements of an admonition and a sincere inquiry. Unfortunately, in a situation of crisis and threat the student is likely to select a response that he thinks will reduce the fury. The results are often expressions of justification, blame, or contrition. That type of response may characterize a student's style under pressure but casts little light on the problem.

An alternative form of inquiry does not attempt to fix blame or responsibility but rather attempts to develop solutions. In this procedure the student is asked to examine what he or she did, in an effort to develop a plan of action that will prevent the incident from happening again. The format is that of an interview with the focus on problem solving. Blame is avoided and solutions are sought. The dialogue starts with some statement of the problem and is immediately followed by a direct request for problem solving. The statement and focus can be as follows: "I have noticed a lot of fighting lately, Peter. What can we do to cut it down or stop it?" Or: "Tammy, your assignments have been late. How can I help so that you get them in on time?"

Another aspect of self-analysis is the inventory of beliefs a student holds about himself. Commonly referred to as the "self-concept," these beliefs or theories about themselves influence the way individuals behave. They tend to be situation- and activity-specific but can give rise to overall self-evaluation. Thus, a person who feels that his skill in football and baseball is very poor may see himself as generally poor in sports, a broad generalization arising from limited experience. Conversely, an individual may have different self-evaluations for the same question asked in different situations. For example, a student who is asked to respond to the comment "I am a good student" may have a different response to "I am a good math student" or to "I am a good physical education student."

Questions on self-concept tests usually explore individual perceptions of skills, aptitudes, attitudes, and values. Questions are direct and require the student to report his or her personal attitudes and feelings. However,

Figure 11-5.
Sample Items from an Open-Ended Self-Concept Survey

Personal Inventory

In each area please give your strongest point and the one that most needs improvement

	Strongest	*Needs improvement*
School subjects	______	______
Written work	______	______
Math work	______	______
Sports	______	______
At parties	______	______
Speaking situations	______	______
Relations with others	______	______
Friendships	______	______
With my parents	______	______
General appearance	______	______
Working in groups	______	______

because the expected average or "normal" answer is easily identified, respondents can falsify or conceal their true feelings. An atmosphere of trust and confidentiality is required in order to receive answers that are candid. A response pattern that provides for strengths as well as weaknesses will encourage comprehensive self-evaluations. The statements in Figure 11-5 are open-ended and allow a student to give a balanced self-report.

The same items can be used to determine the quality of the self-perception. This is accomplished by providing qualitative response options such as the categories "good," "average," and "poor." The student is directed to "Check how you see yourself in the following areas":

	VERY GOOD	GOOD	AVERAGE	POOR	VERY POOR
In school	______	____	_____	____	______
In writing	______	____	_____	____	______
In math	______	____	_____	____	______
In sports	______	____	_____	____	______

The list can be expanded to include a variety of academic, social, sport, interest, and interpersonal areas. A simplified yes or no response pattern can be used with young children or with children with low mental ability. The Yes-No Test in Figure 11-6 was designed to be used with children with limited language.

All indirect procedures tap the personal and partly hidden feelings and attitudes of students. This information can be helpful in providing insight and understanding into why individuals act as they do. It also adds a touch of intimacy to assessment and can provide a glimpse at some underlying constants that give continuity to behavior.

Figure 11-6.
The Yes-No Test

No one pays much attention to me at school.

Yes ☐ No ○

I like to work at school.

Yes ☐ No ○

My teacher helps me.

Yes ☐ No ○

Kids really like me.

Yes ☐ No ○

Teachers like me.

Yes ☐ No ○

Kids pick on me.

Yes ☐ No ○

I am pretty happy.

Yes ☐ No ○

I have good friends.

Yes ☐ No ○

School days are good days.

Yes ☐ No ○

My teacher really cares about me.

Yes ☐ No ○

I am glad to be at school.

Yes ☐ No ○

I like the way I look.

Yes ☐ No ○

I play by myself a lot.

Yes ☐ No ○

I know how to be good.

Yes ☐ No ○

I give up when things get hard.

Yes ☐ No ○

Teachers are good.

Yes ☐ No ○

SOURCE: Developed by Phil Daro as part of a research project in Supplementary Education, State Department of Education, California, 1973. Reproduced by permission of the author.

DIAGNOSTIC EVALUATION OF BEHAVIOR

Both direct and indirect analysis of behavior result in the data upon which decisions can be based. A single procedure, like the sequence sample, can be used to understand behavior and help target interventions. Such procedures not only focus on the student but draw attention to the critical role of the teacher and the impact of other students. A comprehensive analysis, however, includes more than a single incident and often more than one method of analysis.

The diagnostic assessment of behavior examines incidents of behavior within an expanded context of behavioral activity. Such an assessment can ask questions about the onset and duration of the behavior, contrast periods of appropriate behavior, determine the utility of the behavior with a peer or within a family or a culture, identify the relative position of the behavior on a developmental scale, describe the behavior outside of school or in subsets of school life, establish the responsiveness to teacher and peer pressures, or predict the course of behavior.

The diagnostic description of behavior not only identifies a focal point for behavioral change but provides an overall assessment of the student's actions. A general perspective is maintained so that the assessor can understand the problem's place in the student's life. For instance, it could be important to know that Fred, a student from a poor family who does not complete assignments in school, who is careless in his dress and possessions, and who can be belligerent in the school yard, also has a job before and after school to help support his family. His success outside school does not eliminate the need for school changes, but it may explain his listlessness during early morning periods, and it clearly indicates that in some circumstances he is both responsible and resourceful.

A comprehensive analysis of behavior could include a review of these areas:

1. The nature of misbehavior and the circumstances under which it occurs
2. The student's appropriate behavior and when it occurs
3. The onset, circumstances, and duration of the problem
4. The age level or circumstances under which the behavior might be appropriate
5. Patterns of good behavior and misbehavior
6. The quality of a student's interpersonal relations in various school and out of school situations

7. The student's skill level during periods of appropriate vs. inappropriate behavior
8. Coping styles and how they are supported or reinforced in the school setting
9. The willingness to participate in change
10. Assessment of motivation, feelings, attitudes, beliefs, and abilities
11. The student's role in the class and school during different activities
12. Home and peer support for misbehavior.

Behaviors can be organized into those involving social interaction, those involving academic or skill behavior, and those in the areas of feelings and affect. Each of these categories can be further defined by subclasses, which can be rated or otherwise examined. The following lists include some of the common subclasses within each category.

SOCIAL	ACADEMIC/SKILL	AFFECT
Cooperation	Responsibility	Interests
Friendliness	Completion	Moods
Acceptance	Coherence	Patience
Courtesy	Relevance	Frustrations
Helpfulness	Clarity	Emotions
Respectfulness	Attentiveness	Persistence
Talkativeness	Understanding	Angers
	Memory	Fears
	Language	Affections

Several major approaches to behavioral assessment are available. Direct analysis of behavior brings into immediate focus the actions surrounding misbehavior, ineffective behavior, or inappropriate behavior. Indirect assessment provides data on attitudes and feelings that are not readily available to observation. Diagnostic assessment provides a comprehensive examination of a student's behavior and can help identify the interplay among various behavior patterns. Direct methods are the choice when a behavior is clearly disruptive or dysfunctional. Indirect methods are useful when motivational and other personal information will help cast light on the problem. Diagnostic methods are chosen when an overall understanding of the problem is sought, when the assessor wishes to determine the context in which the behavior occurs.

Summary

Behavior assessment is divided between strategies that are drawn directly from actual behavior and those that are based on impressions of behavior. The first type provides the teacher or professional with an exact description of behavior and allows for the careful monitoring of behavior. The frequency count, chronolog, sequence sample, trait sample, options log, and environmental inventory provide data based on direct observation and immediate measurement.

Indirect assessment methods provide behavioral descriptions; these methods include surveys, sociograms, projective techniques, and self-assessments. Each method provides a procedure for reporting beliefs, attitudes, feelings, or knowledge about a student's behavior. These methods are useful procedures in that they provide insight into the general characteristics of a student, and they can help develop self-understanding in the respondent. They also provide a perspective on motivation and behavior that cannot be readily observed.

A diagnostic evaluation provides a comprehensive analysis of student performance. It combines a variety of information in order to arrive at a more complete understanding of the student. It is useful when simpler procedures have failed to produce useful information.

Bibliography

Bursuck, William D. "Assessing Social Problems." *The Directive Teacher* 3, no. 1 (1981): 8–10.

Daughton, David, and Fix, A. James. "The Educational Implications of Five Behavioral Clusters." *The Journal of Special Education* 12, no. 1 (1978): 37–44.

Deno, Stanley L. "Directed Observation Approach to Measuring Classroom Behavior." *Exceptional Children* 46, no. 5 (1980): 396–399.

Epstein, Seymour. "The Stability of Behavior: On Predicting Most of the People Much of the Time." *Journal of Personality and Social Psychology* 37, no. 7 (1969): 1097–1126.

Goodwin, Dwight L., and Coates, Thomas J. *Helping Students Help Themselves.* Englewood Cliffs, N.J.: Prentice-Hall, 1976.

Hecht, Lawrence. "Measuring Student Behavior During Group Instruction." *The Journal of Educational Research* 71, no. 5 (1978): 283–290.

Markus, Elliot J. "Mapping the Social Structure of a Class: A Practical Instrument for Assessing Some Effects of Mainstreaming." *The Journal of Special Education* 14, no. 3 (1980): 311–324.

Mischel, Walter. "On the Future of Personality Measurement." *American Psychologist* 32, no. 4 (1977): 246–254.

Solomon, David, and Kendall, Arthur J. "Dimensions of Children's Classroom Behavior, as Perceived by Teachers." *American Educational Research Journal* 14, no. 4 (1977): 421–441.

Spaulding, R. L. *CASES Manual.* San Jose, Calif.: San Jose State University, 1980.

Stam, Priscilla J., and Stam, James C. "The Effect of Sociometric Grouping on Task Performance in the Classroom." *Education* 98, no. 2 (1977): 246–252.

Stowitschek, Carol E.; Lewis, Beverly L.; Shores, Richard E.; and Ezzell, Debbie L. "Procedures for Analyzing Student Performance Data to Generate Hypothesis for the Purpose of Educational Decision Making." *Behavior Disorders* 5, no. 3 (1980): 136–150.

Walker, Hill M., and Holland, Francine. "Issues, Strategies and Perspectives in the Management of Disruptive Child Behavior in the Classroom." *Journal of Education* 161, no. 2 (1979): 71–88.

Watkins, David. "The Development and Evaluation of Self-esteem Measurements." *Journal of Personality Assessment* 42, no. 2 (1978): 171–182.

Part Four
Special Topics

Informal assessment plays an important role in a variety of classroom-related areas. Part Four examines the application of informal assessment to career exploration, teaching methods, classroom management, materials selection, and environmental control. In addition, Chapter 14 is devoted to the very important area of assessment of minority students.

Chapter 12 considers the development and implementation of a career in education. Occupational categories are listed and worker traits are examined in some detail. The subjects of assessment, task analysis, and success prediction are presented with a focus on application in the classroom setting.

Chapter 13, on teaching and classroom management, provides strategies for the assessment of these critical aspects of teacher performance. In-class observation methods are the basis for most teacher performance evaluations; questionnaires, checklists, and interviews are more appropriate for the examination of classroom materials and environment. The measurement of instructional methods depends on procedures that record student performance.

The use of informal as well as formal assessment procedures with minority students deserves special attention. Chapter 14 discusses the impact of culture and language on behavior, thinking, and achievement. Problems in both the application and interpretation of assessment procedures and data are examined, and improved strategies are presented.

Chapter 12
Careers

Too often high school teachers and counselors ignore what, in the end, is probably the most pressing problem facing the secondary student today—adequate preparation for a future vocation and career. Instead, teaching is often directed at basic skill subjects, and the relation between these and students' eventual life goals is not clarified.

In recent years many advances have been made in secondary education in an attempt to resolve this dilemma, and changes are being instituted in the high school curriculum to reflect a new awareness of students' needs. The problem, however, is even more severe for learning-disabled and other disabled children. Traditionally such students finished high school without adequate skills to get a job. Sometimes they would be referred for vocational rehabilitation services. Sometimes nothing would be done, and they would never realize their full employment potential.

In 1980, the Department of Health, Education, and Welfare was divided into the Department of Education and the Department of Health and Human Services. Surprisingly, the Division of Rehabilitation Services was placed in the Department of Education and combined with the Division of Special Education. The Division of Rehabilitation has traditionally had vocational rehabilitation as a major focus—helping disabled people get jobs—but it had been primarily concerned with adults, that is, those over the age of eighteen. The new coalition pointed out an emerging understanding of the role of career and vocational preparation for every child, as well as adult, and the importance of this long-neglected area of concern for students with learning problems and other handicapping conditions.

The problem has been clearly described by Gellman in 1961:

> The adult or young adult entering the labor market is not automatically employable because he attains physical maturity. Employability is a learned attribute, the culmination of a process of socialization which begins at birth. The family constellation provides the behavioral patterns and motivational systems which induce the child to achieve and become productive. School continues the process of learning to work through school tasks and homework. During the primary school period, the child develops the knack of working with his peers and adapting to authority. As he becomes older, after-school and summer employment succeed household chores. When he begins his formal work life he is prepared for the pressures and tensions of work. He exhibits a work personality which facilitates interpersonal and interactional difficulties in a work situation.
>
> In contrast, the disabled child is deprived of the complex of family chores and responsibilities which develop a sense of productivity and work satisfaction. The birth of a child with an apparent disability induces parental attitudes of overprotection or rejection which limit independent activities. School brings segregation or isolation. Lower standards for the handicapped diminish the achievement drive. Prejudice against disabled persons restricts opportunities for summer or after-school work. As disabled young adults, they lack the knowledge and experience which underpin a work personality. Having learned how not to work, they see themselves as unproductive and unable to work. (p. 632)

THE EXPANSION OF VOCATIONAL EDUCATION

The problem of providing adequate vocational and career programming for handicapped students parallels the development of vocational education in the United States.

When public education was introduced during the colonial period, both the stated and the implicit goals were to pass down the knowledge, culture, and values of the nation and to prepare each citizen to become a productive and contributing member of society. This fairly general statement, interpreted in a variety of ways throughout the years, remains as true today as when it was first projected. Unlike most other Western countries, the right to an education is not guaranteed by the central government—that is, in the case of the United States, it is not guaranteed by the Constitution. While the Preamble is usually interpreted to include support for education, each state has included this important right in its own state constitution and has developed its own educational institutions.

The development of vocational education has followed the development of the country. Originally most jobs were learned through an apprenticeship. Children frequently learned the occupations of their parents by working beside them; there was no need for formal training. Professions such as medicine and law of course required a college education. Since no schooling was required for most careers, secondary schools devoted themselves primarily to the arts and sciences required for college preparation. Increasing population shifts to the cities and the increasing industrialization and specialization of the American economy, however, led to a much greater need for vocational training, and the number of vocational programs began to increase rapidly. The rise in vocational training occurred mostly in the twentieth century, much of it associated with the industrial needs created by World War II and, to a lesser extent, by World War I.

Vocational training programs were quickly developed, most of them "added on" as shop courses to already existing high schools. There was little attempt made to coordinate these courses with those already being offered, and little planning was done to develop a well-rounded curriculum in vocational areas. Because most schools were academically oriented, and vocational programs appeared almost as an afterthought, they did not receive much prestige. Children who took vocational classes were felt to be doing so because they could not succeed in college-bound programs, and a negative attitude emerged toward vocational education.

The United States has often been considered the land of opportunity. As part of a growing and upwardly mobile society, parents were anxious for their children to succeed, and great status was accorded those who "made it." Working with one's hands, however, was not considered "making it" by some segments of society, usually those in the professions, in city or state government, or in other white collar professions; training for manual jobs was somehow considered degrading. On the other hand, many people had jobs in industry, crafts, and business, and found them very satisfying and rewarding. A growing dichotomy emerged between reality in the world of work, and the prevailing attitude of many parents and teachers. At a time when a college education was relatively rare and the employment needs of a growing society were great, such an education was thought to be a passport to a wide variety of jobs. When jobs became more specialized and harder to find, students often found that a general education was not adequate preparation. Many students found that neither their high school nor their college education had provided them with a marketable skill. More and more the disparity between what children learned in school and what they needed to learn became apparent.

THE CONCEPT OF CAREER EDUCATION

In 1971 the concept of career education was spearheaded by Sidney P. Marland, then U.S. Commissioner of Education. Many embraced the idea of changing the curriculum to broaden student experience by introducing students, throughout the school years, to different careers. Career education was envisioned as "the totality of experiences through which one learns about, and prepares to engage in, work as part of his or her life" (Hoyt, 1976). Many felt the American educational system had failed to meet its overall mission; students needed to learn something relevant. The U.S. Chamber of Commerce listed the following reasons why career education could offer necessary educational reforms:

> For too many youth, career exploration begins after leaving school instead of during the early learning years when there is ample time to develop areas of work interest and competence.
>
> Youth unemployment is consistently four times greater than adult unemployment, and turnover is high.
>
> Many students are not provided with the skill and knowledge to help them adjust to changes in job opportunities.
>
> There has steadily developed an increased emphasis on "school for schooling's sake" ... education has become, for many students, simply preparation for more education.
>
> In some schools, much of what happens in the classroom has too little to do with what is happening outside the classroom.
>
> Seventy-six percent of secondary school students are enrolled in a course of study that has, as its major emphasis, preparation for college—even though only 2 out of 10 jobs (between now and 1980) will require a college degree.
>
> The drop-out failure rate among college students remains among the most stable of all statistics in American education. Forty percent of all who enter college this fall will not make it to their junior year, and fifty percent will never obtain a baccalaureate degree. (Chamber of Commerce of the United States, 1975, p. 5)

The concept of career education developed as an educational tool to help youngsters become aware of opportunities in the working world and to define the sequence of steps schools should follow in preparing students to make meaningful career decisions. Some of the purposes and benefits of career education are listed in Figure 12-1.

Figure 12-1.
Career Education Concepts

It extends from early childhood through the retirement years.

It focuses on the full development of all individuals.

It provides the knowledge, skills, and understandings needed by individuals to master their environment.

It emphasizes daily living, personal-social, and occupational skills development at all levels and ages.

It encompasses the total curriculum of the school and provides a unified approach to education for life.

It focuses on the total life roles, settings, and events and their relationships, which are important in the lives of individuals, including work.

It encourages all members of the school community to have a shared responsibility and a mutual cooperative relationship among the various disciplines.

It includes learning in the home, private/public agencies, and the employment community, as well as the school.

It encourages all teachers to relate their subject matter to its career implications.

It includes basic education, citizenship, family responsibility, and other important education objectives.

It provides for career awareness, exploration, and skills development at all levels and ages.

It provides a balance of content and experiential learning, permitting hands-on occupation activities.

It provides a personal framework to help individuals plan their lives including career decision-making.

It provides the opportunity for the acquisition of a saleable occupational entry-level skill upon leaving high school.

It requires a life-long education based on principles related to total individual development.

It actively involves the parents in all phases of education.

It actively involves the community in all phases of education.

It encourages open communication between students, teachers, parents, and the community.

SOURCE: D. E. Brolin and C. J. Kokaska, *Career Education for Handicapped Children and Youth* (Columbus, Ohio: Charles E. Merrill, 1979), p. 104. Copyright © 1979 by Bell & Howell. Reprinted by permission.

VOCATIONAL AND CAREER EDUCATION FOR THE HANDICAPPED

Until recently, little was done to prepare children with learning problems for the world of work, even though their record of employment was worse than that of other groups. Marsh and Price (1980) reviewed the literature and came up with these facts:

1. Only 4 million (36%) of the 11 million handicapped adults capable of competitive employment are working, but 74 percent of the nonhandicapped adult population is employed....
2. Many handicapped persons are unemployed, unable to secure jobs suited to their abilities.... This is undoubtedly true in the case of many mildly handicapped students who leave school.
3. Employment opportunities are linked to the level of educational attainment, grades, and completion of training, as well as aspirations and specific competencies for job-market entry. Without training there is a greater chance that job success will not be realized. Of the 13 million students served in vocational education in 1974, only 2% were handicapped....
4. It is obvious that handicapped students have fewer options, are trained for a limited range of occupational choices, and the jobs are usually low level....
5. Underemployment and unemployment are the greatest indications that schools fail to meet the needs of handicapped students ... (pp. 304–305).

With the advent of P.L. 94-142, the Education of All Handicapped Children Act, and Sections 503 and 504 of the 1976 Amendment of the Vocational Education Act of 1973, which spells out the rights of access to vocational programs for the handicapped, vocational and career education have become important and necessary options for the learning handicapped student. Prior to this, the major focus was in remediating skill areas and on keeping the student in school. With new interest in general education for vocational and career goals, a concomitant interest has developed for children with special needs.

VOCATIONAL ASSESSMENT

The process of assessing students for vocational goals is similar to that which has been described for other areas, *with one important addition:* career exploration. The process is thus expanded to four steps:

1. Exploring careers to determine job(s) to be considered
2. Assessing the student's abilities, strengths, and limitations
3. Making a task analysis of the job or group of jobs being considered by the student
4. Matching the ability levels of the student to the requirements of the job to predict the degree of success

Career Exploration

Most students are not aware of the great number of vocational opportunities available; they have no idea how to prepare themselves for such occupations or how to obtain jobs should they decide on one particular area of interest. Most occupations can be divided into groups, and each group comprises literally hundreds of jobs, any one of which may be a satisfactory possibility for employment. When the time for job hunting comes, there needs to be a match between the jobs available and the jobs the student has displayed an interest in and aptitude for. If the student has been adequately prepared for several related positions, or at least has entry-level skills for a job that provides advancement as he obtains training and experience, the likelihood of staying on the job and finding job satisfaction is greatly enhanced.

The United States Department of Labor publishes the *Dictionary of Occupational Titles* (*DOT*), a multivolume work that lists thousands of job descriptions and the requirements for filling them. The *DOT* arranges jobs into nine occupational categories:

0/1 Professional, technical, and managerial occupations
2 Clerical and sales positions
3 Service occupations
4 Agriculture, fishing, forestry, and related fields
5 Processing occupations
6 Machine trades
7 Benchwork
8 Structural work
9 Miscellaneous

An additional supplement to the *DOT* is the *Guide to Occupational Exploration,* also published by the Department of Labor. It lists traits that are important for success in each job. A useful reference for high school teachers and counselors is the *Worker Trait Group Guide,* developed by the Appalachia Educational Laboratory (AEL, 1978). The *Worker Trait*

Group Guide contains descriptive information about twelve areas and sixty-six groups of occupations. The sixty-six groups, called "worker trait groups," are subdivisions of the twelve areas and represent clusters of occupations requiring similar worker characteristics. The twelve areas are: artistic, scientific, nature, authority, mechanical, industrial, business detail, persuasive, accommodating, humanitarian, social/business, and physical performing. Within each area, the groups are organized according to:

1. Level(s) of General Education Development (GED): GED levels refer to the general educational level required to reason, apply skills that have been learned, and to follow directions. They range from 6 (difficult) to 1 (simple).
2. Amount of specific training and experience required: Some jobs are considered entry level and require no preparation. Others need formal training, on-the-job training, or a combination of both.
3. Types of activities preferred by workers: Jobs have been analyzed, and the activities that are most frequently engaged in by successful workers are listed.
4. Types of work situations: Ten different conditions to which the successful worker must adapt have been identified.
5. Level(s) of aptitude (ability to learn): Jobs have been classified according to eleven aptitudes, with five levels for each area. Workers need to match the aptitudes and levels they display with those that are required by successful workers in any specific job.
6. Types of physical demands: Some jobs require great exertion and strength. Others are more sedentary. The worker needs to match his or her physical abilities with the requirements of the job.
7. Physical surroundings: Jobs have been classified according to the demands that the physical conditions make upon the worker.
8. Complexity with which worker is involved with data, people, and things: Jobs have been classified into six to eight levels of difficulty, in terms of working with data (information, knowledge, facts), people (level of involvement with people or animals that receive care and consideration similar to people), and things (working with tools, machines, or materials).

Most students have limited information on which to base decisions about jobs. Often they have little understanding of the requirements of the job in terms of physical strength, endurance, educational levels, or other areas listed previously. It is important for each student to evaluate his or her interests in a particular job, but it is particularly important that handicapped students and their teachers consider job requirements so that a realistic and viable choice can be made. Table 12-1 lists the areas that are assessed in the *DOT* for each of the occupations listed.

Table 12-1.
Classification of Job Requirements

1. General Educational Development
(SOURCE: U.S. Dept. of Labor, *Dictionary of Occupational Titles*)

LEVEL	REASONING DEVELOPMENT	MATHEMATICAL DEVELOPMENT	LANGUAGE DEVELOPMENT
6	Apply principles of logical or scientific thinking to a wide range of intellectual and practical problems. Deal with nonverbal symbolism (formulas, scientific equations, graphs, musical notes, etc.) in its most difficult phases. Deal with a variety of abstract and concrete variables. Apprehend the most abstruse classes of concepts.	Apply knowledge of advanced mathematical and statistical techniques such as differential and integral calculus, factor analysis, and probability determination, or work with a wide variety of theoretical mathematical concepts and make original applications of mathematical procedures, as in empirical and differential equations.	Comprehension and expression of a level to— —Report, write, or edit articles for such publications as newspapers, magazines, and technical or scientific journals. Prepare and draw up deeds, leases, wills, mortgages, and contracts. —Prepare and deliver lectures on politics, economics, education, or science. —Interview, counsel, or advise such people as students, clients, or patients, in such matters as welfare eligibility, vocational rehabilitation, mental hygiene, or marital relations. —Evaluate engineering technical data to design buildings and bridges.
5	Apply principles of logical or scientific thinking to define problems, collect data, establish facts, and draw valid conclusions. Interpret an extensive variety of technical instructions, in books, manuals, and mathematical or diagrammatic form. Deal with several abstract and concrete variables.		

(continued)

Table 12-1 *continued*

LEVEL	REASONABLE DEVELOPMENT	MATHEMATICAL DEVELOPMENT	LANGUAGE DEVELOPMENT
4	Apply principles of rational systems [such as bookkeeping, internal combustion engines, electric wiring systems, house building, nursing, farm management, ship sailing] to solve practical problems and deal with a variety of concrete variables in situations where only limited standardization exists. Interpret a variety of instructions furnished in written, oral, diagrammatic, or schedule form.	Perform ordinary arithmetic, algebraic, and geometric procedures in standard, practical applications.	Comprehension and expression of a level to— —Transcribe dictation, make appointments for executive and handle his personal mail, interview and screen people wishing to speak to him, and write routine correspondence on own initiative. —Interview job applicants to determine work best suited for their abilities and experience, and contact employers to interest them in services of agency. —Interpret technical manuals as well as drawings and specifications, such as layouts, blueprints, and schematics.
3	Apply common sense understanding to carry out instructions furnished in written, oral, or diagrammatic form. Deal with problems involving several concrete variables in or from standardized situations.	Make arithmetic calculations involving fractions, decimals, and percentages.	Comprehension and expression of a level to— —File, post, and mail such material as forms, checks, receipts, and bills. —Copy data from one record to another, fill in report forms, and type all work from rough draft or corrected copy.

LEVEL	REASONABLE DEVELOPMENT	MATHEMATICAL DEVELOPMENT	LANGUAGE DEVELOPMENT
2	Apply common sense understanding to carry out detailed but uninvolved written or oral instructions. Deal with problems involving a few concrete variables in or from standardized situations.	Use arithmetic to add, subtract, multiply, and divide whole numbers.	—Interview members of household to obtain such information as age, occupation, and number of children, to be used as data for surveys or economic studies. —Guide people on tours through historical or public buildings, describing such features as size, value, and points of interest.
1	Apply common sense understanding to carry out simple one- or two-step instructions. Deal with standardized situations with occasional or no variables in or from these situations encountered on the job.	Perform simple addition and subtraction, reading and copying of figures, or counting and recording.	Comprehension and expression of a level to— —Learn job duties from oral instructions or demonstration. —Write identifying information, such as name and address of customer, weight, number, or type of product, on tags or slips. —Request orally, or in writing, such supplies as linen, soap, or work materials.

2. Preparation and Training Required
(SOURCE: U.S. Dept. of Labor, *Dictionary of Occupational Titles*)

Formal Training Programs include:

1. Graduate: College studies at the graduate level
2. College: Four-year college degree

(continued)

Table 12-1 ***continued***

3. Technical: Community college or technical program beyond high school
4. Vocational: High school level vocational training
5. No formal training: Only general education

Specific Vocational Preparation (SVP) includes training given in any of the following circumstances:

1. Vocational education (such as high school commercial or shop training, technical school, art school, and that part of college training which is organized around a specific vocational objective)
2. Apprentice training (for apprenticeable jobs only)
3. In-plant training (given by an employer in the form of organized classroom study)
4. On-the-job training (serving as learner or trainee on the job under the instruction of a qualified worker)
5. Essential experience in other jobs (serving in less responsible jobs which lead to the higher grade job or serving in other jobs which qualify)

Training Time:

SVP 1. Short demonstration only
SVP 2. Anything beyond short demonstration up to and including 30 days
SVP 3. Over 30 days up to and including 3 months
SVP 4. Over 3 months up to and including 6 months
SVP 5. Over 6 months up to and including 1 year
SVP 6. Over 1 year up to and including 2 years
SVP 7. Over 2 years up to and including 4 years
SVP 8. Over 4 years up to and including 10 years
SVP 9. Over 10 years

---

3. Types of Work Activities
(SOURCE: Appalachia Educational Laboratory, *Worker Trait Group Guide*)

1. Activities dealing with things and objects
2. Activities involving business contact
3. Activities of a routine, definite, organized nature
4. Activities involving direct personal contact to help or instruct others
5. Activities resulting in recognition or appreciation from others
6. Activities involving the communication of ideas and information
7. Activities of a scientific and technical nature
8. Activities involving creative thinking

9. Activities involving processes, methods, or machines
10. Activities involving working on or producing things

---

4. Types of Work Situation
(SOURCE: Appalachia Educational Laboratory, *Worker Trait Group Guide*)

1. Performing duties that change frequently
2. Performing routine tasks
3. Planning and directing an entire activity
4. Dealing with people
5. Influencing people's opinions, attitudes, and judgments
6. Working under pressure
7. Making decisions using personal judgment
8. Making decisions using standards that can be measured or checked
9. Interpreting and expressing feelings, ideas, or facts
10. Working with precise limits or standards of accuracy

---

5. Aptitudes
(SOURCE: Manpower Administration, *Handbook for Analyzing Jobs*)

1. *General.* Understanding instructions, facts, and underlying reasoning. Being able to reason and make judgments. Closely related to school achievement.
2. *Verbal.* Understanding meanings of words and ideas. Using them to present information or ideas clearly.
3. *Numerical.* Doing arithmetic operations quickly and correctly.
4. *Spatial.* Looking at flat drawings or pictures of objects. Forming mental images of them in three dimensions—height, width, and depth.
5. *Form Perception.* Observing detail in objects or drawings. Noticing differences in shapes or shadings.
6. *Clerical Perception.* Observing details and recognizing errors in numbers, spelling, and punctuation in written materials, charts, and tables. Avoiding errors when copying materials.
7. *Motor Coordination.* Moving the eyes and hands or fingers together to perform a task rapidly and correctly.
8. *Finger Dexterity.* Moving the fingers to work with small objects rapidly and correctly.
9. *Manual Dexterity.* Moving the hands with ease and skill. Working with the hands in placing and turning motions.
10. *Eye-Hand-Foot Coordination.* Moving the hands and feet together in response to visual signals or observations.
11. *Color Discrimination.* Seeing likenesses or differences in colors or shades. Identifying or matching certain colors. Selecting colors that go well together.

(continued)

Table 12-1 *continued*

6. Types of Physical Demands
(SOURCE: U.S. Dept. of Labor, *Dictionary of Occupational Titles*)

1. Lifting, carrying, pushing, and/or pulling
2. Climbing and/or balancing
3. Stooping, kneeling, crouching, and/or crawling
4. Reaching, handling, fingering, and/or feeling
5. Talking and/or hearing
6. Seeing

7. Types of Physical Conditions
(SOURCE: U.S. Dept. of Labor, *Dictionary of Occupational Titles*)

1. Inside, outside, or both
2. Extremes of cold plus temperature changes
3. Extremes of heat plus temperature changes
4. Wet and humid
5. Noise and vibrations
6. Hazards/risk of bodily injury
7. Fumes, odors, toxic conditions, dust, poor ventilation

8. Worker Functions: Data/People/Things
(SOURCE: U.S. Dept. of Labor, *Dictionary of Occupational Titles*)

Every job requires a worker to interact to some degree with data, people, and things. The kinds of involvement are given in the following three lists, ranging from relatively simple (at the bottom) to complex (at the top). Each higher relationship includes all that are listed below it.

DATA	PEOPLE	THINGS
0 Synthesizing	0 Mentoring	0 Setting-up
1 Coordinating	1 Negotiating	1 Precision working
2 Analyzing	2 Instructing	2 Operating-controlling
3 Compiling	3 Supervising	3 Driving-operating
4 Computing	4 Diverting	4 Manipulating
5 Copying	5 Persuading	5 Tending
6 Comparing	6 Speaking-signaling	6 Feeding-offbearing
	7 Serving	7 Handling
	8 Taking instructions-helping	

Additional career explorations can be made through visits to various businesses and industry. Once the student has explored the wide variety of occupational choices, these visits can be exceedingly productive. With some preparation and background, the student is then prepared to ask questions that will give him greater insight into a particular job or jobs. This personal contact is probably the most important aspect of career exploration, since it helps the student make the connection between what could be and what is.

Assessment of Abilities, Strengths, and Limitations

Although students participate to some extent in all types of assessment, in vocational assessment student participation is a vital and integral part. The learning handicapped student often feels dependent and helpless in planning for his own future (Goldman, 1961). The assessment process itself can provide him with greater insight into his own ability to make decisions and act on them, since vocational assessment is oriented toward practical questions, that is, toward what will be a real situation. He can see, for example, in a range-of-motion task (lifting, bending, turning, reaching), not only a challenge, but a real situation in which he can get answers about his abilities for the type of work he is considering.

The purpose of the vocational assessment is to predict student success in a specific area of work. Usually the assessment consists of several elements:

1. Paper-and-pencil tests, which evaluate such things as: interests, ability levels, learning capacity, motor speed, finger dexterity, visual-motor coordination, and reasoning ability.
2. Physical tasks to assess such things as: range of motion, endurance, strength, manual dexterity, hand-eye coordination, speed of motion, fine- and gross-motor control, visual acuity, and visual discrimination.
3. Job samples, which consist of mock work situations in a variety of activities, such as: small engine assembly, sorting, clerical skills, filing, and electronic or electrical work. Some job samples are made commercially, and some are homemade. Having the student perform an actual task allows both the evaluator and the student to see if the student can follow directions, pay attention to detail, work consistently without getting distracted, and follow a task to completion.

4. Interpersonal skills, to see how the student gets along with supervisors, co-workers, and the public; and to assess such things as: patience, tolerance for others, ability to receive and accept suggestions and criticism, dependability, and other social forces that influence work behaviors.

Task Analysis

A breakdown of the skills required for any specific occupation are listed in the DOT and the supplementary materials prepared by the Department of Labor. In many instances whether a student possesses the basic abilities to perform a task can be assessed by the vocational assessment. In some instances, however, the student's ability to perform in a work situation can really be assessed only by a situational assessment, that is, by observing him as he works in a real-life situation on the job for which he has expressed an interest, or in one that is similar enough to determine whether or not he possesses the necessary entry-level skills. The situation approach focuses not on the student's physical ability to perform on the job, or on the components of the job, but on the individual's work personality, including such factors as work motivation, work attitudes, and work behaviors.

If a workshop setting is available, the student may have the opportunity to work for an extended period of time in order to assess these factors. If a workshop is not available, a work experience setting may be obtained in the community to provide this opportunity. In both instances, the criterion for determining the student's success will be a comparison of his rate of productivity and that of an average worker who is successful in the environment. Such things as the rate of performance, number of errors, the number of times that instructions must be repeated or are not understood, the amount of productivity and proficiency, can all be measured in terms of what represents normal good performance of workers familiar with a job, and working at a tempo that would be required in competitive employment.

In order to evaluate the student's performance, 100 percent should represent successful completion of tasks by the comparison worker. According to Wegg (1960) the following percentage criteria may apply:

0– 30% Poor or questionable performance. At this point the student is capable only of selected work in a sheltered work or non-competitive setting.

30– 50% Fair performance. The student is capable of sheltered work at this time, but has potential for competitive employment with training and adjustment.

50– 75% Good performance. The student possesses adequate traits for competitive employment.

75–100% Superior performance. The student is potentially an exceptional worker, and capable of competitive employment.

Matching to Predict Success

Brolin and Kokaska (1979) have done extensive research and developed a competency-based model consisting of twenty-two basic skills, which are divided into three areas of basic abilities students need to develop realistic career goals. These twenty-two basic skills include nine daily living skills, seven personal-social skills, and six occupation-guidance and preparations areas. Figure 12-2 outlines these twenty-two career education curriculum competencies, including 102 necessary subskills.

Figure 12-2.
Career Education Curriculum Competencies

1. Managing family finances
   a. Identify money and make correct change.
   b. Make wise expenditures.
   c. Obtain and use bank and credit facilities.
   d. Keep basic financial records.
   e. Calculate and pay taxes.
2. Selecting, managing, and maintaining a home
   a. Select adequate housing.
   b. Maintain a home.
   c. Use basic appliances and tools.
   d. Maintain home exterior.
3. Caring for personal needs
   a. Dress appropriately.
   b. Exhibit proper grooming and hygiene.
   c. Demonstrate knowledge of physical fitness, nutrition, and weight control.
   d. Demonstrate knowledge of common illness prevention and treatment.
4. Raising children, family living
   a. Prepare for adjustment to marriage.
   b. Prepare for raising children (physical care).
   c. Prepare for raising children (psychological care).
   d. Practice family safety in the home.

(continued)

SOURCE: D. E. Brolin and C. J. Kokaska, *Career Education for Handicapped Children and Youth* (Columbus, Ohio: Charles E. Merrill, 1979), pp. 108–109.

Figure 12-2 continued

5. Buying and preparing foods
   a. Demonstrate appropriate eating skills.
   b. Plan balanced meals.
   c. Purchase food.
   d. Prepare meals.
   e. Clean food preparation areas.
   f. Store food.
6. Buying and caring for clothing
   a. Wash clothing.
   b. Iron and store clothing.
   c. Perform simple mending.
   d. Purchase clothing.
7. Engaging in civic activities
   a. Generally understand local laws and government.
   b. Generally understand federal government.
   c. Understand citizenship rights and responsibilities.
   d. Understand registration and voting procedures.
   e. Understand Selective Service procedures.
   f. Understand civil rights and responsibilities when questioned by the law.
8. Utilizing recreation and leisure
   a. Participate actively in group activities.
   b. Know activities and available community resources.
   c. Understand recreational values.
   d. Use recreational facilities in the community.
   e. Plan and choose activities wisely.
   f. Plan vacation.
9. Getting around the community (mobility)
   a. Demonstrate knowledge of traffic rules and safety practices.
   b. Demonstrate knowledge and use of various means of transportation.
   c. Drive a car.

Personal-Social Skills

10. Achieving self-awareness
    a. Attain a sense of body.
    b. Identify interests and abilities.
    c. Identify emotions.
    d. Identify needs.
    e. Understand the physical self.
11. Acquiring self-confidence
    a. Express feelings of worth.
    b. Tell how others see him/her.
    c. Accept praise.
    d. Accept criticism.
    e. Develop confidence in self
12. Achieving socially responsible behavior
    a. Know character traits needed for acceptance.
    b. Know proper behavior in public places.

c. Develop respect for the rights and properties of others.
d. Recognize authority and follow instructions.
e. Recognize personal roles.

13. Maintaining good interpersonal skills
    a. Know how to listen and respond.
    b. Know how to make and maintain friendships.
    c. Establish appropriate heterosexual relationships.
    d. Know how to establish close relationships.
14. Achieving independence
    a. Understand impact of behavior upon others.
    b. Understand self-organization.
    c. Develop goal-seeking behavior.
    d. Strive toward self-actualization.
15. Achieving problem-solving skills
    a. Differentiate bipolar concepts.
    b. Understand the need for goals.
    c. Look at alternatives.
    d. Anticipate consequences.
    e. Know where to find good advice.
16. Communicating adequately with others
    a. Recognize emergency situations.
    b. Read at level needed for future goals.
    c. Write at the level needed for future goals.
    d. Speak adequately for understanding.
    e. Understand the subtleties of communication.

Occupational Guidance and Preparation

17. Knowing and exploring occupational possibilities
    a. Identify the personal values met through work.
    b. Identify the societal values met through work.
    c. Identify the remunerative aspects of work.
    d. Understand the classification of jobs into different occupational systems.
    e. Identify occupational opportunities available locally.
    f. Identify sources of occupational information.
18. Selecting and planning occupational choices
    a. Identify major occupational needs.
    b. Identify major occupational interests.
    c. Identify occupational aptitudes.
    d. Identify requirements of appropriate and available jobs.
    e. Make realistic occupational choices.
19. Exhibiting appropriate work habits and behaviors
    a. Follow directions.
    b. Work with others.
    c Work at a satisfactory rate.
    d. Accept supervision.
    e. Recognize the importance of attendance and punctuality.
    f. Meet demands for quality work.
    g. Demonstrate occupational safety.

(continued)

Figure 12-2 continued

20. Exhibiting sufficient physical-manual skills
    a. Demonstrate satisfactory balance and coordination.
    b. Demonstrate satisfactory manual dexterity.
    c. Demonstrate satisfactory stamina and endurance.
    d. Demonstrate satisfactory sensory discrimination.
21. Obtaining a specific occupational skill
22. Seeking, securing, and maintaining employment
    a. Search for a job.
    b. Apply for a job.
    c. Interview for a job.
    d. Adjust to competitive standards.
    e. Maintain postschool occupational adjustment.

The teacher can determine the extent to which a student has the basic skill necessary for vocational and career training by turning each of the statements in Figure 12-2 into a question, beginning, "Can he or she . . . ?" Replies can be scored by assigning a zero (0) to items in which the student is not proficient, one (1) to items in which the student is partially proficient, and two (2) to items in which the student is proficient. A percentage score can be obtained by dividing the total numerical score by twice the number of items administered. For example, if only the first forty-two items, under "daily living skills," are administered, then the percentage score can be obtained by dividing the student's total score by 84. The percentage score can be evaluated using the guide given in the preceding section on task analysis.

After the student has used the *DOT* or the *Worker Trait Group Guide,* visited business and industry in the community, and identified the occupational area or group in which he or she is interested, the student and the teacher will be able to identify what further training or preparation is necessary. High school courses are often useful preparation for specific jobs. Also, the teacher can work with the student to develop an individualized work-study program that will lead to necessary skills.

Although some jobs are learned best by observation and working on the job, so that formal training may not be necessary, basic skills in practical mathematics (measuring, making change, billing, budgeting), reading (following directions, searching for information, reading graphs and charts), and writing (report writing, keeping notes, writing letters) may be important. If the student knows which of these basic skills are required for a job, and what level of competency is needed, he or she can work, while in school, to acquire them.

Summary

An often ignored, but most important question facing the secondary student is what kind of job he or she will have after graduating from school. Many students who are very capable have had little in the way of career exploration and may not know of the opportunities that exist. Or even if they are aware of the existence of a specific job, they may be ignorant of the skills needed for success in that job. Schools in general have not adequately prepared students with a marketable skill, and the problem is compounded for the special education student, who may have inadequate basic skills and often inadequate interpersonal skills with which to face the world of work.

In recent years the concept of career education, a process by which youngsters are given exposure to work-oriented skills and tasks throughout the school years in order to develop competence and interest in vocational activities, has generated great interest. Research indicates that a little over one-third of the handicapped adults in this country capable of competitive employment are working, as opposed to three-fourths of the nonhandicapped population. These figures point out the great importance of job-related preparation for the handicapped, as opposed to classes in which basic skills that have not been mastered are continually stressed.

A table of basic competencies for independent living or employment is presented so that teachers may assess the level to which a student is able to function. During high school, every effort should be made to ensure that these competencies are achieved; the list allows the teacher to maintain individual records as the competencies are learned.

Career exploration should be a major part of every secondary school program. The *Dictionary of Occupational Titles* is published by the U.S. Department of Labor. Using it, the student can evaluate a job as to the skills required; the educational level needed; and the types of demands, surroundings, and level of complexity required—all before he or she makes any career choice.

Such things as educational level and interest and aptitudes can be assessed via paper-and-pencil tasks, but a workshop evaluation, including such things as simulated job situations, tests of strength, endurance, and range of motion, can be best assessed in a workshop or real job setting. If a student has some particular interest, a task analysis of that job can be made on the job site, and the student's abilities and disabilities matched according to the various elements of the job. With these methods the teacher can identify areas in which the student needs additional training; or, in some instances, a student can be redirected to another occupation if the chosen one appears unrealistic. The task analysis will also help the teacher identify basic skill areas in such things as reading or measurement that can be improved in order to provide job readiness.

Bibliography

Appalachia Educational Laboratory. *Worker Trait Group Guide.* Bloomington, Ill.: McKnight, 1978.

Brolin, D. E., and Kokaska, C. J. *Career Education for Handicapped Children and Youth.* Columbus, Ohio: Charles E. Merrill, 1979.

Chamber of Commerce of the United States. *Career Education: What Is It and Why We Need It from Leaders of Industry, Education, Labor, and the Professions.* Washington, D.C.: Chamber of Commerce of the United States, 1975.

Gellman, W. "The Vocational Adjustment Ship." *Personnel and Guidance Journal* (April 1961): 630–633.

Goldman, L. "Testing Handicapped Clients." *Rehabilitation and Counseling Bulletin* 4, no. 4 (1961): 36–39.

Hoyt, K. B. *Refining the Career Education Concept.* Monographs on Career Education. Washington, D.C.: United States Office of Education, 1976.

Manpower Administration. *Handbook for Analyzing Jobs.* Washington, D.C.: Government Printing Office, 1972.

Marsh, G. E., and Price, B. J. *Methods for Teaching the Mildly Handicapped Adolescent.* St. Louis: C. V. Mosby, 1980.

Public Law 94-142. *Education for All Handicapped Children Act of 1975. Congressional Record.* Washington, D.C.: Library of Congress.

Public Law 94-482. *The Education Amendments of 1976. Congressional Record.* Washington, D.C.: Library of Congress.

United States Department of Labor. *Dictionary of Occupational Titles.* 4th ed. Washington, D.C.: Government Printing Office, 1977.

Wegg, L. S. "The Essentials of Work Evaluation." *American Journal of Occupational Therapy* 14, no. 2 (1960): 65–69.

Chapter 13
Teaching and Classroom Management

The tendency to focus assessment on the student or the task can obscure the influence of the teacher and the environment. Concentration on the act of learning can turn attention away from the act of teaching. It is ironic that while it is readily acknowledged that the teacher is a critical element in student learning, most assessment is aimed at the student. Even when the public complains about poor instruction, the schools are as likely to examine learning as teaching. This chapter presents assessment methods that can be used to improve instruction through an examination of classroom teaching, materials, and environment.

The classroom can be viewed as an ecological system in which learning results from the interaction between student and teacher, student and students, and student and environment. The behavior and learning of a student is intimately related to the teacher's skills, to the attitudes of other students, and to the classroom atmosphere. A shift in the behavior of the teacher or a change in the composition of a class will affect the behavior of the students within that class. A shift in a teacher's attitude toward a student, for example, can have a dramatic impact on the student's performance. Readers can verify the impact others have on their emotions and behavior by imagining their personal reactions in two settings. In one setting the reader is confronted by a negative, disapproving and hostile person; in another the reader encounters a person who is helpful, accepting, and supportive. There is little doubt that behavior changes significantly in each setting; student behavior is no less affected by the behavior of others.

Both teaching and learning are extremely personal processes. They are closely tied to such individual qualities as curiosity, drive, attention, supportiveness, cooperativeness, persistence, and confidence. Both acts are partly under conscious control and can be examined by introspection as well as by external evaluation. Self-examination can provide information not readily available to others, while external evaluation can provide information on how behavior is perceived by others. Both can be used to improve instruction.

Self-examination has the advantage that it can be used to probe any experience at any time. Because it is usually initiated by the individual, self-examination carries with it both an implied willingness to enter into personal exploration and some assurance of a commitment to change. Its disadvantages are the susceptibility to distortion, the difficulty in verification, and the loss of objectivity.

External evaluation, however, can be objective, verified, and repeated. Its focus, though, is often superficial and rigid. It does not necessarily carry with it a teacher's willingness to accept or use the results. In fact, if participation is forced, the results of teacher evaluations can be undermined and discredited. Teacher cooperation is essential to the accuracy and usefulness of external evaluation.

This chapter examines a variety of informal assessment strategies that can be used to examine teaching and management styles. It includes self-evaluations, peer or administrator evaluations, and student self-evaluations. The chapter also considers methods for the examination of class environments, instructional materials, and program effectiveness.

TEACHING STYLE

At least two levels of perception exist about teaching effectiveness. Some perceptions concern the actual way a teacher instructs and manages children; other perceptions concern the way it "ought to be done." The quality of actual performance can be measured through both introspection and external evaluation. The teacher can monitor his or her own performance, while the teaching process itself can assess the results of an instructional activity. The teacher can also submit to a third-party observer and recorder.

The second level of perception is based on idealized expectations about teaching. Both teachers and observers hold ideas about what teaching "should be like." These constitute the standards of excellence against which actual performance can be compared. The discrepancy between observed and ideal performance provides an arena for professional growth.

Several methods of analysis are available for the examination of teaching styles. One set of methods uses predetermined, universal, and fixed criteria against which to judge teaching performance. A second set of methods uses criteria based on the intent of the teacher or on demands and expectations within the setting. The first method is based on identified characteristics of instructional interactions; the second uses criteria bound to the situation.

Analysis with Fixed Criteria

Flanders's (1959) analysis of teacher-student interaction is an example of an assessment method based on identified interactional characteristics. Flanders lists ten categories of verbal communication that occur within classrooms, and he clusters the ten under "indirect teacher influence," "direct teacher influence," "student talk," and "silence." Figure 13-1 is an adaptation of the Flanders analysis; it is designed to allow the assessor to determine an ideal level prior to the actual observations and then to record the actual occurrence within each category.

Teacher communications that are classified as "indirect" tend to encourage a wide range of free and open student verbal participation. Events within the "direct" category involve more teacher domination. "Student talk" is divided into communications that are responses to a direct request from the teacher and those that are initiated by the student.

Another interactional analysis schema that is based on identified characteristics has been developed by Spaulding (1978). In the Spaulding Teacher Activity Rating Schedule (STARS), he uses seven primary categories of teaching styles. These styles occur in either social or cognitive transactions. The categories are described in Table 13-1.

Observational data in a Spaulding analysis are gathered every ten seconds. The observer determines whether the teacher is involved in a cognitive act or in a management act in each ten-second observation and selects the scoring category. A sample recording form is provided in Figure 13-2. In a complete Spaulding observational study the teacher's behavior and student behavior can be recorded together so that the interactional effect is identified.

Figure 13-1.
Observation Frequencies Using Flanders Interaction Analysis Categories

Teacher ______________________ Date ____________ Time ____________

Teacher subject ______________________ Seating arrangement ______________

		Flanders Interaction Categories	Ideal Percent	Actual Frequency Tally	Total *f*	Actual Percent
Teacher Talk	Indirect Influence	1. **Accepts feeling:* Accepts and clarifies the tone of feeling of the students in an unthreatening manner. Feelings may be positive or negative. Predicting or recalling feelings are included.				
		2. **Praises or encourages:* Praises or encourages student action or behavior. Jokes that release tension, but not at the expense of another individual, nodding head or saying "um hm?" or "go on" are included.				
		3. **Accepts or uses ideas of student:* Clarifying, building, or developing ideas suggested by a student. As teacher brings more of his own ideas into play, shift to category 5.				
	Direct Influence	4. **Asks questions:* Asking a question about content or procedure with the intent that a student answer.				
		5. **Lecturing:* Giving facts or opinions about content or procedures; expressing his own ideas, asking rhetorical questions.				

NOTE: "Ideal percent" and "actual percent" should each total 100 percent. "Actual percent" for each of the 10 event categories is calculated by dividing the total frequency (*f*) for that category by the total of the total *f* column.

*There is no scale by these numbers. Each number is classificatory, designating a particular kind of communication event. To write numbers down during observation is merely to identify and enumerate communication events, not to judge them.

	Flanders Interaction Categories	Ideal Percent	Actual Frequency Tally	Total *f*	Actual Percent
Direct Influence	6. **Giving directions:* Directions, commands, or orders which students are expected to comply with. 7. **Criticizing or justifying authority:* Statements intended to change student behavior from unacceptable to acceptable pattern; bawling someone out; stating why the teacher is doing what he is doing; extreme self-reference.				
Student Talk	8. **Student talk-response:* Talk by students in response to teacher. Teacher initiated the contact or solicits student statement. 9. **Student talk-initiation:* Talk initiated by students. If "calling on" student is only to indicate who may talk next, observer must decide whether student wanted to talk.				
Silence	10. **Silence or confusion:* Pauses, short periods of silence and periods of confusion in which communication cannot be understood by the observer.				
		100%			100%

SOURCE: Interaction categories from N.A. Flanders, *Teachers Influence, Pupil Attitudes and Achievement* (Washington, D.C.: U.S. Department of Health, Education, and Welfare, 1959), p. 20.

As a result of his studies Spaulding has characterized over twenty types of teaching styles. These he has given such colorful titles as "the entertainer" and "the controller." Twelve titles with brief descriptions are provided in Table 13-2. These patterns of behavior are easily recognized, and it is not difficult for a teacher to determine a characterization that best describes personal styles at various times during the day.

The stereotypes of common teaching behaviors are given only to illustrate that common patterns do exist and that many variations are available

Table 13-1.
Spaulding Teacher Activity Rating Schedule (STARS)

GENERAL TRANSACTIONS CATEGORIES	
+ Approval	Teacher acts with generally reinforcing effects. Affective character takes priority over cognitive content.
− Disapproval	Teacher acts with generally punishing effects. Aversive character takes priority over cognitive content.
S Structuring	Teacher acts to set or elicit performance goals and action or proscribes certain actions (without aversive effect).
R Restructuring	Teacher acts to repeat, clarify, or modify structuring behaviors; when negative effect, e.g., nagging, is present, it is scored as a disapproval (−).
I Information	Teacher acts to convey information (but does not set or elicit performance [s]).
L Listening and observing	Teacher is nonverbal and attends to child or group.
P Non-Transaction	Teacher is not interacting with students in the class.

SOURCE: R. L. Spaulding. "Spaulding Teacher Activity Rating Schedule (STARS)," (1974). Used with permission of the author.

to the teacher. Some patterns of teaching behavior are not cited. However, teachers are encouraged to identify characteristic patterns in their own teaching or that of others and to personalize their descriptions. Changes in style of teaching will result in changes in student performance.

Another way to assess teaching performance is to sample competency across the many features of the job. This form of assessment is commonly used by supervisors when evaluating a teacher's job performance. The format can also be used as a guide to self-evaluation because it identifies actual teaching areas. The form presented in Table 13-3 covers a range of activities that are important features in teaching.

Students can also provide valuable assessment information about teaching style and methods. It is a common practice at the college and

Figure 13-2.
STARS Data Collection Sheet

School ______ Grade ______ Observer ______

Beginning time ______ End time ______ Date ______

Setting (situation and activity) ______

	Cognitive Structuring						Non-Tran P	Social Behavior Management					
Time	+	–	S	R	I	L		+	–	S	R	I	L
00													
10													
20													
30													
40													
50													
1:00													
10													
20													
30													
40													
50													
2:00													

SOURCE: R. L. Spaulding, "Spaulding Teacher Activity Rating Schedule (STARS)," (1974). Used with permission of the author.

university levels to solicit student evaluations of classroom instruction. Most of the existing formats focus the evaluation on the teacher and hence on teaching style rather than outcomes. The evaluation instrument provided in Table 13-4 is an example of an assessment survey designed for student evaluations when a lecture format has been used. Results are interpreted for indications of possible strengths and weaknesses and can be used to compare one class with another.

Table 13-2.
Selected Teaching Styles

NAME	BRIEF DESCRIPTION
Story teller	Students listen attentively while the teacher reads, narrates, explains, and tells; teacher may also encourage attention, sharing, or other student contributions.
Lecturer	Teacher tells, explains, describes, illustrates, etc., and students attend minimally or show inappropriate behaviors; teacher may ask students to recall or apply what has been described or explained.
Examiner	Teacher directs and rewards attention to content areas and asks for recall or application of specific information; students submit passively to tasks of recall and application; students apply, contribute, or recite as requested.
Entertainer	Teacher frequently digresses from the subject matter while students pay close attention; students also digress. Both teacher and students express own point of view, opinions, or values while not focused in the academic subject matter at hand.
Controller	Teacher uses negative control techniques such as criticism and threat of punishment to keep students on task; appropriate behavior is ignored; [behavior that is] off-task, inattentive, distracted, drowsy, wandering whenever is reprimanded.
Counselor	Teacher responds to help-seeking behavior by listening, setting goals, procedures, giving reinforcers, redirecting behavior, etc.; teacher also elicits student opinions, feelings, attitudes, or values.
Pseudo-Peer	Teacher attends to and reinforces off-task and disruptive behavior of students; also supports such behavior by digressing from the academic task and encouraging and supporting the expression of student opinions, values, and attitudes.

SOURCE: R. L. Spaulding, "Relationships of Inservice Training to Classroom Teaching Models, Management Styles and Student Achievement" (Paper presented at the Annual Meeting of the American Educational Research Association, Boston, 1980.) Used with permission of the author.

NAME	BRIEF DESCRIPTION
Discovery teacher	Teacher focuses student attention on items or arrays of materials or representational data and elicits categorization, grouping, sorting, or other restructuring activities; attention is given to inductive thinking and procedures that encourage attention to goals, objectives, steps that facilitate this process.
Socratic teacher	Teacher focuses students on "givens" and requests deduction of logical implications to be drawn from factual information or premises; generalizing hypothesis generation as well as hypothesis testing is encouraged.
Director	Teacher sets limits and gives directions to students and they comply; has clear rules, expectations, limits, procedures, and standards; gently redirects errant students and greets a positive effect.
Expository teacher	Teacher tells, motivates, focuses attention, and asks students to apply information in an organized, positive manner; students are attentive and contribute appropriately.
Rote processor	Teacher gives bits of information in a repetitious manner; process is fixed and mechanical, student is to be attentive, respond submissively, carry out practice and memorize material.

Table 13-3.
Survey to Evaluate Teaching Competency

	EVALUATION		
COMPETENCIES	EXCELLENT	AVERAGE	IMPROVEMENT COMMENTS
1. Classroom organization			
a. Instructional strategies are varied.	______	______	______
b. All materials are ready when lesson begins.	______	______	______

(continued)

Table 13-3 *continued*

COMPETENCIES	EVALUATION EXCELLENT	AVERAGE	IMPROVEMENT COMMENTS
c. Lessons are planned in accordance with curriculum goals.	______	______	______
2. Instructional objectives			
a. Instructional objectives are identified.	______	______	______
b. Objectives are age- and ability-appropriate.	______	______	______
c. Objectives are in measurable terms.	______	______	______
3. Instruction			
a. Direct instruction is maximized.	______	______	______
b. Assignments are geared so that they meet needs of different abilities.	______	______	______
c. Individualized instruction is well monitored.	______	______	______
d. Instruction involves different student learning modalities.	______	______	______
e. Aides effectively managed.	______	______	______
4. Skill development			
a. Ideas are sequentially developed from simple to complex.	______	______	______
b. Steps in growth are monitored.	______	______	______
c. Teacher's language is clear and appropriate.	______	______	______
d. Questions and activities are appropriate.	______	______	______

COMPETENCIES	EVALUATION EXCELLENT	AVERAGE	IMPROVEMENT COMMENTS
5. Assessment and evaluation			
a. Group tests used to monitor program effectiveness.	______	______	______
b. Individual assessment used to measure pupil growth.	______	______	______
c. Informal assessment of program and pupil movement.	______	______	______
d. Group and individual records maintained in understandable form.	______	______	______
6. Reporting			
a. Parent conferences are preplanned and well organized.	______	______	______
b. Relationship with parents is supportive, cooperative, and informative.	______	______	______
7. Materials			
a. Audiovisual material is used effectively.	______	______	______
b. Aides are used to assist students understand concepts and develop skills.	______	______	______
c. Seat work is appropriate and can be successfully completed.	______	______	______
d. Blackboard is used to present material, illustrate lessons, organize activities, etc.	______	______	______

(continued)

Table 13-3 *continued*

COMPETENCIES	EVALUATION		
	EXCELLENT	AVERAGE	IMPROVEMENT COMMENTS
8. Interaction			
a. Communicates clearly and respectfully with students.	______	______	______
b. Maintains classroom order and discipline.	______	______	______
c. Listens to students and attempts to understand what they say.	______	______	______
d. Is positive and supportive of student accomplishments.	______	______	______

Table 13-4.
Student-designed Survey to Evaluate Lecture-type Class

COMPETENCIES	EVALUATION				
	5 POOR	4 BELOW AVERAGE	3 AVERAGE	2 ABOVE AVERAGE	1 EXCELLENT
1. Instructor communicates clearly to student.	______	______	______	______	______
2. Instructor stimulates thinking.	______	______	______	______	______
3. Instructor motivates students.	______	______	______	______	______
4. Instructor is knowledgeable about the subject.	______	______	______	______	______
5. Instructor demonstrates concern about students.	______	______	______	______	______

COMPETENCIES	EVALUATION 5 POOR	4 BELOW AVERAGE	3 AVERAGE	2 ABOVE AVERAGE	1 EXCELLENT
6. Instructor exhibits high interest in the subject matter.	______	______	______	______	______
7. Instructor makes interesting presentations.	______	______	______	______	______
8. Instructor has organized presentations.	______	______	______	______	______
9. Instructor's written assignments are useful.	______	______	______	______	______
10. Instructor's evaluation and grading procedures are fair.	______	______	______	______	______
11. Instructor's general effectiveness is:	______	______	______	______	______

Analysis with Flexible Criteria

The second type of assessment that is used to analyze teaching styles and procedures is based on situational or individual variables. For instance, instead of being asked to respond to a set of teacher characteristics, students can be asked to judge the value of a teaching activity. The focus of assessment is on specific instruction that has occurred in the classroom. This procedure is illustrated in Figure 13-3 and can result in very direct information. Questions can address various aspects of an activity. Because the focus is on the activity rather than the teacher, the influence of general popularity tends to be neutralized, the teacher is less defensive, and students can be candid.

Activity-focused assessment is easy to construct, adaptable to many situations, and can be repeated frequently. The responses often provide information that can be translated into program modifications. Short assessments can be used to monitor student reactions to features in the

Figure 13-3.
Examples of Evaluation Questions That Address Curriculum

Last week you started to use a new math text. It would help me if you gave me your evaluation of the book and the work that goes with the book.

1. What do you like best about the text?

2. What about the book don't you like?

3. If you could change one thing about the math book and math work, what would it be?

4. Circle which word best describes the book.

   easy average hard

   What about the book makes it this way?

5. What would help you most in math?

6. Other comments

teaching process and allow the students to participate in shaping the course of instruction.

One drawback to the procedure is the time required to read and interpret responses. Simplified forms such as that given in Figure 13-4 can be used when the teacher wants a spot check on an activity. In large classrooms the assessment task can be rotated among the students, so that only five to ten students respond on each evaluation.

Individualized instruction lends itself to another method of assessment: process evaluation. In special education, for instance, each student must have an individual plan that includes goals, objectives, and a time line. A part of the teacher's instructional responsibility is to help the student reach the goal(s) that have been set.

It is possible to monitor the process and activities that are designed and implemented to meet the goals and objectives. In this form of assessment the focus is on the process that leads to student growth. The assess-

Figure 13-4.
Example of a Process Assessment Form

Please give me your reaction to ______________________ activity. Circle the answer to each question and make whatever comments you wish.

In this activity, I learned:

1	2	3	4	5
A lot	Quite a lot	Some	A little	Nothing

I found the work:

1	2	3	4	5
Hard		Medium		Easy

I think other students would learn from it:

1	2	3	4	5
Yes		Maybe		No

I would have learned more if ____

____

____

ment determines the appropriateness and effectiveness of the teaching practices selected and implemented. Figure 13-5 is an example of a process assessment that can be used to evaluate the instructional steps that have been taken on behalf of a student.

Another method of teacher evaluation, the chronolog, requires the help of another teacher, supervisor, or educational professional. This method involves direct classroom observation and can be extremely helpful to a teacher when the following procedures are employed.

1. A verbatim record is made of all statements and actions of the teacher during a period of instruction.
2. The observer records as much detail on interactions and student behavior as possible.
3. All recordings are objective and free of evaluation or judgmental statements.
4. Immediately before or after the observation the teacher indicates the goals and intentions for the period of instruction.

5. The observation is reported verbally to the teacher as soon after the observation as possible.
6. Discussion is encouraged around those teacher behaviors that are not congruent with teacher's goals, intentions, or ideals.
7. A commitment to one or two improvements is encouraged.
8. The observer and teacher schedule a follow-up observation to see if the planned changes have occurred.

Figure 13-5.
Example of Process Assessment of Instructional Plan

Instructional Process Assessment

Student ______________________ Date __________ Room __________

Goal ____

Planned Objectives	Instructional Method	Evaluation Methods

Current Objectives	Instructional Methods	Progress Evaluation

Analysis

1. Preparation/preplanning for instruction
2. Clarity of objective(s)
3. Appropriateness of methods for objective
4. Organization and sequence of activities
5. Flow of activities
6. Selection and utilization of materials and media
7. Options in event of failure
8. Completion of lesson reasonable for students
9. Appropriate evaluation or follow-up.

The chronolog as used in a teacher assessment is a "fault-free" method of observation. The teacher is given a detailed record of his or her performance in the classroom, and can then compare actual and intended behavior to decide if changes are warranted. The observer supports the process, can contribute suggestions, and can provide follow-up. If the observer witnesses a behavior that he or she feels is opposed to good practice, and if the teacher evidences no concern about this behavior during the review period, the observer can point out his or her own concern about the behavior.

A teacher chronolog is similar to the chronolog used with students (Chapter 4). The observer notes the organization and layout of the classroom as well as the general location of the students. The teacher's location, the subject matter under study, and the time of day are all recorded. The primary focus is on what the teacher says and does. Student activity and communications are recorded whenever possible.

The observation is reviewed with the teacher immediately after the recording so that the discussion can easily recapture the mood associated with the instructional period. When the discussion must be postponed until a later time, a few minutes need to be spent setting the scene of the class so that the teacher can reconstruct the episode for himself. This is not an easy task if other instructional experiences have intervened. The format for the observation appears in Figure 13-6.

MANAGEMENT STYLE

Assessment can also be used to provide information on classroom management styles. Spaulding's (1978) STARS, for instance, requires that the observer note whether the teacher is in a cognitive, instructional, or management mode. The same criteria are applied in each mode, but the recording and scoring are separate. The teacher competency scale provided in Table 13-3 also includes management statements such as "communicates clearly" and "maintains classroom order and discipline."

The act of teaching includes both instructional and management activities, and although they are highly interrelated, some separation is useful in analyzing teaching behavior. It is, for instance, possible to find teachers who can provide an excellent curriculum, who have appropriate and properly sequenced materials, but who have great difficulty managing classroom behavior. The reverse can also be found. Some teachers have good management strategies but have limited ability in helping students learn academic subjects. Because of the high degree of overlap in the activities of instruction and management, assessment strategies often combine items related to both functions.

Figure 13-6.
Form for Recording a Chronolog of an Instructional Event

Chronolog of Instructional Interaction

Teacher ____________________ Day ____________ Time ________

Subject ____________________ Method of instruction ____________

____________________ Materials ____________________

Students # ____________________ Location ____________________

Seating arrangement ____________________

Teacher's stated goals ____________________

Running Account

Teacher Comments/Locations/Actions (What does she/he do and say?)	Student Comments/Locations/Actions (What do they do and say?)

After Observation

Observer reads the running acount to the teacher, matching teacher actions with student actions.

Teacher's comments/concerns ____________________

____

Plans for change, if any ____________________

____

Follow-up plan ____________________

____

Strategies for the assessment of classroom management, like those used for instructional assessment, can be divided into those using fixed criteria and those constructed to meet particular needs and reflect individual settings. An example of an assessment method that uses a fixed criteria is given in Figure 13-7. The format allows the viewer to observe actions related to communication, curriculum, and control. The instrument is designed for a quick analysis of classroom management, and if problems are found within any item cluster, a more thorough examination of that area can be undertaken. An in-depth examination could include a teacher interview, a review of work samples and lesson plans, and an inventory of other modes of behavior available to the teacher.

As with all other observational procedures the summary of data must be based on five or more samples of behavior. Multiple observations can either be taken in different settings (e.g., different periods or subjects) or on different days. The reliability of the findings will begin to approach acceptable levels with five observations, but will dramatically increase in significance as twelve or more observations are recorded. Single observations are extremely unreliable unless the teacher who is observed can confirm the finding based on his own observation of his behavior. Such confirmation may eliminate the need for multiple observations.

A second type of management analysis involves the use of the verbatim reporting that was described earlier. The chronolog is an ideal tool for this observation. The focus in this case is on the teacher and on points of the interaction between teacher and students. The procedure will provide information on such managerial elements as the use of directions, authority, acknowledgment, order, and reinforcement. It reveals strengths

Figure 13-7.
Classroom Management Survey

Name ______________________ Date(s) ______________________

Location(s) ______________________ Observer ______________________

Record observation on a five-point scale. Leave blank those statements where an observation or a review is not possible.	1 Never	2 Seldom	3 Sometimes	4 Often	5 Always

(continued)

Figure 13-7 continued

Teacher's Management Style	Performance				
1. Attention and rewards are directed toward appropriate pupil behavior.	1	2	3	4	5
2. Use of punishment is moderate, fair, and timely.	1	2	3	4	5
3. Class rules are clear, reasonable, and consistent.	1	2	3	4	5
4. Alternatives to punishment are available, e.g., contracts or timeouts.	1	2	3	4	5
5. Lesson plans are clear and activities are well organized.	1	2	3	4	5
6. Class assignments can be successfully completed and are well paced.	1	2	3	4	5
7. Student behavior is monitored through eye contact, voice, or position in room.	1	2	3	4	5
8. Communications are clear and responsive to student statements.	1	2	3	4	5
9. Teacher models and demonstrates respect, courtesy, and acceptance.	1	2	3	4	5
10. Statements in group instruction and discussion are directed to group.	1	2	3	4	5
11. Nine out of ten students at work within four minutes of start of activity.	1	2	3	4	5
12. Work assignments are monitored and appropriate work recognized.	1	2	3	4	5
13. Requests and directions are firm and assertive.	1	2	3	4	5
14. Misbehavior is identified and corrected with accuracy and timeliness.	1	2	3	4	5
15. Teacher can attend to two tasks at the same time, e.g., lesson and correction.	1	2	3	4	5
16. Transitions between activities and tasks are smooth.	1	2	3	4	5
17. Group involvement is maintained during single student recitation.	1	2	3	4	5
18. Seat work assignments are within the attention span of the students.	1	2	3	4	5

Analysis

Item Clusters	Scale Profile					Observations
	1	2	3	4	5	
Communication						
8						
9						
10						
13						
15						
Discipline						
1						
2						
3						
4						
7						
14						
Curriculum						
5						
6						
11						
12						
16						
17						
18						

as well as weaknesses in managerial style. It also allows the teacher to see the direct results of particular management actions. Often a teacher is aware of the ineffectiveness of certain actions but has never been able to see the direct relationship between teacher behavior and student behavior. The chronolog not only provides this information but also describes the order of events. With this information a teacher can reconstruct the situation and rehearse other forms of management behavior.

SOCIAL ENVIRONMENT

The environment of a classroom includes the physical and emotional conditions that surround the teacher and the student. Such features as lighting, temperature, noise level, furniture, materials, spatial organization and physical appearance are relatively easy to survey but deceptively difficult to change. The persistence of barriers to the physically handicapped vividly illustrates how difficult some changes are to effect, even when there is agreement about the impact of the problem. The emotional climate of a classroom is more difficult to determine but is in some ways more accessible to the control of the teacher and staff.

Physical Elements

One of the most apparent physical factors is the use of space. Contemporary buildings have attempted to meet the problem of inflexibility with the creation of open spaces that can be rearranged to meet instructional needs. Such arrangements often sacrifice privacy for flexibility and present teachers with new sets of problems, such as elevated noise and visual distractions. Given the limitations of existing plants the assessment question becomes, "Has this room or space been arranged so that it allows for the best instruction and management in this particular activity?" The following checklist identifies some of the characteristics of good space utilization.

- Provides an unobstructed view of all students.
- Can be arranged for small or large group activities.
- Allows for seat-work activities free from major distractions.
- Class discussion can be arranged so that all students can speak face-to-face.
- Teacher can demonstrate or lecture and be easily seen and heard by all.
- There is access to all student stations, so the teacher can move with ease.
- The area can be made relatively free from distracting noise or visual interference.
- Storage areas are located for easy access and minimum classroom distraction.
- Student and teacher seats, tables, etc., are comfortable and can accommodate for physical differences.
- There is an available area for the separation or isolation of a student from the main group.

- Area is available for activity centers that can remain throughout the day.
- Lighting, heat, and ventilation are adequate.
- There is space for the teacher to meet and confer with individuals or small groups of students.

The learning style of students involves a combination of optimal physical, social, and instructional conditions. Most adults recognize that certain physical conditions are conducive to learning. Children are also able to identify those conditions under which they believe that they learn best. Even when students are inaccurate in their perceptions, their involvement in self-assessment can lead them to more effective study practices. The items in Figure 13-8 cover a range of environmental conditions that have some impact on the learning efficiency of individual students and are modeled after the work of Dunn and Dunn (1978).

Social and Emotional Elements

Both students and teachers are often able to determine the student grouping arrangement within a classroom that will lead to effective instructional and management subgroups. The sociogram, described in Chapters 3 and 11 can provide information on student choices for work or play partners. In many situations students are both capable and willing to form groups so that all students are included and yet each group is designed to achieve an effective learning unit. Students who are last chosen or who are isolated from the group can be paired with their first choice or with a supportive, highly chosen student. Measuring the output or growth of each group of students will indicate the degree of success of each cluster.

Group self-assessment can be accomplished either with a self-examination method or by a review of group accomplishments. In self-examination the focus is on individual contributions or satisfactions, and students are asked to determine how their contributions could be changed to improve performance or satisfaction. Commitments are solicited to accomplish proposed changes. A focus on accomplishments, such as an inventory of tasks completed, involves the examination of the rate and degree to which goals and objectives have been met. Group members or the teacher determine what changes might lead to improvements, and a plan and commitment is made. Progress is monitored by observation, testing, rate count, self-reporting, or some other assessment method that can record the impact of change.

Student attitudes about school or class and about physical, social, or

Figure 13-8.
Survey of the Impact of Environmental Conditions on Student Performance

Circle the answer that is most like you most of the time.

I learn best when:

1.	it's very quiet	there are some sounds	there is average noise	it's fairly noisy	it's very noisy
2.	there is no music	there is low music	there is understand-able music	there is loud music	there is vibrating music
3.	there is no talking	there is low talking	there is understand-able talking	there is loud talking	there is shouting
4.	there is faint light	there is soft light	there is room light	there are high lights	there is direct sun
5.	in a dark corner	there is little light	in the middle of the room	near a window	next to a window
6.	it's early morning	it's before noon	it's midday	it's afternoon	it's late night
7.	it's cold	it's cool	it's mild	it's warm	it's hot
8.	in winter	in spring	in all seasons	in fall	in summer
9.	no friend helps	occasionally a friend helps	sometimes a friend helps	a friend often helps	a friend always helps
10.	no teacher helps	occasionally a teacher helps	sometimes a teacher helps	a teacher often helps	a teacher always helps
11.	no parent helps	occasionally a parent helps	sometimes a parent helps	a parent often helps	a parent always helps
12.	there is no encourage-ment	there is occasional encourage-ment	there is some encourage-ment	there is frequent encourage-ment	there is continual encourage-ment
13.	I am not told what to do	I am given suggestions	I am given guidance	I am given outline	I am told what to do
14.	I study by myself	I occasionally study with others	I sometimes study with others	I often study with others	I always study with others
15.	I study alone	I study with one other	I study with two others	I study with three others	I study with a group

16.	in class discussion	in small group discussion	talking with one person	asking some questions	studying by myself
17.	I can often hear what I am to learn	I can sometimes hear what I am to learn	I hear and see what I am to learn	I can sometimes see what I am to learn	I can often see what I am to learn
18.	I listen to others	I do some talking	I listen and watch others	I do some watching	I watch others
19.	I sit quietly	I move around a little	I sit and move around	I am moving around often	I am always moving around
20.	I lie on floor or bed	I sit on floor or bed	I sit in a soft chair	I sit at a table or desk	I stand or move around

Item summary:		
	Sound	1, 2, 3
	Light	4, 5, 6
	Temperature	6, 7, 8
	Support	9, 10, 11, 12, 13
	Interaction	14, 15, 16
	Senses	17, 18
	Location	19, 20

psychological considerations can be determined in a number of ways. Assessment can be conducted through interviews and discussion, through observations and records, and by questionnaires, surveys, and evaluations. The topic areas are unlimited and can include an examination of the climate of the school, the physical facilities, school rules, adult attitudes, seating arrangements, curriculum offerings and methods, student attitudes, teacher behaviors, and so on.

Interview and discussion procedures are often the most direct methods; they can be easily adapted and they can be a forum for the examination of solutions. Adult behavior that includes sincere listening and that restates the student's comments is the most likely to produce frank and open student appraisals. The following brief verbal exchange illustrates a teacher who listens to a student and encourages further elaboration through reflective statements:

Student: Our playing field is no good for baseball.

Teacher: The field isn't right.

Student: Yes, the ground is too rough and the left fence is . . .

Teacher: The ground is too rough and the fence is too close.

Student: That's right. The player has to . . .

The teacher or assessor uses transition statements to move from one phase of evaluative interview to another. For instance, in the previous problem the teacher can summarize the problem and move to a consideration of solutions by saying:

The field needs some improvements if it is to be used for baseball. What changes would be needed so that it can be used?

Once the needed corrections have been fully described by the student, possible solutions can be solicited by a transition statement such as:

There seem to be quite a number of improvements that are needed. What things might we do to get the improvements made?

Subsequent discussion could generate solutions that then need to be examined as to reasonableness, practicability, adequacy, and availability. Listening and restating is used at each step in the discussion and assessment of a problem. Planning and action are the logical outcomes of problem solving.

Observation often provides the first clue to the existence of an environmental problem. Concern or suspicion can occur around such diverse areas as group cohesion, use of space, and time allocation. The examination of the presence or absence of an action or a condition can help to verify or dismiss a concern that has surfaced intuitively. The frequency count is a simple procedure for clarifying a suspicion. A count of positive and supportive versus negative and critical comments, for instance, might be used to describe an element of group cohesion; a count of number of necessary student movements within a room might target one aspect of space utilization; and the number of assignments completed within a time period might be used to determine the adequacy of the time allocation.

Questionnaires can be used to further elaborate on both physical and social environmental conditions. An initial examination can be relatively simple; for example, the teacher can use open-ended questions such as "What do you like best about the lunch program?" and "What do you like least about the program?" This type of data provides an overview of the problem but usually needs to be followed by a more systematic examination. A comprehensive questionnaire can include a variety of elements relevant to the program under consideration. Questions on a lunch program, for instance, might address:

Time of day of lunch
Length of the period
Location and method of seating
Type of supervision
Availability of hot and cold meals
Variety of daily and weekly menu
Appearance and cleanliness of the facility
Taste or quantity of the food
Behavior of the students
Food preferences

The method selected to address any one item will depend upon where the information can be found. In the case of the lunch program, questions related to food preference, taste, and volume might be most accurately judged by observing the type and amount of discarded food. Student preference in supplementary texts can often be determined by the frequency with which each book is chosen. A checkout record card can be an easy method for monitoring text usage.

Direct observation of behavior is usually preferred over solicited opinions. The latter, however, is often the only method available for determining information that is not easily observed. Attitudes, beliefs, and feelings are examples of behavior that can be difficult to observe but is available through personal inquiry. Examples of a variety of inquiries and a sample of possible response patterns are given in Figure 13-9.

INSTRUCTIONAL MATERIALS

The most direct way to evaluate materials and equipment is to observe whether or not they are used and whether they produce the desired learning results. The first observation can be made more accurate by keeping a record card on all materials and equipment. If possible, the card should be attached to the materials and equipment and initialed each time the item is used.

The second observation, that of impact, is more difficult to determine. The most common method is to examine the material and measure the learning that occurs. Student growth is then considered together with the ease of use, the availability and effectiveness of competing materials, and the cost per student. The judgment on the use of the material is usually based on this combination of informal considerations.

Figure 13-9.
Questions Designed to Solicit Opinions

I like eating lunch at school
Always Sometimes Never

The social studies text is
Interesting OK Boring

There is racial prejudice in this school
None A little Some A lot Constant

The rules in this school are strict
Yes No

Teachers
Always listen to you Usually listen to you Seldom listen to you Never listen to you

This room is usually
Too hot A little too hot Just right A little cold Too cold

Select two: This school needs: Better bathrooms
Better play yard
Better library
Better classrooms
Better multipurpose room
Other ________________

Both materials and methods can also be subjected to more careful study. Any one of three basic methods can be used to evaluate the effectiveness of materials or teaching methods. Each method requires that frequent measures be taken on the behavior or learning that occurs. In each method an initial baseline is established in order to determine the level of behavior or learning before the materials or methods are introduced. The baseline is established over five or more days or sessions. Any appropriate behavior can be measured, such as the number of words spelled correctly each day, the length and quality of language papers, the fluency of reading, the number of creative productions, and so on.

The first method of analysis is *reversal.* After the baseline on behavior has been established, a new method or material is introduced. Behavior measurement continues as before. The new procedure is maintained for a period of a week or more in order to establish a stable measure of performance. The new materials are then withdrawn and the previous procedure reintroduced for another baseline period. If a change has occurred during the trial period, the removal of the trial materials or instruction should result in a return to a near baseline performance. A reintroduction of the new instruction, and continued measurement, will again demonstrate the impact of this instruction on performance. A similar procedure used a month or two later can check on the stability of the impact of the materials or method over time. Figure 13-10 illustrates the charting of a reversal procedure.

Figure 13-10.
Arithmetic Production in a Reversal Procedure

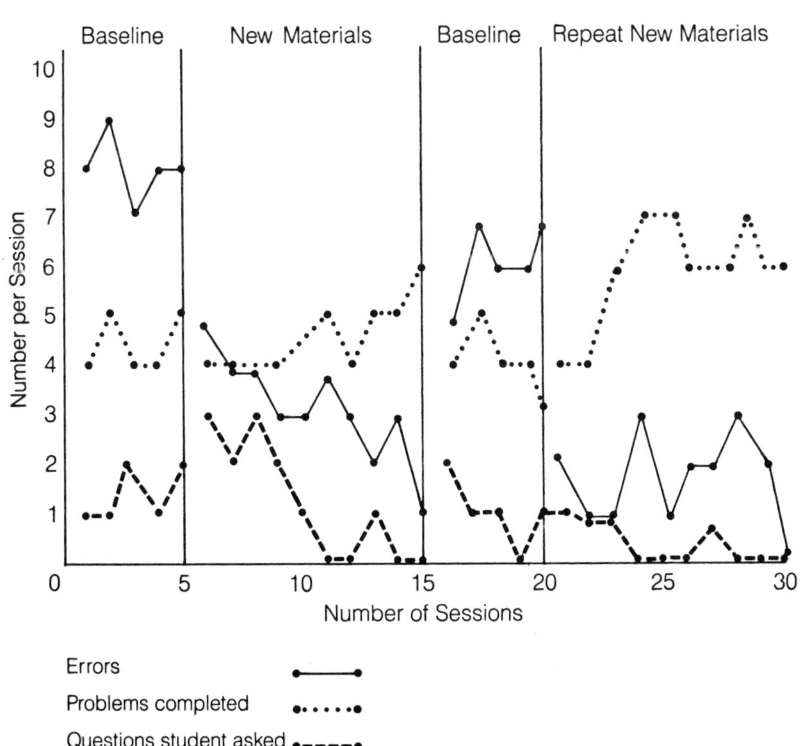

Multiple baseline is a second method for determining the cause of a change in behavior or learning. This method acknowledges that a number of different behaviors can occur as a result of the introduction of new materials or teaching methods. For instance, a decrease in arithmetic error rate may be only one of several ways that new material is expected to affect a student's production. Other changes might include the number of problems completed, number of questions asked, in-seat behavior, or memory over time. It is also possible to measure the performance of each student rather than that of a group. In each case baselines are taken on the behavior of students under consideration. The results will provide a multifaceted view of behavior and change. The charting of multiple baselines can be accomplished by recording the data on separate charts or by plotting the results on the same chart (see Figure 13-10).

A *crossover method* allows the teachers to try one set of materials or procedures on one group and another set on a second group. Instruction is continued long enough for the methods to be reasonably tested (e.g., one or more weeks). The methods are then exchanged and each group receives what the other group had in the first trial period. Measurements are made on both groups throughout the trials, and the results will give an indication of the impact of each method on identical groups. The diagram in Figure 13-11 describes the sequence of events.

Figure 13-11.
Crossover Method of Study for Materials and Methods

Group 1	Arithmetic Method A	Arithmetic Method B
Group 2	Arithmetic Method B	Arithmetic Method A
	September to December	January to April

The selection of good materials can help to eliminate many hours of inefficient learning and needless evaluation. The difference between what is useful and what is soon discarded may rest on such a simple factor as the ease with which students can enter the activity. Figure 13-12 provides a comprehensive checklist of items that can be used in the evaluation of materials.

Figure 13-12.
Important Considerations in Material Selection

General characteristics

- Initial cost is appropriate for use.
- Format is attractive.
- Packaging is convenient.
- Materials are portable or easily managed.
- Upkeep or resupply cost is reasonable.
- Materials are durable.
- Special equipment is available.

Content

- Objectives are clear and obtainable.
- Material is organized and sequenced effectively.
- Material is free from sex, race, ethnic bias.
- Materials satisfy a need in the program.
- Cost-use impact factors are favorable.
- Learner outcomes are appropriate.

Teacher needs

- Manuals or guides are clear.
- Pretraining is identified and provided.
- Method fits teaching style.
- Teaching suggestions are provided.
- Time requirements are reasonable.
- Teacher adaptions are possible.
- Procedures are compatible with good management.

Student needs

- Age and grade identification is accurate.
- Identifies entry-level skills needed.
- Design is for individual or group use.
- Materials have good motivation value.
- Provisions are made for different learning styles.
- Content is relevant to student background and goals.
- Materials foster self-direction and responsibility.

Evaluation

- Materials are field tested and information is provided.
- Claims seem reasonable, sender is reputable.
- Student self-evaluation is possible.
- Student progress can be monitored.
- Users can be contacted for evaluations.
- Pretest period or sample is available.
- Outcome data can be verified.

Summary

The assessment of teaching, management, materials, and environment ranks in importance with student assessment. Learning in schools occurs in an organized environment and that environment has a significant impact on student performance. The actions of the teacher, the quality of the materials, and the physical surroundings each play an important part in student behavior, motivation, and development.

The teacher essentially sets the stage for learning. Through class management, presentation of subject matter, interaction with students, selection of materials, and class atmosphere, the teacher provides the setting where students develop, mark time, or regress. The assessment of these features of instruction provides information on the conditions and processes that lead to learning.

The style of teaching and the management strategies used by the teacher, in large part, determine the achievement and behavior of students in the classroom. Methods that provide information about teacher behavior include teacher-student interaction analyses, teacher instructional checklists, and classroom management surveys. Each evaluates a different aspect of teacher performance, and each area is critical to the overall success of the teacher.

Other methods for improving the effectiveness of instruction include assessments by students, process evaluation, materials evaluation, space utilization surveys, and classroom research procedures. Each is a basic and useful evaluation strategy and a necessary part of a comprehensive assessment repertoire.

Bibliography

Bidwell, Charles E., and Kasarada, John D. "Conceptualizing and Measuring the Effects of School and Schooling." *American Journal of Education* 88, no. 4 (1980): 401–430.

Centra, John A. "Student Ratings of Instruction and Their Relationship to Student Learning." *American Educational Research Journal* 14, no. 1 (1977): 17–24.

Clark, Jonathan, and Jonannet, Pierre. "Observation: A Vehicle for Generating Information Between Partners in Problem Solving." *Journal of Education* 159, no. 4 (1977): 49–61.

Duke, Daniel L. "What Can Students Tell Educators About Classroom Dynamics?" *Theory into Practice* 16, no. 4 (1977): 262–271.

Dunn, Rita S., and Dunn, Kenneth J. "Learning Styles/Teaching Styles: Should They . . . Can They . . . Be Matched?" *Educational Leadership* 36, no. 4 (1979): 238–244.

Dunn, Rita S., and Dunn, Kenneth J. *Teaching Students Through Their Individual Learning Styles: A Practical Approach.* Reston, Va.: Reston Publishing, 1978.

Engelmann, Siegfried; Granzin, Alex; and Sevenson, Herbert. "Diagnosing Instruction." *Journal of Special Education* 13, no. 4 (1979): 355–363.

Epstein, Joyce L., and McPartland, James M. "The Concept and Measurement of the Quality of School Life." *American Educational Research Journal* 13, no. 1 (1976): 15–30.

Fischer, Barbara B., and Fischer, Louis. "Styles in Teaching and Learning." *Educational Leadership* 36, no. 4 (1979): 245–251.

Flanders, N. A. *Teacher Influence, Pupil Attitudes and Achievement.* Washington, D.C.: U.S. Department of Health, Education and Welfare, 1959.

Gesten, Ellis L.; Cowen, Emory L.; DeStefano, Michael A.; and Gallagher, Richard. "Teachers' Judgments of Class-Related and Teaching-Related Problem Situations." *The Journal of Special Education* 12, no. 2 (1978): 171–181.

Hardin, Veralee B. "Ecological Assessment and Intervention for Learning Disabled Students." *Learning Disability Quarterly* 1, no. 2 (1978): 15–20.

Judah, Richard, and Keat, Donald B., II. "Multimodal Assessment: The Classroom Ecology Schedule." *Elementary School Guidance and Counseling* 12, no. 2 (1977): 97–104.

Kratochwill, Thomas R., and Green, Leslie M. "Process Assessment." *Academic Therapy* 13, no. 5 (1978): 563–568.

Spaulding, R. L. "Spaulding Teacher Activity Rating Schedule (STARS)." San Jose, Calif.: San Jose University, 1974.

Spaulding, R. L. "Spaulding Teacher Activity Rating Schedule (STARS)." Revised. San Jose, Calif.: San Jose University, 1978.

Van Horn, Royal W. "Environmental Psychology: Hints of a New Technology." *Phi Delta Kappan* 61, no. 10 (1980): 696–697.

Whitely, Susan E., and Doyle, Kenneth O. "Implicit Theories in Student Ratings." *American Educational Research Journal* 13, no. 4 (1976): 241–253.

Chapter 14 Assessment of Minority Students

The assessment of students with different language, cultural, ethnic, or socioeconomic backgrounds poses unique problems in education. In a pluralistic society where immigration is part of the nation's heritage and where ethnic and racial differences are the rule rather than the exception, teachers and other educational professionals are continually challenged by the need to employ appropriate assessment and instructional procedures. The fact that formal testing is designed and referenced around a representative sample of persons drawn from the major culture limits its usefulness with those students whose experiences set them apart from the norm. In addition, assessment strategies are limited by their susceptibility to the bias or cultural ignorance of the assessor.

The process of assessment with minority students involves several considerations. It is important to understand the student's linguistic and cultural background and his or her current experiences in order to interpret behavior and determine appropriate goals and activities. It is equally important to understand the effect of the minority student on the assessor, including the attitudes, beliefs, and expectations held by the assessor. These factors have a tendency to influence the selection and interpretation of assessment data. It is also critical to know the strengths and limitations of assessment methods as they apply to different minority populations. This information maximizes the chance of proper test selection, administration, and interpretation.

The most blatant misuse of assessment instruments and data has occurred with formal testing. This is not to say that abuses do not occur every day in a smaller way with informal measures, but formal testing traditionally has been used to make the placement decisions that lock a student into special education. Litigation related to the assessment and instruction of minority students gives testimony to the abuses of the past.

LEGAL REQUIREMENTS

Abuses in the testing and special class placement of minority students has led to litigation, laws, and regulations governing these activities. Remedies for the abuses have brought into focus some of the problems involved in minority assessment and have alerted the educational community to the need for more responsible assessment and placement practices. A sample of major legal cases and federal regulations illustrate the serious misuse of testing that has occurred.

Two court cases have had a profound impact on testing and placement practices. The first case involved the language of the children tested, the second case the race of the children. Both involved possible discrimination and denial of equal educational opportunity. In *Diana* v. *California State Board of Education* nine Mexican-American public school children from predominantly Spanish-speaking homes had been tested in English and had been placed in classes for the mentally retarded on the basis of the test results. Subsequent testing, given in Spanish, determined that seven of the nine scored above the retarded range. The plaintiffs, citing *Brown* v. *Board of Education* (1954), the Civil Rights Act of 1964, and Article 9, Section 5, of the California Constitution, contended that the federal government and the State of California should guarantee every citizen the right to an equal educational opportunity. They charged that the testing procedure was discriminatory and inappropriate in that it emphasized verbal skills requiring facility with the English language and ignored abilities in Spanish. The tests were standardized on white, native-born children; and the items were culturally biased.

In an out-of-court decision (1973) the contesting parties agreed that steps should be taken to reduce the inappropriate and unfair use of tests. The agreement in the Diana Remedy Memorandum stipulated that:

1. Children must be tested in their own language and in English.
2. They may be tested on nonverbal sections of intelligence tests.
3. Mexican-American children in Educable Mentally Retarded (EMR) classes should be retested and reevaluated, using nonverbal test sections.
4. School districts throughout the State must submit summaries of the retesting efforts and their plans for transitional programs for children no longer eligible for programs for the educable mentally retarded.
5. A test of IQ that reflects Mexican-American culture would be developed and normed on Mexican-American children.
6. If there is a disparity between the racial-ethnic representation of the district and the EMR classes, to a significant degree, the districts so involved should submit an explanation.

In another Diana Remedy Memorandum, November 1978, the Court further stipulated that "students with physical and mental disabilities be accurately assessed . . . and individuals who do not have those disabilities must not be so identified even though they show learning problems similar to those with such disabilities; they should be helped in other programs." Although the focus of both memoranda is on the mentally retarded, the decisions have broad implications. They stipulate that a test must be conducted in the child's primary language and English, and that tests reflect the culture of the child.

A second class action suit, *Larry P.* v. *Riles* (1971) alleged that several black elementary school children were wrongly placed and held in classes for the mentally retarded. The basic issue focused on the biased nature of tests used to determine the intelligence of black children. The opinion was in favor of the plaintiffs and stated:

> In violation of Title VI of the Civil Rights Act of 1964, the Rehabilitation Act of 1973, and the Education for All Handicapped Children Act of 1975, defendants have utilized standardized intelligence tests that are racially and culturally biased, have a discriminatory impact against black children, and have not been validated for the purpose of essentially permanent placements of black children into educationally dead-end, isolated, and

> stigmatizing classes for the so-called educable mentally retarded. (U.S. District Court for the Northern District of California, 1979, p. 3)

In addition to these cases that directly affect assessment, the case of *Lau* v. *Nicholes et al.* (January 1974) has had a corollary effect on instruction. The suit brought on behalf of Chinese-American students charged that the lack of special language instruction violated Section 601 of the Civil Rights Act (1964) and the equal protection clause of the Fourteenth Amendment. The court ruled in favor of the defendants, as did the U.S. Circuit Court of Appeals. The U.S. Supreme Court found that the schools had violated the Civil Rights Act (1964). The Court assigned responsibility for remedies to the State Board of Education (California). Justice Douglas, in the delivery of the Court's opinion, took notice that the State required education and mastery of English as a requirement for graduation and stated:

> Under ... state-imposed standards there is no equality of treatment merely by providing students with the same facilities, textbooks, teachers, and curriculum; for students who do not understand English are effectively foreclosed from any meaningful education. Basic English skills are at the very core of what these public schools teach. Imposition of a requirement that, before a child can effectively participate in the educational program, he must already have acquired those basic skills is to make a mockery of public education. We know that those who do not understand English are certain to find their classroom experiences wholly incomprehensible and in no way meaningful.

It would seem that assessment conducted in English would also fail to provide "equality of treatment" and that students so assessed would be "effectively forcelosed from any meaningful" evaluation.

Federal regulations related to minority children are most clearly stated in the Education of All Handicapped Children Act of 1975 (PL 94-142). This act addresses the assessment problems associated with language and bias. In the words of the law:

> (c) procedures to assure that testing and evaluation materials and procedures utilized for the purposes of evaluation and placement of handicapped children will be selected and administered so as not to be racially or culturally discriminatory. Such materials or procedures shall be provided and administered in the child's native language or mode of communication, unless it clearly is not feasible to do so, and no single procedure shall be the sole criterion for determining an appropriate educational program for a child. (Section 612, U.S. Public Law 94-142)

ASSESSMENT PROCEDURES

The problems inherent in the assessment of minority children have been recognized for many years. There have been numerous attempts to construct norm-referenced tests that provide an accurate assessment of the student, regardless of race or culture. Five methods typify the efforts with standardized tests.

Culture-free or Culture-fair Tests

Culture-free or culture-fair tests attempt to tap universal indices of development in perceptual, conceptual, or motor growth. The methods, quite logically, avoid the use of language. Most frequently, the tests have employed the perceptual abilities of recognition, memory, reproduction, or creativity. Formal testing procedures have included tests such as the Leiter International Performance Scale, Cattell's Culture-Free Test of Intelligence, the Columbia Mental Maturity Scale, and Raven's Progressive Matrices Test. Each requires a visual-perceptual-conceptual level sufficient to successfully select appropriate visual items and complete a predetermined visual pattern or sequence. Unfortunately, the tests did not match the expectations. Human perception and reproduction of the visual world tends to be tied to culture, as are the required test-taking behaviors that influence the quality of performance.

Mercer (1979) suggests that a few physical indices are stable enough across cultures to be used as *part* of a total assessment. These constitute her Medical Model Measures and include measures of vision, hearing, weight standardized by height, and physical dexterity. Also included are health history and the Bender Visual Motor Gestalt Test. All but the last test are clearly related to health and physical development. The Bender test is a standardized measure that requires the student to reproduce nine line figures with pencil and paper. Mercer reports that sociocultural characteristics accounted for only 2.5 percent of the variance in the Bender score.

Culture Specific Tests

Some tests have been constructed that ask questions or measure skills specifically related to a culture other than the major culture. These measures are very illustrative for the assessor who is outside the minority culture, because they clearly demonstrate the unique learning that occurs within each culture and demonstrate to the assessor his or her own limitations when measured by minority norms. When it is fully developed, this approach could provide information about a student's skill in dealing within a regional or ethnic culture. At this time, however, the following limitations are apparent in this approach: (1) Such instruments are usually developed around material relevant to a particular locale and therefore are appropriate for only a small segment of the minority population. (2) This method has not undergone the research on item selection and standardization required of formal tests. (3) The results seem to have little predictive value in school classes as classes are presently constituted.

Translations and New Versions

What appears to be a simple solution, the translation, turns out to be a flawed approach. It seems relatively easy to take an existing test and translate it into another language. Unfortunately, words, problems, and tasks seldom translate well from one language to another. Even in English a single word like *blanket* has a number of synonyms such as *quilt, cover,* or *comforter*. Each has a different level of familiarity and difficulty. Each word in an English vocabulary list may have different possible translations in another language and each of the translations a different level of familiarity in that language. The sample of words that is representative of the experiences of youth in one culture is very unlikely to be representative of another culture. The translation, at best, is a risky attempt to use a sample of the experiences relevant to one culture and make them language-appropriate for a second language and culture.

A new version of a test differs from a translation in that it draws its item sample from the minority culture and creates new norms based on that population. It is the most adequate form of test conversion. In a new version the framework and the major subtest areas remain intact. New items are selected to represent the new test population, however.

The weakness of this procedure is that it assumes that the underlying framework of the test—the format and subsections—are appropriate concepts in the second culture. That is, the assumption is made that a given format is an appropriate framework to cover a topic area in the second culture and that the topic itself is culturally relevant. It is possible, in fact likely, that in different cultures topics have varying degrees of value, and subsequently the youth have significantly different levels of exposure. Other topics or goals would better represent the development and skills of the minority child and provide better clues as to how the child can be assisted in the classroom. In intelligence measurement, for example, certain topic areas such as verbal skills tend to dominate tests designed for the major culture. In a minority culture this emphasis may not represent the major experiences or needs of the children. A new version of the test that persisted in the verbal emphasis would not adequately tap the abilities of the minority child.

Pluralistic Assessment

The pluralistic approach recognizes that the nation is culturally heterogeneous, accepts that children are culture bound, and recommends cultural norms, particularly in the assessment of learning potential. The procedure of assessment developed by Mercer (1979) uses multiple testing within three model areas: medical, social, and pluralistic systems. In the pluralistic model, the Wechsler Intelligence Scale for Children Revised (WISC-R) scores are converted to Estimated Learning Potential (ELP) scores using normative data gathered on minority group populations. The conversion factors are derived from data based on family size, family structure, socioeconomic status, and urban acculturation. Each of these conditions was found to account for variations between obtained scores and theoretical estimations of learning potential.

The procedure is relatively new, and therefore there is little experiential basis upon which to judge its merits or weaknesses. The entire battery of assessment is thorough and time-consuming. The combination of information from parent and professional reports, from health history to intelligence test scores, may help to offset the problems encountered when only a single test or domain area is considered. The usefulness of the converted ability scores (ELP) has yet to be proven.

Adaptive Behavior

Adaptive behavior refers to a student's ability to cope with the demands and responsibilities of living. It is not tied to the academic skills required in school, but to the development of such behaviors as self-help, self-direction, personal responsibility, communication skills, social skills, physical development, and economic and occupational activity. There are formal scales designed for the measurement of developmental milestones, such as the Vineland Social Maturity Scale (Doll, 1965); of social and emotional behavior, such as AAMD Adaptive Behavior Scale: Public School Version (Lambert et al., 1975); and of social systems, such as Adaptive Behavior Inventory for Children (Mercer, 1979). The data for most instruments are based on interviews with parents, teachers, or guardians. The weaknesses of the scales lie in their dependency on second-hand reporting, the narrow normed age range for many of the instruments, the lack of agreement as to what behaviors should be included, and the limited attention to cultural differences.

The informal assessment of adaptive behavior is a procedure that can be designed to meet unique conditions of the local and the expected behaviors within a minority culture. Direct observation of a student's ability to adapt to nonacademic activities and interaction within the school can also give insight into a particular student's unique ways of behaving. An example is given in Figure 14-1.

Informal Assessment

The strategies and methods of informal assessment are particularly well suited to the assessment of minority students. Interviews, observations, diagnostic assessment, task analysis, developmental histories, and criterion measures are some of the informal methods that can be adapted to cultural differences and designed for a specific task. The procedures are limited, however, by the skill of the assessor and the distortions created by bias and ignorance.

DIFFERENCES AND DISABILITIES

In assessment there is an important distinction between the concepts of differences and disabilities. Differences refers to dissimilarity, uniqueness, and distinctiveness. In language and culture it is applied to the variations that occur in form, characteristics, and behavior. Variations occur between groups because of their different heritage, needs, and experiences. The concept of differences is neutral; it suggests neither goodness nor badness. In assessment it is the most adequate term to describe variations that occur because of language and culture.

On the other hand, the term *disability* has negative connotations. It focuses attention on the inabilities of an individual or group of individuals. It suggests deprivation or inferiority. In matters of language and culture the term has been mistakenly used to suggest that a student raised in another language or culture has a weakness or handicap.

In the school setting, the term *disability* more appropriately refers to a deficit in learning that occurs in spite of persistent instruction or from an inability to participate in ordinary instruction due to physical, mental, or emotional reasons. The disability concept and model is inappropriate for the ordinary and expected differences that occur as a result of differences in background. The danger in the use of the term is that it creates negative attitudes and limited expectations that can adversely affect the progress of minority students. There are, to be sure, minority students who have learning disabilities, as there are children from the major culture with these problems. The error of the past has been to equate difference with disability. Good educational practice and legal requirements caution against this error.

Figure 14-1.
Example of an Informal Adaptive Survey

Student is compared to other youth of same age, culture, language, sex.

Item	Poorer Than Others	Same As	Better Than Others
Home			
Care of clothing	____	____	____
Eating habits	____	____	____
Personal cleanliness	____	____	____
Care of room	____	____	____
Personal appearance	____	____	____
Expression of emotions	____	____	____
Personal ideas	____	____	____
Responsibility for chores	____	____	____
Follows rules/directions	____	____	____
Help others	____	____	____
Attitude toward life	____	____	____
Relations with others	____	____	____

Comments ____
____
____
____

Item	Poorer Than Others	Same As	Better Than Others
Peers			
Liked by others	____	____	____
Leadership ability	____	____	____
Participation with one other	____	____	____
Participation in group(s)	____	____	____
Athletic interest	____	____	____
Interest in opposite sex	____	____	____
Expresses emotions	____	____	____
Social ability	____	____	____
Instigates activities	____	____	____
Makes friends	____	____	____
Understands games	____	____	____
Plays cooperatively	____	____	____

Comments ____
____
____
____
____

Item	Poorer Than Others	Same As	Better Than Others
School			
Follows rules	_____	_____	_____
Relations with adults	_____	_____	_____
Participation on yard	_____	_____	_____
Quality of ideas	_____	_____	_____
Participation in sports	_____	_____	_____
Liked by others	_____	_____	_____
Leadership ability	_____	_____	_____
Sense of time	_____	_____	_____
Takes responsibility	_____	_____	_____
Modulates voice	_____	_____	_____
Knows correct behavior	_____	_____	_____
Appropriate meal behavior	_____	_____	_____

Comments ____
____
____
____

Item	Poorer Than Others	Same As	Better Than Others
Community			
Understands money	_____	_____	_____
Uses transportation	_____	_____	_____
Can purchase lunch	_____	_____	_____
Attends movies	_____	_____	_____
Shops for food	_____	_____	_____
Interested in activities	_____	_____	_____
Takes small jobs	_____	_____	_____
Overnight with peers/relatives	_____	_____	_____
Helps neighbors	_____	_____	_____
Talks with adults	_____	_____	_____
Knows locations	_____	_____	_____

Comments ____
____
____
____
____

The tendency in education to move from a concept of difference to a concept of deficit is relatively easy to understand. The competency and adequacy of both the student and the teacher are intimately linked to success in academic skill areas. In most classrooms the teacher, the materials, and the method of instruction reflect the major culture and language. Students who are unfamiliar with the major culture are likely to perform poorly. When seen from the point of view of the major culture the student appears to be inadequate and a failure. Assessment has helped to contribute to this misperception. For years inadequate and abused intelligence tests have supported the conclusion that the minority student was inadequate.

It is hoped that contemporary assessment avoids the errors of the past. Assessment of students who differ in culture or language should be planned and conducted cautiously, and the results viewed tentatively. Assessment must be performed in the language of the student, and test and assessment strategies must be appropriate to the task or culture. The judgment of disability is reserved for those students where it can be clearly determined that learning and behavioral problems transcend experiential differences that arise from language and culture.

LINGUISTIC DIFFERENCES

The separation of language from culture is admittedly artificial. The two coexist and are in many ways interdependent and inseparable. Language tends to set the parameters of thought and to guide a person's understanding of the world. The words, idioms, and phrases of a language reflect the beliefs, customs, and behavior of the people. However, people of different languages may share many common cultural experiences, and people who share a common language may have distinctly different ethnic experiences.

Differences in language and culture can add richness and variety to human experience. In a world of many languages and cultures, and where movement between regions, nations, and continents is relatively easy, cross-cultural contact is to be expected. In multicultural and multilingual classrooms, students have the opportunity to learn from each other and, in turn, to discover what is unique about their own culture and heritage. At the same time, multiple languages in a classroom can complicate instruction because verbal communication tends to be the medium of instruction.

Language impacts upon the student and the school experience in a number of ways. As the Court has noted *(Lau v. Nichols)* "Students who do not understand English are effectively foreclosed from any meaningful education." In addition to the obvious problems that occur for non-English-speaking students in an English-speaking class, there are potential problems associated with activities closely related to classroom instruction. Appropriate assessment and special instructional assistance may not be available for the student in a second language. Communication between the home and the school may be reduced to such an extent easy access to information and support from parents is denied. The parents' ability to assist the student at home may also be severely limited by language differences. The contrast between home and school may alienate some students from their parents and from the emotional support expected from the home. To reduce these potential problems the school needs to provide assessors fluent in the student's primary language or trained translators, primary language teachers or trained aides, instruction in the primary language, and training and instruction in the secondary language.

TRANSLATORS

The ideal assessment condition is one in which assessment is conducted by a professional who is native and fluent in the student's culture and language and who is also experienced and fluent in the major culture and language. Fluency in the language of the student and knowledge about the culture is another appropriate level of professional competence. Professionals with one of these two levels of skill are currently available in many places but are limited to those non-English languages with large population concentrations and with long histories of immigration. It is less likely that professionals with native or fluent language proficiency are available for smaller groups of non-English-speaking residents. In some cases few of the adults native in these languages have chosen to enter education or allied professions. In still other cases the immigration movement is so recent that there has not been time for the development of bilingual educational professionals. Education of youth, however, cannot be suspended until appropriately trained professionals are available.

When an assessor fluent in both languages is not available, the professional will need to use a translator. The use of a translator is unique in two ways. First, most assessors are not experienced in team assessment, so the introduction of a third party is a novelty. Secondly, assessors need to brief the translator in the purpose and the methods of assessment and to coach the translator during the procedure. The assessor is often ill equipped for the roles of teacher, director, coach, observer, and recorder.

Skillful translation comes with experience and familiarity with the subject matter under consideration. The following general characteristics are essential for a beginning translator:

1. Fluency in the primary language and dialect of the student
2. Fluency in English and the ability to translate words and meanings between the languages
3. Knowledge of the student's culture and of the dominant culture of the school
4. Ability to read and write in the languages several years beyond that expected of the student
5. Ability to converse with ease with children and adults
6. Ability and willingness to follow directions and communicate with the assessor
7. Sensitivity and willingness to follow professional and ethical procedures

It is the assessor's responsibility to select and prepare the translator, as well as to understand the problems inherent in translation. The monolingual assessor will need to verify the translator's fluency in the non-English language. This can be accomplished in several ways. First, the candidate should be asked candidly how well he or she speaks, reads, and writes the language. Second, the history of language learning and usage should be established, as well as the recency of non-English usage. Third, other fluent bilingual speakers should be asked about the candidate's level of fluency. It is important to determine that the translator's language is contemporary, that it is appropriate to the social class of the student, and that accents or dialects will not interfere with translation.

The translator's English fluency is determined during the course of the interview. Questions about the translator's history with the use of English provide some indication as to the possible range and depth of language. Questions about the translator's own experience as a non-English or bilingual student, about cultural differences, child rearing practices, and the role of parents in education, will provide the prospective translator the opportunity to demonstrate English fluency as well as provide the assessor with cultural background information. Good fluency and conceptual ability in English is critical to success in translating. English pronunciation, however, need only be good enough so that the assessor understands all that is said during the English parts of the translation.

In the interview with a prospective translator the assessor provides examples of the verbal material and questions that could be used with a student or parent. A good bilingual translator will be able to tell the assessor which statements can be translated easily and relatively directly, and which will be significantly changed in translation. In all languages there are words and concepts that have no direct counterparts in another language. Examples of this noncorrespondence in languages often emerge even in a brief period of a mock translation. The translator is encouraged to indicate to the assessor any time a phrase, word, or concept must be restated in a significantly altered form. When a major change must be made in translation it will help the assessor to have the translator take the second language statement he has made and retranslate it into English. This will provide the translator with a cross check on what has been communicated. In this way control is exercised over major distortions that may occur in translation. The translator should be encouraged to translate all communications, both verbal and nonverbal, so that the assessor will receive as complete a communication as possible.

The orientation of a translator should contain: (1) the background on the student, (2) the concern of the school and the purpose of the assessment, (3) the type of questions and tests that will be used, (4) time to review standardized or manual presentations of material, (5) a description of the standardized procedures that will be used, (6) the degree of freedom the translator will have in interpreting information, and (7) the need for confidentiality and other ethical considerations.

The assessor and the translator function together in a cooperative manner. The assessor relies heavily on the skill of the interpreter, and the interpreter depends on the assessor to guide the activity, provide the substance of the communication, select alternative statements and tests, and make the professional judgments required in the course of the interview or test. It is the assessor's responsibility to:

1. Select and prepare the interpretor
2. Select appropriate strategies
3. Monitor nonverbal communication
4. Be informed and sensitive to cultural differences
5. Provide the structure and content of the interview
6. Be alert to the needs of the translator, student, and parent
7. Exhibit patience with the process of translation
8. Communicate ethical practices around confidentiality, objectivity, and accurate reporting
9. Communicate the need, purpose, and use of the information
10. Inform the parent and student as to the types of assessments used and the rights and appeals available to the parents

ORAL LANGUAGE ASSESSMENT

Oral language assessment is difficult, even when performed by a trained native speaker with a monolingual student. Formal assessment is time-consuming and complex, often requiring fifty or more speech samples and judgments across numerous linguistic elements. An informal assessment usually concentrates on the functional aspects of language and describes, in general terms, the salient and easily observable aspects of language. The assessment combines information obtained from observations, interviews and tests.

Primary Language Proficiency

The communication patterns between adults and children vary between cultures and depend on the role in which each finds himself. It is nearly universally true, however, that the linguistic forms and codes that are used between adults and children are different from those used between adults. Differences are apparent in grammatical complexity, choice of words, volume and tone, and content. In addition, the adult often uses a different way of standing, a different use of hands and body movement and different facial expressions. Adult statements are often demanding and critical, and therefore inhibit spontaneous speech production. In order to offset possible barriers to maximal student production, speech samples need to be gathered in both adult-child and child-child settings.

Peer observations and records can be made by the interpreter during periods when students converse spontaneously with their friends. A bilingual classroom aide can also be taught to make simple language observations. A monolingual assessor can witness the frequency, spontaneity, and responsiveness of language, but the bilingual observer is needed to determine the complexity, content, and appropriateness of the student's language. Verbatim reports of the student's comments provide a basis for an analysis of the student's language and act as examples of the student's fluency. Records should be kept on the skill levels achieved during each observation. When formal measures of language are available they should be used. A functional assessment can be made by comparing the student's language with that of two other students who have had approximately the same language experiences. A simple analysis framework is provided in Figure 14-2.

When a student cannot be observed speaking with other children who are fluent in the same primary language, the assessor should base the estimate of language development on information from the translator and

Figure 14-2.
Simple Analysis of Observed Language Use

Directions: Record language sample of target student and two other students of like sex, same age, and similar bilingual background.

Content Analysis	Target Student	Comparison Student A	Comparison Student B
Number of sentences in time sample	____	____	____
Length of average sentence	____	____	____
Frequency of verb use	____	____	____
Frequency of noun use	____	____	____
Frequency of modifiers	____	____	____
Percent correct grammar	____	____	____
Appropriate communication	____	____	____
Estimated level of thought (1 low to 5 high)	____	____	____
Estimated complexity of sentences (1 low to 5 high)	____	____	____

the parents. Good verbal rapport between the translator and the student is essential to an accurate language assessment. Ease in communication will result in optimum student production; without it the estimate should not be made.

Parent information can be very useful if data on developmental history and current verbal fluency are candid. Parents must be told the purpose of any questioning, and the assessor needs to be sensitive to parent concerns for their child. Parents, for example, may feel that any time an assessor asks a question of a parent, this attention suggests a problem.

Morphology is the study of word form and structure and includes inflection, derivation, and compounding (see Chapter 8). The morpheme is the smallest meaningful unit of language, such as the word *boy*. The plural *boys* includes two morphemes. A morphological or structural analysis includes an examination of such grammatical forms as tensing (e.g., *-ed*), plurality (e.g., *-s*), possessive (e.g., *-'s*), and adverb endings (e.g., *-ly*). Variations in the forms exist in different languages. The bilingual assessor or translator needs to identify the forms that are appropriate for the language under study and estimate the student's point of development in relation to the normal development within the student's culture.

The importance of using the student's culture as a guide against which to measure growth has been illustrated by B. Merino (1979). She points out that in English the acquisition of the rules for producing plural nouns (i.e., cat becomes cats and house becomes houses) is acquired early in a child's development, generally by the age of six. In Arabic, however, where there are many irregular classes of the plural and many fine distinctions made with different usage, errors in the correct production of some plurals are common as late as age fifteen.

Syntax refers to the way in which words are arranged in an orderly and meanigful system of phrases and sentences (see Chapter 8). Word order is important in most languages. A child's understanding of the meaning of the order of words is basic to the ability to interpret what is heard as well as to express himself clearly. A student who misunderstands the syntax of a direction will respond in a way that acknowledges word understanding but not contextual meaning. For example, the statement, "Your work is completed," could arouse confusion in the student who understands the statement as, "Is your work completed?" A student with syntax difficulty is likely to produce disorganized statements with uncertain meaning.

Semantics is the study of the meaning of words (see Chapter 8). In its simplest form it is measured by a knowledge of the definition of words. At a more abstract level it refers to the comparison of words, word variations, appropriate synonyms and antonyms, and word combinations. At still another level it is the understanding of situational and contextual clues that give added meaning to words. The preposition *up* for instance has a meaning that is enhanced by its context, such as "He ran up the hill" as opposed to "The book is up on the shelf." The words of each language convey thoughts, feelings, and beliefs in their own unique way. Individuals will have a receptive and expressive mastery of the words of their language to varying degrees. This mastery can be examined directly, such as in a vocabulary test, or indirectly, as in the content analysis of a running dialogue.

Other language characteristics are also important to notice and record. For example, in most languages the length of statements increases with increased language skill, and tone and melody add to the meaning of words and phrases. The activity and the type of participants are also important to note. A conversation with adults may be subdued and respectful, while a verbal exchange during a game with peers can be excited and colloquial. Dialects form among peers. In each instance the student chooses a language form that best fits the situation. Figure 14-3 displays the critical characteristics that are included in a language sample analysis.

Any doubt or question about how the student's language compares to the language used by other students of the same age and same language should be resolved through a measured comparison. To do this the translator selects two other students of similar age, sex, and language and takes language samples during the same time period and activity as that

Figure 14-3.
Informal Language Sample Analysis

Language Sample

Student's name ______________ Date ________ Location ________

Activity ______________ Participants ______________

[Space for verbatim language samples]

Language Analysis:

Phonology
(Pronunciation of words and word parts such as vowels, consonants, syllables)

Form and structure
(Grammatical construction, verb tense, sentence complexity, plurals, possessives, adverbs, fluency, etc.)

Semantics
(Correct word usage, size of vocabulary, preciseness in word selection, use of modifiers)

Length
(Word count in sentence, number of sentences used to express topic)

Fit
(Appropriateness in language in context, comparison to the language of peers, style of language initiation and responses)

---

used for the target student. Analyses of the three are then compared. The deviation of the target child will need to be consistent, sizable, and verified in several observations if the finding is to be considered significant.

Bilingual Language Proficiency

The informal measure of bilingual development requires assessors or translators who are themselves fluent in both English and the student's primary language. It is not enough to know the level of development in each language; a judgment of relative proficiency is often needed to make educational decisions. Questions of language dominance and preference also need to be examined.

The issues of proficiency, dominance, and preference are the major focus of informal bilingual language assessment. *Proficiency* refers to the level of development that the student has achieved in each language. At a practical level it is the determination of how well the language skill will serve the student's needs in various settings. It can refer to measures of developmental level, assessments of the language skills available for different tasks, and a comparison of skill levels to that of same-language peers.

Dominance is the judgment as to which of the languages is most fully developed and works most effectively for the student in most settings. It also refers to the language of thought. Cognitive development is closely related to language. In the early stages of the mastery of a second language it is common for the learner to translate from the new to the native language. At this stage, thinking is done in the native language. Some persons continue to think in the native language; others switch to thinking in the language of use, or use different languages for different thoughts, such as using one language for family concerns and another for work. Still other bilingual persons shift much of this thinking to the new language. The dominant language is the one that the student finds is the best for receiving and processing information and the best for expressing thought.

Language *preference* is the language the student would use if given the freedom of choice. This depends as much on the psychological and social needs of the student as on the level of fluency. In the early stages of learning a new language, the constant need to attend, the confusion around new words, and the inability to express oneself are exhausting. Many students need to get away from time to time and require periods of solitude. Once fluency is achieved, however, preference is often related to the social context in which speech is used and to the degree of comfort and assurance a student experiences. Preference can be related to the value placed on a particular language. Measures of preference can be straightforward. When a bilingual choice is available, the chosen language is usually the preferred language. Most bilingual speakers are aware of which language they prefer and will share this information when asked.

A problem encountered in bilingual assessment results from the uneven development of language that characteristically occurs when two languages are learned at the same time. Words learned in one context and in one language may not be known in the other language. For instance, words learned at home in the primary language such as *pillow, underwear,* or *fireplace* may be unknown to the student when they are presented in English. The reverse is true for those learned within a context where English is spoken and where the primary language is not involved.

It was noted earlier that observation is one of the best methods for determining the functional level of oral language. Unfortunately, it is not possible to observe the bilingual student in all, or even a representative sample, of the contexts in which language takes place. The assessor is challenged, therefore, to identify the range of words available to the student and to separate those known monolingually from those known bilingually.

Word lists, pictures, and themes that represent different settings and contexts can be used to encourage the student to respond in whatever language(s) the student holds the information. Preexisting word lists, pictures, and themes that are appropriate to a wide variety of languages and cultures are sometimes not available, and therefore the assessor is left to design his own language list. The most common social systems in which language develops are the home, school, peers, community, and work. Table 14-1 gives a list of the word clusters typically associated with each system. The student whose home and community are essentially non-English-speaking can be expected to have native language vocabulary appropriate for these contexts and may not have an equally well-developed English vocabulary.

Bilingual language analysis is made in the manner suggested in Figure 14-3. Each language is observed and recorded, and a composite description constructed. Notations are made as to the stimuli (vocabulary lists, pictures, etc.) that were used to augment language samples taken in the school or home environment. Words selected from the clusters in Table 14-1 will indicate how comprehensive each language's development has been within each social system.

In addition to these procedures a survey of the student's language history (Figure 14-4) can provide some understanding of the growth of language. A language survey provides information on the course of the second language's development, the social influence on language skill,

Table 14-1.
Social Systems and Associated Language Areas

SOCIAL SYSTEM	GENERIC VOCABULARY AREAS
Home	Intimacy, youth, sleeping, eating, health, customs, religion, heritage, relatives, fantasy, fears
School	School subjects, games, directions, abstractions, writing, reading, social interactions, cross-cultural information
Peers	Play, comradeship, colloquialisms, sports, interests, sex, social terms, profanity
Community	Locations, shopping, entertainment, transportation, jobs, services
Work	Equipment, technology, money, responsibility, organizational structure

the current level of development, and the parents' preference for a dominant language. Information can be provided by the student, parent, or teacher.

Dialects

Many languages, including English, have regional, ethnic, or racial variations called *dialects.* Dialects can exist as major forms of a language that have a common structural form or vocabulary (e.g., standard English and Black English in the United States) or that have a common basis but different vocabulary (e.g., Ilokano and Tagalog in the language of the Philippines). The second type of dialect is often treated as a separate language because of the profound differences between the language of the assessor or teacher and the dialect of the student. Such differences can block direct conversation, and interpreters or professionals with the appropriate dialect may be required.

The first type of dialect allows for far easier communication because of the existence of common words, structures, and sounds. The monolingual assessor can often become proficient in understanding, if not speaking, the dialect. An analysis and interpretation of the characteristic differences between a language and a dialect (as in the example given in Table 14-2) can provide invaluable assistance in learning and understanding dialectal differences.

Figure 14-4.
Example of a Second Language Survey

Student's name __________ Age ______ Date ______

Native language ________ Second language ________ Other ____

Second Language History

Age at time of introduction: Speaking ____ Writing ____ Reading ____
Country in which introduction took place: __________
Years in the United States: ______
Location and degree of prior second language experience:
(Use degree code: None 0, Occasional 1, Frequent 2)

Location	Home	School	Tutor	Peers	Other
Code					

Current Second Language Experience

In-Home Relation	Native Language	Language Used in Home	Second Language Fluency
Mother	______	______	None ☐ Some ☐ Good ☐
Father	______	______	None ☐ Some ☐ Good ☐
Others	______	______	None ☐ Some ☐ Good ☐

Peers

Second Language Fluency
None ☐ Some ☐ Good ☐

Use of Second Language
None ☐ Occasionally ☐ Frequent ☐ Total ☐

Fluency (Check highest level demonstrated)

☐ Survival words
☐ Basic nouns and verbs
☐ Conjugated verbs, nouns, and adjectives
☐ Full sentences, confused forms and structure
☐ Fluent usage, good form and structure

Comments: ____________________

____

____

(continued)

Figure 14-4 continued

Primacy

Dominant language ________ Language of preference ________

Language parents prefer for school instruction ________

Comments ________

School Experience

Native language instruction ☐	Bilingual instruction ☐ Bilingual aide ☐ teacher ☐	All English ☐ instruction
Comments ________	________	________
________	________	________
________	________	________

____

Problems often surround the acceptance of a dialect. A dialect that is a variation of a major language is often associated with a race or an economic class, and the legitimacy of the language is obscured by the attitudes and values held toward the group. It is common, for instance, to associate the Bostonian sound and language with intelligence and wealth while that of the Bronx is associated with lack of education and the working class. Language easily becomes a symbol of differences, and the historical and functional value of the dialect can be overshadowed by preformed ideas including feelings of animosity.

There are several considerations for assessors who work with students with dialects. In many ways the problems they face are similar to those experienced when working with students who are bilingual. Words, sentence structure, and concepts might be understood by the student only in the dialect and be unavailable in standard English. The facility demonstrated in the dialect may be lacking in English, and therefore productions in English will not adequately reflect learning. Ways of thinking, concept development, and belief systems that are a part of dialect and culture can vary dramatically from those experienced by a standard-English-speaking student.

In addition to considerations that are common for all multilingual students, there are significant variations among students who speak a dialect. For some students standard English was the primary language and the dialect was learned from peers. Some students grew up in homes that mixed standard English with the dialect, using each in a different context. Still other students were raised with the dialect as their primary language. These different experiences result in significantly different levels of fluency in standard English and the dialect.

Table 14-2.
Characteristics of Black English That Reflect the Structure of the Dialect

LINGUISTIC CATEGORIES	CHARACTERISTICS	EXAMPLES STANDARD ENGLISH	BLACK ENGLISH
Phonological differences			
Initial position	Merging of /f/ with /th/	thigh	fie
	Merging of /v/ with /th/	Thou	vow
Medial position	Deletion of /r/	Carol	cal
	Merging of /i/ and /e/	pen	pin
	Merging of /v/ with /th/	mother	movver
	Merging of /f/ with /th/	birthday	birfday
Final position	Deletion of /r/	sore	saw
	Deletion of /l/	Saul	saw
	Simplification of consonant clusters:		
	/st/	past	pass
	/ft/	left	leff
	/nt/	went	wen
	/nd/	wind	wine
	/zd/	raised	raise*
	/md/	aimed	aim*
	/ks/	six	sick
	/ts/	it's	it*
	/lt/	salt	saught

(continued)

SOURCE: Diane N. Bryen, "Special Education and the Linguistically Different Child," *Exceptional Children* 41 (1974): 593.

*These items also are morphological differences.

Table 14-2 *continued*

LINGUISTIC CATEGORIES	CHARACTERISTICS	EXAMPLES	
		STANDARD ENGLISH	BLACK ENGLISH
Morphological differences			
Future	Loss of final /l/	you'll	you
Past tense	Simplification of final consonants such as:		
	/st/	passed	pass
	/nd/	loaned	loan
Plural	Deletion of final /s/ and /z/	50 cents	50 cent
		3 birds	3 bird
Syntactical differences			
Auxiliary verb	Deletion of auxiliary	He is going.	He goin.
Subject expression	Repetition of subject	John lives in NY.	John, he live in NY.
Verb form	Substitution of past participle for simple past form	I drank the milk	I drunk the milk
Verb agreement	Deletion of /s/ for third person singular present tense	He runs home.	He run home.
Future form	Substitution of a variation of present progressive tense	I will go home.	I'ma go home.
Negation	Use of double negative	I don't have any.	I don't got none.
Indefinite article	Deletion of /n/	I want an apple.	I want a apple.
Pronoun form	Substitution of objective for nominative case	We have to do it.	Us got to do it.
Preposition	Difference in Preposition	He is over at his friend's house.	He is over to his friend house.
Copula ("be")	Use of durative *be* for *is*	He is here all the time.	He be here.

All the precautions used in the assessment of other multilingual students must be applied to dialect-speaking students. Language fluency, dominance, and preference can be established through observations, interviews, and tests. Test directions and responses, when appropriate, can be given and accepted in both languages. Tests given only in standard English may measure the level of language proficiency more than the subject matter they cover. Nonverbal tests are often less influenced by the language difference, but even these may reflect cultural differences. Assessment related to the skill level in a subject area will provide evidence of the functional level of the student within the context of the materials and language used in the classroom.

The issues surrounding the appropriateness of instruction in dialect versus standard English is beyond the scope of this book. An understanding of how the language affects assessment, however, is most appropriate and has until recent years been neglected in the schools. The impact of the attitudes and beliefs of the assessor is also relevant and will be discussed in connection with culture.

CULTURAL DIFFERENCES

Culture can be defined as the pattern of learned behavior that is shared by members of a society. It includes all systems, techniques, and tools that make up a way of life. It includes the rites, attitudes, beliefs, customs, values, and ideas that are commonly held by a group. Culture is not a static system, but it tends to change slowly so that basic features remain constant over a generation or more. It consists of pervasive patterns of behavior that give unity to a group of people and it sets the parameters that allow for individual variations and change.

The phenomenon of culture is easier to recognize in others than in oneself. The influence of culture is so subtle that individuals have a tendency to accept what has been learned as if it is a basic part of human nature. The social origin and the cultural relativity of ways of thinking, acting, and communicating are not readily apparent in the absence of divergent cultural systems and beliefs. There is almost no human behavior that is not influenced by culture, a fact that becomes evident when an individual is thrust into a new culture.

Culture shock is a term used to label an individual's reactions to a change from a familiar to an unfamiliar culture. The individual becomes confused and overwhelmed; old reliable behaviors are no longer appropriate and present situations are difficult to understand and interpret. Immigrants and travelers experience this shock. Mental and physical reactions attest to the impact of living among people who think and act in ways different from one's own. The physical and emotional shock to a person's system is living testimony to people's lack of preparation for such changes.

Culture shock tends to subside in adults who come to understand or adapt to the new environment. It is common, however, for individuals in a strange culture to gather together with people from their own culture and to protect those elements of the past that have value and utility. The traveler effects this when he seeks out, for example, the "American" hotel or moves about with groups of tourists who help to insulate him from what is foreign and uncomfortable.

The culturally different student faces a similar shock, but because of mandatory school attendance is not able to flee physically. The student also faces possible conflicts between the culture of the home and that of the school. Alienation from the family or the school adds a problem that the student with learning problems can ill afford. Student assessment goes beyond the analysis of skills and behavior. It can identify elements of culture that impact upon student progress. This information can help the teacher, student, and parent understand what is occurring and allow each to make necessary adjustments to improve the situation.

CULTURE VARIATIONS

The range of variations among cultures is inexhaustible. What is taken as a friendly gesture or positive encounter in one culture may be offensive and rude in another. In assessment it is important to recognize that the behavior or attitudes of the assessor's culture are not sacred, unquestionable, or immutable. The focus in assessment is on what exists as a reality for the student, the teacher, and the parents. Therefore, it is important to understand the cultural framework out of which behavior arises and the context in which it occurs. The following list is a brief sample of behaviors and beliefs in other major world cultures.

- The child is asked a question only when there is a problem.
- The act of apology is unheard of and does not exist in word or concept.
- Communication that is straightforward and frank is insulting, disrespectful, and boorish.
- Correcting a student's work in front of other students is an unthinkable affront to the student's dignity.

- In the presence of a raised voice the student lowers his voice out of respect.
- Children, youth, and adults are mutually dependent and supportive; competition is avoided.
- Feeling, sensing, aesthetics, and behavior are of higher value than verbal expression.
- Students are quiet, contemplative, ask no questions, and participate in no class discussion.
- Children lower their heads and eyes as a sign of respect to the adult.

These practices may seem unusual from the point of view of the major culture of the United States, but they are functional and basic features of other cultures. It is easy to see why children from these cultures might: (1) be wary of the adult who asks questions; (2) not understand an apology; (3) be frightened or confused by clear, direct comments; (4) refuse to cooperate with a teacher who corrects them; (5) become inaudible when asked questions in a loud voice; (6) work poorly in independent situations; (7) mix cognitive and aesthetic thought in their productions; (8) be reserved and uncommunicative in class; or (9) avoid looking at the teacher.

The knowledgeable assessor understands the culture of the student and is open to reviewing classroom procedures in light of student needs and expectations. Cultural knowledge comes from direct experience, observations, interviews, informal conversations, shared experiences and attitudes, and readings. Key members of the minority community, older youth, and parents can be invaluable resources to the assessor who is willing to listen and learn.

CULTURAL CHARACTERISTICS

One way to develop a preliminary understanding of a culture is to identify the characteristics that are distinctly different from the major culture. A list of distinguishing characteristics can be developed by a knowledgeable member of the minority community or by someone who is thoroughly familiar with the culture or language. Figure 14-5 is an example of a list that was developed to provide basic cultural information to the majority community during a time of large-scale immigration of Vietnamese families.

Although the information provided in Figure 14-5 can help a professional understand the behavior of a minority child and parent, there are

Figure 14-5.
Characteristics of Some Vietnamese Children and Families Entering the United States in the Mid- and Late 1970s

Some Guidelines to Use in Direct Relations
with Vietnamese Children and Families

1. Vietnamese are part of a proud culture with thousands of years of history.
2. Most children have had years of trauma.
3. Many are painfully aware that thousands of Americans resent their coming, while others are not.
4. Those from the cities have probably studied English for two or more years. Foreign languages begin in grade six (choice of English or French). Vietnamese language is monosyllabic and a tonal language. Word order is similar to English (subject-verb-object). Children from the rural areas have very little education and are mainly from farming families and are not familiar with modern society and technology.
5. Some may not communicate well in speaking or understanding English, yet may be able to read it.
6. Extended family includes all relatives with the father in charge of the household.
7. Social level of teachers is very high in Vietnam; they outrank fathers and are surpassed only by royalty.
8. Mother is main caretaker of the children and has a very specific role to fulfill.
9. There is a minimum of physical education in Vietnam, due to lack of facilities. Some children may be reluctant to take showers. Girls particularly do not like to undress in front of anyone, even another girl.
10. Achievement reflects upon the family and therefore the whole family is made proud. Achievement of the individual is seen as helping the family.
11. Some children have not wanted to eat lunch. Lunch has been the biggest meal of the day in Vietnam; with the siesta it may consume two hours. They may wait until they go home. Some may not like the usual hurried lunch period in this country.
12. Respect for teachers is very important. Children never use a teacher's first name and usually need to attach a title to the last name such as Miss, Mrs. Mr., etc.
13. Parents may be reticent about conferring with teachers, for obvious reasons of language and cultural differences as well as reluctance to deal with authority figures.
14. Stability for these children is extremely important. Recommended that students not change rooms or teachers too often.
15. Most children are more comfortable in highly structured classes. They are also used to strict discipline and not used to relaxed attitudes about classroom procedures.
16. They are also not used to being expected to be spontaneous or raise their hand to ask questions or to recite; rather they expect to be asked by the teacher.
17. Like many other Asian groups, name order is last name, middle name, first name.
18. Usually Vietnamese do not celebrate individual birthdays. But the whole family celebrates Chinese New Year and figures age from that holiday.
19. Adult school: It is wise to assign husband and wife to separate classes, because often he does not wish to be in competition with his wife or children. His authority and self-image should be respected.

SOURCE Adapted by T. Soo-Hoo from a fact sheet compiled and provided by the courtesy of Fatime (Tima) K. Williams at the 1975 Annual Conference of the California School Nurses Organization

20. Sensitivity to social class is advised. Many Vietnamese ladies are very class conscious and may be reluctant to work together or be in the same class with women of a different class. Problems sometimes arise when the wife of an official is reluctant to socialize or work with a prostitute.
21. Touching the top of a child's head is to be *avoided*, even patting them in admiration. Most believe in the immortality of the soul, which resides in the head, and thus touching the top of the head is seen as a violation of that.
22. Do not beckon with a finger or fingers "come here"; this is the way to summon a dog in Vietnam.
23. Avoid bringing your closed fist together with the palm of the other hand. This is an obscene gesture similar to the "finger" in the United States.
24. There are some realistic limitations to how much can be done based on the resources that we have. The important thing to remember is that sensitivity and understanding and genuine caring will be the greatest help in our work with Vietnamese children and families.

---

dangers inherent in the use of such a list. One problem is that the list can act to create a stereotype, an opinion, an attitude, or belief about a group of individuals based on oversimplified information and uncritical judgment. Such opinions are easily remembered and tend to block out new and conflicting information. The listed characteristics are often also seen as innate or inherited, an opinion that runs counter to cultural learning theory.

The changeable nature of cultural characteristics also reduces the validity of lists. For instance, assuming that item 20 in Figure 14-5 was accurate at the time of initial immigration, it seems unlikely that it would remain true for any length of time. Other items can also be expected to change rapidly. Lists must be reviewed and revised frequently, especially during periods of immigration, when many fundamental environmental factors undergo radical changes. Once a minority group has become established within the major society, cultural evolution will often produce changes that distinguish them from newly arrived immigrants.

A third problem with the use of such lists rests in the attempt to apply them to individual members of the group. Within all cultures in-group variations can be significant, and subgroups within a culture may have strikingly different characteristics. Religion, for instance, may play a central role in one family and be ignored in another. Within each family there will be variations among individuals in attitudes, beliefs, customs, and behavior. Lists are useful indices to general group tendencies, but the user is advised to guard against assuming they automatically apply to a particular student.

Assessors can reduce the tendency to stereotype or misapply group information if they:

1. Verify the accuracy and timeliness of available cultural information
2. Determine the amount of variation that occurs within the culture and the likelihood that individuals conform to the characteristics
3. Record new observations about the culture and change expectations accordingly
4. Verify which descriptions are relevant and appropriate to the student under consideration
5. Remain open to the legitimacy of minority behavior that is unlike that of the major culture
6. Appreciate that cultural characteristics are learned and evolve and change over time

CULTURAL VALUES AND ATTITUDES

Cultures differ in beliefs and values, and these differences can have a profound effect on the behavior of students in school. Pepper (1976), for instance, contrasts some general differences between the characteristics of Native Americans and the dominant society:

INDIAN	DOMINANT SOCIETY
Wisdom of age and experience is respected. Elders are revered by their people. Excellence is related to a contribution to the group—not to personal glory. Cooperation is necessary for group survival. Children participate in adult activities. Family life includes the extended family. Time is present oriented—this year, this week—NOW—a resistance to planning for the future. Clocktime is whenever people are ready—when everyone arrives.	Older people are made to feel incompetent and rejected. Competition and striving to win or gain status is emphasized. Competition is necessary for individual status and prestige. Adults participate in children's activities. Family life includes the nuclear family. Time is planning and saving for the future. Clocktime is exactly that. Work is from 9–5 (specified time) and to obtain material possessions and to save for the future. What is mine stays mine.

INDIAN

Work is when necessary for the common good. Whatever Indian people have, they share. What is mine is ours.

Good relationships and mutual respect are emphasized.

People express their ideas and feelings through their actions.

People conform to nature.

Early childhood and rearing practices are the responsibility of the kin group.

Native religion was never imposed or proselytized other groups.

Land gives the Indian his identity, his religion, and his life. It is not to be sold, not owned, but used by all.

Going to school is necessary to gain knowledge. Excelling for fame is looked down upon by the Indian.

Indians have a shorter childhood and the male is held to be a responsible person at the age of 16.

People are usually judged by what they do.

DOMINANT SOCIETY

Success, progress, possession of property and rugged individualism are valued above mutual respect and maintaining good relationships.

People express themselves and attempt to impress others through speech.

People try to dominate and desecrate nature.

Early childhood and rearing practices are the responsibility of the nuclear family.

Religious groups proselytize, coerce, and impose their beliefs on others.

Land is for speculation, for prestige, to be owned, sold, or torn up.

Going to school is necessary to gain knowledge and to compete for grades.

There is an extended childhood and the male is held to be a responsible person at the age of 21.

People are usually judged by their credentials.

The differences described by Pepper touch on such issues as time, competition, expression, age, family, learning, and ambition. The composite picture of a student from the Native American culture is dramatically different from that of a student with the traits of the major culture. Any assessment would need to recognize the legitimate existence of these differences.

The cultural characteristics that tend to be most relevant to school behavior and progress include learning style, relations between children and adults, attitudes toward achievement, the role of the home and the school, and behavioral styles. While these characteristics are important in all students, it is likely that important minority group differences in these areas will be reflected in classroom performance. Table 14-3 provides a framework for examining school-related cultural characteristics.

Table 14-3.
Behaviors and Attitudes in Other Cultures

AREAS	EXAMPLE
Activities	
Pace of activity	Slow, systematic approach to problems
Center of control	Believes that fate controls outcomes
Evaluation criteria	Value placed on style rather than outcome
Role of authority	Leadership is authoritarian and directive
Types of goals	Wish to bring honor on family and group
Classroom vs. yard	Quiet in class, active in sports
Interpersonal relations	
Cooperation vs. competition	Competition avoided; assistance to others
Roles of participants	Leader absolute, all others share in work
Style of communication	Indirect and noncritical conversation
Demonstrations of respect	Silence, agreement, slight bow of head
Friendships	Like sex, across abilities, family ties
Respected persons	Teacher, elders, family, and student class leader
Physical proximity	No social touching, physical distance maintained
Learning styles	
Teacher role	Teacher seen as authority and director
Student-teacher communication	Quiet, wait for directions, no discussion
Praise and correction	Light praise accepted, correction is taken as an affront
Family attitude	Respect education, wish to help, look to teacher as expert

AREAS	EXAMPLE
Degree of conformity	Obeys rules and follows directions
Abilities valued	Aesthetic, artistic, and proper behavior
Personal identity	
Social expression	Self-effacing but social, friendly and talkative with peers
Role of the individual	Duty is to the family, parents guide destiny
Vocational aspirations	Son expected to enter father's occupation; daughter works in the home
Clothing	Major culture clothing adopted
Food	Cultural food in the home
Religion	Religion is at the center of the community activity
Customs	Celebrate holidays of the culture and religion
Language	Native language spoken in most homes; English learned by the working members and school-aged children
Behavioral style	Courteous with adults but little communication outside the home; first generation youth tend to work after high school graduation; little delinquency or drug use

PROFESSIONALS' ATTITUDES

Blatant prejudice and bias against language, culture, race, ability, sex, or ethnic origin is easy to identify in others, and many persons recognize these attitudes and beliefs in themselves. In a system of free, compulsory education both the law and professional ethics strenuously oppose such attitudes and behavior. Bias and prejudice are not allowed to enter into instruction or assessment and can result in litigation against the offending party.

It is not as easy to identify subtle acts of ignorance, bias, or prejudice.

Beliefs and expectations can and do shape the behavior of naive and unsuspecting professionals and work to the detriment of minority students. Such acts of bias are not planned or intentional but are nonetheless harmful. The following examples illustrate acts of subtle discrimination.

- Whenever a dark-skinned student cannot successfully answer a question in class it is asked of a bright, light-skinned student who then answers the question.
- Leadership positions are assigned to students on the basis of their verbal fluency.
- Questions that involve thoughtful responses are addressed to the best and most fluent students.
- Most students screened and found in need of assistance are boys.
- The interpreter used in assessment and instruction is embarrassed by the behavior of minority students.
- Lack of appropriate assessment limits the minority student's access to supplementary assistance.
- There is an overrepresentation of minority students in special education programs for the retarded and an underrepresentation in support programs for the hearing impaired, partially seeing, physically handicapped, and learning disordered.
- Class seating is such that one minority group is clustered at a distance from the teacher.
- Parent conferences are unevenly distributed between majority and minority parents.
- Facial and body language changes in the presence of minority students.
- Individual assessment schedule favors majority group students.
- More school history is recorded for majority group students.

Research and observation will continue to uncover unique forms of discrimination in schools. This discrimination, for the most part, is unintentional and performed by teachers and assessors who profess to be open and free of bias. In the field of minority instruction and assessment all professionals, including minority professionals, need to make periodic reviews of their attitudes and behaviors toward minority students.

There are a number of ways to reduce the amount of personal bias that enters into assessment and instruction. These include peer monitors, cultural immersion, cultural study, and self-examination. The use of professional peers is one way to monitor assessment or instruction. The peer reviews the assessment or instructional materials and procedure in order to detect any bias or favoritism. The peer (hopefully knowledgeable in minority matters) then observes the teacher or assessor during professional performance to determine if a problem does exist. The parameters of the observation are determined in advance, and the focus is concentrated on areas that are influenced by bias or ignorance. Figure 14-6 gives a brief outline of possible points of focus in instruction. Figure 14-7 outlines the focus in assessment.

The immersion method allows the professional to learn, first hand, about the minority group. Full immersion occurs when the professional is able to visit the country of origin of the minority student or is able to live with the minority group in this country. Some teachers, for instance, have spent their summers working and living in migrant camps or with community social service or recreational agencies. A lesser degree of immersion can be accomplished by active participation in home visits, community meetings, advisory boards, religious groups, and personal friendships. The intention of immersion is to increase knowledge and understanding of the minority culture and language.

Figure 14-6.
Multicultural Classroom Behaviors Checklist

Classroom Behaviors	Yes
A. Personal identity	
1. Learning experiences are provided to help students improve their self-concepts.	1. ______
2. Learning experiences are provided to help students identify with their ethnic heritage.	2. ______
B. Curriculum content	
3. Holidays and festivities of different ethnic groups are recognized.	3. ______
4. Magazine and newspaper articles relating to ethnic and cultural experiences and issues are discussed.	4. ______
5. Differing views of conflicts between ideals and realities among ethnic groups are presented for discussion.	5. ______
6. Outside reading assignments include accounts of all cultural and ethnic groups.	6. ______
7. Students explore the literature, music, art, architecture, and/or dance of a variety of ethnic groups.	7. ______

(continued)

SOURCE: Adrienne C. Austin in *Cross-Cultural Educational Assessment Skills Workshop: Training Process and Materials*, ed. A. L. Pasanella, T. B. Sales, and C. B. Volkmor (Los Angeles: California Regional Resource Center, 1978), pp. 286–288. Reproduced with permission of the author.

Figure 14-6 continued

Classroom Behaviors	Yes
8. Information about American ethnic groups is included in all content areas of the curriculum; e.g., social studies, English, literature, physical education, home economics, science.	8. ______
9. Units of study include the experiences of the broad range of ethnic group people instead of focusing exclusively on the "heroes."	9. ______
C. Instructional resources	
10. Bulletin boards and displays reflect the ethnic diversity of American life.	10. ______
11. The classroom library or book collection includes books about American ethnic groups.	11. ______
12. Efforts are made to overcome the deficiencies that may exist in the textbooks' treatment of ethnic minority groups.	12. ______
13. Films, filmstrips, records, and other multimedia resources on ethnic groups are used.	13. ______
14. Material written by and about ethnic groups is used in teaching fundamental skills.	14. ______
D. Instructional strategies	
15. Instructional strategies are designed to provide opportunity for group interaction: e.g., role playing, improvisational dramatics, problem solving, group discussions.	15. ______
16. Instructional strategies are designed to reflect the cultural learning styles of the different ethnic groups within the class.	16. ______
17. A variety of assessment procedures that are appropriate for the cultural and linguistic backgrounds of students are used.	17. ______
E. Language and communication	
18. A student is taught in his or her dominant language or dialect when needed.	18. ______
19. Students are taught about the nature of languages, dialects, and nonverbal communication as cultural behaviors.	19. ______
F. Community resources	
20. Field trips to the various local ethnic communities are provided for students.	20. ______
21. Efforts are made to involve the parents and/or families of students in classroom activities.	21. ______
22. Individuals representing various ethnic groups in the community are invited to participate as classroom resource persons.	22. ______

Figure 14-7.
Multicultural Assessment Checklist

Assessment Items	Yes
A. Materials	
1. Test items are within the experience of the student.	1. ______
2. Test items pose no value conflict for the student.	2. ______
3. Language of the test is appropriate.	3. ______
4. Test format (directions, speed, response mode) is within the experience of the student.	4. ______
5. Statistical information is appropriate for the student's language and cultural group.	5. ______
6. There are a variety of appropriate test materials or procedures available.	6. ______
B. Relationship to curriculum	
7. Student problem is stated in behavioral terms.	7. ______
8. Assessment strategies are selected because they will provide useful information about the problem.	8. ______
9. Alternative methods or procedures are available and have been considered.	9. ______
10. Reporting procedure is appropriate.	10. ______
C. Assessor qualifications	
11. Assessor speaks the native language of the student or has a trained interpreter.	11. ______
12. Assessor is knowledgeable about the culture of the student including attitudes, beliefs, and customs.	12. ______
13. Assessor is familiar with the behavior of student peers with the same language or cultural background.	13. ______
14. Assessor communicates clearly with the student, parent, or interpreter.	14. ______
15. Assessor is sensitive to the needs of bilingual or monolingual students, parents, and the interpreter.	15. ______
D. Parent/student rights	
16. Assessor is familiar with the rights of students and parents and has written materials in the language of the parent.	16. ______
17. Assessor is skilled in explaining the purpose and results of assessment to students and parents through an interpreter.	17. ______
18. Assessor records parent and student reaction to assessment.	18. ______
19. Assessment is discontinued if so requested by the parent or student.	19. ______

Cultural study is a process of learning from a distance, through reading, lectures, visual aids, and discussions. It is a useful procedure and allows professionals to absorb blocks of information. This approach is especially useful at the orientation level of understanding. It can help the professional focus on relevant issues within the study of culture and can break down the rigidity of thinking that is associated with a monocultural upbringing.

No study of culture is complete without some attention to introspection, some attempt at personal examination. The ultimate questions become, "What does this mean to me?" and "How do I behave toward the minority student?" The process of self-examination can be accomplished alone or in a group. Most solitary processes call for relaxed contemplation. Group experiences confront feelings and beliefs in a safe, supportive environment. Individual self-study has the advantage of allowing the person to examine attitudes that would be difficult to share with a group. Group procedures allow the individual to hear how others view cultural differences and to identify models for behavior.

The issues involved in self-examination revolve around beliefs, knowledges, feelings, and behaviors. A format for listing personal understandings of a minority group or person is provided in Figure 14-8. A first step in clearing away bias and ignorance is the recognition of personal attitudes and beliefs and how they influence the action that is taken. The recognition of feelings of discomfort, awkwardness, confusion, anger, and so on might lead to changes in these attitudes but more importantly can lead to conscious changes in behavior and improved teaching or assessment performance.

Figure 14-8.
Self-Examination of Cultural Information and Attitudes

Culture ______________________________

Question	Response	Examples That Support	Examples in Opposition
What information do I have?			

Question	Response	Examples That Support	Examples in Opposition
What beliefs do I hold?			
What feelings do I have?			
How do I actually behave?			
Action needed to change.			

Summary

The most serious challenge in assessment is the attempt to accurately understand the minority student. Legal requirements demand nonbiased assessment and assessment in the native language of the student. Good teaching practice demands that decisions be based on accurate and valid information. In order to achieve these ends teachers and professionals must use knowledge of the culture and language in choosing the instruments and methods of assessment and in interpreting assessment information.

Language differences affect assessment in a number of ways. Lack of familiarity with English obviously renders assessment in English invalid. Thinking is language-connected, and different languages set parameters that define significant beliefs, thoughts, and experiences. Test translations and new versions of tests are inadequate transformations of test materials. Native language assessors and translators can make significant contributions to the knowledge about a minority student.

Cultural differences pose similar problems. People come to view the world through the culture in which they were raised. Samples of behavior based on the expectations of another culture are one way to determine differences but are inadequate for determining deficiencies and abnormalities. The effective assessor moves cautiously and studies cultural and language differences in order to understand more adequately the behavior, development, beliefs, and attitudes of the students who need assistance.

Bibliography

Adeniks, T. Jean, and Brown, Gordon L. "Teacher Attitudes Toward the Education of Black Children." *Education* 97, no. 1 (1976): 102–114.

Bailey, Donald B., Jr., and Harbin, Gloria L. "Nondiscriminatory Evaluation." *Exceptional Children* 46, no. 8 (1980): 590–596.

Chandler, Theodore A.; Shama, Deborah D.; Wolf, Fredric M.; and Planchard, Sara K. "Multi Attributional Causality: A Five Cross-nationals Samples Study." *Journal of Cross-Cultural Psychology* 12, no. 2 (1981): 207–221.

Doll, Edgar A. *Vineland Social Maturity Scale.* Circle Pines, Minn.: American Guidance Services, 1965.

Duffey, James B.; Salvia, John; Tucker, James; and Ysseldyke, James. "Nonbiased Assessment: A Need for Operationalism." *Exceptional Children* 47, no. 6 (1981): 427–434.

Golden, Charles J. "Cross-cultural Second Order Factor Structures of the 16 PF (Personality Factor Questionnaire)." *Journal of Personality Assessment* 42, no. 2 (1978): 167–170.

Herrmann, Douglas J., and Raybeck, Douglas. "Similarities and Differences in Meaning in Six Cultures." *Journal of Cross-Cultural Psychology* 12, no. 2 (1981): 194–206.

Jones, Enrico E. "Black-White Personality Differences: Another Look." *Journal of Personality Assessment* 42, no. 2 (1978): 244–252.

Lambert, N.; Windmilla, M.; Cole, L.; and Figueroa, R. *AAMD Adaptive Behavior Scale: Public School Version.* 1974 revised. Washington, D.C. American Association on Mental Deficiency, 1975.

Mercer, Jane R. *System of Multicultural Pluralistic Assessment Technical Manual.* New York: Psychological Corporation, 1979.

Merino, B. "Diagnosis of Handicap in Limited and Non-English-Speaking Children." Paper presented to an advisory committee of the California Commission on Teacher Preparation and Licensing, Fresno, California, January 1979.

Mowder, Barbara E. "Addressing the Bilingual Handicapped Student." *Psychology in the Schools* 16, no. 1 (1979): 43–50.

Mowder, Barbara. "A Strategy for the Assessment of Bilingual Handicapped Children." *Psychology in the Schools* 17, no. 1 (1980): 7–11.

Oakland, Thomas, ed. *Psychological and Educational Assessment of Minority Children.* New York: Brunner/Mazel, 1977.

Pepper, Floy C. "Teaching the American Indian Child in Mainstreaming Settings." In *Mainstreaming the Minority Child,* edited by Reginald L. Jones. Reston, Va.: Council for Exceptional Children, 1976.

Rodriguez, Roy C. "Effectiveness with Bilingual Children: Approaches for Monocultural Teachers." *Contemporary Education* 50, no. 3 (1979): 134–137.

Singh, Ramadhar; Gupta, Munakshi; and Dalal, Ajit K. "Cultural Differences in Attribution of Performance: An Integration-Theoretical Analysis." *Journal of Personality and Social Psychology* 37, no. 8 (1979): 1342–1351.

Triandis, Harry C. "Reflections on Trends in Cross-cultural Research." *Journal of Cross-Cultural Psychology* 11, no. 1 (1980): 35–58.

Index